Translating Texts

Clear and accessible, this textbook provides a step-by-step guide to textual analysis for beginning translators and translation students. Covering a variety of text types, including business letters, recipes, and museum guides in six languages (Chinese, English, French, German, Russian, and Spanish), this book presents authentic, research-based materials to support translation among any of these languages.

Translating Texts will provide beginning translators with greater text awareness, a critical skill for professional translators. Including discussions of the key theoretical texts underlying this text-centered approach to translation and sample rubrics for (self) assessment, this coursebook also provides easy instructions for creating additional corpora for other text types and in other languages.

Ideal for both language-neutral and language-specific classroom settings, this is an essential text for undergraduate and graduate-level programs in modern languages and translation.

Brian James Baer is Professor of Russian and Translation Studies at Kent State University and Leading Research Fellow at National Research University School of Higher Economics in Moscow, Russia. He is co-editor of *Beyond the Ivory Tower: Rethinking Translation Pedagogy*, author of *Translation and the Making of Modern Russian Literature*, and founding editor of the journal *Translation and Interpreting Studies*.

Christopher D. Mellinger is Assistant Professor of Spanish Interpreting and Translation Studies at the University of North Carolina at Charlotte. He is co-author of *Quantitative Research Methods in Translation and Interpreting Studies* (Routledge) and the managing editor of the journal *Translation and Interpreting Studies*.

Translating Texts

An Introductory Coursebook on Translation and Text Formation

Edited by Brian James Baer
and Christopher D. Mellinger

LONDON AND NEW YORK

First published 2020
by Routledge
2 Park Square, Milton Park, Abingdon, Oxon OX14 4RN

and by Routledge
52 Vanderbilt Avenue, New York, NY 10017

Routledge is an imprint of the Taylor & Francis Group, an informa business

© 2020 selection and editorial matter, Brian James Baer and Christopher D. Mellinger; individual chapters, the contributors

The right of Brian James Baer and Christopher D. Mellinger to be identified as the authors of the editorial material, and of the authors for their individual chapters, has been asserted in accordance with sections 77 and 78 of the Copyright, Designs and Patents Act 1988.

All rights reserved. No part of this book may be reprinted or reproduced or utilised in any form or by any electronic, mechanical, or other means, now known or hereafter invented, including photocopying and recording, or in any information storage or retrieval system, without permission in writing from the publishers.

Trademark notice: Product or corporate names may be trademarks or registered trademarks, and are used only for identification and explanation without intent to infringe.

British Library Cataloguing-in-Publication Data
A catalogue record for this book is available from the British Library

Library of Congress Cataloging-in-Publication Data
Names: Baer, Brian James, editor. | Mellinger, Christopher D. (Christopher Davey), editor.
Title: Translating texts : an introductory coursebook on translation and text formation / edited by Brian James Baer and Christopher D. Mellinger.
Description: 1. | New York : Taylor and Francis, 2019. | Includes bibliographical references and index. |
Identifiers: LCCN 2019025278 | ISBN 9780415788083 (hardback) | ISBN 9780415788090 (paperback) | ISBN 9781315225609 (ebook)
Subjects: LCSH: Translating and interpreting–Study and teaching–Methodology.
Classification: LCC P306.5 .T724 2019 | DDC 418/.02–dc23
LC record available at https://lccn.loc.gov/2019025278

ISBN: 978-0-415-78808-3 (hbk)
ISBN: 978-0-415-78809-0 (pbk)
ISBN: 978-1-315-22560-9 (ebk)

Typeset in Sabon
by Swales & Willis, Exeter, Devon, UK

This book is dedicated to the founder of the translation program at Kent State University and co-author with Albrecht Neubert of *Translation as Text*, Gregory M. Shreve. For the editors of this volume and for many of its contributors, you have been an unforgettable teacher, mentor, and friend. What began during your sabbatical year at the University of Leipzig in 1985–86 continues to bear fruit.

Contents

Contributions		*viii*
Editor and contributor biographies		*ix*
Acknowledgments		*xii*
1	**Introduction: Translating texts**	**1**
	Why now?	2
	Toward a research-based translation pedagogy	3
	What is a text?	4
	How texts are made	6
	Theory in the translation classroom	10
	How to use this textbook	11
TEXT TYPES: SAMPLES WITH TEXT ANALYSIS		**15**
2	**Recipes**	**17**
3	**Instruction manuals**	**60**
4	**Museum guides**	**104**
5	**Patient education materials**	**141**
6	**News reports**	**183**
7	**Business letters**	**219**
	Appendix A: Sample grading rubric	*259*
	Appendix B: How to build a corpus	*261*
	References	*268*
	Index	*274*

Contributions

This volume would not have been possible without the collaboration of experts in the field who lent their expertise to the project in each of the following languages. These authors were responsible for the compilation, analysis, and interpretation of each of the specialized comparable corpora in their respective languages. More information on corpus compilation and analysis is provided in the introduction and in the appendices.

Introductions to text types: Kelly Washbourne, Erik Angelone, and Jeffrey Killman
English: Jeffrey Killman and Leonardo Giannossa
Chinese: Sanjun Sun
French: Loubna Bilali and Andrew Tucker
German: Erik Angelone
Russian: Tanya McIntyre
Spanish: Kelly Washbourne

Editor and contributor biographies

Erik Angelone is Associate Professor of Translation Studies at Kent State University. He received his Ph.D. in Translation Studies from the University of Heidelberg and his M.A. in Intercultural Communication from the University of Maryland, Baltimore County. His primary research interests include process-oriented translator training, translation pedagogy, intercultural communication, and online teaching and learning. He co-edited the volume *Translation and Cognition* (with Gregory Shreve) and the volume *Bloomsbury Companion to Language Industry Studies* (with Maureen Ehrensberger-Dow and Gary Massey). He has over 15 years of experience in training translators at Kent State University, the Zurich University of Applied Sciences, and the University of Heidelberg.

Brian James Baer is Professor of Russian and Translation Studies at Kent State University, where he teaches translation-related courses at the undergraduate, Master's, and doctoral levels. He is also Leading Research Fellow at National Research University School of Higher Economics in Moscow, Russia. He is founding editor of the journal *Translation and Interpreting Studies* (*TIS*), general editor of the Kent State Scholarly Monograph Series in Translation Studies, and co-editor, with Michelle Woods of the book series Literatures, Cultures, Translation (Bloomsbury). He is author of the monographs *Other Russias: Homosexuality and the Crisis of Post-Soviet Identity* (2009), which was selected as a Choice Outstanding Academic Title by the American Library Association in 2011, and *Translation and the Making of Modern Russian Literature* (2015). In addition, he has edited a number of collected volumes: *Beyond the Ivory Tower: Re-thinking Translation Pedagogy*, with Geoffrey Koby (2003), *Contexts, Subtexts and Pretexts: Literary Translation in Eastern Europe and Russia* (2011), *No Good without Reward: The Selected Writings of Liubov Krichevskaya* (2011), *Russian Writers on Translation. An Anthology*, with Natalia Olshanskaya (2013), and *Researching Translation and Interpreting*, with Claudia Angelelli (2015). He is also the translator of Juri Lotman's final book-length work, *The Unpredictable Workings of Culture* (2013). He is currently working on an annotated translation of Andrei Fedorov's 1953 *Introduction to Translation Theory*.

Loubna Bilali is Assistant Professor in Translation Studies at Kent State University. She holds a Ph.D. in Translation with a focus on localization from Kent State University, Master's degrees in Translation (French–English) from Kent

State and in Cross-Cultural Communication and Translation Studies from Chouaib Doukkali University in Morocco, where she also completed her undergraduate studies in English Linguistics. As part of her teaching responsibilities, she is responsible for the translation technology courses and serves as the coordinator for the lower division Arabic courses within the Modern and Classical Language Studies Department. She is also an English–Arabic grader for the American Translators Association (ATA). Her research interests include localization training, terminology management, corpus-based research, and translation pedagogy.

Leonardo Giannossa earned a Ph.D. in Translation Studies from Kent State University with a dissertation that investigates lexical cohesion in English and Italian using a combined corpus-based and statistical analysis approach. At Kent State, he worked on building an electronic bilingual glossary of legal terms through the analysis of French and English parallel texts from the UN-sponsored website of the *International Court of Cambodia* and taught several Italian language classes. After graduating, he was a Visiting Lecturer in Translation Studies at the Center for Translation Studies at the University of Illinois, Urbana-Champaign, where he taught Terminology, CAT tools, Theory and Practice of Translation and Bilingualism and contributed to the development of the Center's online M.A. program. His research interests include corpora as applied to Translation Studies, terminology, discourse analysis, paratexts, and lexical cohesion. He is the author of "Text-Based Approaches to Translation" in the Wiley-Blackwell *Encyclopedia of Applied Linguistics*. He is currently an instructor of Italian and English at the Mandela Intercultural Center in Taranto, Italy.

Jeffrey Killman received his Ph.D. from the University of Málaga, Spain and is currently an Assistant Professor of Spanish Translation at the University of North Carolina at Charlotte, where he teaches a range of topics including translation practice, translation technologies, and translation theory. He has also taught translation practice courses at the American University and the University of Texas at Brownsville. His research centers mostly on legal translation and translation technologies, and his publications have appeared in various edited volumes and journals such as *Babel, Perspectives*, the *Journal of Internationalization and Localization*, and *Translation and Interpreting Studies*. He is a member of the scientific committee of *EntreCulturas* and the advisory board of *Professional Communication and Translation Studies* (PCTS) and is currently the vice-president of the American Translation and Interpreting Studies Association.

Tanya McIntyre received her Ph.D. in Translation Studies from Kent State University in 2012. She also holds a bachelor's in Linguistics and Foreign Language Pedagogy from Tver State University, Russia and Master's degrees in Russian Translation and TESL from Kent State University. Her research interests include corpus-based translation studies, discourse analysis in translation, and the pedagogy of translation and Russian as a second language. In addition to teaching undergraduate and graduate Russian and translation courses at Kent State University, Dr. McIntyre is a co-director of the KSU STARTALK Foreign Language Academy.

Christopher D. Mellinger is Assistant Professor of Spanish Interpreting and Translation Studies at the University of North Carolina at Charlotte. Dr. Mellinger holds a Ph.D. in Translation Studies from Kent State University. He is the managing editor of the journal *Translation and Interpreting Studies* and co-author with Thomas A. Hanson of *Quantitative Research Methods in Translation and Interpreting Studies* (Routledge). He has co-edited special issues on community interpreting and technology (*Translation and Interpreting Studies*, 2018) and on translation process research (*Translation & Interpreting*, 2015). In addition to his teaching at UNCC, Dr. Mellinger has experience teaching Spanish for healthcare, translation, interpreting, computer-assisted translation, and localization at the graduate and undergraduate levels at Wake Forest University, Kent State University, and Walsh University.

Sanjun Sun received his Ph.D. in Translation Studies from Kent State University in 2012. He is Associate Professor of Translation Studies at Beijing Foreign Studies University, Beijing. Currently, he is co-editor of the Chinese journal *Translation Horizons* and director of the MTI (Master of Translation and Interpreting) program, which enrolls around 80 students a year. He has co-authored two books in Chinese on translation and language studies, and published articles in journals such as *Meta*, *Target*, *and Perspectives*. His research interests include cognitive translation studies and translation technology. He has years of experience working in translation companies and as a freelance translator.

Andrew Tucker is a Ph.D. Fellow in Translation Studies at Kent State University, where he teaches translation and researches online translator education. He received his Master's in Hispanic Studies and Bachelor of Arts in Spanish from Auburn University, as well as a Certificate in Translation from New York University. Andrew makes extensive use of specialized corpora when translating and has presented on their benefits to translators at professional association conferences. He has additionally designed coursework on corpora in legal translation for the Universidad Nacional Autónoma de México (UNAM). Andrew's research interests include online teaching and learning, translation pedagogy, corpora in translation, and legal translation.

Kelly Washbourne is Professor of Spanish Translation at Kent State University. His work centers on literary translation, and translator training and education. He recently co-edited the *Routledge Handbook of Literary Translation* with Ben Van Wyke (2018). He is an associate editor of the journal *Perspectives: Studies in Translation Theory and Practice*, and the series editor of both the *Translation Practices Explained* series and the newly launched Routledge *Guides to Teaching Translation and Interpreting*. He is currently collaborating on the translation of Tang dynasty poetry in English and studies of its anthologization.

Acknowledgments

We would like to express our thanks to a number of people without whom this volume would not be possible. In particular, we'd like to express our gratitude to the two anonymous peer reviewers and colleagues at Kent State University and the University of North Carolina at Charlotte for their constructive feedback. Kelly Washbourne, Erik Angelone, and Jeffrey Killman are thanked not only for their language-specific analyses, but also for helping provide introductory comments for each of the text types. Their expertise in specific text genres was particularly useful as the different chapters took shape. Also, Leonardo Giannossa's corpus-building and analysis instructions were instrumental to this project. Special thanks to Allison Braden for her editorial support at various stages. And we greatly appreciate Louisa Semlyen and Eleni Steck for their patience and guidance throughout.

The authors and publishers wish to thank the following for permission to reproduce the sample texts appearing in this book:

Calliope and Isabelle De Ridder for "La Lettre d'affaire – Exemple la lettre française," www.calliope.be/french/res/FRmodules.html

Groupe Renault for the extract of "CLIO – Notice d'utilisation"

N.V. Filonova for "Ne boiat'sia, a znat'! (profilaktika onkologicheskikh zabolevanii)"

Dr. Marlies Höck for "Information für Patienten und Angehörige. Information Krätze (Skabies)"

Thomas Heinemann for "Bienendieb in Menden"

Volker Römer for "DDR Museum Pforzheim"

Institut d'Education Médicale et de Prévention and Dr. Bruno Assouly for "Ne laissez paz le diabète vous priver de vos yeux"

Musée de la Résistance et de la Déportation de Besançon – Citadelle

rachaelray.com for "Raspberry Cheese Coffee Cake"

"Understanding and Managing High Blood Pressure," reprinted with permission from the American Heart Association. Brochure content has been discontinued; for more current content, go to www.heart.org

While every effort has been made to trace copyright holders, this has not been possible in all cases. Any omissions brought to the publisher's attention will be remedied in further editions.

1 Introduction

Translating texts

One of the unique features of this coursebook is that, while it can certainly be used in the kind of professional translation program that gave birth to it, it is also designed to be used in the new contexts of translation pedagogy that have emerged over the past 10 years, specifically in departments of foreign languages, comparative literature, and world literature. At the same time, it seeks to address the new modalities of translation pedagogy that have arisen within professional education programs, including online instruction, typically asynchronous, as well as non-language-specific models. Within traditional contexts of professional translator education, this textbook could be used in an introductory course on translation or in a course on text formation, common in European translation programs. As for the new contexts of translation pedagogy, this textbook could be used in a stand-alone course on translation practice or integrated into a second-language composition course. In terms of the new modalities of translation pedagogy mentioned above, this textbook could easily be used in non-language-specific courses given the fact that it contains material in six languages and includes instructions for how to add on additional material in other languages, as needed.

Another distinguishing feature of this textbook is that it is research-based in a number of ways. First, it addresses what empirical studies have shown us about novice-level behaviors – and, increasingly, about novice-level conceptions of translation, and of language. It does so by developing the textual awareness necessary to guide the translator's decision-making with the goal of fostering in novice translators the kind of top-down processing that characterizes the expert. Moreover, that textual awareness, or the sensitivity to what Gayatri Spivak refers to as "the protocols of the text" (2005: 107), is no less relevant to building translation proficiency as it is to building writing proficiency in another language.

This coursebook is also research-based in its use of corpora, defined by Federico Zanettin as a "collection of electronic texts assembled according to explicit design criteria" (2002: 11) – the design criteria in our case being genre-specific texts created over the last 10 years so as to ensure they document current conventions. These corpora allow for the systematic investigation of text types or genres as a whole and are useful for identifying the macro-level features of specific texts. Rather than relying solely on bilingual dictionaries, student-translators can use corpora to provide a more holistic understanding of how texts are made. At the same time, text-type- or genre-specific corpora are an effective way to instill in language learners a keener understanding of register and rhetoric while also challenging a structuralist understanding of language as a fixed and discrete code. They also offer a convenient vehicle for introducing digital humanities into the curriculum. For these reasons, a number of scholars have, over the past 20 years, advocated for the use of corpora in both translation (Bowker and Pearson 2002; Olohan 2004; Zanettin, Bernardini, and Stewart 2000) and foreign language courses (Hidalgo, Quereda, and Santana 2007; Sinclair 2004; Vyatkina and Boulton 2017). Moreover, those calls now have the support of a growing body of empirical research on the development, use, and integration of corpora in the translation classroom (e.g., Biel 2017; Laursen and Pellón 2014; Rodríguez-Inés 2014).

Therefore, with the primary purpose of developing the text awareness that we know to be crucial in supporting translators' decision-making, this textbook provides stylistic and rhetorical analysis of a series of pragmatic genres, including recipes, instruction manuals, museum guides, patient information, news reports, and business letters in six languages: Chinese, English, French, German, Russian, and Spanish. The analysis is based on a series of corpora created for this purpose. Moreover, instructions for building corpora of this kind are provided in Appendix B so that students or teachers may develop their own for other text types and languages. However, a textbook such as this one – addressing both translation proficiency and second-language proficiency – would not have been possible even 15 or 20 years ago when certain beliefs regarding the relationship between translation and second-language acquisition remained firmly entrenched, namely, that translation activities necessarily interfered with second-language acquisition and that translation training should occur only after a certain level of language proficiency was achieved. And so, before describing the organization of this textbook and how to use it in the various contexts referred to above, let us first sketch out the factors that have made a textbook such as this one possible.

Why now?

In 2007 the Modern Language Association, the largest organization of language teachers in the U.S., issued a report titled "Foreign Languages and Higher Education: New Structures for a Changed World," which urged departments of foreign languages to re-imagine the goals of foreign language instruction. The authors encouraged foreign language departments to reorient themselves away from the unrealistic goal of "replicat[ing] the competence of an educated native speaker, a goal that postadolescent learners rarely reach," toward "the idea of translingual and transcultural competence, [which] places value on the ability to operate between languages" (MLA 2007). These authors also strongly encouraged language departments to offer courses on translation to diversify course offerings and better connect language proficiency with employment opportunities – with translation and interpreting being among the fastest-growing sectors in the global economy.

At roughly the same time, researchers began turning their attention to the relationship of translation to second language acquisition, demonstrating that exposure to translation training, once banished from the communicative language classroom, can actually enhance language learning (Laviosa 2014; Malmkjaer 1998; Rocha 2010). And while not all such studies were conclusive in establishing a direct link between translation activities and improvement in second-language acquisition, there are now many studies documenting a positive reaction to translation activities among second-language students (Carreres 2006; Conacher 1996; Hervey, Higgins, and Haywood 1995/2002; Lavault 1985), suggesting a role for translation in increasing motivation and, by extension, persistence. Informed by this growing body of research, Colina and Lafford (2017) have advocated for the inclusion of translation as a "fifth skill" in the language classroom, alongside speaking, listening, reading, and writing.

All this was happening against the backdrop of impressive growth in the sector of the economy often referred to as the language industry. In fact, a 2016 Forbes report listed translation as one of the 20 fastest-growing jobs in the country (Sola 2016), and in 2019, the U.S. Bureau of Labor Statistics projected translation and interpreting to grow at a much faster rate than all other professions, at about 18% growth over a 10 year period (BLS 2019). Since then increasing numbers of foreign language departments, as well as departments of comparative literature and world literature, have begun to offer courses in the theory and practice of translation. While this is laudable, many departments are relying on faculty with degrees in foreign languages and literature and with little training or experience in translation or familiarity with translation studies. This textbook is designed to fill that specific but urgent need for research-based teaching materials that can be easily used by instructors with little or no training in Translation Studies, allowing language programs to take the "translational turn" (Backmann-Medick 2009) in a pedagogically-sound way while also providing a unifying structure in translation courses that are non-language-specific.

While the continued growth in the language industry has provided the most obvious justification for introducing translation into foreign language programs – connecting students with career paths – it is not the only one. More and more scholars are making the argument that translation pedagogy is not just for professional translators. The fact that translations are ubiquitous in our lives – whether we are aware of it or not – underscores the need for a more sophisticated understanding of the task of the translator on everyone's part. Translation literacy is now seen as a key aspect of global literacy (Takeda and Yamada 2019) and, as such, no less relevant than information and digital literacy. Evidence for this growing emphasis on translation literacy can be seen in new academic programs, such as the University of Iowa's minor in "Translation for Global Literacy" with its gateway course "Translation and the Global Society." This notion of translation literacy underscores the idea that translation pedagogy is not just for professional translators. As Anthony Pym comments, "Translation scholars may need to break the unspoken pact that they have developed with the translation professions. They should instead adopt a view where *everyone can translate*, not just professionals, and everyone can be trained to translate better" (Pym 2018: 1; emphasis added).

Toward a research-based translation pedagogy

Another defining feature of this coursebook is that it is research-based in the sense that it was designed to address as directly as possible what we know from empirical research about students' initial understanding of the task of the translator and the behaviors associated with that understanding. For example, Presas and Martín's (2014: 273) study of "the implicit theories of translation students" revealed very mechanistic views of the act of translation as exchange, "which do not reflect the complexity of translation phenomena" (Presas and Martín 2014: 273). Moreover, these implicit theories of translation held by students suggest implicit theories of the nature of language, namely that natural languages are more or less equivalent codes and that all languages reflect the "same" reality so that, if one searches long enough and with the help of a big enough bilingual dictionary, a close equivalent for source texts, words and constructions can eventually be found.

These implicit theories of translation, and by extension of language, align well with what we know from a now rather extensive body of research on novice translator behavior, as opposed to that of experts or professionals. For instance, novice translators tend to translate small units (words, phrases) to the detriment of textual cohesion (e.g., Lörscher 1991; Tirkkonen-Condit 1992); they fail to check dictionary meanings against the context (e.g., Lörscher 1991, 1996); they lack a strategic orientation to solving problems (e.g., Göpferich 2010); and they overuse bilingual dictionaries, ignoring other resources, such as parallel texts, background reading, or targeted research (e.g., Krings 1986; Kussmaul 1995). Taken together, these behaviors are said to represent bottom-up processing, as opposed to the behaviors of experts or professionals, which are described as more top-down. In other words, the decision-making of professionals is guided by a keen awareness of the genre conventions of the text they are translating, among other things.[1]

In addition to empirical studies of translator behaviors, there exists a rather extensive body of anecdotal evidence suggesting the kind of conceptual support novices need in order to better address "the complexity of translation phenomena" (Presas and Martín 2014: 273). Unsure of what should guide their decision-making, student-translators are often reluctant to alter source-text patterning, resulting in awkward-sounding texts lacking in cohesion, which are typically labeled "translationese." If novice translations are, as researchers have shown (e.g., Kumpulainen 2018; Malkiel 2009), an effect of "bottom-up" processing, then our pedagogical approaches in introductory courses must be aimed primarily at developing a more complex understanding of translation as decision-making, providing the conceptual tools necessary to guide that decision-making, and thereby supporting the development of top-down processing, which begins and ends with *text*, hence the title of this textbook.

This textbook is designed specifically to address these behaviors and to inculcate more top-down processing by re-focusing student attention onto the *text* as the primary unit of translation. To that end, it offers corpus-based analysis of various text types, moving from the smallest units of translation (words and phrases), which is where students typically begin, and spiraling up to ever-higher levels of text, ending with a discussion of such "global" or supra-sentential textual features as cohesion and discourse organization. This spiraling up is meant to leave students with an awareness of the text *as text* before beginning the actual translation, which increases the likelihood they will exhibit greater top-down processing.

What is a text?

By *text*, we are referring to "units of language larger than a single sentence, typically comprised of several written sentences or spoken utterances grouped together in a particular sequence," one that is "non-random" (Shreve 2018: 165). That is, the sentences that comprise a text "have been brought together deliberately for communicative purposes by a text producer in order to carry out a 'definable communicative function'" (Crystal 2008) (Shreve 2018: 165); or, as Halliday and Webster (2014: 183) put it, texts are "coherent and interconnected pieces of language, as distinct from unorganized strings of sentences." The definition of individual texts, however, almost invariably bleeds into the notion of text types or genres insofar as the creation of a text is governed by conventions:

> The properties of the grouping [of texts] can vary according to the communicative setting in which it is used; variation in these properties can be used to classify texts into different *text types* for instance, an endeavor called *text typology* pursued both in text linguistics and translation.
>
> (Shreve 2018: 165)

While this text-based approach to translation is commonly associated with scholars working at the University of Leipzig in the 1970s and 1980s, such as Otto Kade and Albrecht Neubert, their insights are shared by scholars from many cultures and historical periods. The Russian literary scholar Mikhail Bakhtin, for example, offered a concept similar to text types with his notion of speech genres. According to Bakhtin (1986: 64), speech genres are produced when "a particular function (scientific, technical, commentarial, business, everyday) and the particular conditions of speech communication specific for each sphere give rise to particular genres, that is, certain relatively stable thematic, compositional, and stylistic types of utterances." For Bakhtin, speech genres were a natural outgrowth of his dissatisfaction with Saussure's "too rigid a conception of code" (Holquist 1986: xxi), as represented by his idea of *langue*. As Bakhtin points out, this code is an abstraction, which no individual speaker can know in its entirety, except, perhaps, "the Biblical Adam, dealing only with virgin and still unnamed objects, giving them names for the first time" (1986: 93). As Bakhtin argues, speakers typically interact not directly with the abstract language system but rather with socio-culture "genres" or text types, which grow and evolve in specific socio-cultural contexts. "When we select words in the process of constructing an utterance," Bakhtin explains,

> we by no means always take them from the system of language in their neutral, *dictionary* form. We usually take them from *other utterances*, and mainly from utterances that are kindred to ours in genre, that is, in theme, composition, or style. Consequently, we choose words according to their generic specifications.
>
> (1986: 87)

Bakhtin then suggests the pedagogical implications of a text-based understanding of language when he writes: "Words are strung together only in the first stage of the study of a foreign language, and then only when the methodological guidance is poor" (Bakhtin 1986: 86). Translation pedagogy that is not text-based would be, by analogy, akin to bad foreign language instruction that allows novice learners to pluck individual words directly from the abstracted code through the use of a dictionary and string them together in a way that

Introduction

typically reflects L1 patterning and often leads to the production of "texts" that are not only awkward but incomprehensible. The novice translator's overreliance on bilingual dictionaries produces a similar effect.

Gayatri Spivak (2005: 94), too, lends theoretical support to a text-based approach to translation when she writes:

> Grasping the writer's presuppositions as they inform his or her use of language, as they develop into a kind of singular code, is what Jacques Derrida, the French philosopher who has taught me a great deal, calls entering the protocols of a text – not the general laws of the language, but the laws specific to this text. And this is why it is my sense that translation is the most intimate act of reading.

Like Bakhtin, Spivak contrasts Saussure's abstract *langue* to the "singular" code of a text, which can only be deciphered by entering the protocols of that specific text or text type. This ability to enter the protocols of a text – to realize that words acquire a specific valence within a text – is in fact a key *aha* moment in the development of translator proficiency. Growing awareness of textual protocols will lead students to become dissatisfied with bilingual dictionaries alone and so move on to consult other, more context-dependent resources, such as thesauri, corpora, concordances, and parallel texts. Moreover, such context-specific resources underscore the idea that textual protocols do not exist autonomously, but are always at the service of the underlying message(s) or purpose(s) of the text.

To the extent that text types represent "language in use and text in context" (Hatim 1997: xiii), textual competence combines linguistic and cultural competence into an indissoluble whole, making it, one could argue, the mother of all translation competences. Moreover, it is the premise of this textbook that textual competence, understood as a deep understanding of textual protocols and rhetoric as the ultimate unit of translation, addresses either directly or indirectly all the novice translator behaviors mentioned above. Rather than focusing on individual words and phrases, awkwardly strung together, students begin to reference the text to guide their decision-making at every level, from the selection of words to discourse organization. By authorizing novice translators to move beyond source-text patterning, a focus on the text also encourages them to make use of resources beyond the bilingual dictionary, up to and including corpus-based tools, which capture language in contexts, as well as parallel texts, which are texts written by target language speakers for target language speakers. Texts also provide the verbal context against which students can check dictionary definitions and through which students can understand the limits of dictionaries, the abstracted definitions of which are regularly challenged and continuously stretched by real-world usage.

How texts are made

As mentioned above, texts can be described as "a non-random" grouping of sentences. But what tells us that certain linguistic units are assembled in a way that is non-random? What is the conceptual and linguistic glue that holds these

Introduction 7

linguistic units together in such a way as to produce a verbal artifact that is perceived as a text? For the translator who is tasked with recreating a text in another language for a different readership in a different cultural context, knowing how that text is made – or "the protocols of the text," as Spivak put it – is fundamental. And knowing how they are made differently across languages and cultures is perhaps even more important, for it is this text awareness that distinguishes the bottom-up processing of the novice from the top-down processing of the professional, with the understanding that the "top" in top-down processing is the text as a whole. In fact, the dreaded *translationese* of the novice translator is often an effect of words "strung together," as Bakhtin put it, without the necessary conceptual and linguistic glue to make those words into text. And so, a familiarity with the textual conventions of the source and target cultures lies at the very foundation of professional translation practice.

Although we all deal with texts throughout our daily lives, and most of us recognize texts when we see them – and are able, often intuitively, to compose texts in our native language – many of us would be hard-pressed to say what specific properties or features turn a random assortment of words, phrases, and sentences into a text. Cohesion is one such property, although it is one of the hardest things to pinpoint. As Le notes, "How coherence works [at the macro level, i.e., between units larger than the sentence] is generally overlooked and never demonstrated" (Le 2004: 260). This can be explained at least in part by the fact that the linguistic "glue" that is cohesion is often invisible. As W. A. André Wilson (1972: 135, quoted in Beekman and Callow 1974 and Baker 2018) noted in regard to the first translation of the Christian bible into Dagbani:

> For a native speaker it was difficult to express what was wrong with the earlier version, except that it was "foreign." Now, however, a comparison … has made clear that what the older version mainly suffers from are considerable deficiencies in "discourse structure," i.e., in the way the sentences are combined into well-integrated paragraphs, and these in turn into a well-constructed whole – that is, a text.

So, in order to make visible the conceptual and linguistic features that create texts out of words, phrases and sentences – what linguists refer to as *coherence* and *cohesion*, respectively – we will need to employ some analytical terminology. Those terms we will group into three categories as they relate to (1) the purpose or communicative function of the text, or *what texts do*; (2) the nature of the text, or *what texts are*; and (3) the building blocks of text, or *what texts are made of*. These analytical terms are used throughout the volume and presented in bold to facilitate reading and analysis.

What texts do

Roman Jakobson (1960) provides terminology for describing what language does, that is, the communicative function of language, designating six different types. We draw on four of those functions in this coursebook, namely **conative**, **phatic**, **poetic**, and **metalinguistic**, to understand the overall purpose of a text. According to Jakobson, the *conative function* of language aims to persuade the readership to

Introduction

do something or act in a certain way. The type of language used to accomplish this end is typically associated with imperative or vocative constructions. The *phatic function*, in contrast, tries to establish contact or continue communication with the reader by creating a psychological connection. The *poetic function* of language is the creative use of language to focus on the message of the text, while the *metalinguistic function* uses language to speak about the text itself. This last function of language may manifest in a number of ways in a text, such as language that attempts to clarify or disambiguate a term or word.

Understanding the communicative function of language helps us to understand the communicative purpose of the text as a whole, which Katherina Reiss (1971/ 2000, 1981/2004) categorized with the terms: **informative, expressive**, and **operative**. *Informative texts* would be texts primarily focused on the content and relaying information or facts, while *expressive texts* aim to evoke a specific feeling or emotion, perhaps shifting the focus of the text to the author or the speaker and emphasizing the aesthetic quality. *Operative texts*, in turn, are persuasive texts that attempt to influence readers or users, compelling them to do something or to act. One would expect to see a high degree of referential language in texts whose primary purpose is informative, a high degree of emotive or even poetic language in texts whose primary purpose is expressive, and a high degree of conative and phatic language in texts whose primary purpose is operative. Texts, however, do not neatly fall into these three categories and may pursue multiple communicative purposes, but the categories are useful in fostering greater awareness of what texts (and language) do and providing a metalanguage to discuss that.

What texts are

The next category of terms describing the nature of texts relies heavily on Halliday and Hasan (1976) and their description of register. For them, register comprises **field, mode**, and **tenor**. The first concept, *field*, describes the content of the text and the specific field of discourse or domain to which a text belongs. The *mode* of a text, in contrast, focuses not on the content but on the way in which language is used. For instance, the mode might take into account whether a text is to be read or to document events. The *tenor* of a text focuses on the relationship held between the author and the audience. The tenor might describe an expert-to-nonexpert relationship or a specific difference in power or social standing between author and reader. These three concepts help to describe what a text actually is.

Closely related to the idea of register is the structural organization of the text. In this coursebook, we have chosen to use Swales' (1990) and Bhatia's (1993) term **rhetorical move** to describe the various rhetorical parts of a text. These textual features differ across text types and genres, and may be mandatory or optional in a certain text type. For example, a greeting would be a mandatory rhetorical move in a business letter. These moves are provided at the beginning of each chapter in both English and the target language to support discussion in language courses.

What texts are made of

The last category of terms deals with the building blocks of texts, namely words and phrases. The text analyses presented in each chapter identify high-frequency nouns, verbs, and phrases as a starting point for discussion about what texts are made of. These lists can provide the most relevant vocabulary in a language course and can point students to the major themes or topics of a text, providing a foundation for discussions of field, mode, and tenor, as described above.

These lexical building blocks, and the relationships among them, often referred to as lexical webs, are key to creating textual coherence. In order to describe relationships among words, we will use some familiar terms, such as **synonym** and **antonym**, and some not so familiar terms, such as hypernym, hyponym, meronym, and metonym, which we will define below. A **hypernym**, or superordinate, refers to a general word or term as opposed to its opposite, a **hyponym**, which describes a more specific word. For example, *game* is a hypernym for the concepts poker, rummy, or craps. **Meronyms** describe parts of a whole. For example, the cornea is a meronym of an eye and bark is a meronym of a tree. Whereas meronym is a linguistic descriptor, a **metonym** is a poetic or rhetorical device, by which a part can be used to substitute for the whole. For instance, the White House might be used to refer to the President of the United States, or the hearth may be used to refer to the home. So, while all the parts of a whole are meronyms, not all meronyms can function as a metonym. For example, all the specific rooms in the White House are meronyms while only the Oval Office can function as a metonym to refer to the president or the office of the presidency.

This is relevant for translation in a number of ways. With target languages that may lack a specific lexical item, a translator may choose to use a hypernym, or general word, accompanied by an adjective. At the level of stylistics, however, languages exhibit greater or lesser tolerance for repetition. French, for instance, is less tolerant of repetition than English. Therefore, many French texts often employ a range of word types, such as synonyms, metaphors, and metonyms. France may be referred to in a single article as France, the Republic, and the Hexagon, whereas the metonym Hexagon may not be readily comprehensible to an Anglophone audience.

In addition to the word types described above, Halliday and Hasan (1976) identify other devices at the word level that can be used to create textual cohesion: **reference, substitution, ellipsis,** and **conjunction**. The term *reference* describes a semantic relationship between two items, such as a comparison or a means of identifying another item. In English, for example, references may be demonstrative (e.g., this, that, those, these, here, there) or personal (e.g., personal pronouns). *Substitution*, as a cohesive device, is the replacement of a word or phrase with another to avoid repetition. In certain text types or languages, **repetition** may be valued as a cohesive marker for clarity and concision, while in other contexts, it may be frowned upon and avoided, as in the example above. Consequently, *repetition* and *substitution* are two cohesive devices that merit closer examination when analyzing a text. Related to these two devices is **ellipsis**, which refers to a specific type of substitution in which a word or phrase is replaced with nothing. These types of omissions are marked in the sample analyses using the symbol Ø. *Conjunctions*, as the term implies, join together words and sentences and can be classified in a number of ways. For instance, conjunctions can be additive, adversative, causal, and temporal.

Two final analytical terms that are commonly used throughout the coursebook come from corpus linguistics: **collocation** and **collocate**. As Olohan (2004: 198) describes, *collocation* generally refers "to the likelihood that a word will occur near another word." When working in specific fields or domains, collocations are particularly important to keep in mind since words may be used differently depending on their contexts. For instance, the German section of the recipe chapter describes how specific collocations in English may be rendered as compound nouns in German. The various words that make up a collocation are called *collocates*.

Theory in the translation classroom

Although theories of learning and of translation as text are already embedded in this textbook, we understand that learning can be enriched and proficiency can be enhanced by explicit discussion of theoretical texts, provided those texts directly address what we know to be beginning students' "misconceptions" about translation. The justification then for including theoretical texts in the curriculum would be to support learners' conceptualization of their given field of practice rather than relying on learners to construct a conceptualization inductively from activities alone. Such an approach is also supported by educational theory, which stresses the need to connect new knowledge with students' previous knowledge by creating what Vygotsky terms a *zone of proximal development*. By recognizing that students do not enter the classroom tabula rasa, but with conceptualizations of translation and some familiarity with text conventions (see Baer 2016), instructors can scaffold learning activities that move students progressively up Bloom's taxonomy of learning toward higher-level engagement with the material. Therefore, based on the existing research on novice behaviors and conceptualizations, described above, one can derive three guiding principles for the selection of theoretical readings: (1) to dismantle a model of translation as exchange in favor of a model that sees translation as a complex decision-making process; (2) to offer guidance to novice students in their decision-making; and (3) to provide an in-depth understanding of how texts are made.

A text that is especially helpful in laying the foundation for a new, more sophisticated understanding of translation among students is the semiotician Juri Lotman's *The Phenomenon of Culture* (1978/2019). In this short and very clearly presented essay, Lotman distinguishes between two models of translation – translation between equivalent codes and translation between non-equivalent codes. A translation produced within the first model, when back-translated, will always reproduce the original utterance or text intact, and any distortion in the message is caused by a breakdown in the technology of transmission. This model aligns closely with the conceptualizations of beginning translation students as outlined by Presas and Martín (2014). Natural languages, however, belong to a different model as they are non-equivalent or asymmetrical codes, which is the basis of Mona Baker's textbook *In Other Words* (1992/2018). Translation between non-equivalent codes, when back-translated, will not – and cannot – predictably reproduce the original utterance. Rather than associating such translation with loss and distortion, however, Lotman claims that only translation between asymmetrical codes can generate new messages. Translation between non-equivalent codes, Lotman goes on to argue, is at the basis of all creative intelligence, as symbolized by the two asymmetrical hemispheres of the human brain – and, as such, requires complex and creative decision-making on the part of the translator.

Once that fundamental distinction has been made, an understanding of the nature of the translator's decision-making can be introduced via Jiří Levý's (1966) seminal essay "Translation as a Decision Process." (For a less academic introduction to translation as decision-making, see Chapter 6 of Robert Wechsler's *Performing Without a Stage: The Art of Literary Translation* (1998), titled "Decisions, Decisions.") Students can then be encouraged to reflect on their own decision-making and the various social, political, and cultural factors affecting it – that is, what makes a solution "feel" right? Without such critical reflection, the largely unconscious forces affecting a translator's decision-making will inevitably reproduce existing power asymmetries. This focus on decision-making, in turn, encourages a shift in the way students conceptualize translation quality – from right/wrong or good/bad to an evaluation of the decision-making process underlying the translation: is it responsible, informed, and consistent?

In regard to principle 2, above, effective texts for guiding student decision-making are Catford (1965), where he introduces the concepts of obligatory and optional linguistic shifts, as well as Vinay and Darbelnet's (1995) translation strategies, especially those they define as "indirect" as they produce changes to source-text patterning. Both of these texts are grounded in the premise that natural languages are asymmetrical or non-equivalent codes, which requires a variety of indirect, often quite creative, solutions. Giving a name to the specific operations or shifts, such as transposition and modulation, is an effective way to authorize novice translators to move away from source-text structures, which they are initially very reluctant to do. These concepts can, of course, be expanded and extended as Hatim does with Catford's notion of linguistic shifts, underscoring the "multi-layered nature of 'shifts'": "There will be a shift simultaneously from one linguistic system to another, from one socio-cultural system to another, and from one literary or poetic system to another" (Hatim 2001/2013: 65). In this way, one can spiral up to a discussion of shifts at ever broader levels.

Other texts that help to guide novice decision-making, but at the level of text, are the many writings related to skopos theory, or the notion of purpose-driven translation. Writings by Vermeer (1989), Reiss (1981/2004), and Nord (1988) are especially helpful in drawing novice translators' attention to phenomena that are visible only at the level of text since they do not appear at the sentential or sub-sentential level, such as coherence and cohesion, discourse organization, and thematic progression. Also effective here is Blum-Kulka's (1986) work on implicitation in translated works, which can lead students to a more nuanced understanding of text as a combination of the words on the page and the assumed knowledge of the intended readership; when the amount of shared background knowledge decreases, the number of words typically increases, producing the phenomenon of explicitation.

How to use this textbook

This textbook is designed to be used both in the more traditional contexts as well as these emerging contexts, and by seasoned instructors of translation as well as by foreign language instructors who have little or no experience with

Introduction

translation, and by practitioners who have little or no experience with teaching, as explained below. Just as the pedagogy of the volume is already embedded within the volume itself, we have also aimed to scaffold the progression of chapters in a way that aligns with research on text-based approaches to translation. Bnini (2016: 94), in his review of Hatim and Mason's (1997) work on text type and translation curriculum, asserts that these authors "suggest a graded multi-stage curriculum design which is further refined by Hatim (2001:182)." This tiered approach to translation teaching places instructional texts early in the curriculum on the basis of two dimensions, namely *evaluativeness* and *markedness*. The first dimension, evaluativeness, creates a gradation between expository and argumentative writing. In this sense, recipes or manuals might be considered more informative or expository in nature and less "evaluative," while news reports may be considerably more evaluative. The second dimension, markedness, is related to how formulaic or standardized a text might be and the expectation that a reader might have of the text type. A text with a high degree of markedness is less formulaic or standardized.

With these two dimensions in mind, we have ordered the text types as follows: recipes; instruction manuals; museum guides; patient information; news reports; and business letters. The first three text types are largely expository in nature and have relatively fixed rhetorical moves. In contrast, the later chapters raise questions related to argument and ideology and are likely to vary considerably in terms of their content and rhetorical moves. Consequently, we chose to present the texts in this order to move learners progressively toward more complex textual analysis and decision-making during the translation process.

While the order of these text types is intentional in the coursebook, it is possible to use chapters independently from one other. Depending on the context in which the coursebook is used, there may be merit in using only a few chapters, and the analyses in each chapter allow for this piecemeal approach. The terminology used in each chapter is in bold and defined above in this introduction.

Translation courses

As evident in the title of the volume, translation courses are perhaps the most readily apparent context in which the volume can be used. Each of the six languages included in the coursebook can serve as either source or target language, expanding the number of language combinations that can be taught. Since each set of materials is drawn from content drafted originally in the language under discussion, the text types can also serve as a model for drafting texts. We explicitly avoid providing translations of the sample texts to allow students to use the modeled analysis to guide the translation process. Moreover, the metalanguage introduced in the volume allows students and instructors to discuss their decision-making in more meaningful ways.

The ways in which the volume can be integrated into translation courses can vary, from scaffolding learning activities related to reflective practices either in groups or individually (e.g., Pietrzak 2019) to the creation of new corpora based on the guidelines provided in Appendix B. Students could be asked to find an example of one of the text types and then discuss how prototypical their example is, based on the genre analysis provided in the coursebook. Then, as a final project, students could work in groups to create a corpus for another text type, analyzing it according to the models provided. Instructors may also task students with translating specific texts based on a variety of pre-determined requirements, sometimes referred to as a *translation brief*, to elicit different renditions. When assigning the translation of patient education materials, the instructor may change the target audience from nonexpert to expert, or the instructor might ask students to adapt a museum guide for use with children. In a similar vein, recipes might be translated inter-semiotically, rendering the translation of each step into a series of visuals accompanied by limited text in the target language. Still another potential variation would be the translation of a business letter into an advertisement, encouraging students to move a primarily operative text into a more expressive form.

For programs that offer courses in translation for several different language pairs, the volume can be used to provide structural unity across language combinations by providing a common approach to text-type analysis. Programs may wish to standardize their introductory courses across a range of languages to help facilitate common learning outcomes and objectives.

The sample rubric that appears in Appendix A may also prove useful when discussing the evaluation of translations with students. Each of the categories included in the rubric aligns with micro-textual and macro-textual features that are discussed in the various chapters, allowing students and instructors to focus on a more holistic view of translations rather than specific micro-textual errors. While detailed feedback on a translation is certainly useful, this type of rubric may help foster a dialogue between student and instructor and move beyond a detect-and-correct approach to translation evaluation (Washbourne 2014).

Non-language-specific translation courses

Another emerging context in which this coursebook could be used is in non-language-specific translation courses or workshops. In this configuration, students with a range of language pairs are included in the same class rather than having language-pair-specific practice courses. This type of class is perhaps most common in MFA programs or literary translation courses, but an increasing number of language programs have adopted this model as a means to offer translation to interested students regardless of their source language (e.g., Cheshire et al. 2018). While impossible to provide language-specific feedback for each student, the coursebook provides a common framework within which students can analyze texts and translations and rely on the language-specific examples used throughout the volume. In addition, reading examples across multiple languages within a specific text type may help students to develop greater textual awareness or consciousness of how languages and written discourse work in general.

Beyond this non-language-specific configuration, the coursebook also allows for languages other than English to serve as the source or target language. Given the range of languages in the volume, a greater number of language pairs can be included. For instance, courses on Chinese–German translation are possible with this type of volume. The same holds true for any of the language combinations, since the materials do not presuppose a specific direction in which translation students are required to work. Consequently, the volume has the

Introduction

potential for adoption in a range of settings that extend beyond the U.S. context where the editors are based.

Language courses

A third context in which the coursebook is particularly applicable is the language classroom, in which students can use the text types features as models for drafting their own texts in that language. While many European institutions have courses explicitly related to text formation, U.S. institutions often emphasize writing in the target language within the context of content-based courses or within upper-level language courses. The coursebook offers support for language instructors who wish to integrate specific text types into their courses, providing the requisite rhetorical moves in each of the text types. Likewise, the high-frequency vocabulary included in each section allows instructors to focus on vocabulary that is most likely to appear in each text type. Instead of a decontextualized list of words that often accompany language learning materials, each chapter provides guidance on terminology that is drawn from authentic texts that can be integrated into written assignments. Moreover, such a course is an effective way to provide scaffolding for subsequent courses in literature. Understanding the nature of these conventional, pragmatic text types offers a benchmark for students to evaluate literary style and innovation. Moreover, the instructions on how to develop specialized corpora and models for analysis allow instructors to incorporate components of language for specific purposes that are unique to their context and language combination.

Notes

1 Decision-making, however, is not only guided by an awareness of textual conventions, but also by an awareness of the nature of the task and by a sufficient number of cognitive inputs to allow for the creation of a robust situation or mental model against which to judge choices for sense in the local and global context.

Text types

Samples with text analysis

2 Recipes

Almost everyone – even people who do not cook – knows what a typical recipe looks like, not only because they are everywhere in our food-obsessed culture but also because recipes are a highly standardized text type. The fact that most people will recognize a recipe when they see one does not, however, mean that they know how to write a recipe, or that they will be able to tell the mandatory parts of a recipe from the optional parts. Moreover, recipes are often regarded as a simple text type, though they can be deceptively complex, revealing layers of culturally marked, if not culture-bound, content. A recipe needs to be primarily functional. *Designata* and *denotata* – linguistic signs in the text and actual things in the world – must be bridged; indeed, proof of a recipe's success lies "in the pudding." Both writers and translators have in fact been known to test source and target recipes in the kitchen (Epstein 2009), what scholars of translation assessment call *performance testing*. In some ways a recipe is a source text; the prepared meal, its translation.

Recipes contain distinctive features specific to their genre, country of origin, and even writer or publisher. Recipes may show traces of oral history, collective memory, and individual stylistic variation; there are even literary recipes. Recipes may even show interdiscursive and intertextual ties, that is, connections to other recipes and to texts from the same cultural system as well as to the source from which they were collected. Across different languages and cultures and even within a given language community, recipes may vary in terms of the implicit versus explicit propositional content they provide and in terms of to whom they are directed. Whether a text was written for amateur enthusiasts or seasoned professionals will provide for varying levels of detail; the under-explicit recipe can be frustrating to the wrong reader, the overexplicit one, tedious. Textual features that may appear in a recipe are subheadings for ease of readability/usability, rhetorical structure, cohesive ties, and enumeration. Physical features include layout and typography, both font type and size. Recipes may also be multimodal, employing visual cues to illustrate the finished product or different steps of its preparation. With the inclusion of both written text and visual aids, recipes are frequently multi-semiotic.

ENGLISH

The culture of cooking in the English-speaking world is very dynamic and rapidly diversifying, with recipes being developed for various audiences, ranging from "foodies" to novices. Despite this diversity, there remain certain stable elements. In order to understand the current state of English-language recipes, a corpus of 25 texts was collected from 11 different sources, all published in the last 5 years to ensure they document current textual conventions. Another macro-textual feature worth mentioning is the average length of this text type. A recipe is typically a short piece of writing, which is supported by the mean value (in terms of words) of the recipes included in the English corpus, which is exactly 353.76 words. A quick look at the range of lengths of the 25 corpus recipes shows that the minimum length is around 150 words and the maximum around 833, depending on the complexity of the recipe. However, most of the recipes range between 200 and 500 words. Indeed, only two recipes in the whole corpus were longer than that, at 664 and 833 words.

Macro-textual features

At the macro-textual level, we begin by isolating the mandatory features of English-language recipes, or what Swales (1990) and Bhatia (1993) call **rhetorical moves**. They are:

1. Title
2. Servings
3. Ingredients
4. Directions/instructions/preparation

As evident from the list above, the fourth move has three different labels. The recipes in our corpus showed all three with no clear-cut preference – the labels "directions" and "preparation" each occurred 8 times in the corpus, whereas the label "instructions" occurred 7 times.

In addition to these mandatory moves, which were found in all 25 corpus recipes, another rhetorical move seems to be mandatory as well: the *Servings* information. This section was found in all but one of the texts and usually appears right before the ingredients. Despite being a frequent rhetorical move, this macro-level textual feature varies considerably in the way the information is presented. The variants encountered in the corpus under analysis were: makes; yield; serves; and servings. Other optional moves that may be found in a recipe are:

1. Author's name (found in 15 recipes)
2. Date (found in 7 recipes)
3. Prep time (found in 7 recipes)
4. Total time (found in 12 recipes)
5. Cook time (found in 6 texts)
6. Level (of difficulty – found in 4 recipes)
7. Nutritional Information (found in 7 recipes)

The above-mentioned information is not mandatory because it is not vital to the success of a recipe. The author's name, for instance, is provided in 15 of the 25 recipes whereas the date is only present in 7. Moreover, as for the times required to complete a recipe or the various steps, they are usually specified in the directions, instead of in a separate move. All of these optional moves are usually found before the list of ingredients with the only exception being the "nutritional information" move, which is either placed after the ingredients or at the very end of a recipe.

In terms of register, it is worth looking at the three aspects which Halliday (1993) claims define a register, namely: the **field** of discourse, or what the text is about; the **mode** of discourse, or how the language is used; and the **tenor** of discourse, or the relationship between the author and the audience.

As far as the **field** is concerned, one way to find out about the topic of a text and the discipline a given text type refers to is by looking at its terminology and, more generally speaking, its lexical items. A quick look at the frequency word list makes it clear that the terminology and lexical items used in this text type primarily relate to baking. Some of the high-frequency words which point to this are:

High-frequency lexical items	Frequency	High-frequency lexical items	Frequency
cup	86	cook	44
add	65	cream	43
heat	64	oven	39
sugar	60	pepper	38
butter	58	bowl	37
salt	58	dough	36
pan	54	teaspoon	36
chocolate	44		

All of the lexical items in the table above describe either ingredients, equipment, or the process of making the recipe, which we see through verbs such as "add" or "heat."

As for the **mode** of discourse, recipes are meant to be read as users interact with the text while preparing the recipe. Recipes are mostly limited to the essential ingredients and steps that are necessary for users to prepare the culinary item in question and therefore tend to be sparing in words.

Finally, the **tenor** tells us about the kind of relationship that exists between the author and the text recipients, which can be one of equality or inequality (i.e., expert-to-expert or expert-to-nonexpert). When it comes to recipes, both relationships may be present as the author is usually an expert in the field and users may or may not be experts. Indeed, just as nonexperts use recipes to learn how to prepare a meal, experts also may use recipes to learn how to cook new dishes. The fact that recipes can be understood by experts and nonexperts alike is further stressed by the step-by-step, instructive nature of recipes.

20 **Text types**

The **communicative function** of the recipe is primarily **informative**. It is highly factual in that the purpose of a recipe is to transfer knowledge and information about how to cook a dish rather than persuade the audience to buy or do something. However, it is also possible to state that recipes have a certain degree of **conative** language, shown by the use of the imperative, which is aimed at triggering a certain action or reaction from readers.

Micro-textual features

At the micro-textual level, the corpus data point to a preference for the imperative mood and tense in recipes. In particular, the corpus shows approximately 362 instances of the imperative, roughly 100 instances of the present tense, 12 instances of the present perfect, 11 instances of the future (will) and 0 instances of the past tense. The use of the future tense is used to describe possible consequences for certain actions on the part of the recipe user (i.e., "Do not stir; stirring will cause the meatball to break apart") or to provide additional but not crucial information. This is also confirmed by the fact that in 5 out of 13 instances where the future is used, such information is placed in brackets.

Regarding **cohesive devices**, the definite article seems to be the preferred method of referencing. Indeed, *the* occurs 549 times in all of the texts, although this number is high since *the* appears quite frequently as well when its use is mandatory as the definite article and it is not being used for cross-referencing. Other referencing devices that appear in the corpus are *these* (1 time), *that* (which appears 4 times in the corpus, but it is used only twice as a referencing device), *this* (11 times but it is used only twice to refer to ingredients), *here* (1 time, and it is not even part of the recipe), *them* (occurring 9 times in a total of 7 texts), *they* (occurring 4 times in a total of 3 texts), *it* (occurring 43 times in a total of 13 texts) and *its* (occurring 5 times in only 3 texts). By contrast, a cohesive device which is scarcely used in the recipe corpus is substitution. For example, there are only 6 occurrences of *each* and 1 instance of *another* used as substitution devices. Substitution does not appear to be a widely used cohesive device in recipes, perhaps because, as we will see next, priority is given to ellipsis, which is another cohesive device similar to substitution but different in that the part of a sentence it refers to is omitted rather than replaced with a substitute expression. Ellipsis is used in 34/39 cases after the verb *cook*, 53/108 cases after the temporal conjunction *until*, 10/15 cases after the verb *bake*, 21/28 cases after the verb *stir*, 11/15 cases after the verb *mix*, and 35/37 cases before the verbs *serve/serving/serves*. The recipe corpus also extensively employs additive and temporal conjunctions as evidenced in the following table.

In particular, the additive conjunction *and* is the second-highest frequency word in the corpus after the definite article *the*. The other highly recurring type of conjunction is the temporal (*until, then, when, before, once, after, first, yet*). Based on these findings, we see that the two types of conjunction most typical of recipes are additive and temporal. As a result, the two types of sentences that can be said to be typical of recipes are compound and complex sentences.

Conjunctions	Frequency
and	361
until	108
or	91
then	36
if	15
when	11
before	9
but	6
once	5
after	1
first	3
yet	1

As far as lexical cohesion is concerned, a quick look at the list of high-frequency nouns in the corpus shows that repetition is a predominant lexical cohesive device in recipes, as revealed in the following table:

High-frequency nouns	Frequency	High-frequency nouns	Frequency
cup(s)	112	dough	36
minutes	91	teaspoon(s)	71
sugar	60	garlic	33
butter	58	water	31
salt	58	cake	30
pan	54	cheese	30
chocolate	45	flour	29
cream	43	grams	26
heat	40	ingredients	26
mixture	39	chicken	24
oven	39	inch	24
pepper	38	oil	24
bowl	37	egg	23

Other cohesive devices such as synonyms or pronouns might cause more confusion than any potential gains in style, which is why repetition is the main lexical device used to link concepts in a recipe.

The table above also points to a high occurrence of nouns in recipes. The nouns used in recipes can be further classified into four domains: (1) nouns describing ingredients (salt, pepper, chocolate, etc.); (2) nouns describing quantities (cups, teaspoons, etc.); (3) nouns describing equipment (oven, pan, etc.);

Text types

and (4) nouns describing the products of cooking or mixing ingredients together (dough, batter, etc.).

In addition to nouns, another word category that is highly recurring in this genre is verbs, as shown in the table below:

Verbs	Frequency
add	65
cook	44
place	37
stir	28
set	28
heat	24
cut	24
make	22

Sample text – English recipe

Raspberry Cheese Coffee Cake
Makes one 9" cake

Ingredients

Cake:

- 2 1/4 cups flour
- 1/2 cup sugar
- 1/4 cup light brown sugar
- 3/4 cup salted butter, softened
- 1 cup sour cream
- 1 large egg
- 1/2 teaspoon almond extract
- 1/2 teaspoon baking soda
- 1/2 teaspoon baking powder

Filling:

- 1/4 cup sugar
- 1, 8 ounce package of cream cheese, softened
- 1 egg
- 1 1/2 cups fresh raspberries, divided
- 1/2 cup seedless raspberry jam
- 1 cup sliced almonds

Preparation

In a large mixing bowl, stir **the** flour and sugars together with a whisk. Then add **the** butter, and mix Ø on low until a crumbly mixture forms.

Remove 1 cup of **the** crumbly mixture and set it aside. To **the** remaining crumb mixture, add **the** sour cream, egg, almond extract, baking soda, and baking powder. Beat Ø on low until Ø smooth.

Place **the** mixture in the refrigerator until you're done making **the** filling. Preheat your oven to 350°F.

Recipes 23

In a small mixing bowl, combine **the** cream cheese, egg, and sugar on low speed until Ø smooth. Then gently fold in Ø 1 cup of **the** fresh raspberries and set Ø aside. Hold **the** remaining 1/2 cup of raspberries for garnish.

Measure out your raspberry jam, and stir Ø with a spoon until it's smooth and pourable. Set it aside.

In a small bowl, toss together **the** reserved 1 cup of crumb mixture and 1 cup of sliced almonds.

Then, in a 9" springform pan, evenly spread butter on **the** bottom and about 2" up **the** sides and lightly flour Ø. Pour **the** batter into **the** pan and spread it evenly. Then, create a shell in which to pour your filling by gently pushing **the** batter up **the** sides of **the** pan from **the** center of **the** pan, making a well in **the** middle.

Bake **the** shell for about 15 minutes to help set it, then remove Ø from **the** oven. Pour in Ø **the** cream cheese filling to your indentation, so **the** filling is even with the sides of the crust. Then drizzle in Ø **the** raspberry jam and swirl with a knife.

Top Ø with **the** reserved crumb mixture and then add **the** sliced almonds. Bake Ø for 55-65 minutes until **the** cream cheese is set and **the** top is golden brown.

Let **the** cake cool in **the** pan for at least 15 minutes before Ø releasing **the** side of **the** pan. **The** center will sink a little as it cools.

Once Ø completely cooled, top Ø with fresh raspberries, slice Ø, and enjoy Ø. Store **the** cake in **the** refrigerator.

Key: conjunctions – highlighted in gray; definite article (reference device) – bold
Source: rachaelray.com

Sample English recipe analysis

All of the above-mentioned macro-textual characteristics are exemplified in the sample cheesecake recipe that will be analyzed in detail. The recipe was taken from Rachael Ray's official website. Rachael Ray is a popular chef in the U.S. and host of several TV cooking programs and author of more than ten cookbooks. The recipe in question includes every mandatory move (title "Raspberry Cheese Coffee Cake"; ingredients; and instructions – "preparation" in this particular case) as well as several non-mandatory moves: the author's name (Maria Betar), date (December 19, 2016), and serving information ("Makes one 9" cake"). The text is 432 words long, which falls within the average length range of this genre. The mode of discourse is informative and the tenor of discourse points to an expert-to-nonexpert as well as expert-to-expert relationship. As for the field of discourse, it is possible to narrow it down to chocolate cake cooking. This is not only given away by the title; it is also evidenced by the high occurrence of such lexical items as raspberry (8) – which is the most highly occurring one – cake (5), and cream cheese (4). Lastly, the communicative function is informative based on the reasons elaborated above.

As far as micro-textual features are concerned, the mood, as well as the tense, that prevails in the sample text is the imperative, although the indicative mood is also used but not as frequently. Indeed, the sample recipe has 29 instances of imperatives (mainly used to give directions while cooking), 6 instances of present tense and 1 of future tense (will).

In terms of cohesive devices, the preferred method of referencing in the text is the definite article *the*. In the sample text, *the* is mostly used anaphorically (to refer back to something previously mentioned) as in the first paragraph, which says "stir the flour and sugars," where *the* refers to the previously mentioned quantities required for those ingredients in the "ingredients" move. The definite article is used a total of 37 times in the text as a reference device (bolded text), whereas ellipsis (represented by the symbol Ø in the sample recipe), the preferred form of substitution in this genre, is used 18 times. As for conjunctions, the sample recipe makes use of the following items:

Conjunctions	Frequency
and	16
then	7
until	6
so	1
together with	1
before	1
as	1

The sample recipe makes ample use of additive and temporal conjunctions. Temporal conjunctions help organize the several steps of a recipe in a logical and sequential way, whereas additive conjunctions help join the different ingredients and steps. As a result of this extensive use of temporal and additive devices, the sample recipe is characterized mainly by compound and complex sentences. Indeed, the text above displays 4 simple sentences, 9 compound sentences, and 12 complex sentences.

Finally, as far as lexical cohesion is concerned in the sample recipe, the two most frequent types of lexical cohesive devices are repetition and hypernyms (also known as *superordinates*). In the sample recipe, there are no synonyms, and all of the terms mentioned in the "ingredients" move, which are quite detailed in that they are preceded by units of measurement, are then repeated throughout the preparation steps. In many cases, however, this occurs in a more general way without including the exact same units of measurement provided in the ingredients list. One could argue that these generalized repetitions function as hypernyms that are being used to generically refer to previous instantiations that are more specific. For example, in terms of lexical items relating to ingredients and equipment, the sample recipe contains 12 instances of hypernyms and 23 instances of repetitions, as shown in the table below:

Repetition	Frequency	Hypernym	Frequency
cream cheese	3	pan (instead of springform pan)	5
sour cream	1		
cake	4	egg (instead of a large egg)	1
baking soda	1		
baking powder	1	raspberries (instead of fresh raspberries)	1
egg	1		
fresh raspberries	2	raspberry jam (instead of seedless raspberry jam)	2
sugar	2		
sliced almonds	2	sugar (instead of light brown sugar)	1
flour	1		
teaspoon	2	butter (instead of salted butter)	2
almond extract	1		
oven	1		
refrigerator	1		

As for the lexicogrammatical features of the mandatory moves, the title "Raspberry Coffee Cheese Cake" is like the majority of the other recipe titles in the corpus: it is a noun phrase and does not include any definite articles. The ingredients move is also characterized by noun phrases pre-modified by units of measurement (cups, teaspoons, tablespoons, etc.) or quantities in general (slice, clove, stick, stalk, sprig, etc.) and post-modified by adjectival phrases. Like the title, the ingredients move also does not contain the definite article, which is also in line with the majority of the recipes in the corpus. As for the directions move, two main word categories prevail, namely nouns (84 instances) and verbs (47 instances).

26   **Text types**

CHINESE

Cuisine is an important part of Chinese culture and is central to the Chinese way of life. That being said, it is also marked by great regional variety and distinct regional flavors. Chinese dishes range from simple to extravagant, and accordingly the recipes range from concise to complex. In order to understand the current state of Chinese-language recipes, a corpus of 40 texts was collected from 12 different sources, all published in the last 5 years to document current textual conventions. Recipes are typically short, and the average number of Chinese characters of the recipes included in the Chinese corpus was about 255 characters. These texts ranged from 136 characters to 647, depending on the complexity of the recipe.

Macro-textual features

At the macro-textual level, we begin by isolating the conventional features of Chinese-language recipes, or what Swales (1990) and Bhatia (1993) call **rhetorical moves**. They are:

1. Title (菜名)
2. Ingredients (材料/用料/食材明细)
3. Directions (做法/步骤)

As is evident from the list, moves 2 and 3 have different labels. The recipes corpus showed that among the labels in move 2, 材料 was preferred, with 15 occurrences, while 用料 and 食材明细 occurred 7 and 5 times, respectively. It should be mentioned that in move 2 there were typically two or three sub-moves: 主料 (main ingredients), 辅料 (minor ingredients) and/or 调料 (seasonings). In move 3, the label 做法 was preferred to 步骤 based on the number of occurrences.

In addition to these three conventional moves, which were found in all 40 recipes in the corpus, there are a few optional moves: (1) 菜谱简介(features, found in 3 recipes), which usually appear before the ingredients; (2) 烹饪难度 (level of difficulty, found in 2 recipes); (3) 烹饪时间 (cook time, found in 2 recipes); (4) 小诀窍/小窍门/烹饪技巧 (tips or note, found in 8 recipes), which is often placed at the end of a recipe; and (5) 使用的厨具 (major utensils used, found in 1 recipe). Unlike recipes in English, Chinese recipes typically do not contain such moves as servings, author's name, date, and nutritional information. These moves are not vital to the success of a Chinese recipe.

In terms of **register**, it is worth looking at the three features of register put forward by Halliday and Hasan (1985), namely: the **field**, or what the text is about; the **mode**, or how language is used; and the **tenor**, or the relationship between the author and the audience. As far as the **field** is concerned, one way to find out about the topic a text describes and the discipline it refers to is by looking at its terminology and, more generally speaking, its lexical items. A quick look at the frequency word list makes it clear that the terminology and lexical items used in this text type relate to cooking. Some of the high-frequency words which point to this are:

High-frequency lexical items	Frequency	High-frequency lexical items	Frequency
适量 (appropriate amount)	86	生抽 (soy sauce)	23
放入 (add)	66	主料 (main ingredients)	22
分钟 (minute)	46	鸡蛋 (egg)	21
辣椒 (chili)	36	备用 (for later use)	20
少许 (a little)	32	胡椒 (pepper)	19
洗净 (wash)	32	面粉 (flour)	18
翻炒 (stir fry)	27	猪肉 (pork)	18
料酒 (cooking wine)	26		

All of the lexical items in the table above describe either ingredients, amount, or the process (through verbs such as 放入 (add) or 翻炒 (stir fry)).

As for the **mode**, recipes are usually texts written to be read by the users, who interact with the text while preparing a certain recipe. One more element pointing to the fact that recipes are usually conceived of as written texts is the fact that there is no dialogue between the author of the text and the audience and there are none of the signs of spontaneity you would see in spoken language, such as fillers and pauses.

Finally, the **tenor** tells us about the kind of relationship existing between the author and the audience, which can be one of equality or inequality (i.e., expert-to-expert or expert-to-nonexpert). When it comes to recipes, this relationship can be both insofar as the author is usually an expert in the field and the audience may or may not be experts. Indeed, just as nonexperts use recipes to learn how to prepare a meal, experts also may use recipes to learn how to cook new dishes. The fact that recipes can be understood by experts and nonexperts alike is further underscored by the non-technical nature of the cooking terms used in recipes, as evident from the list of lexical items above.

The **communicative function** of recipes is **informative**. They are highly factual in that the purpose of a recipe is to transfer knowledge and information about how to cook a dish rather than persuade the audience to buy or do something. However, it is also possible to state the recipes have a certain degree of **conative** language that attempts to elicit a certain action or reaction from the readers.

Micro-textual features

At the micro-textual level, the corpus data point to a preference for the imperative mood in recipes. Almost all the sentences in the directions were imperative, and pronouns such as 我 (I) and 你 (you) were rarely used. Regarding **cohesive devices**, the use of **reference** is rare in Chinese recipes. Personal pronouns including 我 (I), 你 (you), and 自己 (oneself) occur 18 times in 9 out of the 40 recipes. Among demonstrative reference devices, 这 as the Chinese equivalent for this appears in many words or phrases in the corpus such as 这个 (this one), 这一步 (this step), 这样 (this way), 这时 (at this moment), and 这道菜 (this dish). A close reading shows that only 这 (this, occurring once), 这一步 (this step, occurring twice), 第一步 (step 1, occurring once), and 这道菜 (this dish, occurring twice) functioned as reference devices. The Chinese equivalents for

28   Text types

that, *those*, *these*, and *there* did not appear at all in the recipe corpus. The cohesive device of **substitution** is also rarely used in the Chinese recipes; in this regard, only 3 occurrences of 其他 (other) were found. By contrast, **ellipsis** is often a widely used cohesive device in Chinese, in which subjects and objects are optional if they can be implied by the context. In the case of recipes, simple sentences starting with a verb are the norm; the omission of objects occurred at least 3 times in compound sentences in the corpus of Chinese recipes. The recipe corpus also makes use of additive, causal, and temporal **conjunctions**:

Conjunctions	Frequency
然后 (then)	15
接着 (then)	8
并 (and, also)	4
如果 (if)	3
所以 (therefore)	3
而且 (moreover)	2
不仅 (not only)	1
为了 (in order to)	1
以便 (so as to)	1
因为 (because)	1
只要 (as long as)	1

Generally speaking, the use of conjunctions is less frequent in Chinese than in English. Also, directions in the Chinese recipes are in the form of a list of successive steps, which reduces the need for conjunctions. **Lexical cohesion** is arguably the most commonly used form of cohesion in Chinese. In the case of recipes, each step is described by one simple sentence or one compound sentence; in compound sentences, lexical repetition occurs 16 times in the Chinese recipe corpus to help provide cohesion.

In the Chinese recipe corpus, there is a high occurrence of nouns, as shown in the following table:

High-frequency nouns	Frequency	High-frequency nouns	Frequency
适量 (appropriate amount)	86	调料 (seasoning)	16
分钟 (minutes)	46	锅 (wok)	16
辣椒 (chili)	36	椒粉 (pepper powder)	16
少许 (a little)	32	白糖 (white sugar)	15
料酒 (cooking wine)	26	酱油 (soy sauce)	14
生抽 (soy sauce)	23	香菇 (mushroom)	14
鸡蛋 (egg)	21	小火 (low heat)	14

(Continued)

Recipes 29

(Continued)

High-frequency nouns	Frequency	High-frequency nouns	Frequency
胡椒 (pepper)	19	砂糖 (granulated sugar)	13
面粉 (flour)	18	葱花 (chopped green onion)	12
猪肉 (pork)	18	花椒 (Chinese red pepper)	12
材料 (material)	17	肉片 (sliced meat)	12

The nouns used in the Chinese recipes can be classified into three domains: (1) nouns describing ingredients, such as 辣椒 (chili), 料酒 (cooking wine), 生抽 (soy sauce), etc.; (2) nouns describing quantities, like 适量 (appropriate amount), 少许 (a little); (3) nouns describing time, such as 分钟 (minute) and 小时 (hour). In addition to nouns, another word category that is highly recurring in this genre is verbs, as evidenced in the table below:

Verbs	Frequency
放入 (add)	66
加入 (add)	40
倒入 (pour in)	36
洗净 (wash)	32
翻炒 (stir)	27
搅拌 (stir, mix)	15

Sample text – Chinese recipe

鱼香茄子（非油炸）
　食材明细：
　茄子2根，香醋（料汁）1勺，姜少许，生抽（料汁）1勺，白糖（料汁）1/2勺，泡红辣椒（料汁）2个，葱花（料汁）少许，蒜2瓣，郫县豆瓣酱1勺，水淀粉适量，料酒1勺，香葱少许
　做法步骤：

1. 茄子洗净切长条，放入少许盐，用手抓Ø拌均匀腌制片刻后挤出水份备用。
2. 葱、姜、蒜切碎。泡红辣椒切碎。
3. 取一小碗倒入调料汁中的所有食材搅拌均匀成鱼香汁备用。
4. 锅中倒入比平时炒菜稍多点的油，放入挤干水份的茄子翻炒。
5. 炒至茄子变软呈透明时倒出备用。
6. 锅中另倒入少许油，放入葱、姜末爆香。
7. 加入1勺郫县豆瓣酱翻炒出红油。
8. 倒入炒好的茄子翻炒均匀。
9. 加入1勺料酒继续翻炒。再倒入小半碗水盖盖焖煮2分钟左右。
10. 倒入调料碗中的鱼香汁不停翻炒。
11. 加入蒜炒出香味。
12. 淋入水淀粉炒匀。

30 Text types

> 13. 最后加入香葱碎。
> 14. Ø出锅Ø装盘。
>
> 小窍门：豆瓣酱和泡红辣椒都有**盐**味，不必另加**盐**了。泡红椒是鱼香菜的灵魂，最好不要省略。
>
> 使用的厨具：炒锅
>
> Key: connectors – underline; lexical repetition – highlighted in gray

Sample Chinese recipe analysis

All of the above-mentioned macro-textual characteristics are exemplified in the sample recipe that will be discussed hereafter when analyzing the micro-textual features of recipes. The recipe was taken from meishichina.com, a Chinese food-themed website, which contains thousands of illustrated recipes. The sample recipe is for 鱼香茄子（非油炸）(Yuxiang eggplant, non-fried), which is a popular Chinese dish. The recipe includes every conventional or obligatory move: title 鱼香茄子（非油炸), ingredients (食材明细), and directions (做法步骤); it also includes some optional moves: tips (小窍门) and major utensils used (使用的厨具).

The text has 398 characters and is a bit longer than the average (255 characters) for this genre. The mode of discourse is informative and the tenor of discourse points to an expert-to-nonexpert as well as an expert-to-expert relationship. The communicative function is informative as per the reasons elaborated in the section above.

As far as the micro-textual features are concerned, the indicative mood and the present tense are used for giving directions while cooking. In terms of cohesive devices, the use of short sentences and a set of numbered steps reduces the need for cohesive devices in each step in the directions. Reference and substitution are absent in the sample text; ellipsis (represented by the symbol Ø in the sample recipe) is used 3 times; conjunctions are not used whereas connectors (see words highlighted in gray in the sample text) such as 再 (then) and 最后 (finally) are. Within-step lexical repetition (see underlined words in the sample text) appears 3 times, while there are no hypernyms or synonyms; in the whole recipe, there are instances of repetitions as shown in the table below:

Repetition	Frequency
料汁 (dressing)	5
茄子 (eggplant)	5
鱼香 (yuxiang)	3
泡红辣椒 (pickled red chilies)	2
豆瓣酱 (bean paste)	2

(Continued)

(Continued)

Repetition	Frequency
淀粉 (starch)	1
料酒 (cooking wine)	1
香葱 (chive)	1
鱼香汁 (yuxiang juice)	1

The sample recipe is characterized mainly by simple sentences; in the sample, there are 11 simple sentences and 5 compound sentences.

As for the lexicogrammatical features of the conventional moves, all titles, with the exception of one, are characterized by noun phrases. The ingredients move is also characterized by noun phrases followed by units of measurements (克 grams, 汤匙 tablespoons, etc.) or quantities in general (适量 appropriate amount, 少许 a little, etc.). As for the directions move, two main word categories seem to prevail, namely nouns (75 instances) and verbs (31 instances).

32   Text types

FRENCH

Gastronomy and the art of cooking have always been objects of great pride in French culture. With its abundance of artisan wines and cheeses and the richness and sophistication of its ingredients, flavors and cooking techniques, French gastronomy was added to UNESCO's list of the Intangible Cultural Heritage of Humanity[1] in 2010 in recognition of its cultural importance and impact. French cooking styles were subject to Italian and Portuguese influences over the centuries and have significantly contributed to Western cuisines. In order to understand the structure and characteristics of contemporary French-language recipes, a corpus of 25 texts was collected from 14 different resources, all published in the last 5 years in order to reflect the current textual conventions of this text type.

Macro-textual features

At the macro-textual level, four major features, also known as **rhetorical moves**, are evident:

1. Title (*Titre*)
2. General information (*Informations générales/Info pratiques*)

   a. Number of servings (*Nombre de portions*)
   b. Preparation time (*Temps de préparation*)
   c. Cooking time (*Temps de cuisson*)

3. Ingredients (*Ingrédients*)
4. Preparation (*Préparation/Préparation de la recette/Étapes/Étapes de la recette/Réalisation*)

The second rhetorical move appeared in 21 recipes and was labeled either *informations générales* (found in 4 recipes) or *info pratiques* (found in 2 recipes) or did not contain any label (in 15 recipes), simply listing information about servings, levels of difficulty, prep and cook time, and cost/budget. Given the nature of the texts' sources (web pages), this information sometimes appeared in the form of graphics (icons indicative of time, cost, or difficulty level) either at the top or on the side of the recipe page and, therefore, did not always require a label *per se*. The type of information provided varied significantly depending on the recipe author or publishing source. The following are some of the optional moves that appeared under general information:

1. Author's name (found in 10 recipes)
2. Date (found in 4 recipes)
3. Level of difficulty (found in 13 recipes)
4. Cost (found in 3 recipes)
5. Notes (found in 6 recipes)
6. Chef bios (found in 3 recipes)

The information yielded by these moves does not necessarily interfere with the making of a recipe or the success of a dish (i.e., author's name, bio, date, and cost).

The fourth rhetorical move has six different labels with no noticeable preference for one over the others. The label *preparation* occurs 11 times, while *préparation de la recette* and *étapes* each occur 3 times in the corpus; the label *réalisation* is used twice and *étapes de la recette* once, while four of the recipes do not have a label for the preparation or instructions section. These sections directly accompany the ingredients section.

All recipes in the corpus are accompanied by illustrations, either of the step-by-step preparation or a picture of the final product or served dish. Two of the recipes contain videos in which the chefs walk viewers through the recipes.

As a text type, recipes are generally concise and tend to observe a similar structure. The average length of the recipes in the French corpus is 285.72 words. Most recipes range between 200 and 400 words, with only three recipes outside this word range, at 511, 564, and 624 words, respectively. If we look at the range of lengths of the 25 recipes, we notice that the minimum length is around 113 words and the maximum is around 711, depending on the complexity or difficulty of the recipe.

As for the **register** of this text type, there are three aspects worth considering: the **field, mode**, and **tenor** of discourse (Halliday and Hasan 1985). The **field** of discourse can be determined by looking at the lexical field, the terminology used, and the frequency of lexical units. The table below contains a list of high-frequency lexical items that all relate to cooking, ingredients, or equipment.

High-frequency lexical items	Frequency	High-frequency lexical items	Frequency
minutes	47	*ingrédients*	28
sel	42	*poivre*	26
sucre	38	*temps*	25
faire	37	*jus*	24
cuisson	35	*bien*	24
citron	35	*feu*	23
beurre	33	*laisser*	23
four	33	*œufs*	23
ajouter	33	*plat*	23
crème	32	*mettre*	23
cuire	30	*pâte*	21
préparation	29		

In terms of **mode**, recipes are texts designed to be read and followed in order to prepare a dish. They are highly structured and compact and do not allow for interaction or a back-and-forth between the audience and the author. As for **tenor**, recipes are texts that address both experts and nonexperts alike, since the language used is accessible to an audience with different levels of expertise and familiarity with cooking.

34 Text types

With respect to the **communicative function**, recipes are **informative**, providing information about which ingredients and items are needed and describing how to cook and prepare a meal. They may also make use of **conative** language to a certain degree, since much focus is placed on the audience through the use of imperative sentences (i.e., orders) urging users to follow steps or perform certain tasks.

At the micro-textual level, the imperative mood and tense are prevalent in recipes. The imperative is used to give orders, advice, and recommendations. These same functions are also expressed using the infinitive form in French (known as *infinitif jussif*, which is a non-temporal form of the verb used instead of the imperative to express an order or command). The French corpus consists of 276 instances of the imperative, 544 instances of the infinitive, 2 instances of the future, and 0 instances of the past tense.

As far as **cohesive devices** are concerned, the definite articles *le*, *la*, and *les* were highly ranked in terms of frequency and appear to be the preferred method for referencing, with a total of 728 occurrences throughout the corpus. However, in 82 of these occurrences, the articles served as direct object pronouns functioning as a substitution device to avoid repetition. The third-person subject pronouns *il* and *elle* were used 16 times, 4 out of which *il* acted as a substitute for other words.

A number of referents were also used, such as the determiner *ce* (20 times in 12 texts); *cette* (11 times in 7 texts); *ces* (4 times in 3 texts); *ça* (2 times in 2 texts); *cela* (1 time in 1 text); *leur* and *leurs* (3 times in 3 texts); *vous* and *votre* (3 times in 2 texts); and *vos* (1 time in 1 text). Similar to the substitutive function served by the pronouns *le*, *la*, and *les*, *y* is another pronoun that replaces prepositions indicating location. This pronoun appeared 13 times in a total of seven texts. *En* is also a pronoun that replaces nouns introduced by a partitive, an indefinite determiner, or an expression of quantity. *En* occurred 97 times in a total of 21 texts, in 2 of which it served as a substitute. Ellipsis is also a widely used cohesive device. It was used 22 out of 23 times after the verb *laisser*, 5 out of 6 times after the verb *remuer*, 27 out of 30 times after the verb *cuire*, 10 out 18 after the verb *mélanger*, 9 out of 9 after the verb *refroidir*, 12 out of 12 after the verb *saler*, and 8 out of 8 after the verb *servir*.

The French recipe corpus makes use of additive and temporal **connecting words**, as indicated by the lexical items in the table.

Connecting words	Frequency	Connecting words	Frequency
et	280	*quand*	5
avec	59	*mais*	4
pour	58	*après*	2
puis	37	*aussitôt*	2
pendant	27	*aussi*	2
ou	17		

(Continued)

(Continued)

Connecting words	Frequency	Connecting words	Frequency
jusqu'à	14		
ensuite	13	lorsque	1
ainsi	8	enfin	1
avant	7	déjà	1
si	7		
alors	6	sinon	1

The additive conjunction *et* is the second-highest frequency word in the corpus after the partitive article *de*. Other highly recurrent items are temporal (e.g., *puis, pendant, jusqu'à, ensuite, avant, quand, après, aussitôt, enfin, lorsque, déjà, enfin*) as well as causal (*pour, ainsi, alors*). These items suggest that compound and complex sentences are the types of sentences typically found in recipes. Regarding **lexical cohesion, repetition** appears to be the most prevalent lexical cohesive device used in recipes, as evidenced in the table below.

High-frequency nouns	Frequency	High-frequency nouns	Frequency
minute (s)	50	oeufs	23
sel	42	plat	23
sucre	38	eau	23
citron	35	pâte	21
cuisson	35	personnes	20
beurre	33	recette	20
four	33	huile	18
blanc (s)	33	terrine	18
crème	32	thym	17
préparation	29	min	16
ingrédients	28	persil	16
poivre	26	sauce	16
temps	25	vanille	16
jus	24	tranches	15
feu	23	cl	15

Préparation refers to the steps required to complete a recipe and serves as a label denoting one section of a recipe. The same applies to the word *ingrédients*, which refers to the actual listing of ingredients needed, and the word *recette*, which very often appears in the title of recipes specifying what the recipe is about (e.g., *recette de ...*). The remaining words all refer to different concepts. Thus, repetition is the main lexical device used to connect concepts in a recipe.

The high-frequency nouns can further be classified in terms of the semantic fields to which they belong. We distinguish between (1) nouns referring to ingredients (*sel, sucre, citron, beurre, crème, poivre*, etc.); (2) nouns describing quantities (*cl*,

36   Text types

etc.); (3) nouns describing equipment (*four, terrine, plat*, etc.); and (4) nouns describing the products of cooking or mixing items (*pâte, sauce*, etc.). Besides nouns, verbs are another lexical category that is predominant in recipes, as indicated here:

Verbs	Frequency	Verbs	Frequency
ajouter	58	*saler*	16
faire	57	*couper*	16
laisser	41	*réserver*	14
mélanger	31	*laver*	13
cuire	30	*passer*	11
verser	24	*poivrer*	10
mettre	23	*incorporer*	10
manger	22		

Sample text – French recipe

Cailles farcies au foie gras et aux cèpes

Préparation 30 min | Cuisson 20 min | Plat | Facile | Noël

Ingrédients (4 personnes)

4 cailles
200 g de foie gras en bloc
10 g de cèpes séchés
2 échalotes
15 cl de vin blanc
2 cuillères à soupe de Porto
1 branche de thym
40 g de beurre
Sel
Poivre

Préparation

Réhydratez **les** cèpes dans un bol d'eau chaude. Désossez **les** cailles en **les** incisant par **le** dos et en enlevant **la** carcasse.

Égouttez **les** cèpes et faites-**les** sauter Ø sur feu vif avec **la** moitié du beurre et **la** moitié des échalotes ciselées, dans une poêle. Salez Ø et poivrez Ø, puis faire revenir Ø jusqu'à ce que l'humidité des champignons s'évapore.

Coupez **le** foie gras en dés et mettez-**le** dans un saladier. Arrosez Ø avec **le** porto et ajoutez-y **les** cèpes refroidis. Farcissez **les** cailles avec **ce** mélange et ficelez-**les** fermement, en croisant leurs cuisses.

Ciselez **le** reste des échalotes et faites-**les** suer dans une sauteuse avec **le** reste de beurre. Faites dorer **les** cailles sur toutes **les** faces puis déglacez Ø avec **le** vin blanc. Ajoutez **le** thym, couvrez Ø et faites cuire Ø pendant 20 minutes sur feu moyen. Servez Ø chaud.

> Key: referencing (definite articles) – bold; connecting words – highlighted in gray; pronouns – underline
> *Source: www.academiedugout.fr/recettes/cailles-farcies-au-foie-gras-et-aux-cepes_7545_4*

Sample French recipe analysis

One recipe from the corpus will be used to exemplify the macro- and micro-textual characteristics that were discussed earlier. The recipe was published in an online French cooking encyclopedia named *L'Académie du Goût*. It is an online platform created by one of the leading chefs in France, Alain Ducasse, who brought together a number of prestigious French chefs to share their knowledge, expertise, advice, and recommendations with gastronomy fans and experts and to contribute to the collection of thousands of signature recipes. At the macro-textual level, the recipe in question includes every mandatory move (*titre: Cailles Farcies au Foie Gras et aux Cèpes; ingrédients*; and *préparation*) as well as several non-mandatory ones: author's name (*Académie du Goût* team); prep time (*30 min*); cook time (*20 min*) number of servings (*4 personnes*); and level of difficulty (*facile*). In addition, the recipe includes illustrations for each step of preparation along with an image of the final product. The text has a length of 198 words. The mode of discourse is informative, and the tenor of discourse suggests an expert-to-expert as well as an expert-to-nonexpert relationship. The field of discourse is poultry cooking. Lastly, the communicative function is primarily informative and uses language that is conative.

At the micro-textual level, predominant mood and tense are imperative. There are 25 total instances of the imperative, 5 of which take the form of *infinitif jussif*. As for cohesive devices, the preferred method of referencing in the sample text is through the use of definite articles (*les, le,* and *la*), which are in bold in the sample text. These articles were used 22 times throughout the text (*les,* 11 times; *le,* 8 times; and *la,* 3 times). In 18 out of 22 cases, the definite articles were used anaphorically to refer back to something previously mentioned, as is the case in the first paragraph, where the definite article in *Réhydratez les cèpes dans un bol d'eau chaude* replaces the quantity of penny bun mushrooms needed for this ingredient since the quantity is mentioned in the *ingrédients* list (*10 g de cèpes séchés*). In addition to referencing, there were a few instances of substitution using the definite article *les* (4 out of 22 times), where it functions as a direct object pronoun to avoid repetition. The pronouns *y* and *leurs* were also used once each for substitution purposes in order to prevent repetition. One demonstrative determiner, *ce*, was used to serve the same purpose. Ellipsis occurs 9 times in the sample text (represented by the symbol Ø in the sample text). The following connecting words (highlighted in gray) are found in the sample text:

Text types

Connecting words	Frequency
et	10
avec	5
puis	2
jusqu'à	1
pendant	1

The text makes use of additive conjunctions, which help to connect ingredients with step-by-step cooking instructions and temporal words that provide a logical organization and sequencing to the different steps of the recipe. The use of these words reflects the proliferation of simple and complex sentences identified in this recipe. Only 2 out of the 11 sentences that make up the text are simple sentences. The remaining 9 are either compound (7) or complex (2).

As far as lexical cohesion is concerned, the two types of lexical cohesive devices prevalent in the sample text are repetition (50 instances), by far the most common, followed by hypernymy (2 instances; *champignons* instead of *cèpes séchés* and *thym* instead of *branche de thym*). There are no instances of meronyms.

Repetition	Frequency	Repetition	Frequency
cailles	5	*branche*	1
cèpes	5	*carcasse*	1
beurre	3	*champignons*	1
échalotes	3	*cuillères*	1
foie	3	*eau*	1
gras	3	*cl*	1
blanc	2	*cuisses*	1
feu	2	*dos*	1
moitié	2	*mélange*	1
porto	2	*minutes*	1
thym	2	*poêle*	1
vin	2	*soupe*	1
bloc	1	*saladier*	1
bol	1	*poivre*	1

Regarding lexicogrammatical features related to mandatory moves, 18 out of 25 recipe titles use noun phrases (e.g., *Cailles Farcies au Foie Gras et aux Cèpes* and *Dinde aux Marrons et Fruits Secs*). Seven recipe titles use definite articles, and five of these titles mention the name of the chef who apparently created the recipes. The ingredients move is characterized by noun phrases pre-modified by units of measurements (*kg, cl, cuillères à soupe, cuillères à café, pincée*, etc.) or quantities (*tranche, branche, gousses,* etc.) and post-modified by adjectival phrases. No definite or indefinite articles are used in this move. However, the partitive article *de* often precedes mass, or uncountable, nouns. Finally, the two most prevalent parts of speech observed in the preparation move are nouns (53 instances) and verbs (25 instances).

40 Text types

GERMAN

Cuisine from German-speaking parts of the world is reaching a broader audience than ever before by virtue of recipes appearing in large, ever-expanding online databases housed on the websites of national television stations, food companies, and cooking magazines. Moreover, international-ization and localization trends have resulted in a greater demand for recipe translation. By providing insights into how German-language recipes are prototypically structured, corpus-based text analysis can provide support both for translation and monolingual writing. To illustrate this, a small-scale corpus of German-language recipes consisting of 40 texts from 14 different sources was compiled. All of the recipes appeared online and were published within the past 5 years, thereby providing a contemporary snapshot of prototypical text conventions.

Macro-textual features

At the macro-textual level, the following **rhetorical moves** emerge as prototypical in German-language recipes based on our representative sample:

1. Title (*Titel*)
2. Ingredients (*Zutaten/Einkaufsliste*)
3. Preparation (*Zubereitung/Rezept*)

As section headings, moves two and three are more or less terminologically standardized. *Einkaufsliste* (shopping list) appears in only 3 of the 40 texts and in 1 of the 14 sources. The same holds true for *Rezept* (recipe). The degree of standardization for these headings seems to be higher than what we see in English, where there is more tolerance for lexical variation.

Additional common moves found in German-language recipes include a one to two-sentence description of the food item immediately following the title (in 21 of the 40 texts) and preparation time (in 20 of the 40 texts). Other optional moves for the recipe genre in German include a "goes well with" passage (appearing in 11 out of 40 texts), and "difficulty level" (appearing in 9 out of 40 texts prior to the list of ingredients). There is typically no mention made of nutritional information. Such information appears in only 3 of the 40 texts and only in 1 source.

At the level of average text length for this genre, the mean value in words for the 40 recipes is 187.45 (with the lowest length at 140 words and the highest at 478). This average is approximately half of what was found in the English-language recipe corpus, a finding that can be explained in large part by a preference for compounds in German. Corpus data reveal that 1,430 words consist of ten or more letters (~14% of the corpus). It is not uncommon for two-word collocations in English to be rendered as one-word compounds in German, as seen in the following examples from the corpus:

German term	English equivalent	Frequency
Backpapier	parchment paper	19
Tomatenmark	tomato paste	12
Butterschmalz	clarified butter	9
Ahornsirup	maple syrup	8
Pflanzenöl	vegetable oil	8

In terms of the **mode**, recipes can be classified as written texts to be read with a primarily didactic function in that the reader is guided in the creation of a food item. German-language recipes, in particular, are highly formulaic in both their lexical and syntactic constituents, as will be discussed later when examining micro-textual features. Controlled vocabulary and strategic utilization of **ellipsis** and **substitution** contribute to enhancing readability and text economy.

The **tenor** of German-language recipes often involves communication between a nationally-known sender (such as a food or media company) and an anonymous general public receiver. The intended receivers are experts and nonexperts alike. While the terminology is not particularly specialized, readers need to be aware of field-specific meanings presented by seemingly general language vocabulary, as illustrated by the following examples:

Word	Meaning in general contexts	Meaning in recipe context
geben (v)	to give	to add
würfeln (v)	to roll the dice	to dice
ziehen (v)	to pull	to run through

As previously mentioned, the **communicative function** of recipes is primarily didactic or **informative** in nature. Informative features, such as the list of ingredients, preparation time, and difficulty level, deliver factual information that illustrates the **conative** function of language and in the service of the overarching purpose of the text.

Micro-textual features

At the micro-textual level, the preparation steps in German recipes are generally built around a noun (direct object) + verb (infinitive form) template core. These infinitive form action verbs render an imperative mood. Many of the infinitive verbs consist of a root along with a range of attached prefixes that establish semantic variation, for example, rühren (to stir), *an*rühren (to blend), *durch*rühren (to churn), *ein*rühren (to stir in), and *unter*rühren (to mix in). We do not see the verb initial imperative constructs that typify English-language recipes. The majority of the sentences are present tense compound sentences linked by the additive conjunction "and." An analysis of the first step in each of the 40 recipes yields the following results in terms of sentence types: 29/40 compound,

Text types

8/40 simple, and 3/10 complex. Corpus statistics reveal an average sentence length of 11.65 words.

Substitution is used frequently in German-language recipes. This strategy primarily comes in the form of pronominal adverbs, such as *darin* (in it), *damit* (with it), *darüber* (over it), *dazu* (to it), which serve as anaphoric placeholders for concrete nouns. We find 94 of these in the corpus. Such *da*-compounds are often difficult to translate into English. There seems to be a greater preference in English for avoiding such placeholders by introducing additional verbs, as illustrated via the following example:

German passage
Milch erwärmen und Butter oder Margarine darin zerlassen.

Literal English translation
Heat milk and melt butter or margarine *in it*.

Idiomatic English translation
Heat milk. *Add* and melt butter or margarine.

Another cohesive device used frequently in German-language recipes to enhance text economy is **ellipsis**. In a random analysis of 40 multi-sentence steps in the corpus, 23 made use of ellipsis and 17 did not. Substitution seems to be preferred over ellipsis in German recipes.

In examining **hypernym** and **hyponym** distributions based on corpus wordlist data, it becomes evident that recipes call for lexical and semantic precision. While semantically broad hypernyms are used, we often see similarly high frequencies for corresponding hyponyms when quantified in the aggregate:

Hypernym	Frequency	Hyponyms	Total frequency
braten (to fry)	11	*anbraten* (to brown), *andünsten* (to sauté), *anschwitzen* (to sauté), *bräunen* (to brown), *anrösten* (to brown)	48

These data would also seem to reveal a preference for **synonymy** in German-language recipes. However, within a given recipe (as opposed to across recipes), this is not evident. Each source uses controlled vocabulary rooted in lexical recurrence. This mitigates ambiguity and fosters predictability. The widespread distribution of **hyponyms** highlights a preference for lexical and semantic precision in German-language recipes, particularly at the level of verb + noun collocations.

Paralleling the frequently occurring word *Minuten* are a number of temporal conjunctions, including *dann* (then), appearing 33 times, *bis* (until), appearing 26 times, and *erst* (first), appearing 7 times. These underscore a potential linguistic and cultural preference for linearity and temporal signposts in German-language recipes.

Recipes 43

Sample text – German recipe

Curryschnitzel auf *Süßkartoffelpüree* und *Kokosbutter*
Portion(en): 3 **Vorbereitungszeit**: 20 **Min.** *Zubereitungszeit*: 15 **Min.**

Zutaten

- 6 Scheiben Toastbrot (alternativ *Semmelbrösel* oder besser Pankomehl)
- 1 Ei (Größe L)
- 1 TL *Currypulver*
- 3 *Putenschnitzel*
- Jodsalz, Pfeffer
- 1–2 EL Mehl
- 2–3 EL Öl (z.B. Erdnussöl)
- 2 EL Butter
- 600 g *Süßkartoffeln*
- 2 TL KNORR Gemüse Bouillon
- 2 TL Honig
- 1–2 EL *Kokosraspeln*

Zubereitung

1. Toastbrot entrinden und in einer *Küchenmaschine* fein mahlen. Ei mit Curry verrühren. Fleisch salzen und pfeffern. **Erst** in Mehl wenden, **dann** in der Ei-Curry-Mischung und **zuletzt** in den *Toastbrotkrumen*.
2. Schnitzel in einer Pfanne in Öl und 2 EL Butter *beidseitig* jeweils 2–3 **Minuten** knusprig braten, dabei das Fett während des Bratens über die Schnitzel schöpfen. Auf *Küchenkrepp* abtropfen lassen.
3. *Süßkartoffeln* schälen und 2–3 cm groß würfeln. In kochender KNORR *Gemüsebouillon* weich kochen, abgießen und stampfen oder durch eine Presse drücken. Mit Salz und Honig abschmecken. In einer Pfanne *Kokosraspeln* rösten und über das Püree geben.

Dazu passen *Limettenspalten* und zum Beispiel gebratener Brokkoli.

Key: temporal conjunctions and time constructions – bold; compound nouns over ten characters long – italics; general language verbs used in field-specific contexts – underline
Source: www.knorr.de/rezepte/detail/2647/1/curryschnitzel-auf-suesskartoffelpueree-und-kokosbutter

---

Sample German recipe analysis

A sample recipe will be used to contextualize the aforementioned macro-textual and micro-textual conventions typically found in German-language recipes. The recipe for Curry Schnitzel with Mashed Sweet Potatoes and Coconut Butter was taken from the Knorr online recipe database. Knorr is a German food brand with international operations in over 30 countries around the world. The recipe adheres to the three prototypical rhetorical moves of "title," "ingredients," and "preparation" and contains the optional moves of "portion size," "preparation time," and a "goes well with" statement at the end. The recipe consists of 191 words. The average sentence

44 Text types

length is 8.6 words per sentence, around three below the corpus mean of 11.65. It contains numerous compound nouns consisting of ten or more characters (italicized), thereby exhibiting a prototypical feature of German-language recipes:

German compound	No. of characters	EN equivalent
Curryschnitzel	14	curry schnitzel
Süsskartoffelpüree	18	mashed sweet potatoes
Kokosbutter	11	coconut butter
Vorbereitungszeit	17	preparation time
Semmelbrösel	12	breadcrumbs
Currypulver	11	curry powder
Putenschnitzel	14	turkey schnitzel
Süsskartoffeln	14	sweet potatoes
Kokosraspeln	12	coconut flakes
Küchenmaschine	14	food processor
Ei-Curry-Mischung	17	egg-curry mixture
Toastbrotkrumen	15	toasted white breadcrumbs
Küchenkrepp	11	paper towel
Gemüsebouillon	14	vegetable bouillon
Limettenspalten	15	lime wedges

With the exception of one sentence, all preparation steps adhere to the noun (direct object) + infinitive (end) verb syntactic template typical of German-language recipes.

Of the 11 sentences constituting recipe steps, 5 are compound, 3 are simple, and 2 are complex. Seven of the eleven sentences contain the additive conjunction *und* (and). The text type conventions of temporal conjunctions and other time constructs are particularly prominent in this sample recipe (see content highlighted in bolded text). In the last sentence of the first step, we see the juxtaposition of three temporal indicators in the very same passage: *Erst in Mehl wenden, dann in der Ei-Curry-Mischung und zuletzt in den Toastbrotkrumen* (*First* coat in flour, *then* in the egg-curry mixture, and *finally* in the toasted white bread crumbs). Additionally, we see two noun compounds containing the word *Zeit* (time), *Vorbereitungszeit* (preparation time) and *Zubereitungszeit* (cooking time). *Minuten* (minutes) occurs 3 times. Collectively, these temporal signposts suggest a monochronic cultural mindset.

Ellipsis is a frequently used cohesive device in this text, occurring at least once in each of the preparation steps. We see one example of substitution in the form of a *da*-compound (*dabei* while doing so) to replace the lengthiest instruction in the recipe, which immediately precedes it and consists of 17 words. This is found in the second step.

Out of the 118 words appearing in this recipe, only 28 (~24%) occur more than once. Recurrence is generally restricted to situations where ingredients are repeated verbatim in the preparation steps. None of the verb forms in the steps recurs, pointing toward lexical and semantic precision. We see only one noun recurring in the steps (*Schnitzel*), which is the primary food item being prepared. This food item also represents the only lexical item for which we see a hypernym (*Fleisch*/meat). There are no occurrences of synonyms.

RUSSIAN

In recent years, the genre of recipes in Russian culture has been undergoing rapid change. In the pre-internet era, recipes were primarily found in printed cookbooks, such as *Kniga o vkusnoi i zdorovoi pishche* (Book of Tasty and Healthy Food 1953) and *Kulinariia* (Culinary Art 1955), or passed on from generation to generation as written notes or oral stories. Most Russians were accustomed to cooking and needed no basic directions, such as how to boil an egg or add salt "to taste." Thus, unlike English recipes, Russian recipes tended to be imprecise and resembled storytelling rather than clearly laid-out instructions. When Russia's political borders opened following the collapse of the Soviet Union and the internet became widely available, Russians had unprecedented access to Western-style recipes from numerous websites and blogs, which began to influence the way Russian recipes were structured. To understand the current dynamic state of Russian recipes, we analyzed a corpus of 15 recipes from 8 different sources, all published between the years of 2014 and 2016.

Macro-textual features

We begin our analysis with macro-textual features of the recipes and look at the **rhetorical moves** that occur in all the recipes in the Russian corpus:

1. Title
2. Ingredients (Игредиенты)
3. Directions (Приготовление, Способ приготовления, Пошаговый рецепт приготовления, Инструкция приготовления, or no explicit heading for the steps)

The directions are referred to in five different ways, which points to a certain inconsistency in modern Russian recipes. The least common were Инструкция приготовления (1 occurrence) and the absence of a heading (2 occurrences). The most common was Пошаговый рецепт приготовления (6 occurrences, 5 of which were from the same source). It appears that Приготовление (4 times) and the related Способ приготовления (2 times) remain typical for referring to directions in recipes, while Пошаговый рецепт приготовления (Step-by-step recipe) may be a reflection of the English-language tradition of dividing recipes into steps, which is not typical for older Russian-language recipes.

In addition to the three mandatory moves, a variety of optional features were found in the recipe corpus:

1. The number of servings (Рецепт на 12 персон, 6 порций, Количество порций) (found in 4 recipes)
2. Name or nickname of the author (found in 12 recipes)
3. Date published (found in 8 recipes)
4. Prep time (Подготовка) (found in 2 recipes)
5. Time (Время готовки or приготовления) (found in 3 recipes)
6. Level of difficulty (Сложность приготовления – легко, средне, сложно) (found in 2 recipes)

7. Nutritional information (Калорийность или энергетическая ценность на порцию (found in 1 recipe)
8. Type of cuisine (Кухня) (found in 1 recipe)
9. Advice or story accompanying a recipe (Совет к рецепту, История к рецепту, or an introduction without a heading) (found in 12 recipes)
10. Bon appetite or another wish (Приятного аппетита! Благополучия и достатка в новом году!) (found in 5 recipes)

Interestingly, most recipes provide the name(s) of the author(s) and a story and/or advice from them, which typically precede the ingredients and steps. We also notice a tendency to conclude recipes with a closing line, such as "Bon appetite" or even "Best wishes for the New Year." Indications of difficulty, preparation time, type of cuisine, and number of servings are not frequently found in the corpus. Only 2 recipes indicated whether a dish was vegetarian or not. Only one contained nutritional information.

The analysis suggests that a certain degree of imprecision persists in Russian recipes. Five recipes (which is one-third of the corpus) contain the lexeme примерно (approximately).

Another notable macro-feature that characterizes this text type is the length of texts. The total word count for the recipe corpus was 6,994 words, with an average of 466.27 words. The shortest recipe was 161 words, while the longest was 1,002 words, which suggests that Russian recipes display significant variation in length. We should keep in mind that since Russian recipes often include authors' stories, the average length may be longer than English-language recipes.

We analyzed **register** using the three aspects put forward by Halliday and Hasan (1985): **field, mode,** and **tenor.** The prevailing lexical items, or terminology, give us a good idea of the text type's topic or **field** of discourse. As we see in the table below, the high-frequency words and their forms relate to the field of cooking.

High-frequency lexical items	Frequencies of each item	Total frequency
Масло (масла, маслом, масле)	19 + 15 + 7 + 1	42
Добавить (добавляем, добавьте, добавив, добавляемых, добавляйте, добавляю, добавляют, добавляя)	18 + 8 + 5 + 1 + 1 + 1 + 1 + 1 + 1	37
Перец (перца, перцев, перцы, перцем, перчик, перчика)	25 + 7 + 4 + 2 + 1 + 2 + 1	32
Сыр (сыром, сыру)	17 + 9 + 2	28
Блюдо (блюда, блюд, блюду)	12+10 + 3 + 2	27
Рис (рисом, риса)	18 + 6 + 2	26
Лук (луковица, лука, лук-порей)	16 + 4 + 2 + 3	25
Сахар (сахара, сахаром, сахару)	14 + 5 + 2 + 1	22
Соль (солью, соли)	14 + 2 + 6	22
Чеснок (чеснока, чесноком)	14 + 6 + 2	22

(Continued)

Recipes 47

(Continued)

High-frequency lexical items	Frequencies of each item	Total frequency
Перемешать (перемешивая, перемешивают, перемешивайте, перемешиваем))	13 + 3 + 1 + 2 + 2	21
Тесто (теста, тестом)	13 + 5 + 1	19
Картофель (картофеля, картофелем, картошка)	11 + 4 + 2 + 2	19
Яйцо (яйца, яйцом, яйцами)	8 + 8 + 1 + 1	18
Молоко (молоком, молока)	13 + 3 + 1	17

The lexical items in the table above describe ingredients (milk, pepper, etc.) or process (to add, to mix). The word "dish" is also quite frequent.

In terms of the **mode** of discourse, recipes are written. The ultimate purpose of a recipe is to help readers prepare a dish according to the directions in a recipe. The **tenor,** or the relationship between the author and the audience of recipes, may be two-fold. On the one hand, the authors are typically experts in cooking, while the audience may or may not be experts. Ideally, recipes should be written in a way that both experts and nonexperts could follow them, unless otherwise indicated.

In terms of their **communicative function**, recipes are **informative** texts by means of which the authors transfer their knowledge and skills to the audience. The authors' notes may be meant to persuade the readers to choose their dish, which indicates a degree of **conative** function in recipes.

Micro-textual features

At the micro-textual level, our analysis points to a variety of verb forms used in the corpus. The infinitive, which used to be the standard for Russian recipes (e.g., перемешать (occurs in four texts), нарезать (six texts), выложить (six texts)) still prevails. However, we see the emergence of new verb forms in recipe writing. One is the use of the first-person plural form of verbs in the present tense (добавляем (three texts), выкладываем (three texts)). Another noticeable form is the imperative or directive used in the second-person plural, something that may have entered Russian recipes from English (e.g., выложите (two texts), посолите (two texts)). Very infrequent are sub-jectless perfective future forms (украсим зеленью – we'll decorate with herbs). The imperfective future tense (будет(е)) and the past tense appear mostly in the author's stories (e.g., Мнение моих домашних разделилось [My family's opinions (regarding the dessert the author made) were split]). Another example: У меня есть идеальный рецепт, который будет хорош с любым другим мясом (I have an ideal recipe that will be good with any other type of meat). The table below shows the dynamic state of verb-form use in Russian recipes.

Verb tense	No. of texts
Infinitive (e.g., нарезать)	7
Present first-person plural (e.g., нарезаем)	4
Imperative (e.g., нарежьте)	3
Mixed forms in one recipe (e.g., нарезать, нарежьте, нарезаем)	1

Regarding **cohesive devices**, Russian recipes use a variety of different devices, including reference, substitution, and conjunctions. For instance, personal reference such as я occurs 29 times and его 22 times. Other examples include ee (12 times), их (10 times), вы (9 times), он (7 times), мой (2 times), and several forms of personal reference pronouns that were not frequently employed in the corpus (моей, моем, мне, etc.). Demonstrative referents are also used, such as это (17 times) and forms of это/этот/эта/эти (22 times).

Substitution in Russian may refer to the use of personal pronouns он/она/оно/они to refer to objects or people they represent. Russian nouns have grammatical gender, which makes it possible to use personal pronouns to refer to inanimate objects. In our case, we classify them as referential cohesive devices. Halliday and Hasan's (1985) framework of cohesion was developed for the English language, and thus is not fully applicable to Russian, e.g., Halliday and Hasan's substitutive devices "one" and "do/does/did" are not found in Russian. Russian may have its own cohesive devices not typical for English or other languages (e.g., the use of verbal adjectives as substitutions for relative clauses and verbal adverbs as substitutions for temporal clauses). Ellipsis, as a cohesive device, is not seen in recipes, since this type of cohesive device is more frequently seen in dialogue or oral speech.

Conjunctions, however, are a cohesive device that are abundant in the recipe corpus. The most frequent conjunctions in the analyzed corpus are:

Conjunctions	Frequency
и	251
до (тех пор, пока)	37
или	32
а	24
если	21
что	21
чтобы	18
но	14
пока	8
то	8
затем	6
когда	4
потом	3
далее	2

The additive conjunction и (and) is by far the most frequent one in the corpus, which may be due to the nature of the cooking process (following steps, adding one ingredient to another, mixing ingredients, etc.). Similarly, temporal conjunctions are also frequent (until, while, then, when, etc.). The frequent use of additive and temporal conjunctions suggests that Russian recipes contain primarily two types of sentences – complex and compound sentences.

Lexical cohesion is created primarily through repetition. The table below provides a quick look at the frequently repeated words. Various forms of the same lexeme are included in the total count.

High-frequency nouns	Frequency	High-frequency nouns	Frequency
грамм (г.)	51	лук	25
шаг	46	приготовление	25
масло	42	салат	24
минута (мин.)	40	соль	22
штука (шт.)	33	чеснок	22
перец	32	сахар	22
стакан (ст.)	32	духовка	22
сыр	28	вода	22
блюдо	27	рецепт	20
ингредиент(ы)	27	тесто	19
вкус	25	картофель	19
рис	26	яйцо	18
соус	26	морковь	18

The word Ингредиенты is a superordinate form for produce/products used in cooking and indicates a parts/whole relationship. Non-produce items refer to measurement units (грамм, штука) or cooking utensils, such as сковорода (10 times) and кастрюля (9 times). Some nouns, such as тесто (dough), are products of combining ingredients together. The noun шаг refers to steps in the cooking process and is typically followed by a cardinal numeral (one, two, etc.).

From the standpoint of lexical cohesion, it is interesting to note that Russian often uses diminutive forms of nouns to indicate the small size of an object, endearment toward someone or something, as well as politeness on the part of the speaker. Russian recipes, it turns out, are no exception. Here are some diminutives we found in our recipe corpus: форма – формочка, ложка – ложечка, кусок – кусочек, кастрюля – кастрюлька, орехи – орешки, перец – перчик.

Russian particles (же, ведь) also play an important role in textual cohesion, since they help identify emotional tones in texts. Recipes, however, did not make frequent use of particles. Ведь occurred only twice, while же was not used at all.

It is notable that recipes tend to use a high number of nouns. Verbs, however, are not as frequent. The verbs vary in their prefixes (солить – посолить). Below are several verbs that occurred most frequently in our recipe corpus.

Verbs (and their conjugated forms)	Frequency
добавить	34
приготовить	27
перемешать	18
нарезать	15
выложить	15
измельчить	11
смешать	10
(по)солить	9

Overall, our analysis suggests that Russian recipes are changing under the influences of open borders and the internet. We live in exciting times when linguists can witness these changes first-hand. Twenty-five years ago, who would have predicted that we would see a Russian recipe explaining to the reader how many milliliters are in an American measuring cup (Американская мерная чашка – 237 мл.)?

Sample text – Russian recipe

29 ноября 2016 / Анна Гомон

Рагу из курицы с овощами и сырными булочками

Сытное блюдо. Для меня это – в первую очередь, комфортная еда, которая состоит из простых ингредиентов и её легко приготовить. Рецепты этих блюд стабильны, проработаны и качественны. Как правило, в состав Ø обязательно входят сезонные продукты. И очень неплохо, если блюдо готовится в одной посуде. Эта еда принесет в вашу жизнь ощущение радости, защищенности и уюта. И у меня есть идеальный рецепт, который будет хорош с любым другим мясом и овощами на ваш вкус. Курица, приготовленная таким способом, получается сочной, а булочки пропитываются соусом и замечательно дополняют рагу.

Ингредиенты

филе куриных бедер 500 г	*кабачок 1/2 шт.*	*тыква 300 г*
морковь 3 шт.	болгарский перец 1 шт.	луковица 2 шт.
зубчик чеснока 2 шт.	острый перец 1 шт.	овощной бульон 400 мл
сливки 10% 100 мл	тимьян, розмарин, шалфей 1 ст. л.	соль, перец 2 ч. л.
кукурузная мука 2 ст. л.	пшеничная мука 180 г	сливочное масло 60 г
пармезан 40 г	молоко 80 мл	разрыхлитель 1,5 ч. л.
соль 1/4 ч. л.		

Пошаговый рецепт приготовления

Шаг 1

Срезать с мяса лишний жир и сухожилия, нарезать Ø крупными кубиками. Кукурузную муку посолить, обвалять в ней курицу, излишки Ø стряхнуть. Лук нарезать полукольцами, морковь Ø – тонкими кружочками, болгарский перец, тыкву и кабачок Ø – кубиками. Чеснок измельчить. Тимьян, розмарин и шалфей мелко порубить.

Шаг 2

Нагреть небольшое количество оливкового масла в кастрюле с толстым дном, обжарить курицу на сильном огне. Переложить Ø в миску.

Шаг 3

В этой же кастрюле обжарить овощи в течение 5 минут. Посолить Ø, приправить Ø пряными травами.

Шаг 4

Добавить курицу и влить бульон. Тушить Ø под крышкой на среднем огне около 20 мин.

Шаг 5

Влить сливки, уменьшить огонь и тушить Ø еще 5–10 мин. до загустения.

Шаг 6

Смешать муку с маслом, сыром, солью, разрыхлителем.

Шаг 7

Постепенно вливая молоко, замесить крутое тесто.

Шаг 8

Выложить тесто на слегка посыпанную мукой поверхность, собрать Ø в шар.

Шаг 9

Сформовать из теста шарики размером с куриное яйцо, расплющить Ø в лепешки и выложить Ø на рагу.

Шаг 10

Запекать рагу с булочками при температуре 190 градусов 25–30 мин. Булочки увеличатся в объеме и станут золотистыми.

Шаг 11

Достать кастрюлю из духовки и сразу же подать Ø.

Key: various features discussed in sample analysis – highlighted in gray
Source: www.gastronom.ru/recipe/38710/ragu-iz-kuricy-s-ovoshchami-i-syrnymi-bulochkami

Sample Russian recipe analysis

The sample recipe for our analysis was published in 2016 on gastronom.ru, a popular Russian-language cooking website that provides recipes, cooking advice, diets, and more. At the macro-textual level, the recipe contains the three mandatory rhetorical moves typical for Russian recipes (the title Рагу из курицыс овощами и сырными булочками [Chicken stew with vegetables and cheese buns], the list of ingredients (Ингредиенты), and directions, Пошаговый рецепт приготовления [Step-by-step recipe]), as well as some of the optional rhetorical moves, such as the author's name (Anna Gomon), publication date (November 29, 2016), level of difficulty (сложно [difficult]), and a story accompanying the recipe (in this case, an introduction briefly discussing the recipe and its advantages). Each step has a picture illustrating it, and is numbered (Шаг 1, Шаг 2, etc.). The length of the sample recipe is about 360 words, which is within the average range for recipes. In terms of the mode of discourse, the ingredients' list and the directions are informative, while the introduction is both informative and conative. The tenor of discourse appears to be both

52   Text types

expert-to-nonexpert and expert-to-expert. As for the field of discourse, the sample recipe is about making stews with chicken and vegetables, as well as rolls to accompany the dish. It is seen from both the title and the list of frequent lexical items, which includes nouns and adjectives related to chicken (курица, куриный) (7 occurrences) and to vegetables (овощи, овощной) (4 occurrences), as well as in the repetition of the words рагу (stew) (4) and булочки (rolls) (4).

At the micro-textual level, the instructions in the recipe are primarily phrased using infinitives (about 30 instances), which is traditional for Russian recipes. Seven of the fifteen recipes in the corpus use infinitives for instructions. The introduction is written primarily in the present tense (состоит [consists of], готовится [is prepared]) and the future (e.g., будет хорош [will be good], принесет радость [will bring joy]). Some verbal adjectives and verbal adverbs are used throughout the recipe (приготовленный [cooked], вливая [while pouring in]).

As for grammatical cohesion, the sample recipe uses some reference devices (mostly pronouns) and conjunctions. Since the steps are numbered, few conjunctions are used. The additive conjunction *и* is by far the most frequent in the sample recipe (17 occurrences). The conjunctive referential pronoun который is used twice, while the conjunctions *а* and если are each used once. Verbal adverbs and adjectives also perform a cohesive function indicating temporal relations between the actions.

However, the main grammatical cohesive device in the sample recipe is ellipses (marked with the symbol Ø in the sample text). In 2 instances, a dash is used in the sample recipe to indicate that a lexical item was omitted. From the standpoint of syntax, the sample recipe appears straightforward. It contains few complex or compound sentences, preferring simple sentences instead, especially when outlining the preparation steps.

In terms of lexical cohesion, the recipe contains numerous repetitions, e.g., the names of ingredients being reiterated in the various steps. Some instances of hypernymy are found, where a hypernym, or a reference that changes the type of a concept, is used; e.g., one of the main ingredients, listed in the ingredients section as филе куриных бедер (bone-free chicken thighs), is referred to as курица (chicken) or мясо (meat [of chicken, in this case]) throughout the rest of the text. While it is clear to the reader that the recipe refers to the boneless chicken thighs (and so this may not be hyponymy per se), it may also be consistent with the introduction, which specifies that other meat can be substituted for chicken thighs.

From the description above, it may appear that the sample recipe we analyzed is precise. However, manual analysis shows that, as may be typical for some Russian recipes, the sample recipe trusts the reader to use common sense. For example, the list of ingredients lists spicy peppers as an ingredient; however, the directions never mention them, assuming that the reader should know to add it to other vegetables when preparing them.

SPANISH

The cultural specificity of recipes affects the translatability of this text type in a fundamental way. The first caveat for the translator revolves around the most basic decision of whether a recipe is materially feasible to translate *as a recipe*: the Peruvian penchant for tortoise or guinea pig may make for fascinating culinary history or historical linguistics but would be a low relevance text for would-be cooks where key ingredients are scarce or not part of the cultural palate. Or consider what is perhaps Spain's best-known cookbook, *1080 recetas* (Ortega 1972), which has a section called "Variety Meats" featuring disembodied tongue and peeled sheep skulls – all culturally authentic but ill-advised for the sensibilities of the American market. Recipes in the original Spanish featuring liquor – which the Spanish text calls "especially appropriate for children's afternoon snack" – are bowdlerized in the English, and, through addition, humane hints for cooking lobster appear (Abend 2007). Abend, when reviewing the translation, faults the workaday pragmatism of the original text, which does not lend itself to food "fetishization" and thus fails to inspire a translation relevant to today's foreign connoisseur (ibid.). Such examples bear out Cronin's (2017: 61) observation that "translation foregrounds the buried cultural and linguistic complexity of items that are frequently taken for granted in the culture of origin."

In order to perform a data-driven analysis of the current state of recipes authored between December 2015 and December 2016 in Spanish, a corpus of ten texts from ten different sources was collected from Mexican digital sources. The length of the Spanish recipe in our corpus is on average 22.34 words; the minimum is 15.52 words, and the maximum, 29.16 words. A notable feature of these texts is their average word length of 4.35 characters, with a range of 4.0 to 4.66 in the corpus, a remarkable consistency. The corpus shows an average of 16.1 sentences per recipe, and a mean number of words per text of 359. We will begin in our analysis of the corpus with the broad conventions called macro-textual features.

Macro-textual features

The macro-textual features of a recipe include the following **rhetorical moves**:

1. Title (*Título*)
2. Author/source (*Autor/Fuente*)
3. Ingredients (*Ingredientes*)
4. Preparation (*Preparación*)

In addition, several optional moves or variations are present in the corpus data, including:

1. Author's name (*Nombre del autor*)
2. Date (*Fecha*)
3. Yield (*Porciones* or *rendimiento*)
4. Prep time (*Tiempo de preparación*)
5. Cooking time (*Tiempo de cocción*)

Text types

6. Level of difficulty (*Dificultad*)
7. Storage (*Conservación*)

In one text, the author's name and date appear; in three texts, prep time is given; in at least five texts the yield was given (although using different terms, *Porciones* and *Rendimiento*, and in one case the text simply notes "12 personas," without a heading); in one text, method of storage; none recorded the level of difficulty. The communicative goals of each of these sections are self-evident, although it can be observed that level of difficulty – and other information – in a sense function as a kind of metadata, allowing the user to gauge the text's appropriateness for use, and even for the source site to catalogue it accordingly. Nutritional information does not often appear and may be said to be not characteristic of Spanish recipes, as in many cases it is a response to legislative requirements or cultural prioritization. However, it does appear in one text in our corpus. A subheading to the title of the recipe may also appear, such as, *Aquí la receta con la que sorprenderás a todos la noche del grito*, referencing the tradition of *chiles en nogada* being served on a specific occasion in Mexico, in this case, Independence Day.

One could also add to these steps a contextualization or framing, in which the author explains a tradition, or offers a historical or personal meaning of a dish in a narrative introduction, often including tips; in online fora, recipes may also have a "2.0" component whereby feedback is suggested by readers who have tested, varied, or perhaps refined a dish.

The context of the situation is frequently examined using Halliday and Hasan's (1985) three **register** variables of **field, mode,** and **tenor.** High-frequency lexical items make the subject matter, or **field** – in this case, cooking – easily discernible:

High-frequency lexical items	Frequency	High-frequency lexical items	Frequency
hasta que	28	*sal y*	11
a fuego	17	*se agrega*	11
de la	17	*y el*	11
en una	15	*de pollo*	10
cucharadas de	14	*la mezcla*	10
taza de	14	*que la*	10
con la	11	*al gusto*	9

We find the temporal conjunction, *hasta que*, to have the highest frequency in the cluster corpus. This is a logical finding, as in cooking actions have to be limited by reactions or an end to actions, lest everything burn or boil over. It also suggests the prototypical use of subordinating conjunctions, and thus complex sentences, despite their brevity. The other high-frequency nouns are measurements, temperatures, and, unexpectedly, a passive construction (*se agrega* is added) that serves as an implied command. *Al gusto* (to taste) constitutes the most frequent complete terminological unit in the findings, a term that introduces not an objective measure but a vague invitation to determine for oneself, through flavor, when a step is complete. In the raw frequency list, the prepositions and **conjunctions** *de, que, con, para* predominate, as do nouns denoting ingredients; in descending order of occurrence, they are: *sal, agua, fuego, manteca, pavo, ajo, carne, pollo, azúcar, chiles, leche.*

Mode describes the degree of oral and written discourse elements characterizing a text. Recipes are usually written to be performed rather than learned; procedural texts, recipes are read sequentially rather than, say, consulted ad hoc as an aid to troubleshooting.

Tenor describes the relationship between the author and the reader and the familiarity or distance between them, for example, expert-to-expert or expert-to-nonexpert or layperson. That relationship is made manifest in many psychological features, including references to the readers' motivations for cooking (e.g., one recipe in the corpus promises no less than impressing one's family at the holiday meal: *Así que ¿listos? Disfruten a lo grande esta rica y sencilla receta que los hará quedar muy bien con la familia y amigos en las celebraciones de Navidad y Año Nuevo*). A discourse feature that clearly indicates tenor is the empathetic question *¿listos?* (ready?), which is in the interrogative mode and mimics oral discourse. Conceivably the function of this type of language is **phatic**, that is, a way of "holding the floor" during a key transition in the process being described. These questions are also instances of mood management. We might compare this strategy to *emotionally intelligent signage* common today, in which street signs inform but also build empathy as they prompt certain actions from the reader. In addition to adding didacticism into the procedural, as reinforced by the plural form of address, used as if to address a classroom of students, our sample recipe employs all-important tonal markers that suggest the recipe author's encouraging supervision. The recipe actually guides the reader through the most difficult step by counseling *ánimo y no se desesperen* (take heart, don't despair). The language, we may observe, is not clinical, as in a technical installation manual, but evocative, full of deliberately expressive features such as appetizing language, as we can see in the *siempre rico* in the very name of a recipe.

Micro-textual features

At the micro-textual level, the data show that the most common verbs reveal a mixture of formal and informal forms of address, and overall variability in the singular, plural, and infinitive forms of commands:

Verb	Frequency
agrega	20
pon	9
deje	7
agregar	5
hacer	5

(Continued)

Text types

(Continued)

Verb	Frequency
deja (as a command)	4
añadan	4
caliente	4
cocinar	4
cocinen	4
dejar	4
hervir	4
pueden	4
puedas	4

Sixty-two instances of *se* occur in the corpus, but only two texts use passive *se* constructions as commands (imperative mood); one maintains it all the way through and one alternates with infinitives. The most typical use of present subjunctive mood occurs after just such temporal conjunctions as *hasta que* (e.g., *hasta que espese*) or causal constructions such as *para que* (7 instances in 40% of texts).

Material reality is frequently reflected in recipes, whether of locally sourced ingredients (e.g., *flores de cempasúchil*, an indigenous borrowing that has been lexicalized in the Spanish and therefore is not marked with italics) or of cooking procedures such as broiling, which is not as common in Latin cookery as it is in the Anglo world.[2] Spanish adapts by combining two methods: *asar a la parrilla*, "to roast on the grill"; conversely, the Spanish cook more frequently *a la plancha*, i.e., on a round flat top range with equally distributed heat. Other terms such as the dish named metaphorically *Manchamanteles de Jalisco* (The Jalisco Tablecloth-Soiler) that appears in one of the recipes in our corpus might need a cultural note to explain this thick tropical-style *mole*, the latter a term which itself is used reductively as a loanword and a superordinate term to mean *mole poblano,* though it actually covers many kinds of sauce in Mexico. Conventional lexicographic senses of terms can be deceiving, as the same term, or cognate term, can have different referents. For instance, Spanish *pimentón*, technically paprika, is vastly more varied (and flavorful). It is a matter of debate how near-synonymy in recipes affects the food. World knowledge, however, is vital in determining what kinds of chili peppers, for example, may make for reasonable substitutions. Complicating matters further, names of staples such as beans can vary widely (*habas, frijoles, habichuelas*) across the more than 20 Spanish-speaking countries. It is virtually certain that Spanish-language recipes, moreover, feature more traditional cookware implements, such as wooden bowls, than English recipes do.

Invariably in the recipe genre the precision of measurements will be different across cultural systems – Spanish often prefers "to pre-heat" rather than providing more precise oven temperatures despite the precision in our sample. Weights and measures are given in metric units.

Sample text – Spanish recipe

El tradicional (y siempre rico) pan de muerto

Ingredientes

- 3 1/2 tazas de harina
- 225 gramos de mantequilla
- 3 huevos
- 1 1/4 tazas de azúcar
- 1/2 taza de agua
- 2 cucharadas de ralladura de cáscara de naranja
- 22 gramos de levadura
- 7 yemas de huevo
- 1/4 de cucharadita de sal
- 1 cucharada de agua de azahar (si no encuentran pueden sustituirlo por 2 cucharadas té de anís preparado y bien cargado)

Preparación

En un recipiente poner la levadura junto con media taza de azúcar y el agua que debe estar tibia (cuidado que no esté caliente) para que la levadura se active. Al poco tiempo comenzarán a salir burbujas de la mezcla y eso quiere decir que la levadura ya está "despierta" pero si eso no ocurre hay que repetir el proceso.

Sobre la mesa de casa o en una batidora (para hacer pan), poner el harina, 1/4 de taza de azúcar, la ralladura de naranja, la sal, mantequilla y agua de azahar o el té anís e integrar los ingredientes poco a poco; agregar los dos huevos enteros así como las yemas y la levadura.

Amasar hasta que la mezcla este suave y sea manejable. No se preocupen si al principio la mezcla parece una especie de engrudo que no se logra despegar de la mesa, es normal. Deben amasar hasta que la mezcla se separe de la mesa pero eso lleva su tiempo así que ánimo y no se desesperen.

Una vez que lograron la masa deben dejarla descansar tapada con un paño húmedo, o con papel film, en una parte tibia de la cocina hasta que doble su tamaño gracias al efecto de la levadura – consideren esto a la hora de elegir el recipiente donde la pondrán para que cuando doble el tamaño la mezcla no se desborde –.

El siguiente paso es desgasificar la masa, es decir amasen de nuevo eliminando el gas que se formó. Ahora hay que separar una parte de la masa para las decoraciones (o huesitos) y con el resto formar los bollos del tamaño que quieran que sean sus panes y colocarlos en una charola con suficiente espacio entre ellos, considerando que van a duplicar su tamaño.

Con la masa apartada hacer los huesitos y el cráneo (la bolita) del pan. Batir el huevo que no se utilizó y a forma de pagamento usarlo para colocar los huesos al pan así como la bolita del centro.

Dejar reposar los panes, aproximadamente durante una hora, en una zona tibia de la cocina para que dupliquen su tamaño.

Precalentar el horno a 200 grados Celsius, meter los panes durante 15 minutos y bajar la temperatura a 180 grados para hornear por 20 minutos más o hasta que el pan esté listo. Dejar enfriar.

Aparte mezclar un cuarto de taza de agua y otro de azúcar y llevar al fuego hasta que el azúcar esté disuelta. Con el jarabe obtenido barnizar los panes y espolvorear el azúcar restante.

Text types

> Si quieren darle un giro interesante a su pan, pueden sustituir la ralladura de naranja por alguna de limón, toronja o mandarina. Además pueden darle otro sabor si le agregan los pétalos de dos flores de cempasúchil, lo que además le otorgará un color único.
>
> Key: various features discussed in sample analysis – highlighted in gray

Sample Spanish recipe analysis

We start with a macro-level analysis of the sample recipe. If we apply the Fernández-Huerta Reading Ease index (Modified Flesch Reading Ease),[3] some general data about our sample emerge (and note that some data are slightly different from those found using Wordsmith Tools): The average word is short (4.35 letters); is under two syllables (1.94); and there are approximately 17 (16.66) words per sentence, consistent with the corpus as a whole. Measured on five different readability metrics, the sample text was scored as indicated in the table below; a roughly fifth-grade reading level, and a reading time of roughly two and a half minutes (2.665 minutes):

Text Readability		
Index	Value	Difficulty
Fernández-Huerta	73.45	Fairly easy
Gutiérrez	46.61	Average
Szigriszt-Pazos	69.44	Fairly easy
INFLESZ	69.44	Fairly easy
µ readability	65.22	Average

Grade level (Crawford): 4.9 (years of school needed to understand the text).

In our sample text, we find the following "rare or misspelled words" (and in fact one actually is misspelled: *pagamento [for *pegamento]): *desgasificar, desesperen, pagamento, engrudo, barnizar, sean, amasen, desborde, cempasúchil*, and *charola*.

Let's consider some of this terminology and phraseology at the micro-textual level. The name of the dish *pan de muerto*, or Mexican bread of the dead, marks the occasion for cooking this food. Terms that may themselves be cultural borrowings such as *agua de azahar* ("orange blossom water" or "orange flower water") appear in our sample; the ingredient is North African and Middle Eastern in origin (*ma' el zhar*). A lexical item or phraseme is employed that is at once a technicism, a metaphor, and a fixed or habitual collocation – *la levadura ya está "despierta"* (the yeast at this point is "awakened"), which may differ from how other languages encode the idea, whether in metaphor or not (e.g., "activated" yeast in English). Curiously, the text uses two different words for describing a paste-like consistency ("pagamento" [*pegamento*] and *engrudo*).

The verb *desgasificar*, flagged in our readability index as low frequency, might suggest something like "to degas" or a similar technical term denoting the process of removing air bubbles from dough; however, we must be cognizant of how abstraction and concretion, and particularization and generalization, play a role in analyzing such terms. In English, for example, we might use "to punch down the dough" or, less informatively, "to remove the air bubbles from," or the specific technique used to achieve the result of removing air bubbles, namely "to knock back the dough."

An important principle in the drafting of procedural texts, including recipes, is that of iconicity. Steps should appear on the page or screen in the order they should be carried out in the phenomenal world. The most obvious example in a recipe in the Anglo-American world is the ingredients list, where the ingredient may be listed as, for example, "butter, melted" in order to indicate that the step should be taken during prep work, before the procedures given in the recipe. In our sample text under consideration, the paragraph in bold notifies the Spanish-speaking reader to choose a large container in which to place the yeast, due to the dough doubling in size; ideally, the bowl size should be noted *before* any instructions to let the mixture rest are given.

As for cohesive ties, in our sample recipe, the steps are not numbered, as they might be for a more novice readership. Numbers, then, are conspicuous for their absence here, although paragraphing serves a similar purpose. Finally, there is world knowledge assumed in the exophoric references to skull-shaped foods and their symbolism in Day of the Dead culinary traditions. The text virtually self-translates at intervals between the literal and figurative levels of representation: e.g., the instruction regarding *el cráneo* (*la bolita*) (the skull [the little rolled dough-ball]). The reference to edible cempasuchitle flowers, a word derived from the Nahuatl and Hispanicized as *cempasúchil*, creates intratextual coherence in that these Mexican marigolds are known as the *flor de muerto*, which the Mexican reader will know are a part of the celebration. Such cohesive ties demonstrate the *hermeneutic circle*: the part drawing meaning from the text as a whole, and the whole in turn depending on the interpretation of the component parts.

Regarding the mood and verb tenses used in the recipe, there is rather unsystematic use. For instance, generic imperatives, in the form of infinitives, and plural commands are both used. The subjunctive is used wherever a contingency is involved (e.g., do x until y). The preterit tense used for the phrase *Una vez que lograron la masa deben dejarla descansar* (Once you have made [pret., plural] the dough, let it rest), an unusual construction for a recipe where the reader will expect subjunctivity to be expressed in the more common future past perfect subjunctive (*hayan logrado*), or perhaps an ablative absolute ([*Una vez*] *hecha la mesa* … etc.). This single instance, or hapax legomenon, of a preterit (pl.) occurs in the corpus, and of a second-person familiar verb conjugation. Nouns of note in the corpus include the abbreviations *tz* and *pzas*, which are conventional measurements.

Notes

1 See ich.unesco.org/en/RL/gastronomic-meal-of-the-french-00437.
2 Cultural substitutions are a common procedure in translating recipes. Cronin (2017: 63) describes an illustrative case in which a cookbook translator found that ingredients were not available in the target culture; the publisher recommended substitutions be used, which the translator found to be distorting; a compromise was found in rendering the original ingredients plus a list of possible substitutes.
3 Huerta Reading Ease = $206.84 - (0.60 * P) - (1.02 * F)$. P = Number of syllables per 100 words; F = Number of sentences per 100 words (https://legible.es/).

3 Instruction manuals

The user manual (or user guide) is a kind of technical communication and one of the most common forms of user assistance. This text type typically accompanies a physical product and has a variety of functions, such as enhancing the brand of the product, meeting legal requirements, reducing product liability, showing users how things work, and warning them of risks. Schäffner (2001: 49) draws a useful distinction between different types of user information: "installation manuals (predominantly for experts), operating leaflets (for both experts and laypeople), [and] user manuals (predominantly for laypeople)."

Manuals are not read like novels, just as novels are not read like technical manuals. User manuals are read *efferently* – for the information that may be extracted and used, or, in Rosenblatt's (1978: 15) words, for "the information to be acquired, the logical solution to a problem, the actions to be carried out." By contrast, literature, for example, is read *aesthetically*, to experience *how* a work is written, fostering a subjective relationship to the text in the act of reading. At the same time, reading to perform a task is different from reading to gain general knowledge. The former is time-bound – the reader is seeking to apply knowledge immediately – and thus the reading is for just-in-time learning. Because of this task focus, technical manuals are often consulted, not read linearly, if they are read at all, even though users are routinely told to read all instructions *first*. They are usually read while installing, assembling, maintaining, operating, storing, or repairing a complex device or piece of equipment. The user manual's focus is on *how* things work rather than *why*.

Within the context of English-language traditions, user manuals must be intuitive, unambiguous, clear, and simple. They must also present information step-by-step. For optimal utility, they must have useful illustrations of steps and parts, including unique diagrams such as exploded views, callouts, flowcharts, tables, numbered lists, or checklists. The adjective most often associated with effective technical documentation is *user-friendly*. Pragmatically, then, such texts must be organized with subheadings and different fonts and font sizes. User manuals are frequently printed in consecutive, multilingual format and are published in online and hard-copy formats.

However, variation is possible, and even expected, when working with user manuals in different languages. In some cases, user manuals in languages other than English follow the structure of English manuals since they may be translations. Likewise, user manuals are often authored or translated anonymously by non-native speakers. In other cases, English user manuals are written with translation in mind to comply with a range of regulatory and legal requirements. The length of user manuals can sometimes make it impossible to rely solely on human translation, and machine translation may be used to generate the initial draft of the translation to be then edited by a target language specialist. Yet unedited machine translation may be used as is, and as a result these texts may have faulty grammar more than perhaps any other text type except product packaging and signage. Technical manuals are often usability tested with test users and with a prototype of the product in order to determine user needs and potential problems.

Who is the target user of the user manual? Backinger and Kingsley (1993: 2) provide U.S. government guidelines for the developer: "your goal should be to provide *the least competent user* with the information necessary to use your device in the most safe and effective manner possible" (emphasis added). In practice, the degree of obfuscation in many user manuals would call into question how widely observed this principle of user-centeredness is. Moreover, the imperative to be user-friendly is often at odds with the need to meet all legal requirements or to fully explain how a product works. Many instruction manuals can also be described as consumer-oriented, meaning they provide documentation for products intended for home purchase, such as recreational vehicles, appliances, vehicles, home entertainment devices, and tools.

ENGLISH

Instruction manuals accompany many different types of product and can be referred to in different ways (e.g., user's/owner's manual, instructions for use, or user guide). In most cases, they are intended to be read by the general public. This genre of text can be characterized as primarily *exhortative* with a certain degree of *conative* language, meaning that manuals seek primarily to motivate the user to operate, set-up, or maintain a given product optimally. Furthermore, in order to effectively motivate such conduct, instruction manuals are also instructive, providing as much knowledge or information as necessary. The corpus under study in this analysis comprises ten recently published manuals, taken from nine different sources. Their corresponding products include a smartphone, computer hardware in a couple of cases, an activity tracker ("smartwatch"), a microwave, a security camera system, a Bluetooth stereo transmitter, an astrophotography digital camera, a streaming media player, and a power wheelchair. Given the electronic nature of these products, examples of frequently occurring vocabulary include "screen" (418 instances, 80% of the texts), "device" (356 instances, 80%), and "power" (334 instances, 100%).

Macro-textual features

While the main function of instruction manuals is for the reader to perform an action on the product they accompany, manuals may very well feature other communicative goals, as evidenced by the following **rhetorical moves**, observed to different extents in the corpus:

1. Warnings, precautions, or safety notices (found in all 10 manuals)
2. Table of contents (found in 9 of the manuals)
3. Troubleshooting/product support (found in 7 of the manuals)
4. Promotion/advertising of the product purchased (found in 7 of the manuals)
5. Legal notices, such as copyrights or trademarks (found in 4 of the manuals)

In the case of the first move, it is standard to include warnings, precautions, or safety notices to alert the consumer to any potential risks or accidents associated with setting up, maintaining, or using the product. The second move also tends to be standard, as evidenced in all but one case in the corpus: a computer monitor manual, which happens to be thematically organized primarily around images of certain features (e.g., "front panel controls") and parts (e.g., "power cable"), which serve the purpose of directing the user to relevant linguistic information or instructions. Instruction manuals often include graphics and images and, like in the case mentioned, may be more "image-based" than "text-oriented" (Risku and Pircher 2008: 156). In any event, tables of contents are a common means of facilitating the user's access to the instructions or information, especially because instruction manuals are often divided into individual sections that can be read on their own without the reader needing to read a previous section. The third move, the inclusion of troubleshooting sections or product support information, can often be found in manuals to allow the user to trace and correct potential faults in the product. The fourth move is also common, as manufacturers often take advantage of any occasion to advertise their brand, encourage consumers to purchase from them again, or reassure them of the value of the product they have already purchased. In the case of three texts included in the corpus, the consumer is even "congratulated" for purchasing the product, which Byrne (2012: 160) regards as a "rather strange feature of some instruction manuals [which] other cultures may regard ... as insincere flattery which is both irritating and patronizing." Despite the corpus results of the fifth move, one may reasonably expect to find legal notices that protect the rights of product creators (in the case of copyrights) or identify the source of the product (in the case of trademarks). Moreover, such notices are frequently found on the product packaging or products themselves, which may explain, at least in part, why a little more than half of the texts included in the corpus do not contain legal notices.

Consistent with the instructive nature of manuals and their primary purpose to incite the reader to do something with the product they have purchased, there are several micro-textual features which give instruction manuals their unique flavor and enable them to serve their purpose. The fifth and sixth most frequently occurring words in the corpus are the second-person pronouns "your" and "you," respectively, preceded only by words such as "the," "to," and "and," which may very well be among the most frequent in any variety of English corpus. Moreover, these two pronouns occur in all ten of the manuals comprising the corpus.[1] The use of the second person pulls the reader into the action so to speak and tends to be one of the main distinguishing characteristics of any "how-to" or technical genre of writing. Likewise, imperative verbs, which are also par for the course, directly involve the reader with the instructions. For instance, "press" appears quite frequently in the imperative in all but seven ("you press") of its 254 total appearances in the corpus, and it appears as such in each of the manuals. Though "use" appears in 410 instances and in all ten manuals as well, thereby surpassing "press" in frequency, "use" occurs frequently enough in the corpus as a noun, in the infinitive, in conjunction with auxiliary verbs, or in the present tense that its use as an imperative is less frequent than that of "press," leaving it in second place. Evidence of "press" and "use" in the imperative can be verified in frequently appearing clusters in the corpus such as "press the" or "press OK" or "use the" or "do not use." The translator of instruction manuals in English may very well have to exercise caution when translating the second person (verbs/pronouns) or the imperative. In other languages, there may be different ways to convey the second person (e.g., formal/informal, plural/singular) and the imperative (e.g., formal/informal, plural/singular, infinitive), and the translator may need to select one way or another depending on the context or corresponding translation project specifications.

Micro-textual features

Given the exhortative nature of instruction manuals, it is worth mentioning the use of modal verbs, which are used to communicate that something has to or can/cannot be done, or that something is the right or correct thing to do. Frequent examples in the corpus include "need to" (46 instances, 100% of the texts), "may not" (34 instances, 70% of the texts), "you may" (33 instances,

64 **Text types**

70% of the texts), "you must" (32 instances, 60% of the texts), "must be" (29 instances, 80% of the texts). From a translation point of view, care must be taken to select an equivalent that conveys the intended meaning. Depending on the language, a change in the tense (e.g., present vs. conditional) of the same verb might indicate "must" or "should," for example. There might be more than one way to convey the meaning of the source modal along similar lines as "should" or "ought," where one option is more frequent than another or more typical or preferred in a particular context.

The last area of verb usage that should be pointed out has to do with the level of description that accompanies instruction manuals. Manuals make considerable use of the to-infinitive as an adverb to instruct the user as precisely as possible. A few frequently occurring to-infinitives in the corpus are "to adjust," "to remove," and "to avoid." In the majority of cases, they are used as adverbs, such as in the following constructions: "To adjust this setting, swipe to …," "To remove a shortcut, press and hold …," or "To avoid damaging the components and cards, handle them …" Only in a few cases are they used in other ways, for example, as direct objects ("The … adjustments allow you to adjust your monitor …") or adjectives ("Note the lever to remove SIM 2"). Also worth noting is how the to-infinitive may frequently be placed at the beginning of the sentence rather than at the end. Initial positioning of these adverbials situates them as a point of departure. In genres of writing with how-to themes, the placement of these adverb structures at the beginning of the sentence is especially common. Translators, in such cases, may have to weigh carefully whether preserving this syntactic pattern in the target language can be done without causing distortion.

At the sentential level, there is evidence of varying degrees of complexity, that is, these texts are not composed of simple sentences alone, despite the emphasis on making things clear and comprehensible. Take, for example, the subordinating conjunction "if," which has a relatively high frequency of 506 and occurs in all the texts of the corpus in sentences such as "If unintended movement or brake release occurs, turn the power chair OFF as soon as it is safe." Another example is the temporal conjunction "when," which also occurs quite often (369 times) and in all the texts as well, in sentences such as "When prompted, touch Reset phone …" When working with such conjunctions, translators may, depending on their languages, experience some tension between being accurate and sounding natural.

Sample text – English user manual

Version 7.0

Illustrations in this guide are provided for reference only and may differ from actual product appearance. Product design and specification may be changed without notice.

Important information
The lightning flash with arrowhead symbol, within an equilateral triangle, is intended to alert the user to the presence of dangerous uninsulated voltage within the product's enclosure that may be of sufficient magnitude to constitute a risk of electric shock.

The exclamation point within an equilateral triangle is intended to alert the user to the presence of important operating and maintenance (servicing) instructions in the literature accompanying the product.

...

WARNING: To reduce the risk of fire or electric shock, do not expose this product to rain or moisture. This product should not be exposed to dripping or splashing. No objects filled with liquids, such as vases, should be placed on or near the product.

WARNING: Do not expose batteries to excessive heat such as sunshine, fire, and so forth.

...

Cable TV installer notice of proper grounding
This reminder is provided to call your attention to Article 820–40 of the National Electrical Code (Section 54 of the Canadian Electrical Code, Part 1) which provides guidelines for proper grounding and, in particular, specifies that the cable ground should be connected to the grounding system of the building as close to the point of cable entry as practical.

Installation location
To assure adequate ventilation for this product, maintain a spacing of 4 inches from the top and side of the TV receiver and 2 inches from the rear of the TV receiver and other surfaces.

Also, make sure the stand or base you use is of adequate size and strength to prevent the TV from being accidentally tipped over, pushed off, or pulled off the stand. This could cause personal injury and/or damage to the TV. Refer to the Important Safety Instructions on the following pages.

...

Note: In situations where the power plug or appliance coupler is used as the disconnect device, the disconnect device shall remain readily accessible and operable.
Product information
Keep your sales receipt to obtain warranty parts and service and for proof of purchase. Attach it here and record the serial and model numbers in case you need them. These numbers are located on the product. Model No.

...

The new standard in Smart TVs
Welcome to TV like you've most likely never seen before – a home screen that you can personalize with your favorite devices and streaming channels. Choose from hundreds of thousands of streaming movies and TV episodes, plus music, sports, kids, family, international, and much more.

Source: This text is excerpted and modified from Roku TV, www.roku.com

Sample English instruction manual analysis

To further analyze and contextualize the textual features described above, a sample instruction manual has been selected from the corpus under study. The manual is for a smart TV product that streams media. The company is well-known for pioneering television streaming, which receives video and audio data over a computer network, then plays it back while continuing to receive subsequent data. The manual stands out in that it exemplifies all five of the rhetorical moves described above, as well as the micro-textual features discussed.

66 **Text types**

At the macro-textual level, regarding the first move, the manual contains a good deal of warnings and notices, the majority of which precede the table of contents perhaps to ensure they are read first and are not overlooked by the user eager to begin using the product. The very first such warning/notice describes an arrowhead symbol with a lightning flash to alert to a risk of electrical shock. Notice the level of description and detail contained in this warning, surely included as a means to avoid risk of harm to the user and to minimize potential liability. The warnings are even geographically localized in a couple of cases to be in compliance with certain codes or regulations in specific areas of the world. An example of such (not shown in the text sample) is "Warning: This product contains chemicals known to the State of California to cause cancer and birth defects or other reproductive harm."

In the case of the second move, the table of contents is both extensive (some 110 topics) and detailed in the description of the contents covered in each case. This is mainly because the product offers a good number of different set-up options and features that can be personalized to suit the purchaser's needs. An example of a detailed topic in the table of contents is "Blocking Movie Store, TV Store, and News (U.S. TV models only)," which directs the reader to page 27 of the manual. The full table of contents is not listed for considerations of space, but detailed topics such as these are common in many instruction manuals in English.

Exemplifying the third move, which has to do with product support or trouble-shooting, the company points the user to external product support resources, as opposed to some other manuals, which may include a self-contained trouble-shooting section in the guide itself. In one case, the manual prompts the user to visit a support website as well as the support section of the company's website to access frequently asked questions (FAQs). Directing users to websites for trouble-shooting and project support helps limit the length of the manual and allows companies to regularly update their support documentation. In another case, the manual instructs that a "representative must troubleshoot your problem over the telephone or through email before receiving service."

The fourth move, promotion or advertising, is especially present in the sample manual as opposed to some of the other manuals. In one case, it manifests as a congratulations for purchasing a new television. This introductory promotional statement is included as the first set of content in the first section of the manual, titled "Welcome." Another advertising move in the same section, included after stretches of content about the updates the device periodically receives, takes the form of:

> The new standard in Smart TVs. Welcome to TV like you've most likely never seen before – a home screen that you can personalize ... Choose from hundreds of thousands of streaming movies ... and much more. You should never run out of things to watch.

As mentioned in the previous section, manufacturers will often promote their products whenever possible and attempt to counter buyer's remorse and dis-courage customer returns.

Finally, the fifth move, copyrights and trademarks, is situated both at the beginning and the end of the manual. Take the following excerpt, for example, selected from the final section of the manual:

All content and services accessible through the TCL Roku TV belong to third parties and are protected by copyright, patent, trademark and/or other intellectual property laws ... Without limiting the foregoing, you may not modify, copy, republish, upload, post, transmit, translate, sell, create derivative works, exploit, or distribute in any manner or medium any content or services displayed through the TCL Roku TV.

As observed in this excerpt, this move may closely resemble the all-inclusive descriptive discourse commonly found in legal texts.

At the micro-textual level, the manual contains examples of all the features described in the previous section. It makes frequent use of the second-person pronouns "you" and "your." An example in which both occur is "You can even personalize the names of each input and move tiles around so your most often used devices and streaming channels are only a click away." The manual also directly involves the reader in the action by frequently using the imperative. "Switch," for example, is used in the imperative in "Switch to a TV input to access the device connected to that input ..." This same example exhibits use of the to-infinitive as an adverb ("to access"), which is frequently used to enhance the level of description in this how-to genre. To-infinitive adverbs are also placed at the beginning of the sentences as a point of departure in a number of cases (e.g., "To change network settings ... navigate to ...," "To repeat the channel scan ..., navigate to ..."). The manual is also no exception in that it often uses different modal verbs to assist in carrying out its conative function of language, such as "must" (e.g., "you must configure," "you must connect"), "need" (e.g., "you'll only need to," "you need only select"), and "can" (e.g., "you can configure," "you can change your network").

Finally, the manual presents complexity in several cases at the sentence level. Proof of such complexity is the use of the subordinating conjunctions "if" and "before" in "If you turn on the TV again before it has entered the very low power mode, it turns on immediately" or the temporal conjunction "when" in "When you've highlighted the channel you want to watch, press OK."

68   **Text types**

CHINESE

A manual is a book or booklet that gives the user practical instructions on how to do or use something, which accompany electronic goods, computer hardware and software, vehicles, and home appliances. In Chinese, a manual is referred to as 用户指南, 用户手册, 使用说明书, or 操作手册.

The Chinese corpus includes 11 manuals and contains 243,760 Chinese characters. In terms of length, they vary considerably, ranging from 991 characters to 128,018. Of the 11 manuals in the Chinese corpus, 5 are for Chinese online systems, 3 are for Chinese software programs, and the remaining 3 are for a Chinese personal computer, a Chinese car, and a Chinese mobile phone service.

Macro-textual features

Different types of manuals have different **rhetorical moves**. The typical moves are as follows:

1. Name of product (产品名称)
2. Name of institution (机构名称)
3. Release date (发布日期)
4. Version (文件版本)
5. Table of contents (目录)
6. Introduction (前言)
7. Warnings/precautions/tips (警告/注意事项/温馨提示)
8. How to install (安装说明)
9. How to use (使用说明/操作说明)
10. Care and maintenance (维护保养事项)
11. Troubleshooting tips (常见故障及处理方法)
12. Appendix (附录)
13. Contact us (联系我们)
14. Index (索引)

In the Chinese corpus, moves 1 and 9 are mandatory, and most of the other manuals contain moves 2, 3, and 5. The other moves appear in four or fewer manuals in the corpus. Moves 10 and 11 appear only in the personal computer manual and the car owner's manual.

As far as the **field** is concerned, looking at a text type's terminology and lexical items can help determine the topic and discipline. The word frequency table makes clear that the terminology and lexical items used in this text type relate to manuals. All the lexical items in the table describe either instructions or processes (through verbs such as 使用 or 输入).

Lexical items	Frequency	Lexical items	Frequency
项目 (project)	1136	数据 (data)	496
系统 (system)	1015	编辑 (edit)	492
选择 (select)	783	显示 (display)	481

(Continued)

(Continued)

Lexical items	Frequency	Lexical items	Frequency
操作 (operate/operation)	709	登记 (registration)	455
图 (figure)	676	用户 (user)	420
信息 (information)	670	使用 (use)	419
申请 (application)	628	输入 (enter)	415
按钮 (button)	602	数字 (digital, digit)	407
点击 (click)	601	文件 (file)	388

As for the **mode** of discourse, manuals are usually texts written for reading as the audience interacts with the text while preparing to use a new machine or device. Manuals are usually seen as written texts, which points to the fact that there is no dialogue between the author of the text and the audience. There is none of the spontaneity you would see in spoken language, as reflected in fillers and pauses.

When it comes to the **tenor** of the discourse of manuals, the relationship between author and audience is one in which the author is an expert and the audience may or may not be experts. Indeed, just as nonexperts use manuals to learn how to use a machine or a product, experts also may use manuals to learn how to use products. The fact that experts and nonexperts alike can understand manuals is further underscored by the non-technicality of the operational terms used in a manual.

The communicative function of Chinese manuals is **informative**. It is highly factual in that the purpose of an instruction manual is to transfer knowledge and information about how to operate a new product rather than persuading the audience to buy something. However, manuals also exhibit a certain degree of **operative** function, as evidenced in the use of **conative** language in the imperative to trigger action from the reader.

Micro-textual features

At the micro-textual level, the corpus data illustrate a preference for the imperative mood in Chinese manuals. Most of the sentences in the directions are imperative, and pronouns like 我 (I) and 你 (you) are rarely used. Politeness is also stressed in manuals because readers are clients.

The use of **reference** is relatively common in the manuals. Personal pronouns, including 你/您 (you) and 我 (I), occur 198 times in the corpus. Among demonstrative reference devices, 这, the Chinese equivalent for *this*, appears 137 times in many words or phrases in the corpus, such as 这些 (these), 这样 (this way), 这种 (this kind), 这个 (this one), and 这类 (this type). By comparison, the Chinese equivalents of *that, those,* and *there* occur 14 times in total in the corpus. The cohesive device of **substitution** is rarely used in the manuals; there are no obvious Chinese equivalents for *one, ones,* and *same*. By contrast, **ellipsis** is a widely used cohesive device in Chinese, in which subjects and objects are optional if they can be implied by the context. In the case of manuals, compound sentences starting with a verb are the norm; the omission

Text types

of objects occurs at least 5 times in compound sentences in this corpus. The manuals in the corpus also make use of additive, causal, and temporal **conjunctions** (see table).

Conjunctions	Frequency
和 (and)	897
或 (or)	795
如果 (if)	382
并 (and/also)	303
及 (and)	204
然后 (then)	105
若 (if)	98
而 (while/yet/but)	73
否则 (otherwise)	71
或者 (or)	58

Generally speaking, the use of conjunctions is less frequent in Chinese than in English. Also, directions in manuals are in the form of a list of successive steps, which reduces the need for conjunctions. **Lexical cohesion** is arguably the most commonly used form of cohesion in Chinese. In the case of manuals, each step is described by one simple sentence or one compound sentence.

In the Chinese corpus of manuals, there is a high occurrence of nouns.

High-frequency nouns	Frequency	High-frequency nouns	Frequency
项目 (project)	1136	文件 (file)	388
系统 (system)	1015	文本 (text)	370
图 (figure)	676	命令 (command)	338
信息 (information)	670	时间 (time)	320
按钮 (button)	602	数据库 (database)	318
数据 (data)	496	许可证 (license)	313
编辑 (editing)	492	功能 (features)	295
用户 (user)	420	状态 (status)	291
数字 (digit/number)	407	内容 (content)	280

The nouns used in the Chinese manuals can be classified into two domains: (1) nouns describing the products and their components, such as 系统 (system), 数据库 (database), and 按钮 (button); and (2) nouns describing the operational process-related items, such as 命令 (command), 图 (Figure), and 状态 (status). Another highly recurring word category in this genre is verbs (see table).

Verbs	Frequency	Verbs	Frequency
选择 (select)	783	设置 (configure)	289
申请 (apply)	628	进入 (enter)	289
点击 (click)	601	打印 (print)	288
显示 (display)	481	填写 (fill in)	273
使用 (use)	419	检索 (search)	248
输入 (enter)	415	注销 (log out)	224
变更 (change)	336	保存 (save)	219
查询 (search)	322	打开 (open)	218
检查 (check)	320	说明 (describe)	204

The verbs used in the manuals corpus mainly describe the operation process. Verbs give the instruction for each step. The frequency of some verbs, such as 使用 (use), indicates that they are typical of this text type.

Sample text – Chinese instruction manual

某大学VPN服务使用手册

一、VPN服务的用途：
  1、提供从公网安全地访问校园网电子资源的快捷通道；
  2、通过VPN安全通道登录办公系统实现移动办公。
  3、通过VPN安全通道登录校内其他应用系统。
二、哪些用户需要使用VPN服务：
  1、家住在校外(含家属院)的用户、到外地出差的用户，请点击https://vpn
    .xyz.edu.cn访问。
  2、在校内办公区和学生区上网的计算机无需使用VPN服务。
三、使用VPN服务的前提条件：
  一台已经接入到公网的计算机及一个校园门户帐号。
  VPN系统目前支持Windows 7、Windows10，OSX等操作系统，支持IE浏览器8.0以上版本。
四、VPN系统的具体使用步骤：
  1. 用浏览器输入网址：https://vpn.xyz.edu.cn如图所示。在页面中，输入Ø用户名和密码，第一次Ø会提示下载并安装插件和客户端。
  2. "VPN安装程序"安装(安装期间，自动弹出的所有权限请求，Ø都选择肯定含义的那个选项，给予该程序所需要的权限。)后，桌面上会出现 "EasyConnect" 图标的快捷方式，如下图所示。
  3. 运行桌面上 "EasyConnect" 图标的快捷方式，需要输入的"服务器地址"为 "https://vpn.xyz.edu.cn"，并"连接"。如下图所示。
  4. 使用用户名和密码登录。（登录期间，自动弹出的所有权限请求，Ø都选择肯定含义的那个选项，给予该程序所需要的权限。)(注:若有提示连接不到服务器，Ø是因为windows的防火墙或安装的卡巴斯基等防火墙拦截的原因，请关闭防火墙后再点上图的"连接"按钮)。提示所需输入的用户名和密码为我校"信息门户"的用户名和密码(若信息门户密码遗失，请到 http://my.xyz.edu.cn 页面找回密码)。
  5. 登录成功后，桌面右上角会出现一个四方小图标。鼠标指向该图标，(1) Ø可以看到 "SSL VPN 已连接"且"流速：发送和接收"有数据流量：
  另外，Ø可以查看此时本机的IP地址(如下图所示)，(2) 确认是否成功获得(如下图)IPv4 地址 2.1.1.*(查看ipv4地址方法，见下图所示:控制面板->网络和 internet->网络连接 或者查看ipv4地址方法是：控制面板->网络和共享中心->更改适配器设置),这样说明VPN已连接成功（注，若不满足(1)和(2)条件，说明安装 VPN 安装程序(即步

> 骤2.的操作)时，程序没有获得所需权限。<u>此时</u>，用户需要返回vpn.xyz.edu.cn页面，点击"VPN卸载程序"(SSL VPN修复工具->快速修复->客户端控件卸载->确定)，用该程序完全卸载本程序；<u>然后</u>重新按照该篇使用流程进行安装操作，<u>直到</u>满足(1)<mark>和</mark> (2)条件。）。
>
> 　　此时关闭自动弹出的浏览器页面(如下图所示)，另外打开浏览器(注：推荐使用IE、360等IE核心的浏览器：不要使用谷歌浏览器、火狐浏览器、Microsoft　Edge浏览器)，直接输入学校资源的网址(如my.xyz.edu.cn<mark>或</mark>lib.xyz.cn)，访问校内资源。
>
> 五、咨询电话：8889198
>
> 网络中心
2017年3月18日
>
> Key: connectors – underline; conjunctions – highlighted in gray

Sample Chinese instruction manual analysis

This sample manual is for a Chinese university's VPN service. At the macro-textual level, it includes six moves: 产品名称 (name of the product), 机构名称 (name of institution), 发布日期 (release date), 安装说明 (how to install), 使用说明 (how to use), and 联系我们 (contact us), although those exact titles are not used. The text has 991 characters and is the shortest manual in the Chinese corpus. The mode of discourse is informative, and the tenor of discourse suggests an expert-to-nonexpert as well as expert-to-expert relationship. The communicative function is informative, based on the reasons outlined above.

As far as the micro-textual features are concerned, the indicative mood and the present tense are used to give directions related to the product. The use of short sentences reduces the need for cohesive devices. A personal pronoun, 我 in 我校 (our university), appears only once in the text. Among demonstrative reference devices, 那个 (that) appears twice, while the Chinese equivalent for *this* never appears. Substitution is absent in the sample text; ellipsis (omission of the subject in this case) appears 7 times (represented by the symbol Ø in the sample text); conjunctions (see words highlighted in gray in the sample text) are often used, such as 和 (and) and 或 (or). Connectors (see underlined words in the sample text) are also used, such as 此时 (at this time) and 然后 (then). Instances of repetition in the corpus are listed by frequency (see table).

Repetition	Frequency	Repetition	Frequency
使用 (use)	9	如下图所示 (as shown below)	6
安装 (install)	8	登录 (log in)	5
程序 (program)	8	地址 (address)	5
浏览器 (browser)	8	权限 (permission)	5
用户 (user)	8	输入 (enter)	5
服务 (service)	7	系统 (system)	5
连接 (connection)	6	需要 (require)	5
密码 (password)	6		

The sample manual is characterized mainly by sentences that start with a verb. Simple, compound, and complex sentences each account for about 1/3 of the total number of sentences in the sample. All manual titles in the corpus except for one are characterized by noun phrases.

74 Text types

FRENCH

User manuals (*manuels d'utilisation/mode d'emploi*) constitute a major genre of technical communication. These at times book-length documents contain operating instructions on how to install, use, and troubleshoot a piece of hardware or software, a product, or a system of any sort. Some guides also include tutorials or getting-started kits with guidance on how to use a device or product. This type of documentation is user-centered, and its content and length depend on the target audience and the complexity of the product itself (e.g., a one-page leaflet vs. a booklet vs. an entire manual). Manuals may be procedural, focusing on the step-by-step instructions on how to use a product, or they may function as reference guides, describing the parts, functionalities, and features of a product. User manuals can be found in print, electronic format (usually as a PDF), or online containing hyperlinks (as a web page or online help). They may also feature quick response (QR) codes linked to online videos.

To better understand the features of French user manuals, we will analyze a corpus of 11 manuals published by 11 separate sources within the last 5 years. The text type length in this corpus varies considerably, from 1,342 to 12,443 words. The mean text length is 5,405 words. Size differences may be due to the depth of the information that the manuals provide and to the varying complexity of the devices, products, or systems they describe. A user manual for a car is different than a user manual for a smartphone, camera, piece of software, or dishwasher. Even though the information provided may fall under the mandatory rhetorical moves described below, the amount of information needed to explain the different facets of a given product varies widely. Moreover, many user manuals contain graphics (illustrations, charts, or diagrams) with callouts, the textual content of which was not included in our corpus.

Macro-textual features

At the macro-textual level, we begin by isolating the mandatory features that characterize the user manual as a specific type of technical documentation. Essentially, user manuals display the following **rhetorical moves**, whose sequencing may change depending on the product:

1. Cover page (*Page de garde*)

   - Name of product (*Nom du produit*)
   - Product reference and details (*Référence au produit, et au modèle concerné*)
   - Version information (*Numéro de version du manuel*)
   - Copyright information (*Droit d'auteur et de reproduction*)

2. Contents page (*Sommaire*)
3. Introduction (*Introduction*)
4. Body of the manual (*Corps du manuel*)

   - Warning/precautions/safety regulations/notices (*Avertissement/précautions/consignes de sécurité/avis*)
   - Product parts (*Parties du produit*)

- Features (*Caractéristiques des fonctions*)
- Installation (*Installation*)
- Care and maintenance (*Mesures de prévention/d'entretien*)
- Troubleshooting (*Dépannage*)

5. Warranty information (*Garantie*)
6. Appendix (*Annexe*)
7. Table of contents (*Table des matières*)
8. Index (*Index*)

Typically, user manuals have a cover page that displays information related to the product name (e.g., *La TV d'Orange Guide d'utilisation* or *Guide d'utilisation Cardi-3 Electrocardiographe Une marque de DUPONT MEDICAL*), model, and manual version (e.g., *Version française2*), as well as any copyright information or terms and conditions specified by the company. The table of contents (*table des matières*) in French user manuals appears at the end of the manual and includes a detailed outline with different parts or sections, paragraphs and their page numbers, while a concise version called a *sommaire* is placed at the beginning of the manual and lists major sections or chapters. A hierarchical numbering scheme is used in both the full and abbreviated tables of contents to indicate sections and sub-sections (i.e., first-level headings, second-level headings, and so on). Some manuals use different numeral types and fonts to differentiate between higher- and lower-level sections.

The introduction usually contains a description of the product, the objective of the manual, its structure, and how to navigate it. Introductions may also provide an overview of product parts and occasionally an image or drawing of main parts, along with their functionalities, features, and any specialized terminology or abbreviations. The body of the manual contains core information related to the functioning of the product and its use. Generally, warnings, precautions, and safety regulations are displayed using icons and text boxes to indicate actions that users should refrain from taking or recommendations on how to handle the device or product. Such elements are introduced at the beginning of the manual and then mentioned throughout the manual to reinforce what users should or should not do. It is very common to use a variety of symbols for components and parts in compliance with accepted industry standards, such as symbols for electronic circuits.

The listing of product parts includes visuals (graphics with callouts) explaining part names, functionalities, and advanced features (lists of menus if applicable). The product parts section is followed by another section, dealing with how to install/assemble the product, if relevant. This move often adopts the format of step-by-step instructions, with or without visuals, to guide users. Manuals also include information regarding how to take care of products and maintain their optimal functionality, plus a troubleshooting section detailing potential issues or errors and how to handle them. Moreover, manuals provide warranty information, along with terms and conditions. They also include an appendix containing additional information about the product and containing graphics and scenarios as well as additional help. A detailed table of contents is located at the end and may contain an alphabetized index or glossary, depending on how large the document is.

Text types

In addition to these mandatory moves, optional moves include manual revision information (*date de révision du manuel*) (e.g., *Indice de révision: 20,130,520; Français (CA). 10/2014. Rev.1.0*), author or technical writing team members' names (*nom de l'auteur/de l'équipe de rédaction*), a preface (*préambule*) containing details related to the document and key pointers to be read before using the product, an FAQ section (*foire aux questions*) addressing common user questions, and links to tutorials (*tutoriels*) and training videos for additional guidance on how to operate a given device.

To describe the **register** of French user manuals, we will look at three aspects: **field, mode**, and **tenor**. Based on lexical item frequency, the **field** of discourse primarily corresponds to products and devices covered by user manuals as well as product or device specifications, features, and means of use. Many of the words in the table below are associated with the macrostructure of the text, for example, a description of features (*caractéristiques des fonctions*) may contain phrasing such as *cette fonction vous permet de valider immédiatement une prolongation de votre contrat*, menus (*menus*) (e.g., *pour cela utilisez les boutons du menu de la page d'accueil; sélectionner le menu équipement en cliquant sur l'icône correspondante*), and usage (*utilisation*) (e.g., *un minimum de 2 Go de RAM est nécessaire pour une utilisation habituelle*). The table shows how many times these terms appear in the corpus as well as the number of texts in which each item appears.

High-frequency items	Frequency	No. of texts	High-frequency items	Frequency	No. of texts
équipement(s)	325	4	*menu(s)*	145	11
personnaliser	316	2	*prise*	141	9
fonction(s)	308	11	*réglages*	130	6
scénario(s)	211	5	*batterie*	127	6
utilisation	197	11	*groupes*	125	1
écran(s)	190	11	*page(s)*	122	11
appareil(s)	183	7	*sécurité*	115	7
télécommande	177	2	*enregistrement*	114	11
manuel(s)	175	11	*téléphone*	105	7
bouton	173	11	*touches*	100	4
utiliser	171	11	*contrôle(s)*	94	10
projet(s)	169	5	*liste(s)*	93	10
alarme(s)	148	6			

An examination of **mode** – how a text will be used – reveals that user manuals are typically meant to be read before or while operating a device, or sometimes when a user needs guidance on how to troubleshoot an issue. Given the type of information user manuals cover and how their sections address different aspects of product use and maintenance, this type of documentation can be checked on a need-to-know basis and at any point when the product is being used. Finally, the **tenor**, which characterizes the relationship between the author of a user manual and the audience (users), points to an expert-to-nonexpert relationship, as reflected in the degree of precision, transparency, and detailed explanations and instructions outlined for users who may have no prior knowledge of the product. The **communicative function** of French user manuals is **informative**, as indicated by the factual, precise, and objective language used, as well as the highly structured outline reflecting the rhetorical moves employed. The sole intent of technical writing in general and user manuals in particular is to convey neutral information as correctly and concisely as possible. Some of the texts in our corpus adopt an interactive style, structured to answer user queries (e.g., *comment utiliser ce mode d'emploi; comment effectuer des réglages; qu'est-ce que le MIDI ?*) or to directly address the user with headings employing second-person possessive pronouns (e.g., *personnaliser votre appareil; personnalisation de votre système*), thereby establishing a sense of personal ownership and suggesting how to optimize product use. Manuals also contain several icons that draw a reader's attention to warnings, safety regulations, and preventive measures; here, the user is directly addressed and prohibited from engaging in certain behaviors or uses. Manuals also use notices and notes (*remarques*) to provide key information and recommendations.

Micro-textual features

At the micro-textual level, and based on the corpus, the predominant mood of French user manuals is the indicative. The present indicative is used in statements describing products and their characteristics and functionalities (e.g., *des instructions detaillées sont disponibles sur notre site*). The future indicative is minimally used to refer to the results of an action undertaken by the user (e.g., *la barre de contrôle sera maintenue par la ceinture de sécurité du pilote*). The imperative is used to give commands on how to operate, install, and configure or change settings on a device (e.g., *sélectionnez [mes préférences] à l'aide des touches de direction, puis validez avec ...*). There is also a marked use of infinitive verbs, especially in headings expressing how-to statements (e.g., *pour mettre à jour un élément, il suffit de cliquer sur le bouton; afficher les informations d'aide*).

Verbs	Tense	Frequency	No. of texts	Verbs	Tense	Frequency	No. of texts
est	présent	666	11	permet	présent	70	10
personnaliser	infinitif	316	2	cliquez	impératif	66	5
être	infinitif	207	11	validez	impératif	62	5
utiliser	infinitif	171	10	appuyer	infinitif	60	4
sont	présent	135	11	appuyez	impératif	60	6
peut	présent	117	11	peuvent	présent	55	8
sélectionner	infinitif	97	7	supprimer	infinitif	55	7
doit	présent	95	9	cliquer	infinitif	49	5
pouvez	présent	91	9	gérer	infinitif	49	4
lancer	infinitif	88	9	vérifier	infinitif	48	10
faire	infinitif	86	10	placer	infinitif	47	6
sélectionnez	présent	83	4	sera	futur	47	9
piloter	infinitif	75	2	changer	infinitif	44	8
modifier	infinitif	70	9	accéder	infinitif	42	5

Text types

An analysis of **cohesive devices** shows that French user manuals use both articles and demonstratives for referencing. The definite articles *la* (1,900), *le* (1,556), *les* (1,206), and *l'* (1,172), and the indefinite articles *un* (838) and *une* (449) are used to refer to different sections of manuals or to the features, buttons, menus, interface elements, or versions of a particular device. The demonstrative adjectives *ce* (166), *cette* (98), *cela* (48), *ces* (39), and *cet* (37) are used when describing manuals, equipment, procedures, functionalities, settings, or illustrations. The most frequent personal pronoun in the corpus is *vous* (629), which is used to address users formally and guide them through the process of operating a device (e.g., *vous pourrez ultérieurement modifier les données introduites; si vous disposez d'une connexion internet active*). The impersonal *il* (211) is also used, though mostly to provide recommendations (e.g., *il est préférable de nettoyer votre sollette de temps à autre; il est impératif que les électrodes ne se touchent pas; il ne faut pas mouiller la boîte des dérivations*). *Nous* appears 95 times across nine texts in reference to manufacturers. This first-person plural personal pronoun is used to introduce sections of manuals (e.g., *nous allons dans ce chapitre procéder à la creation d'un projet; nous allons donc commencer par voir comment procéder dans ce cas*), to emphasize recommendations (*Nous recommendons des sauvegardes régulières sur un support non réinscriptible; nous vous conseillons vivement d'entrer immédiatement les caractéristiques ...*), or to provide contact information and invite users to get in touch with the company support team (e.g., *vous pouvez nous contacter par téléphone ou mieux par courriel, nous essayons de traiter les problèmes dans les 24 heures*). Possessive pronouns such as *votre* (315) and *vos* (49) emphasize user ownership of a product and its different uses (e.g., *sauvegardez régulièrement votre projet sur un autre support; assurez-vous que votre enregistreur soit raccordé au 220V; pour visionner vos enregistrements*).

The visual support that user manuals provide in the form of icons and graphics leads to **substitution**, as certain icons are used to express warnings (*avertissements*) and notices (*notes* or *remarques*) or serve as navigation items (hypertexts) to move from one section of the manual to another or return to the front page or to specific menus. Icons found at the beginning of manuals are accompanied by definitions of what they represent, and they stand in for a variety of linguistic labels.

In addition to visual/iconic substitution, lexical substitution occurs minimally through the use of possessive pronouns such as *leur* (20 times in six texts), which is used to refer back to processes or functionalities already mentioned (e.g., *afin d'assurer leur bon fonctionnement, vous devez impérativement insérer la carte*). Cohesive devices, ellipsis and substitution may not be used often so as to maintain the clarity of the instructions and to avoid any assumptions or ambiguities.

As far as **conjunctions** are concerned, both coordinating and subordinating conjunctions are used in the user manual corpus. *Et* is the most frequently used additive conjunction. The second most used conjunction begins with the preposition *pour*, which is used in headings and in the body of the text to indicate how to operate devices or systems. The conditional *si* is used to present alternative results and different outcomes depending on how users combine functionalities. The corpus analysis also displays a significant use of temporal conjunctions indicated by the words *puis, lorsque, lors*, and *ensuite*, which suggest the step-by-step nature of the instructions that users must follow to assemble, install, use, fix, or disassemble a product.

Coordinating connecting words	Frequency	No. of texts	Subordinating connecting words	Frequency	No. of texts
et	1056	11	pour	622	11
puis	172	10	si	210	11
ou	46	8	lorsque	93	10
mais	39	10	ainsi	67	10
donc	25	6	comme	49	10
aussi	24	9	lors	47	8
ensuite	19	7	alors	45	8
			afin	41	9
			depuis	37	11
			quand	27	5

The predominance of coordinating and causal conjunctions reflects the extensive use of compound and complex sentences that characterizes the style of user manuals.

With respect to **lexical cohesion,** a look at high-frequency nouns shows that the repetition of lexical items is an important lexical cohesive device in user manuals (see table). The most visible examples of **repetition** are reflected in the manual macrostructure via the references to devices, functionalities, menu items, and product operation found in the body of a user manual.

Lexical item	Frequency	Lexical item	Frequency
équipement(s)	325	menu(s)	145
fonction(s)	308	prise	141
scénario(s)	211	réglages	130
utilisation	197	batterie	127
écran(s)	190	groupes	125
appareil(s)	183	page(s)	122
télécommande	177	sécurité	115
manuel(s)	175	enregistrement	114
bouton	173	téléphone	105
projet(s)	169	touches	100
alarme(s)	148		

Sample text – French user manual

CLIO
NOTICE D'UTILISATION

Bienvenue à bord de *votre* véhicule

Cette notice d'utilisation et d'entretien réunit à *votre* intention les informations qui *vous* permettront :

80 **Text types**

– de bien connaître *votre* véhicule et, par là même, de bénéficier pleinement, et dans les meilleures conditions d'utilisation, de toutes les fonctionnalités et de tous les perfectionnements techniques dont il est doté.

– de maintenir son fonctionnement optimum par la simple mais rigoureuse observation des conseils d'entretien.

– de faire face, sans perte de temps excessive, aux opérations qui ne requièrent pas l'intervention d'un spécialiste.

Les quelques instants que *vous* consacrerez à la lecture de cette notice seront très largement compensés par les enseignements que *vous* en tirerez, les fonctionnalités et les nouveautés techniques que *vous* y découvrirez. Si certains points restaient encore obscurs, les techniciens de notre Réseau se feraient un plaisir de *vous* fournir tout renseignement complémentaire.

Pour *vous* aider dans la lecture de cette notice *vous* trouverez le symbole suivant :

⚠ Pour indiquer une notion de risque, de danger ou une consigne de sécurité

La description des modèles, déclinés dans cette notice, a été établie à partir des caractéristiques techniques connues à la date de conception de ce document. **La notice regroupe l'ensemble des équipements (de série ou optionnels) existant pour ces modèles, leur présence dans le véhicule dépend de la version, des options choisies et du pays de commercialisation.**

De même, certains équipements devant apparaître en cours d'année peuvent être décrits dans ce document.

Enfin, dans toute la notice, lorsqu'il est fait référence au Représentant de la marque il s'agit d'un Représentant RENAULT.

Bonne route au volant de *votre* véhicule

Traduit du français. Reproduction ou traduction, même partielle, interdite sans autorisation écrite du constructeur du véhicule.

RENAULT S.A.S. SOCIÉTÉ PAR ACTIONS SIMPLIFIÉE AU CAPITAL DE 533 941 113 € / 13-15, QUAI LE GALLO

92100 BOULOGNE-BILLANCOURT R.C.S. NANTERRE 780 129 987 — SIRET 780 129 987 03591 / TÉL. : 0810 40 50 60

NU 853-8 – 99 91 008 86R – 03/2012 – Edition française

S O M M A I R E

Key: verb tenses – highlighted in gray; preferred method of referencing – italics; connecting words – underline

Source: www.groupe.renault.com

Sample French instruction manual analysis

To illustrate the features of French user manuals discussed above, we will analyze an assembled excerpt from a user manual for a car, the Renault Clio, published by French automobile manufacturer Renault. At the macro-textual level, the manual includes every mandatory move specified in this analysis. It makes use of headings to mark key content, and numbered and bulleted lists to help users scan information, special notices for warnings and precautions, graphics to reference components, and tables with detailed information about specific features. The cover page displays the name of the car along with the Renault logo and the title of the manual, *Notice d'utilisation*. The second page of the manual contains a recommended brand for car lubricants and fluids (*RENAULT préconise les lubrifiants ELF homologués pour vos vidanges et appoints*). The following page provides an introduction to the manual and its objectives (*les informations qui vous permettront de bien connaître votre véhicule ...*). The list of manual objectives is followed by a hazard symbol and definition (*Pour indiquer une notion de risque, de danger ou une consigne de sécurité*). The introduction also includes a disclaimer regarding the content of the manual, the different features discussed and how they relate to different models, and the requirements of the countries in which the car is sold. The introduction ends with copyright information (*Traduit du français. Reproduction ou traduction, même partielle, interdite sans autorisation écrite du constructeur du véhicule*), information about the company including the address and telephone number, and the manual version (*NU 853–8 – 99 91 008 86R – 03/2012 – Edition française*). A short version of the table of contents is provided, followed by a more extensive table of contents for Chapter 1. This manual uses detailed tables of contents to start each chapter. The manual also makes use of an extensive number of visuals and tables to explain parts, functionalities, warnings, and recommendations. It provides maintenance information, an appendix, and an alphabetized index. The text is 29,413 words long (264 pages). The mode of discourse is informative in the sense that the manual is providing facts about the car and how to make the best use of it. The tenor of discourse points to an expert-to-nonexpert relationship since the automotive company is offering useful information to its user on how to use a car it manufactures. The field of discourse relates to the automotive industry and, more particularly, to car parts and features.

As far as the micro-textual features are concerned, the mood and tense that prevail in this sample are indicative present and future (verbs highlighted in gray). In terms of cohesive devices, the preferred method of referencing (italicized items) in this sample seems to be definite articles (*la*, 1,104; *le*, 978; *l'*, 609; *les*, 406), indefinite articles (*un*, 391; *des*, 408, *une*, 167); demonstratives (*ce*, 59; *cette*, 26; *ces*, 27), and personal pronouns (*vous*, 248; *votre*, 103; *nous*, 19). Substitution is marked using definite articles, which function as direct object pronouns to avoid repetition (*le* was used 42 times; *la*, 14; *les*, 8; and *en*, 4 times for this purpose). Graphics and icons are sometimes used as substitutes for linguistic content. As for connecting words (underlined words), the sample user manual makes use of the coordinating conjunction *et* for addition (422 occurrences), the preposition *pour* (292 occurrences) for expressing intent, *puis* (59 occurrences) for marking subsequent steps, and a number of others, such as *ou* (21), *afin* (18), and *ensuite* (11). Finally, a large number of both compound and complex sentences can be found in the user manual.

82   Text types

GERMAN

The controlled vocabulary and syntactic templates typically found in instruction manuals have resulted in a current industry trend in which the translation of this particular genre is handled in large part by machines for many language pairs, including German to English. That said, corpus-based analysis of instruction manuals can provide valuable insight into lexico-grammatical patterns of relevance when authoring such manuals in preparation for optimal machine translation. The empirical documentation of such conventions can also inform the translation of web-based tutorials, which now either replace or complement print manuals. A corpus of six full-length German-language electric toothbrush manuals was compiled for this purpose. These manuals were retrievable online in PDF format on the respective company websites in 2016.

Macro-textual features

A comparative analysis calls attention to the following **rhetorical moves**, which are prototypical for the user manual genre, as they appear in at least four of the six texts:

1. Company and product name (with a visual depiction) (*Hersteller und Produktbezeichnung*)
2. Customer greeting (*Begrüßung*)
3. Important safety precautions/warnings (*Sicherheits- und Warnhinweise*)
4. Schematic overview of parts/features (*Abbildung*)
5. Technology specifications (*Technische Daten*)
6. Instructions (*Beschreibung der Bedienung/Art der Vewendung*)
7. Warranty/contact information (*Garantie/Kontaktinformationen*)

Whereas a customer greeting is typical, scope and content are not standardized. One of the welcome messages is congratulatory, two thank the reader, and a fourth simply encourages the reader to enjoy the toothbrush, as rendered in the table of greetings.

German customer greeting
Sehr geehrter Kunde,
wir beglückwünschen Sie zum Kauf Ihrer neuen GRUNDIG Schallzahnbürste CleanWhitePlus TB 8030 Power Edition.
English translation
Dear Customer,
Congratulations on the purchase of your new GRUNDIG Ultrasound Clean-White-Plus TB 8030 Power Edition ultrasonic toothbrush

---

German customer greeting
Sehr geehrte Kundin, sehr geehrter Kunde,
vielen Dank für den Kauf dieses Zahnbürstensets
English translation
Dear Customer,
Thank you for purchasing this toothbrush set

(Continued)

(Continued)

German customer greeting
GENIESSEN SIE IHRE ZAHNBÜRSTE
English translation
Enjoy your toothbrush

It is worth noting that 43 exclamation marks occur within the "safety pre-cautions" rhetorical move, distributed across four of the six manuals. This is a commonly used punctuation convention in German-language texts for framing warnings as crucial must-read content. The customer greeting, instructions, and warranty information moves are marked by widespread direct address using the formal you (_Sie_). This level of formality and social distancing is prototypical for the manual genre, despite the deliberately direct nature of instruction steps.

The mean sentence length in number of words for this genre is 13. Each of the six manuals constituting the corpus analyzed here has a mean sentence length that falls within a range of 12 ± 3 words. This narrow range highlights the prototypical syntactic patterns of instruction manuals, where sentence length is relatively fixed.

The **mode** of discourse for the instruction manual genre is first and foremost didactic, with the communicative intent to get the readers to utilize the product. The table of frequently occurring action verbs found in the corpus reveals this didactic function.

German action verb	English translation	Frequency	No. of texts
reinigen	to clean	37	6
verwenden	to use	25	6
drücken	to press	23	6
laden	to charge	22	5
ziehen	to pull	21	5
stellen	to place	20	6
schalten	to switch	18	5

As far as **tenor** is concerned, communication in an instruction manual takes place between a company whose product is purchased and an anonym-ous consumer. As mentioned, this reader is often directly addressed by way of the formal "you" (_Sie_). We see the author self-address in the form of _wir_ (we) or _uns-_ (us) a total of 23 times, primarily in the context of greeting or congratulating the reader and, to a lesser extent, in the warranty section. Controlled vocabulary, in conjunction with the aforementioned syntactic tem-plates, enhances readability and predictability from the perspective of a lay or nonexpert audience. This high-frequency, controlled vocabulary, as depicted in the table, also establishes the **field** of discourse.

Text types

German term	English translation	Frequency	No. of texts
Zahnbürste	toothbrush	134	6
Ladestation	charging station	103	5
Gerät	device	98	6
Akku/-s	battery/-ies	81	6
Borsten	bristles	46	4
Wasser	water	46	6
Zähne	teeth	37	6
Bürstenkopf	brush head	34	4
Netzstecker	power plug	30	6
Gebrauch	use	28	6
Steckdose	electric outlet	27	6
Bedienungsanleitung	instruction manual	26	6

Micro-textual analyses reveal that the vast majority of sentences in the corpus, as one might expect, involve imperatives. An examination of the first two sentences in the instructions section of each of the six manuals in the corpus reveals the following prototypical syntactic template:

imperative verb + *Sie* (you) + direct object + prepositional phrases

It is interesting to note that the word order found in this template varies from what we see in German-language recipes, which also contain instructions, where the verb is an infinitive form and comes at the end of the sentence. Perhaps the prototypical word order pattern in instruction manuals is a pre-editing (authoring) strategy in preparation for machine translation into English, where this same word order is prototypical.

Micro-textual features

A micro-textual analysis of syntactic patterns in the safety precautions/warnings move indicates some interesting deviations from the aforementioned template and encompasses typical distancing strategies in German-language manuals. These include using passive (instead of active) voice and using nominalized constructs where one might find verb equivalents in English. While both the safety precautions/warnings and instructions moves make use of the imperative, we only see more extensive use of the passive and *bitte* in the former, as seen in the following examples:

German passage	Literal English translation	Modulated English translation
Das Gerät darf nicht in Betrieb genommen werden, wenn …	The device is not to be put into use if …	Do not operate the device if …

(Continued)

(Continued)

German passage	Literal English translation	Modulated English translation
Bei Beschädigung der Leitung ist das Gerät zu verschrotten	In the event of damage to the cable, the device is to be disposed of	Dispose of the device if the cable is damaged
Lassen Sie das Handteil nicht herunter fallen	Prevent the handle from dropping	Do not drop the handle

We see some variation in preferred sentence type when comparing the safety precautions/warnings move and the operating instructions move. An analysis of the first two sentences of safety precautions in the six manuals reveals the following breakdown: ten simple, two compound, and two complex. There is a clear preference for a clear and concise message. In the operation instructions, we see the following breakdown: five simple, five compound, and two complex, revealing greater tolerance for syntactic variation.

The most prominent **cohesive device** in this genre, as shaped by deliberate utilization of controlled vocabulary, is lexical recurrence or **repetition**. An analysis of the first two sentences of instructions in the six manuals reveals that four of the six texts repeat the same noun form verbatim across juxtaposed sentences. Utilization of synonymy is limited. We occasionally see instances of **hyponym/hypernym** relations, such as *Zahnbürste* ("toothbrush") and *Gerät* ("device"), with the former used more frequently in the operating instructions and the latter used more extensively in the safety precautions. It could be that the safety precaution language is based on devices and appliances in a broader sense and is used verbatim across manuals and devices.

Further indication of controlled vocabulary and an operative text function comes in the form of extensive antonymy as a cohesive device, as rendered in the following examples from the corpus:

German antonym pair	English antonym pair equivalent
aufsetzen/trennen	to attach/to detach
ein/aus	on/off
eingeschaltet/ausgeschaltet	turned on/turned off
einschalten/auschalten	to turn on/to turn off
entsorgen/(auf)bewahren	to dispose of/to keep
geschränkt/uneingeschränkt	limited/unlimited
nass/trocken	wet/dry
niemals/immer	never/always
oben/unten	up/down
öffnen/schliessen	open/close

In several of these examples, we see how antonymy is morphologically established through prefix variation, as is common in the German language. Getting

86   **Text types**

these prefixes right is one of the primary challenges facing the German–English translator when working with this genre.

Sample text – German user manual

Zahnbürstenset

Munddusche, Spiegel + 8 Aufsätze NC- 49 9 0 - 675

Sehr geehrte Kundin, sehr geehrter Kunde,
vielen Dank für den *Kauf* dieses **Zahnbürstensets** mit Munddusche, Spiegel und 8 Aufsätzen für die umfassende Zahnreinigung und -pflege.
Bitte lesen Sie diese Bedienungsanleitung und befolgen Sie die aufgeführten Hinweise und Tipps, damit Sie Ihr neues **Zahnbürstenset** optimal einsetzen können.
  Lieferumfang
  Aufbewahrungs- und Ladesystem
  Elektrische Zahnbürste
  2 Aufsteck-Zahnbürsten
  2 Aufsteck-Zungenbürsten
  2 Aufsteck-Interdentalbürsten
  2 Aufsteckköpfe für Zahnseide
  Mundspiegel (beleuchtet)
  Munddusche
  Wassertank (165 ml)
  2 Aufsteck-Düsen für die Munddusche
  Bedienungsanleitung
  Zusätzlich benötigt: 2 **Batterien** Typ AA (für die Munddusche), 1 **Batterie** Typ AAA (für den beleuchteten Spiegel)

  Batterien einlegen
  Die Munddusche und die Spiegelbeleuchtung werden mit **Batterien** betrieben.
  Öffnen Sie das jeweilige **Batterie**fach auf der Unterseite der Munddusche und auf der Unterseite des **Spiegels.**
  Legen Sie die **Batterien** ein: 2 **Batterien** Typ AA in das **Batterie**fach für die Munddusche und 1 **Batterie** Typ AAA in das **Batterie**fach des **Spiegels.** Achten Sie beim *Einlegen* der **Batterien** auf die korrekte Polarität.
  Schließen Sie die **Batterie**fächer abschließend wieder, indem Sie die Abdeckungen aufsetzen.

  Elektrische Zahnbürste verwenden

1. Stellen Sie das Aufbewahrungs- und Ladesystem auf eine stabile, ebene Fläche und verbinden Sie es über das Stromkabel mit der Stromversorgung. Stellen Sie die elektrische **Zahnbürste** auf Ihren Steckplatz. Der Ladevorgang beginnt automatisch.
2. Stecken Sie die Aufsteckzahnbürste auf das Handstück der elektrischen **Zahnbürste** auf. Befeuchten Sie den Bürstenkopf unter fließendem Wasser und tragen Sie die Zahnpasta auf.
3. Schalten Sie die **elektrische Zahnbürste** über die Ein/Aus-Taste ein.
4. Führen Sie die **elektrische Zahnbürste** mit leichtem *Druck* von einem **Zahn** zum anderen und putzen Sie jeden **Zahn** einige Sekunden lang. Führen Sie die **Zahnbürste** über die Außen- und die Innenseite der Zähne sowie über die

Kaufflächen. So _ent_fernen Sie Plaque gründlich – auch an schwer erreichbaren Stellen.

5. In eingeschaltetem *Zustand* können Sie durch *Drücken* der Ein/Aus-Taste zwischen drei verschiedenen Vibrations- und Putzbewegungen wechseln und die **elektrische Zahnbürste** _aus_schalten.

6. Nach zwei Minuten ist die empfohlene Putzdauer erreicht und die **elektrische Zahnbürste** schaltet sich automatisch aus.

HINWEIS:
Anstelle der **Zahnbürste** können Sie auch die Zungenbürste für die *Reinigung* der Zunge, die Interdentalbürste oder den Zahnseide-Kopf für die *Reinigung* der Zahnzwischenräume auf das Handstück der **elektrischen Zahnbürste** aufstecken.

Bezugsquelle:

PEARL.GmbH
PEARL-Str. 1-3
79426 Buggingen
Tel. 0180/ 555 82
www.pearl.de

Key: imperative verbs – highlighted in gray; separable prefixes – underline; lexical recurrence – bold; nominalized forms – italics
Source: Excerpted from www.pearl.de/pdocs/NC4990_11_134737.pdf

Sample German instruction manual analysis

The sample instruction manual is for the Pearl NC 4990 electric toothbrush. It was retrieved from the company's website in 2016 and consists of 1,172 words with an average sentence length of 13.6 words, which puts it right at the mean for the texts in our corpus. At the macro-textual level, this sample exhibits six of the seven moves identified as prototypical in German-language instruction manuals, with only warranty information not included. The reader is addressed using the formal "you" (*Sie*) a total of 70 times, primarily as a distancing strategy in the context of instructions, where it also softens the impact of juxtaposed imperative verbs. In this manual, there is no self-address from the author. These imperative verbs (highlighted in gray) often contain separable prefixes (underlined), which come at the end of the sentence. The separable prefix verbs in this sample manual highlight the tendency for German-language texts to establish semantic variation along morphological lines.

In addition to the widespread use of the formal you, a second distancing strategy in the sample manual involves the deliberate use of passive voice constructs, as found in the following two examples. We would likely see these modulated in English-language manuals to avoid the passive voice:

German passive construct	Literal English translation	Modulated English translation
... *werden mit Batterien betrieben*	... are operated by batteries	... are battery operated
... *damit die Pumpe keinen Schaden nimmt*	... so that the pump does not obtain any damage	... to avoid damaging the pump

Text types

The most common cohesive device used in this sample text is lexical recurrence. We see the term *Batterien* (batteries), for example, appearing a total of 21 times. The base form *Batterie-* (text in bold) is also frequently used in contexts involving other constructs (i.e., *Batteriefach*, or battery compartment) as partial recurrence. At the level of terminology, we see a strong lexical preference for nominalized forms (text in italics), which would likely be transposed into verbs in English (see table).

Nominalized German construct	Literal English translation	Transposed English translation
vielen Dank für den Kauf dieses Zahnbürstensets	Thank you for your purchase of this toothbrush set	Thank you for purchasing this toothbrush set
Achten Sie beim Einlegen der Batterien	Pay attention during the insertion of batteries	Pay attention when inserting batteries
... durch Drücken der Ein/Aus-Taste	By the pressing of the on/off button	By pressing the on/off button
Anstelle der Zahnbürste können Sie auch die Zungenbürste für die Reinigung der Zunge	As an alternate to the toothbrush, you can also use the tongue brush for the cleaning of the tongue	As an alternate to the toothbrush, you can also use the tongue brush to clean your tongue

RUSSIAN

Scientific and technological advances, as well as a sharp increase in international trade after World War II, have contributed to an increase in the flow of technical documentation across international borders. Consequently, translation and localization of user technical manuals has gained momentum. This section focuses on the analysis of a corpus of ten original user manuals in Russian, collected from ten different sources. All texts were published between 2015 and 2016.

Macro-textual features

Based on analysis of this corpus, we isolated the following mandatory macro-textual **rhetorical moves** and their Russian variants:

1. Name of product and its manufacturer
2. Table of contents (which was, interestingly, missing in one of the manuals)

- Содержание

3. Warnings and safety regulations

- Техника/требования безопасности
- Безопасность

4. List of product parts

- Комплектность
- Комплект поставки

5. Information on how to assemble or install the product

- Порядок настройки
- Подготовка к работе
- Подготовка к использованию
- Порядок подготовки к работе
- Монтаж и подключение
- Подключение и настройка
- Порядок установки

6. Information on how to use the product and its various features

- Правила пользования прибором
- Устройство и принцип работы
- Порядок/условия эксплуатации
- Управление и настройка
- Назначение и принцип действия
- Использование по назначению

90   **Text types**

7. Protocols related to storage, maintenance, and transportation

- Транспортирование (транспортировка) и хранение
- Техническое обслуживание
- Правила хранения
- Уход

8. Warranty information

- Гарантии изготовителя (may include гарантийный талон, a form to fill out in case of product malfunction)
- Гарантийные обязательства
- Сведения о гарантии

The above list demonstrates a remarkable variation in the wording of section headings in the corpus, particularly in the sections concerning information on installation and usage. It may indicate that specifications for technical writing in Russia are currently in flux. Moreover, it may point to a preference for synonymy in Russian vs. a preference for consistency in English-language texts.

In addition to the mandatory moves outlined above, the following are optional rhetorical moves:

- Serial or model number (Серийный номер/Модель)
- Date ("01.02.2016" (date/month/year), "07.2016" (month/year) or "2016" (year))
- Introduction (Введение/Общие сведения)
- Technical specifications (Технические параметры/Технические характеристики/Техническая информация/Технические данные)
- Troubleshooting (Устранение неисправностей/Возможные неисправности и методы их устранения)
- Information regarding recycling (Утилизация)
- Manufacturer's country (Сделано в России)
- Appendix (Приложение)
- Contact information and website (Адрес/Информационный телефон/Реквизиты)
- Information regarding quality control and adherence to GOST standards (Свидетельство о приемке, Штамп ОТК)
- Acknowledgment of sale/purchase (Отметка о продаже, Подпись, Штамп)
- Addresses of service providers (Адреса сервисных центров)

Moreover, five manuals contain a section that addresses the buyer directly (Уважаемый покупатель! [Dear customer,] Благодарим Вас за … [Thank you for …]), and two manuals include a glossary of terms and a list of abbreviations.

The order in which the rhetorical moves occur varies, the only exception being the product and manufacturer names on the title page. The table of contents is located either at the beginning or end of the document.

In addition to text, user manuals contain many pictures and graphs to aid in product assembly and operation. Text formatting varies in terms of capitalization, list formats, font types and sizes, bolding, italicizing, and highlighting. The use of warning images, such as an exclamation point or a raised pointed finger, is also common.

As for the **register** of Russian user manuals, the word frequency list points to the **field** of technical discourse. The table lists the most frequent lexical items found in the corpus, with their grammatical variations included in the number of occurrences (notably, all of them, with the exception of необходимо, are nouns). The most frequent item, эксплуатация (use), occurred most often as part of the collocation руководство по эксплуатации, the Russian equivalent for "user manual."

Lexical item	Frequency	Lexical item	Frequency
эксплуатация (use)	87	необходимо (is necessary)	41
работа (work, functioning)	80	подключение (installation, connection)	39
устройство (device)	75	напряжение (voltage)	38
стабилизатор (regulator, stabilizer)	69	управление (operation)	34
руководство (manual)	54	изделие (product)	33
прибор (device, appliance)	52	сигнализатор (signaling indicator)	32
велосипед (bicycle)	47	внимание (attention)	29
режим (setting (of a device))	43	сеть (power supply, network)	28

As for the **mode**, user manuals are written for an audience preparing to use a certain technology or software device. In terms of the publication venue, user manuals are typically printed or published online, which leaves little room for dialogue between the author and the addressee. The **tenor**, or the relationship between the author and the addressee, is either expert-to-expert or expert-to-nonexpert. The terminology found in user manuals is, however, more technical than that found in other instructive genres, such as recipes, since the latter targets a wider audience. Indeed, most people can make a simple meal, while fewer people can (or want to) put together a motorcycle or a sauna stove.

The main **communicative functions** of user manuals are **informative** and **instructive**, as they contain information about a device and provide directions for its use, assembly, care, storage, and other related aspects. Safety warnings are of great importance, although, in comparison with U.S. user manuals, Russian-language manuals may contain fewer of them. Some manuals also include marketing of their company's products, which adds a degree of *conative* language. Based on Offord's (2005) classifications of styles, user manuals relate to both the scientific style (научный стиль) and official style (официальный стиль), which are among higher-register writing styles.

User manuals, like recipes, aim at getting their target audience to intake information and follow instructions. However, from a pragmatic standpoint, both user manuals and recipes become instructive only when their addressees familiarize themselves with the content and implement the directions. In terms of consequences for the failure to implement these directions, user manuals may have higher safety risks than recipes.

92 Text types

Micro-textual features

At the micro-textual level, the corpus data point to an abundance of passive structures, primarily (1) constructions with a short past participle of a perfective verb serving as the predicate, such as сенсор установлен (a sensor is installed); (2) constructions with the reflexive suffix -ся for imperfective verbs, such as рекомендуется очистить (it is recommended to clean); and (3) constructions with third-person plural verbs with an omitted subject, such as переводят ([they] transfer). As is typical for Russian instructive structures, infinitives and imperatives are used to express steps in a process, e.g., установить (install, infinitive form) and разблокируйте (unblock, imperative form). Safety warnings show a preference for repeating the word запрещается (it is prohibited), with 22 occurrences found in the corpus. Russian safety warnings also often contain negative structures, such as не допускается (it is not allowed to) or не предназначен (not meant to) and imperatives (удостоверьтесь [make sure]), which are also frequently negated, such as не используйте (do not use) or не вскрывайте (do not open).

Interestingly, some manuals are more interpersonal than others. One of the manuals, for instance, makes use of the pronoun мы (we) to represent the manufacturer, e.g., Мы рекомендуем выполнять сложные проверки в сервисном центре (We recommend the implementation of complex checks at a service center). In impersonal writing, a passive structure with рекомендуется would be used. The same manual uses a capitalized version of the second-person plural pronoun Вы and its related forms to refer to customers and their purchase, e.g., приобретенный Вами мотоцикл (the motorcycle you purchased). As the service industry develops, we anticipate an increased use of personal appeal, especially in user manuals targeting a broad customer base (e.g., for vehicles, software, or home appliances and electronics).

Consistent with Russian official style, other features of user manuals include:

- Terminology

  - Generic, occurring in three and more texts, such as устройство (device, 75 occurrences), прибор (device, 52), режим (mode, 43), напряжение (voltage, 38)
  - Specialized, confined to one text, such as роллета (roller window blinds) (70 occurrences in one text), стабилизатор (stabilizer) (69), сигнализатор (entry alarm) (32)

- Verbal nouns, such as эксплуатация (87), стабилизатор, напряжение, сигнализатор, подключение, индикатор (indicator) (29), назначение (intended use) (20)
- Noun chains, порядок работы роллеты (order of operation of roller blinds) (10), поворот ключа (turn of a key) (16), батарея питания (power battery) (5)
- Verbal adjectives, such as поврежденный (damaged), оснащенный (equipped), соответствующий (corresponding), возникший (emerged), смонтированный (assembled), включенный (turned on)
- Abbreviations commonly found in official style and scientific writing, such as и т.д., и т.п., шт., см., вкл., выкл., кг., км, кВА (kVA), мм рт. ст.

Instruction manuals   93

- Acronyms, such as ТО (Техническое обслуживание), ОТК (Отдел технического контроля), ПО (Программное обеспечение)

Regarding **cohesive devices,** user manuals show the following tendencies. The use of personal pronouns is rare, which is consistent with the official style and impersonality of user manuals, as discussed in the description of the corpus. In contrast, demonstrative pronouns are employed rather frequently, e.g., это and its forms occur about 40 times in the corpus. The use of ellipses, or complete omission of a lexical term, might be hypothesized as creating cohesion in a user manual. However, analysis of the corpus revealed that while there are instances of ellipses, manuals tend to repeat lexical items, possibly to aid the reader in following instructions by avoiding any potential ambiguity. Lists, which are used in all manuals in the corpus, may be considered ellipses, since they explicitly indicate omission of the first part of the sentence.

The most frequent **conjunctions** are: и (all texts); или (all texts); а (all texts), чтобы (eight texts); если, то (eight texts); где (three texts); and до тех пор, пока (two texts). The relative pronoun который often has a conjunctive function (29 instances). Extensive use of lists and sections, often numbered, may be considered a type of cohesion in a text. User manuals contain both simple and compound/complex sentences, with the actual instructional part gravitating toward simple sentences and lists.

As for **lexical cohesion, repetition** prevails, which is evident from the frequency data. At times, synonymy is used. Notably, we found instances of synonymy that is established explicitly, e.g., в дальнейшем – сигнализатор или прибор (further referred to as an alarm or device), as is also typical for official legal texts (официально-деловой юридический стиль). Also of note is the lack of diminutive forms in the corpus; none were used in any of the texts.

Sample text – Russian user manual

Научно-производственная фирма «Радиус»
Прибор «Квант»
Руководство по эксплуатации, паспорт

1. Назначение и принцип действия
Прибор «Квант» предназначен для контроля тока нагрузки и определения мест повреждения в распределительных электросетях.

1.1. Прибор обеспечивает:

- контроль исправности прибора;
- контроль наличия напряжения на воздушных линиях (ВЛ) электропередач 6–35 кВ;
- контроль тока нагрузки на ВЛ 0,4–35 кВ;
- определение места замыкания на землю в сетях 6–35 кВ;
- определение места обрыва провода в сетях 6–35 кВ;
- определение опоры, находящейся под напряжением 6–35 кВ;
- световой и звуковой контроль исправности обесточенных предохранителей или целостности электрической цепи.

На рис. 1 приведена структурная схема прибора.

1.2. Контроль исправности прибора
В режиме «КОНТР.» напряжение источника питания подается на выходной преобразователь 7 (рис. 1), нагрузкой которого служит микроамперметр. При исправности источника питания и выходного преобразователя стрелка прибора отклоняется на 90–150 делений шкалы (в настоящем ТО деления шкалы приводятся для приборов с полной шкалой 200 делений).

1.3. Контроль наличия напряжения 6–35 кВ осуществляется с помощью встроенной электрической антенны. Электрической антенной служит металлическая пластина, расположенная в передней части прибора (рис. 2).
...

2. Правила пользования прибором «КВАНТ»
Внешний вид прибора показан на рис. 2.
Включение питания осуществляется переключателем «ВКЛ/ОТКЛ». Выбор режима работы осуществляется последовательно, путем нажатия кнопки «РЕЖИМ», которое подтверждается коротким звуковым сигналом. При этом загорается соответствующий выбранному режиму светодиод.

2.1. При включении питания прибор переходит в режим «КОНТР.».
Пользоваться прибором можно при отклонении стрелки в этом режиме на 90–150 делений шкалы.

2.2. Для контроля наличия напряжения на ВЛ 6–35 кВ оператор должен подойти к ВЛ на расстояние 5–6 м и сориентировать прибор перпендикулярно оси ВЛ (рис. 4).
В режиме «U kV» при наличии напряжения прибор должен показывать не менее 60 делений шкалы.
При контроле напряжения следует учитывать влияние электрического поля соседних ВЛ и экранирующее действие людей, техники или других объектов, расположенных между прибором и ВЛ.

2.3. Для контроля тока нагрузки на ВЛ 0,4 и 6–35 кВ оператор должен подойти к ВЛ на расстояние соответственно 2–3 и 5–6 м. Сориентировать прибор перпендикулярно оси ВЛ (рис. 4). Выбрать необходимый режим контроля тока. Контроль тока нагрузки на ВЛ 0,4 кВ может производиться на пределах: «20 А», «50 А» и «100 А». Значение тока при этом определяется путем деления показаний прибора на коэффициенты 10, 4 и 2 соответственно для каждого из пределов.
...
Контроль тока нагрузки на ВЛ других конфигураций производится на тех же пределах с учетом поправочного коэффициента, определяемого опытным путем.

2.4. Для определения места замыкания на землю на ВЛ 6–35 кВ используются режимы 1:1000, 1:100, 1:10 и 1:1 в зависимости от уровня тока замыкания на землю.
Определение места замыкания начинается с определения поврежденной ВЛ. Для этого необходимо произвести измерения магнитного поля вблизи всех ВЛ, отходящих от шин питающей подстанции. Оператор должен подойти к одной из отходящих ВЛ, вблизи выхода ее с территории подстанции, на расстояние 5–8 м от оси ВЛ (рис. 4). Встать лицом к ВЛ, держа прибор перед 4 собой перпендикулярно оси ВЛ (руки оператора должны быть расположены в районе органов управления прибора).
...

> 2.6. Для определения места обрыва провода ВЛ 6–35 кВ оператор устанавливает режим «U кV» и производит контроль электрического поля на расстоянии 5–6 м от ВЛ. Показания прибора за местом обрыва возрастают в 5–10 раз по сравнению с показаниями до места обрыва.
>
> *Source: Excerpted from Прибор «Квант». Руководство по эксплуатации/Appliance "Kvant." User Manual, www.rza.ru/upload/iblock/df2/kvant.pdf*

Sample Russian instruction manual analysis

The sample user manual deals with a device called *Kvant*, which is used to control load current and detect places of damage in powerlines. The PDF of the manual is published on the manufacture's website www.rza.ru. At the macro-textual level, the manual contains all the mandatory rhetorical moves with the notable exception of the table of contents. It starts off with the name of the product and the manufacturer, followed by two sections on how to use the product (Назначение и принцип действия and Правила пользования прибором). The manual also contains the list of parts, as well as the sections on storage, transportation, and warranty. In terms of optional rhetorical moves, we see technical specifications (Технические характеристики), the manufacturing number (заводской №), information regarding quality control (Контролер), and acknowledgments of sale/purchase (Дата продажи, М.П. (место печати)). True to its genre, the manual contains images with drawings and graphs.

The text is about 1,450 words long, which is typical for the texts included in our corpus. One must keep in mind that the length of user manuals may vary greatly, depending on the complexity of the device and the level of detail that a manufacturer prefers. The mode of discourse is informative and the tenor of discourse points to an expert-to-expert relationship, since in order to use this device one ought to be familiar with powerlines and load currents. As for the field of discourse, the use of technical terms points to a technical domain, specifically, electricity and powerlines (e.g., воздушные линии электропередач [aboveground powerlines], электрическая цепь [electrical chain], электрическое поле [electrical field], ток [current], etc.). Lastly, the communicative function is informative and instructive, with instances of safety warnings.

From the standpoint of micro-textual features, the mood and tense tend to be represented by impersonal passive constructions, primarily (1) short past participles for perfective verbs, such as прибор предназначен (the device is designed for); (2) the reflexive suffix -ся, e.g., контроль осуществляется (control is implemented); (3) impersonal plurals, e.g., прибор переводят (the device is re-adjusted); and (4) passive verbal adjectives, such as настроенный (is adjusted to), расположенный (is located). The imperative tone of the manual is delivered via the use of (1) infinitives, e.g., встать лицом к ВЛ (stand facing the powerline); (2) adverbs of necessity, e.g., должен подойти (must approach), необходимо провести (necessary to carry out); and (3) imperatives, e.g., подключите кабель (attach the cable). The primary tense is present. In terms of punctuation, an exclamation mark is used with warnings.

The user manual under analysis is dry and impersonal. There is not a single instance of the pronouns мы (we) or вы (you). This may be due to the

Text types

expert-to-expert tenor of this particular manual, which tends to be quite formal in Russian.

In terms of cohesive devices, referential devices are scarce. The referential pronoun *это* (and its forms) is used 9 times. Ellipsis is present in the form of lists. The use of numbering is also a form of connecting parts of the text. Conjunctive devices are primary sources of grammatical cohesion:

Conjunctions	Frequency
и	28
или	6
а (а также)	5 (2)
если	2
но	1

For the most part, additive conjunctions are used (и and а также). These conjunctions frequently form complex sentences. The text, however, often resorts to simple sentences, which makes sense from the standpoint of the directness and clarity expected of instructional manuals.

In terms of lexical cohesion, repetition is prevalent, again for the purpose of clarity. In addition, we note instances of phrases followed by their abbreviated versions (e.g., воздушная линия электропередач, referred to as ВЛ). The table below exemplifies the abundance of repeated words, phrases, and abbreviations.

Repeated items	Frequency	Repeated items	Frequency
Прибор	48	Квант	10
ВЛ	38	Предохранитель	9
Ток	15	Режим	7
Замыкание	14	Электрическое поле	5
Напряжение	13	Магнитный датчик	4
Гц	10	Магнитное поле	4

SPANISH

The file size for the ten texts in the corpus is 244,938 characters, for an average of almost 24,500 characters per file, the size of a booklet. The smallest is 10,702 characters, or 859 words; the largest is 44,348, or 3,421 words. The mean number of words per sentence is roughly 17 words. There are 2,000 words between 10 and 17 letters long in the sample. Ten representative digital texts from Argentina, published online from December 2015 to December 2016, were collected in order to analyze their composite features, or rhetorical moves (Swales 1990b).

Macro-textual features

The following are the **rhetorical moves** one may find in a user manual:

1. Name of product (*Nombre del producto*)
2. Table of contents/summary/quick start guide (*Tabla de contenido/resumen/ guía*)
3. Introduction (*Introducción*)
4. Warnings/precautions/contraindications/safety regulations or notices (*Advertencias/precauciones/contraindicaciones/avisos de seguridad*)
5. Environmental protection and disposal/recycling (*Protección del medio ambiente y desechos/ Reciclaje*)
6. Product purpose/indications for use (*Indicaciones del uso*)
7. Product description (parts and accessories)/technical specifications chart (*Descripción del producto (piezas y accesorios)/especificaciones técnicas*)
8. Conditions that may affect use (*Condiciones*)
9. Explanation of how to install the product (*Cómo se utiliza el producto*)
10. Explanation of how to use features (*Cómo funcionan las características*)
11. Care and maintenance measures (*Cuidado y mantenimiento*)
12. Storage (*Almacenamiento*)
13. Troubleshooting tips/FAQs (*Preguntas más frecuentes*)
14. Appendix (*Anexo*)
15. Guarantee or warranty information/limitations of the product (*Garantía/ limitaciones del producto*)
16. Contact information and soliciting action (*Información de contacto*)

Virtually all of these inclusions are mandatory, although they occur in different proportions. The order and presence of these moves, too, varies vastly from text to text; in one, a diagram and summary are given, followed by an explanation of symbols, then safety information. In most cases, however, the order roughly follows the moves above, although often safety or a "before starting" sequence comes in the first three moves.

In terms of **register**, which includes **field, mode,** and **tenor,** the **field** of the technical manual – its topic and degree of specialization – has been plotted on a line of thematic complexity from simplest to most complex: small appliances, large appliances, sound and image devices, telephones, computers, and, finally, complex systems such as automobiles. Documentation for the latter two,

Text types

computers and complex systems, are often considered handbooks and have a more didactic purpose than the others (Gamero Pérez 2001: 92). The **field** of a user manual is technical rather than scientific since the product descriptions have an objective correlative: They are "about" an actual product, not a theoretical one or a class of products as a whole. The most frequent nouns appear in the table.

Lexical item	Frequency	Lexical item	Frequency
uso	65	seguridad	43
producto	58	electrodoméstico	40
heladera	57	batería	36
instrucciones	56	funcionamiento	35
artefacto	53	tiempo	35
garantía	53	agua	34
cable	51	instalación	33
temperatura	51	caso	32
botón	49	equipo	32
manual	49	forma	32

These nouns reflect aspects of the function of the text type as noted above – the safe and effective installation, assembly, maintenance, operation, storage, or repair of a consumer product: product (*producto, artefacto*); processes (*uso, instalación*); purpose (*instrucciones*); general and specific parts (*artefacto, equipo, cable*); product functions or features (*temperatura*); safety (*seguridad* and verb forms such as *asegúrese* [19 instances]); and legal liability (*garantía*), the latter of which appears in seven of the ten texts. Nouns such as *falla* (17 in six texts in the corpus) and *daños* (24 in eight texts) suggest the commonness of the troubleshooting sub-move, which may also be related to safety and liability. Other nouns that are more abstract, though countable, are *deterioro* (4) and *desgaste(s)* (6), which are measurements of wear and tear, and important for product liability. *Servicio técnico autorizado*, a set phrase, is used in six texts, and serves as part of a hold-harmless clause – the nonexpert may void the warranty if he or she attempts certain kinds of repairs. In at least one case, further action – a fill-in section – is required in order to activate product warranties. In another text, the gas installer or electrician is meant to fill in their license number and billing information for reference. *Póngase en contacto* (8 in five texts) evinces sub-move #15, offering customer service. The **mode** of the user manual, that is, its position on the written/oral discourse continuum, is written, highly structured, and frozen language. The use of commands presupposes an implied author who is an expert authority, usually a designer, engineer, or marketing specialist. The **tenor** of these texts underscores the inequality between the participants; a neutral stance; an unmarked, impersonal style; and a formal form of address (*Ud.*). Users are not invited to interact or improvise; they are told 5 times in four different texts to *respetar* (follow) all instructions, with warnings about failure to do so.

The **communicative function** of Spanish user manuals has been classified as "directive," a subcategory of **informative** texts; that is, they are designed to instruct addressees how to do something (Rolf 1993). The user manual is a reference tool, however, not a training tool (Abdelhak, Grostick and Hanken 2016: 365). The conative, expressive, metalinguistic, poetic, and phatic functions of language are rare enough to catch the reader's attention when they do appear. The closest approximation of the **metalinguistic** function of language in the manuals is the self-referential *este manual*, or "this manual" (5 instances).

Micro-textual features

At the micro-textual level, imperative verb forms are used frequently, as we will discuss below. Nouns are often used interchangeably to refer to performance breakdown: *falla(s)* (22), *anomalías* (1), *desperfecto(s)* (3), *problema(s)* (12), or *accidente(s)* (8). Spanish has been slower to adopt inclusive language, although it does appear in the product limitations or warnings to users in one text (*Personas con capacidades diferentes o reducidas ...*). We also find prohibition words: *nunca* (15 instances); *jamás* (2); forms of *peligr-(o/oso/osa/osos/osas)* (14); *precaución* and variations (13); and emphatic headings stressing safety: *importante(s)* (20), almost invariably used in bold or with exclamation points in the respective texts. *En caso de* (22 instances in eight texts) suggests potential malfunctions for troubleshooting. Conditional limits to actions are suggested by terms such as *sólo* (11 instances). The prepositional construction *antes de* + [infinitive] has high frequency, with collocates (*... utilizar/usar/realizar/*) appearing in five, six, and seven different texts, respectively. Adverbs are perhaps most revealing of the emphasis on proper procedure (see table for the most salient examples).

Adverbs	Frequency	Adverbs	Frequency
correctamente	15	*atentamente*	2
completamente	8	*brevemente*	2
cuidadosamente	4	*estrictamente*	2
solamente	4	*exclusivamente*	2
adecuadamente	3	*fácilmente*	2
detenidamente	3	*inmediatamente*	2
firmemente	3	*periódicamente*	2
regularmente	3	*suavemente*	2
potencialmente	3	*suficientemente*	2
únicamente	3	*convenientemente*	1
absolutamente	2	*debidamente*	1

These describe *manner, place,* and *time* of use, maintenance and repair, all of which modify the extent, limit, or way in which actions are to be performed. The 59 instances of *cuando* (in all ten texts), when used as an adverb and with adverbs of time, attest to this, although some are used conjunctively. *Siempre* (19 in nine texts) acts similarly, as an adverbial. Many nouns, too, in technical

Text types

texts describe qualities that relate to quality control, for example, *estanqueidad* (3 instances), which refers to being airtight or watertight.

In Spanish user manuals, the preferred **cohesive devices** include: definitive articles; the anaphoric reference *estos*, which is used twice, *dichos*, 4 times; the deictic *abajo* (3) is used but not *aquí* (Spanish prefers *presente* (7)); *ellos/ellas* are not used (0); *algunos/as* (2), *mucho* (5), *ningún* (10).

Examples of **conjunctions** include *y* (378 instances, the sixth most common word out of 3,315), *hasta* (21), *o* (228), *luego* (15), *si* (79), *cuando* (59), *antes* (52), and *pero* (3). We find avoidance of repetition through words like *aparato* (22 in four texts), *dispositivo* (9 in five texts), *electrodoméstico* (40 in two texts), and *electrodomésticos* (4 in four texts). The texts are clear when specific tools are *not* required, as suggested by the frequency of *cualquier tipo de* (5 instances).

The most common verbs and verb forms in the sample appear in the frequency table.

Verb	Frequency	Verb	Frequency
debe	54	*realizar*	21
puede	49	*asegúrese*	19
ser	46	*evitar*	19
utilice	39	*limpie*	19
coloque	29	*sea*	19
encuentra	29	*muestra*	17
utilizar	29	*deben*	15
presione	25	*tenga*	15
pueden	24	*enchufe*	14
ajuste	22	*deje*	13

Nine of these top verbs are imperatives, and 269 passive constructions using *se* are found in the corpus, accounting for the appearance of *encuentra* (7 of its 29 instances) and *muestra* (17). At least one verb is used invariably with cautions (*evitar*, 19). Finally, the infinitive is also used imperatively, although it tends not to be used in the steps but in the soliciting action sections (e.g., *En caso de necesitar repuestos o asesoramiento, dirigirse a etc.*).

Sample text – Spanish user manual

Manual de instrucciones

Características

FELICITACIONES POR HABER ADQUIRIDO ESTE PRODUCTO Y MUCHAS GRACIAS POR CONFIAR EN NOBLEX PARA SATISFACER SUS NECESIDADES TECNOLÓGICAS EN AUDIO.

• ROGAMOS LEER CUIDADOSAMENTE ESTAS INSTRUCCIONES ANTES DE USAR LA UNIDAD. • CONSERVE ESTE MANUAL DEBIDO A QUE PODRÍA NECESITARLO EN EL FUTURO. • LAS ILUSTRACIONES Y GRÁFICOS DE ESTE MANUAL SON DE REFERENCIA Y SUJETOS A CAMBIOS SIN PREVIO AVISO.

Los auriculares HP1962RS con banda de sujeción variable son cómodos y resistentes para un uso personal confortable y seguro.

Gracias a su sistema de plegado y cable desmontable permiten llevar tu música a cualquier parte de manera fácil y cómoda.

Son ideales para ser usados en la reproducción multimedia digital de dispositivos MP3, MP4, reproductores de CD/DVD/Blu-ray, Tablet, Smartphone o PC notebook.

Precauciones

Este sistema de auriculares se diseñó y fabricó para garantizar la seguridad personal; sin embargo, el uso inadecuado de la unidad puede causar algunos riesgos evitables.

Para evitar averías o mal funcionamiento:

• Nunca abra los auriculares ni el control multifunción. • No intente desarmar y reparar la unidad usted mismo. Solicite el servicio a personal capacitado. • No añada accesorios que no hayan sido diseñados para estos auriculares. • Si hace ajustes o realiza procedimientos diferentes de los especificados en este manual, puede quedar expuesto a riesgos peligrosos o provocar cortocircuitos que podrían ocasionar que inutilicen el sistema de auriculares en forma permanente y definitiva. • No exponga la unidad a un calor excesivo ni lo coloque cercano a objetos con llamas, como por ejemplo velas encendidas o de fuentes de calor, como cocinas, radiadores, calefactores, estufas u otros elementos que produzcan calor.

Uso

De esta forma al estar ligeramente separados del oído generan una mayor sensación natural del campo estéreo y una reproducción de frecuencias más lineal y precisa.

Tener en cuenta la diferencia entre el auricular derecho (R) e izquierdo (L) y colocar el auricular correcto en la oreja correspondiente. Ajuste el volumen del dispositivo conectado a un nivel seguro.

Garantía

Esta garantía comprende nuestra obligación de reparar sin costo la unidad, en los términos de la Ley 24.240 y su reglamentación, siempre que la falla se produzca dentro de un uso normal doméstico de la misma y que no hayan intervenido factores ajenos que pudieran perjudicar a juicio de NOBLEX ARGENTINA S.A. su buen funcionamiento.

NOBLEX ARGENTINA S.A. no está obligada en ningún caso al cambio de la unidad completa, pudiendo reemplazar las piezas defectuosas de manera que la misma vuelva a ser idónea para el uso al cual está 2. destinada. Durante la vigencia de la garantía regirán normativas establecidas por la ley 24.240, el Decreto 1798/94 y normas concordantes.

...

12. Si se modificara el documento de compra de cualquier forma o si se hubiera dañado, alterado o retirado de la unidad las etiquetas de identificación que ésta posee o cuando presenten enmiendas o falsedad de alguno de sus datos, significará sin perjuicio de las acciones civiles y/o penales que por derecho correspondan, la inmediata revocación de la presente garantía.

Key: various features discussed in sample analysis – highlighted in gray
Source: Excerpted from Noblex Argentina

Sample Spanish instruction manual analysis

The text we selected for analysis, *Manual de instrucciones: Noblex auriculares (Rolling Stones Limited Edition)* contains many of the above-mentioned textual features and will be used to demonstrate the micro-textual features of user

102   **Text types**

manuals. The text was taken from www.noblex.com.ar, and its length is 2,347 characters (which in this text type often include symbols such as the pound sign or numerals). The mode and tenor of discourse are fairly typical for the text type, although the use of the possessive pronoun *tu* is notable, as it represents a strategy of reducing the distance between the company and the presumably youthful buyer. Legal language indemnifying the company appears throughout the text, e.g., *SUJETOS A CAMBIOS SIN PREVIO AVISO*. The company's environmental awareness is signaled in its notes, using extensive enumeration, *El mismo al final de su vida útil, requiere de un procedimiento adecuado para su tratamiento, recuperación, reciclado, reutilización y/o disposición final en instalaciones especiales*. The multiple near-synonyms, while perhaps compliant with legal requirements for product documentation and product life-cycle management, also suggest a desire to project an eco-friendly ethos to the customer, while persuading them to reuse, recycle, or dispose of the product properly. These clauses are sometimes written with an international audience in mind (*tenga en cuenta las leyes vigentes en su país*).

One instance of the conative function of language occurs where purchasers are congratulated on their good taste (*Felicitaciones por haber comprado este producto y muchas gracias por confiar en Noblex para satisfacer sus necesidades tecnológicas en audio*). Three texts use constructions with *gracias* for the same purpose.

In terms of mood, the declarative, imperative, and subjunctive are all present. In the final clause of the warranty (clause no. 12), the tenses and moods are used strategically:

> *Si se modificara el documento de compra de cualquier forma o si se hubiera dañado, alterado o retirado de la unidad las etiquetas de identificación que ésta posee o cuando presenten enmiendas o falsedad de alguno de sus datos, significará sin perjuicio de las acciones civiles y/o penales que por derecho correspondan, la inmediata revocación de la presente garantía.*

For instance, the pluperfect subjunctives are used as counterfactuals here (viz. should the receipt have been altered, etc.), and the main clause following this *if*-clause becomes the legally binding contingency, a "shall" clause, whereby the warranty is voided (*revocación*). The only indicative mood in the sentence of five or more subjunctives is *significará*, the subjunctives indicating non-specificity or futurity.

In terms of cohesive devices, personal pronouns do not appear, and demonstrative references (*esto, eso, esos, estos, aquí, allá*) are very few. *Lo* is used in 34 texts, however, referring to the antecedent, the product. *El usuario* is used 10 times in five texts, substituting for forms of "you" (the formal *usted* appears 6 times in four texts). The types of sentences are compound, especially in the itemized subclauses of the warranty. The tips and installation steps use simple sentences with univocal meanings.

Regarding tense, the imperative is the signature verb form in the user manual, both in the positive and negative forms, including for prohibitions. Phrasal verbs such as "should" appear as well, though less often (Schäffner 2001: 51–2). Accordingly, the modal *debe* appears 54 times in the corpus, in all ten texts:

deben (15), *deberá* (12), *deberán* (2), and *debería* (1). Contingencies, particularly harmful ones, are marked by the conditional, e.g., *podría* + verb. The noun appears in the text, often in the passive voice, to indicate states of operation: *Se encenderá una luz verde cuando el aparato haya alcanzado la temperatura final; cuando* or *si* are used to describe the conditions of the state in question. The present tense used will impart a sense of obligation ("shall"), and the subjunctive mood works concordantly in the warranty section to illustrate the conditions under which the warranty is invoked: *Esta garantía comprende ... siempre que la falla se produzca dentro de un uso normal doméstico de la misma y que no hayan intervenido factores ajenos que pudieran perjudicar a juicio de NOBLEX ARGENTINA S.A. su buen funcionamiento*. The word "no" appears 254 times, in all ten texts, and in connection with both product limits and prohibitions. The imperative itself appears with the greatest frequency at the beginning of each instruction.

In terms of textual cohesion, the use of *el mismo* for *el producto* constitutes a double substitution: the former for the latter, which in turn is a substitution for the actual product name. Regarding noun phrases, the use of borrowings (*drivers, backup*) is evident. Still, others appear out of necessity, as they must correspond to the labeling on the product itself (e.g., the term is *el botón power* because the device's "on" button literally reads "Power" in the graphic).

Note

1 "Your" and "you" rank fifth (1,707 instances) and sixth (1,447 instances) in the corpus, respectively, and occur in all the texts comprising it. The only corpus in which "your" ranks higher is that of patient education materials, where it ranks fourth (just one spot higher) but does not occur in all the texts. Though "you" ranks the same in the corpus of business letters, it also does not occur in all the texts.

4 Museum guides

Museum guides are one of a number of texts that assist visitors in making sense of a vast array of artifacts, from the most pragmatic aspects, such as how to make your way through a physical exhibition space, to the more complex tasks of cultural education and dissemination. Museums must also manage rotating exhibits with their object labels or "captions," a range of publications from brochures to catalogues, and behind-the-scenes documents, including legal materials related to accessioning and curating. Museums manage texts that reach well beyond their walls as well, including art encyclopedia entries and museum webpages (Neather, forthcoming). Increasingly, museums have to comply, morally if not legally as well, with media accessibility considerations so that all patrons can enjoy what is on display. This may involve audio descriptions or other accommodations for the deaf and hard of hearing.

Today's museums may have social media communications directors, press officers, publications departments, and tour guides. The fact that so many of the objects in museums have to be recontextualized from where they were originally found and "used," as well as the inescapable need to interpret them and the varying levels of visitors' expertise to do so, make Ravelli's (2009) invitation to consider *museums as texts* an intriguing point of entry for our analysis. Museums exercise a pedagogical function in that they shape how we order, understand, and construct meanings, and how, through selection and even exclusion, they invite the visitor to occupy positions from which to view not only knowledge but their own identities in relation to it (Trofanenko and Segall 2014: 2). Like other educational environments, such as libraries, museums are shifting their focus to technology, interactivity, and customization. University-museum collaborations involve research and dissemination efforts. For example, museums frequently have physical classrooms and generate many textual materials related to outreach, including digital captioning for virtual classrooms, leaflets, and worksheets.

Museum communication is the broad category or genre under which museum guides are one form of text. Twenty-first-century museums may have oral communication services in place, such as interpreters (combination tour conductor-docent-historian-programming specialists, not to be confused with language interpreters), or audio guides, scripted text recorded to audio files or an interactive web app using GPS for use on a handheld device. Many written texts such as *museum press releases*, *e-news*, *blogs* and *web presentations*, and public relations form part of the contemporary museum's communications arsenal (Lazzeretti 2016: 1–10). *Press kits*, which may include contact sheets, fact sheets, annual reports, press releases, and diverse media such as images may also be available. These combine to perform informative, persuasive, and promotional functions (ibid: 6).

This chapter will focus on museum guides specifically and outline the prototypical features of this ubiquitous text type.

ENGLISH

Museum guides allow visitors to learn about a museum's attractions, facilities, rules, and policies, serving as a reference for visitors to make the most of their visit. The corpus in this chapter includes guides from 12 museums: the American Museum of Natural History, National Archives Museum, United States Holocaust Memorial Museum, de Young Museum, Mütter Museum, Smithsonian American Art Museum/National Portrait Gallery, National World War II Museum, Revs Institute, Smithsonian, Franklin Institute, Phillips Collection, and the National Infantry Museum. The guide lengths vary considerably, ranging from 608 to 6,537 words, and the average length is 1,595 words. Of the 12 corpus texts, eight range from 990–1,667 words. The remaining four texts contain 361, 608, 786, and 6,537 words.

Macro-textual features

Museum guides often include the following eight **rhetorical moves**:

1. Name of the museum
2. Museum introduction
3. Goals or mission statement
4. Detailed information on exhibitions, galleries, and attractions
5. Visiting information
6. Visitor rules/policies
7. Persuasion to visit/participate/purchase
8. Frequently asked questions (FAQs)

Ten of the twelve guides single out the name of the museum, the first move, which is typically found toward the beginning of the guide. The remaining two guides only mention the museum name in passing, assuming readers will already be at the museum. An introduction or information about the museum itself, the second move, is found in nine of the guides, whereas in the other three guides, the introduction contains information about logistics in two cases (e.g., how long visitors should plan to spend in each gallery or how the museum is designed for self-guided tours and how the brochure helps with planning) or, in the remaining case, only contains information about the exhibitions themselves.

The third move, the goals or mission statement, is explicit in five cases (one guide shy of half the texts). Here is an example of a mission or goal statement: "In the spirit of inquiry and discovery embodied by Benjamin Franklin, the mission of The Franklin Institute is to inspire a passion for learning about science and technology." In eight of the guides, detailed information about exhibitions, galleries, or attractions (the fourth move) is included for at least the museum's most noteworthy attractions. The other four guides either list the exhibitions, galleries, or attractions or include only practical information about the venue, such as the temperature, so that visitors can dress accordingly. The fifth move, visiting information, appears in all 12 guides, for obvious reasons: a main communicative function of museum guides is to facilitate visiting these institutions. This information may be more or less detailed depending on the venue. While it is standard to include the address, hours, and information about admissions and accessibility, in certain cases there is information about parking, how to get there, "trip planners," "visitor tips," lockers, etc.

Rules or policies on visitor conduct, the sixth move, appears in all but two texts. They may refer to policies on taking photos (with or without flash) or filming, tripods, cell phone use, food or drink in galleries or exhibitions, smoking, pets, guide dogs, backpacks, purses, shoes/cleats, jogging strollers, rollerblades, and skateboards, among others. Eight of the guides exhibit the seventh move and directly attempt to persuade people to visit the museum in general or specific exhibitions, to become a member of the museum or participate in activities, or to purchase food and drinks or memorabilia. For example, one guide says, "Inspire your inner artist and browse books, jewelry, décor, and more" in an effort to entice visitors to swing by its gift store. Another includes glowing visitor testimonials. Though the remaining four guides do not attempt to directly persuade visitors, their descriptions of the venue or its attractions may include a persuasive tone or specific highlight. For example, in one such description, visitors learn that "each automobile on display ... is of considerable historic importance," which reinforces that idea that the museum is worth the trip. The last move, a section of frequently asked or typical visitor questions, exists as such in only one of the guides (e.g., "Why isn't photography allowed?"). The other guides may not include such a section because information about rules, policies, directions, ticketing, galleries, etc. is deemed comprehensive enough on its own or because space limitations do not permit its inclusion. Nevertheless, in a few instances, visitors are directed to a website or designated staff should they have any questions.

The overall **communicative function** of museum guides is **informative**, in that the focus is on the content, and the content is primarily about the venue and the attractions. The venue and attractions are described in detail, in many instances to get people to come and enjoy them, and information about location, visiting hours, and directions are often provided. Evidence of such descriptions can be seen in the particularly extensive use of prepositions indicating the relationship of one word to another to form phrases acting as adverbs, adjectives, or nouns. For example, the most frequent preposition in the corpus is "of." It appears 481 times, ranks fourth as the most frequent word, and occurs in 100% of the texts.[1] "In" and "at" are location/direction and/or time examples of prepositions with high frequency in the corpus, ranking 8th (250 instances) and 15th (115 instances), respectively, and appearing in each of the museum guides.[2] These three frequent prepositions also appear in clusters that are among the most frequent in the corpus and which happen to be spread across all of the texts: "of the" (the most frequent cluster with 145 appearances), "in the" (the second most frequent cluster with 106 appearances), and "at the" (the sixth most frequent cluster with 56 appearances).[3] Examples of descriptive utterances in which "of" or "of the" is used are "the evolution of constitutional rights," "the art of different cultures and eras," "within walking distance of the Castle," "of the likes of," "of the museum." In fact, this last example ranks 28th as a cluster with 15 appearances spread across 75% of the texts. Usage examples of "in" and "in the" include "Also in the tower," "the museum is in the middle of the block," "Trip Planner kiosk in the Visitor

108   Text types

Center," and "sealed in the most scientifically advanced housing." Finally, "at" and "at the" feature in examples such as "at the intersection of," "closes at 4:30 pm," "at the Tickets counter." Though "including," a preposition used to indicate that someone or something is part of the whole that is being referenced, is not used as frequently as these three prepositions in the context of this corpus and in general, its presence in the corpus is nonetheless considerable, ranking 54th, with 22 appearances spanning 83% of the texts.[4] It is typically used to introduce examples or as a means to provide a more complete description. Take for example, "Millions more, including homosexuals, Jehovah's Witnesses, Soviet prisoners of war, and political dissidents, also suffered grievous oppression and death under Nazi tyranny." Translators working with these prepositions and others must pay particular attention to the immediate context in which they are used, as accurate and idiomatic renditions will vary accordingly.

Micro-textual features

Though museum guides are primarily informative, as demonstrated above, there is also a significant presence of first- and second-person pronouns as a means to personalize the visitor experience or achieve immediacy between the reader and the text. The inclusion of such pronouns can relate to the seventh rhetorical move: persuasion to visit the museum, galleries, or exhibitions, to become a member or participate in activities, or to make purchases. Examples of this are "you" (95 instances, 83% of the texts), "your" (61 instances, 100% of the texts), "we" (29 instances, 50% of the texts), and "us" (18 instances, 58% of the texts). "You can," for instance, is a cluster featuring "you" that occurs in 14 instances spread across 33% of the texts, in phrases such as "In the Wexner Center, you can learn about recent genocides." "Your" appears in the cluster "your visit," which occurs in 8 instances spread across 42% of the texts, in phrases like "to make sure your visit is inspiring and enlightening." An example of "we" in the corpus is "We all experience museums differently," and "us" occurs in phrases like "a range of activities that help us recognize that we all share responsibility for creating a more just world." Unlike in instruction manuals, where first-person plural pronouns typically refer to the manufacturer, here the pronouns are inclusive, referencing everyone. While the use of the first and second person may, as these examples show, introduce inclusiveness, the translation of these forms may be complicated by a range of factors, such as target genre or context expectations of person, formality, or number. That is, the translator may have to deviate from the first or second person and opt for a different way to convey such forms appropriately in the target text. Along these lines, Baker (2011: 252) reminds us that "under the vast heading of 'context' is the language user's sense of what is socially and textually appropriate or normal."

Another micro-textual feature worth analyzing is the heavy presence of proper nouns and adjectives. This is because museums are places that house and display historical, artistic, scientific, or cultural objects, which are often designated as particular or unique, and the fourth move provides related details. In addition, museum guides often include visiting information, the fifth move; such information often includes the names of the museums, galleries, or attractions themselves, as well as nearby places of interest, street names, or transportation.

In any event, proper nouns and adjectives in museum guides may refer to historical periods/events/figures, places, peoples, paintings, collections, exhibitions, art genres/movements, plant/animal species, scientific works/inventions/discoveries (eponymous or not), or cultural movements/groups. Some examples from the corpus are "Impressionism," "Mexico," "California," "Sepik," "Amazonas," "the American Indian Museum," "Amtrak," "Appledore," "Aspirin," "Battle of the Bulge," "Boatmen on the Missouri," "Buchenwald," "Buddha," "Bundesarchiv," "the Cosmic Pathway," "the Declaration of Independence," "Expressionist," "Gilded Age," "the Golden Gate Park," "Jewry," "the Neolithic," "the New Deal," "the Rockefeller Collection," "Roma (Gypsies)," "Tyrannosaurus," "WWII," and "Yehuda." The task of translating proper nouns is often not straightforward. Sometimes equivalents are already established[5] and should be used because target readers will expect them in their languages, while in other cases no such equivalents are available, and the translator is faced with the dilemma of formulating target renderings. In such cases, provided the museum does not have a set policy or established precedent in this regard, it may be wise to bring the item as-is from the source language to the target language, especially if a rendering in the target language would confuse or disorient the reader. However, the translator may accompany the borrowed item with a brief explanation in the form of, say, a clause or with a target rendering in parenthesis. An accompanying explanation or translation may very well enhance the reader's understanding.

The conjunction "and" is the third most frequent word (657 appearances) in the corpus and occurs in all the texts.[6] This particularly high frequency, as in the case of the prepositions, has to do with the considerable amount of detail often included in museum texts. "And" may link items of the same part of speech (e.g., "presents larger-than-life movies, documentaries and stage presentations") or related clauses (e.g., "Of those, 10 were ratified and are known as the Bill of Rights," "Nearly a quarter of its resident animals are endangered species, and the zoo serves as a leader in conservation, animal care, protection, and visitor education."). Particularly in the latter case, "and" is indicative of complex sentence structure in that it gives rise to compound sentences. Translators working with such sentence structures may either have to replicate the complexity or deconstruct it, depending on the devices available in the target language and discourse patterns considered contextually appropriate.

Sample text – English museum guide

PHILLIPS: YOUR GUIDE TO THE MUSEUM

ENHANCE YOUR VISIT

Free App
The app includes audio guides and videos about works of art in the permanent collection and special exhibitions, event and exhibition schedules, a map, and more. Available for Apple and Android devices.

Audio Tours
Hear about works of art in the permanent collection and special exhibitions through our audio tours, available on the Phillips app or via cell phone in the galleries. Look for this symbol:

Our contemplation audio tour guides you through a mindful experience with the permanent collection and special exhibitions. These stops invite you to slow down and connect with the art. Look for this symbol:

...

COLLECTION HIGHLIGHTS
1 A Little Help from My Friends #178 #75
In Luncheon of the Boating Party (1880–81), Pierre-Auguste Renoir painted his real-life friends. That included his new girlfriend, Aline Charigot, at lower left. While everyone at the luncheon seems focused on flirting, Renoir shows Charigot looking at her dog, perhaps because dogs are a traditional symbol of loyalty.

AMERICA'S FIRST MUSEUM OF MODERN ART
The Phillips Collection is home to a growing, world-class collection of more than 3,500 works of modern and contemporary art. Housed in Duncan Phillips's boyhood home and additions to it, the museum organizes internationally acclaimed exhibitions, offers lively programming for adults and children, and conducts important scholarly research on the history of art.

Phillips referred to the museum as an "experiment station," and today it retains the founder's personal stamp in a gathering of art that combines tradition, idiosyncrasy, and daring. One of the great pleasures of the Phillips is the unconventional way in which works by artists of different nationalities, periods, and styles coexist happily in visual conversations within its galleries.

THE COLLECTION
Duncan Phillips (1886–1966), the grandson of a Pittsburgh steel magnate, built the extraordinary collection you see today. When the museum opened in 1921 as The Phillips Memorial Art Gallery, in honor of Phillips's father and brother, the collection included work by American Impressionists and their French counterparts. A major coup was the 1923 purchase of Pierre-Auguste Renoir's sumptuous Luncheon of the Boating Party.

Phillips continued adding significantly to the collection through the second half of the 20th century, acquiring major works by Europeans such as Ben Nicholson and Nicolas de Staël, and Americans such as Willem de Kooning, Adolph Gottlieb, Philip Guston, Morris Louis, and Joan Mitchell.

GENERAL INFORMATION

Hours
Tuesday–Saturday, 10 am–5 pm
Sunday, Noon–7 pm
Thursday extended hours, 5–8:30 pm

Accessibility
All areas of the museum are accessible. Complimentary wheelchairs are available at the coat check. Assistive listening devices are available for tours and programs in the auditorium.

Join Us!
Members receive unlimited free admission and discounts. To learn more, stop by the membership desk, visit phillipscollection.org/support, call 202.387.3036, or e-mail membership@phillipscollection.org

Source: Excerpts selected from phillipscollection.org

Sample English museum guide analysis

A sample from the corpus of museum guides has been selected to contextualize and further analyze the textual features discussed above. The guide is for The Phillips Collection, an art museum located in Washington, D.C. At the macro-textual level, its name, the first rhetorical move, is featured on the first page of the guide, which also includes the second move, an introduction. The introduction is particularly comprehensive in this case, spanning some two paragraphs. The first sentence of the first paragraph reads: "The Phillips Collection is home to a growing, world-class collection of more than 3,500 works of modern and contemporary art."

The third move, a mission statement, takes the following form: "Phillips referred to the museum as an 'experiment station,' and today it retains the founder's personal stamp in a gathering of art that combines tradition, idiosyncrasy, and daring." Though the guide does not directly state that the museum's mission is to preserve Phillips's vision, this is what it suggests by conscientiously retaining the founder's vision ever since he opened the museum in 1921.

The Phillips Collection guide fully addresses the fourth move of providing detailed information about its collection. It includes a "Collection Highlights" section, which contains passages such as: "Phillips was so captivated by the luminous paintings of American Abstract Expressionist Mark Rothko that he designed the Rothko room in 1960" and "In the sculpture courtyard are two works of distinctly different aesthetic sensibilities that use the same traditional material – bronze." The guide also points to its website, where visitors may go if they have trouble finding their favorite work, "to see if it is on view and where it is located."

The Phillips Collection guide includes comprehensive visiting information, the fifth move. In addition to hours and admission, it provides information about accessibility (wheelchairs, assistive listening), a free audio guide app, audio tours, gallery talks, how to become a member, share photos, and so on. At the same time, the guide facilitates information about visitor rules and policies, the sixth move. For example, it tells visitors to silence their mobile phones in the galleries; that "non-flash photographs for personal non-commercial purposes of permanent collection works are allowed"; to "leave backpacks, backpack-type child carriers, umbrellas, food and drink, large bags and packages, tripods, easels, and other large items in the complimentary coat check"; and to "keep a distance of at least two feet from the art."

While the overall tone and descriptive nature of the guide could generally be said to have a persuasive effect on readers, enticing them to visit the facilities, the guide, in fulfillment of the seventh move, also features direct soliciting or advertising. For example, the slogan of The Phillips Collection is "America's First Museum of Modern Art." The introductory paragraph also boasts its "more than 4,000 works of modern and contemporary art" and points out that it "organizes internationally acclaimed exhibitions, offers lively programming for adults and children, and conducts important research on the history of art." Pointing out the volume of its collection and the use of qualifiers such as "first," "more than 4,000," "internationally acclaimed," "lively," and "important" are instances of intentionally persuasive language. Moreover, the guide also includes a "Join Us!" section where readers are tempted with the benefits of membership and instructed how to learn more about them.

Though the Phillips guide does not include the eighth and final move, an FAQ section, it does include a good amount of information about its collection, facilities, tours, rules, admission, accessibility, and so on. In any event, visitors are directed to "Phillips volunteers" or its website should they have any questions or need additional information about exhibitions, events, and directions. In keeping with museum guides' informative nature, the Phillips guide includes extensive use of the prepositions and prepositional clusters discussed in the previous section: "of" (39 instances), "in" (35), "at" (7), "including" (3), "of the" (10), "in the" (10), "at the" (3), and "of the museum" (2). Examples of their usage in this guide: "Pierre-Auguste Renoir's Sumptuous Luncheon of the Boating Party;" "has been replicated in the additions to the museum;" "everyone at the luncheon;" "American and European artists, including: Milton Avery, Pierre Bonnard, Georges Braque...;" "All areas of the museum are accessible."

The Phillips guide includes first- and second-person pronouns to provide a more personal visit. There are 3 instances of "you" and "your," two of "our," and one each of "us" and the cluster "your visit." Usage examples include "Our contemplation audio tour guides you through a mindful experience" and a couple of sections entitled "Enhance Your Visit" and "Join Us!" Not only does the use of such pronouns create an inviting tone, it also has a persuasive effect on readers and may be viewed as a manifestation of the seventh move.

The Phillips guide is no exception in that it references a substantial number of proper nouns and a few proper adjectives. They refer to titles of collections (e.g., A Moving Story), art genres/categorizations (e.g., Abstract Expressionist), titles of specific works (e.g., Luncheon of the Boating Party), architecture (e.g., Georgian Revival), names of facilities (e.g., Center for Art and Knowledge, Phillips Memorial Art Gallery), holidays/days of the week (e.g., Thanksgiving Day, New Year's Day, Sunday), and peoples (e.g., Europeans, Americans). These items contribute to the highly descriptive nature of the guide, as well as enhance the visiting information (i.e., the fifth move).

Finally, this museum guide makes ample use of the conjunction "and." In a number of cases, "and" links items of the same part of speech (e.g., "The app includes audio guides and videos about works of art in the permanent collection and special exhibitions," "These stops invite you to slow down and connect with the art."). This type of link allows the guide to include more detail in its descriptions. It also links related clauses (e.g., "Phillips's marriage to painter Marjorie Acker and friendships with artists helped develop his taste, and he worked enthusiastically to train his eye.").[7] While the conjunction also allows for more information to be included, it also considerably complicates the sentence structure.

CHINESE

Museums are enormously important institutions in contemporary China. In recent decades, along with developing the economy, tourism, and cultural exchanges, China has been rebuilding and expanding old museums, adding new buildings, increasing collections, and modernizing exhibition facilities. There are estimated to be around 2,000 museums of all varieties in China. In order to understand the current state of Chinese-language museum guides, a corpus of 52 texts (such as guides to the China Art Museum, the National Museum of China, and the Suzhou Museum) was collected from various sources, all published in the last 5 years so as to document current textual conventions. A museum guide is typically a short piece of writing; the average length of a Chinese museum guide, in terms of characters, included in the Chinese corpus is 278 characters. The lengths of the 52 museum guides in the Chinese corpus range from a minimum of 23 characters to a maximum of 1,230.

Macro-textual features

At the macro-textual level, we begin by isolating the conventional features, or **rhetorical moves**, of Chinese museum guides:

1. Name of the museum/gallery (博物馆名称)
2. Opening and closing times (开放时间)
3. Admission fees (门票情况)
4. Group visits/Contact number (预约参观/联系电话)
5. Address (地址)

As indicated in the list above, move 4 has two different labels. The museum guide corpus shows that among the labels in move 4, 预约参观 was preferred, with 33 occurrences, while 联系电话 occurred 10 times.

In addition to these five conventional moves, which were found in all 52 guides in the corpus, there are a few optional moves:

1. Type of museum (所属分类) (found in 13 museum guides)
2. Route (路线) (found in 7 museum guides)
3. Introduction to the museum/gallery (博物馆介绍) (found in 13 museum guides)
4. Tips (注) (found in 5 guides, often placed at the end of a museum guide)
5. Gallery/museum guidelines (入馆要求) (found in 1 museum guide)

Unlike guides in English, Chinese museum guides typically do not contain such moves as services, parking, or security and accessibility information. These moves are not vital to the success of a museum guide.

The frequency word list (see table) makes clear that the terminology and lexical items used in this text type relate to museum guides.

Text types

High-frequency lexical items	Frequency	High-frequency lexical items	Frequency
博物馆 (museum)	122	闭馆 (close)	33
开放 (open)	77	门票 (admission ticket)	32
参观 (visit)	59	展览 (exhibition)	31
时间 (time)	41	历史 (history)	29
预约 (appointment)	40	文化 (culture)	28
免费 (free)	35	开馆 (open time)	26
地址 (address)	33	位于 (location)	22

All of the lexical items in the table describe visiting information, introduce the museum, or solicit action (mainly through nouns such as 时间 or 地址).

As for the **mode** of discourse, museum guides are usually texts written to be read by museum visitors. One element pointing to the fact that museums are usually conceived as written texts is that there is no dialogue between the author and the audience, and there are none of the signs of the spontaneity you would see in spoken language, such as fillers and pauses. Finally, the **tenor** of discourse tells us about the relationship between the author and the audience, which can be one of equality or inequality (i.e., expert-to-expert or expert-to-nonexpert). When it comes to museum guides, this relationship can be both, in that the author is usually an expert and the audience may or may not be experts. Indeed, just as nonexperts use museum guides to learn how to visit a museum, experts may also visit museums to conduct, for example, academic research on historic buildings. The fact that museums can be visited by experts and nonexperts alike is further stressed by the non-technical nature of the informative terms, as is evident from the table of lexical items.

The **communicative function** of Chinese museum guides is **informative** and uses **conative** language. They tend to be highly factual in that the purpose of museum guides is to transfer knowledge and information about how, where, when, and why to visit a museum and to persuade the audience to purchase admission and, perhaps, membership. However, museum guides might also be said to have a certain degree of phatic function, in that the inclusion of telephone numbers aims to establish contact or continuing communication between the addresser and addressee.

Micro-textual features

At the micro-textual level, the corpus data point to a preference for the declarative or indicative mood in museum guides. Almost all the sentences in the directions were declarative or indicative, consisting mainly of statements.

As regards **cohesive devices**, the use of **reference** is rare in the Chinese museum guides. The personal pronouns 我 (I) and 自己 (oneself) never occur in the Chinese corpus, while 你 (you) occurs only once. Among demonstrative reference devices, 这 (the Chinese equivalent for *this*) appears in many words or phrases in the corpus, such as 这座 (this building), 这些 (these), 这次 (this time), 这样 (such), and 这里 (here). A close reading shows that only 这座 (this building, occurring 4 times), 这里 (here, occurring 3 times), 这些 (these, occurring 1 time), and 这次 (this time, occurring once) worked as reference devices. The Chinese equivalents for *that, those,* and *there* did not appear at all in the museum guides corpus. The cohesive device of **substitution** is also rarely used in the Chinese museum guides; only其他 (other) was found once. By contrast, **ellipsis** is a widely used cohesive device in Chinese, in which subjects and objects are optional if they can be implied by the context. In the case of museum guides, simple sentences starting with a verb are the norm. The omission of subjects occurred at least 5 times in compound sentences in the corpus. This corpus also makes use of additive, causal, and temporal **conjunctions** (see table).

Conjunctions	Frequency
和 (and)	80
并 (and, also)	10
或 (or)	8
而 (and, also)	8
同时 (meanwhile)	7
不仅 (not only)	5
而且 (but also)	3
但 (but)	1
因此 (therefore)	1

Generally speaking, the use of conjunctions is less frequent in Chinese than in English. Also, visitor information in Chinese museum guides is typically presented in the form of concise lists of information, such as the address, route, and opening time, which reduces the need for conjunctions. **Lexical cohesion** is arguably the most common form of cohesion in Chinese. In the case of museum guides, each step is described by one simple sentence or one compound sentence; in compound sentences, lexical repetition occurs 17 times in the Chinese museum guides corpus.

In the Chinese museum corpus, there is a high occurrence of nouns, as shown in the table below.

High-frequency nouns	Frequency	High-frequency nouns	Frequency
博物馆 (museum)	122	藏品 (collection)	14
时间 (time)	41	公众 (public)	14
地址 (address)	33	基地 (base)	14
历史 (history)	29	文物 (cultural relics)	13
文化 (culture)	28	分类 (type)	13
教育 (education)	22	观众 (audience)	13
建筑 (architecture)	16	名称 (name)	12
地区 (district)	15	联系电话 (contact number)	12
展厅 (exhibition hall)	15		

Text types

The nouns used in the Chinese museum guides can be classified into three domains: (1) nouns describing visiting information (directions, address, maps, opening and closing times), such as 时间 (time), 地址 (address), 地区 (district), and 联系电话 (telephone number); (2) nouns describing certain museum types, such as 历史 (history), 文化 (culture), and 教育 (education); and (3) nouns describing exhibitions in the museum, such as 建筑 (architecture), 藏品 (collection), and 文物 (cultural relics). In addition to nouns, another highly recurring word category in this genre is verbs (see table).

High-frequency verbs	Frequency
开放 (open)	77
参观 (visit)	59
预约 (make an appointment)	40
闭馆 (close)	33
收藏 (collect)	30
开馆 (open)	26
展示 (exhibit)	23
陈列 (exhibit)	21
介绍 (introduce)	16
成立 (establish)	14

Sample text – Chinese museum guide

博物馆名称：中国美术馆
地址：北京市东城区五四大街1号（100010）
所在地区：东城区
开放时间：9:00—17 :00无休息日
所属分类：文化艺术类
路线：420、 8 、803、810、814、84 路美术馆站下
联系电话：64006326
博物馆介绍：中国美术馆是以收藏、研究、展示中国近现代艺术家作品为重点的国家造型艺术博物馆。1963 年 6 月，毛泽东主席题写"中国美术馆"馆额，明确了中国美术馆的国家美术馆地位及办馆性质。主体大楼为仿古阁楼式，黄色琉璃瓦大屋顶，四周廊榭围绕，具有鲜明的民族建筑风格。主楼建筑面积 22379 平方米，一至五层楼共有 20 个展览厅，展览总面积 7000 平方米，展线总长 2110 米。中国美术馆收藏各类美术作品近10万余件，藏品中主要为近现代美术精品，其中有对 20 世纪中国传统绘画产生重要影响的画家及作品。收藏品类有绘画、雕塑、陶艺、民间美术等数十个品类。其中包括年画、剪纸、玩具、皮影、彩塑、演具、木偶、风筝、民间绘画、刺绣等民间美术品。建馆 40 年来　Ø共举办各类美术展览和国内外著名艺术家作品展览 3100 多个，Ø接待观众数百万人次，中国美术馆已成为向大众实施美育的重要艺术殿堂。

Key: repetitions – highlighted in gray

Sample Chinese museum guide analysis

All of the above-mentioned macro-textual characteristics are exemplified in the selected sample museum guide. The museum guide was taken from http://exhibit .artron.net/, a website that contains thousands of well-known museum guides. The example museum guide for the purposes of this study is for 中国美术馆 (Chinese Art Gallery), a famous Chinese museum. The museum guide in question includes every conventional move: 中国美术博物馆 (name of the museum/ gallery), 开放时间 (opening and closing times), 门票情况 (admission fees), 预约 参观/联系电话 (group visits/contact number), and 地址 (address). It also includes some optional moves: 所属分类 (museum type), 路线 (route), and 博物馆介绍 (introduction to the museum/gallery).

The text has 446 characters, a bit longer than the average of 278 characters in this genre. The mode of discourse is informative, and the tenor points to an expert-to-nonexpert relationship, as well as expert-to-expert. The communicative function is **informative** for the reasons given above and exhibits **conative** language.

As far as the micro-textual features are concerned, the declarative or indicative mood and the present tense are used for statements or to give directions.

Conjunctions are rarely used in this sample; the additive conjunction 及 (and) occurs only once. There are no hypernyms or synonyms. In the whole museum guide, there are instances of repetitions, as shown in the table (see words highlighted in gray).

Repetition	Frequency
博物馆 (museum)	3
东城区 (east district)	2
主体大楼 (main building)	2
展览 (exhibition)	2
藏品 (collection)	2
收藏 (collect)	2
其中 (including)	2
作品 (work)	2

The sample museum guide is characterized mainly by simple sentences. In the sample, there are four simple sentences and two compound sentences.

As for the lexicogrammatical features of the conventional moves, all titles, with the exception of two, are characterized by noun phrases. The address and opening time moves are also characterized by noun phrases, followed by descriptions of place (大街 (avenue), 区 (district) etc., or nouns describing time (无休息日). As for the introduction move, two main word categories seem to prevail: nouns (60 instances) and verbs (11 instances).

118   Text types

FRENCH

France is known for its museums, which house collections that cover subjects ranging from priceless art to the history of regional coal mining operations. Because museums attract a variety of visitors from both within France and abroad, museum guides (*guides de visite*) must inform a wide audience of the historical and cultural significance of a museum and its exhibitions. To gain an understanding of the current textual features of the French museum guide, we compiled a corpus of 20 texts published within a 5-year period by 20 different sources. The length of the texts included in the corpus varies considerably, ranging from 277 to 2,293 words. Differences in the running length of each text are due to the detail with which museum contents are described. Two guides also contain translated text (English and German), which naturally increases their length. Only the French text of those guides was included in the analysis.

Macro-textual features

We begin at the macro-textual level by outlining the following **rhetorical moves**:

1. Museum name (*Nom du musée*)
2. Museum introduction (*À propos du musée*)
3. Exhibitions/collections (*Expositions/Collections*)
4. Visiting information (*Informations pratiques*)
5. Contact information (*Contacts*)

The organizational structure of a French museum guide is not always labeled. For example, a museum's name (*nom du musée*) is customarily indicated by a logotype. Moreover, moves are not always arranged in a consistent order due to the significant effect of graphic design on layout. Guides taking the form of websites feature a clear organizational structure in which each move is housed on a parent page in the website's primary navigation. However, the name each move receives depends on the guide, with the museum introduction (*à propos du musée*) receiving as many as four distinct headings (*musée, le musée, bienvenue,* and *bienvenue au musée*) in our corpus. Information on a museum's permanent collection and exhibitions is often split into *collections* and *expositions*. Visiting information, frequently labeled *informations pratique*, but also *infos pratique, venir au musée,* and *en pratique*, contains the greatest number of subdivisions. The most common sub-rhetorical moves found here are the museum's address (sometimes labeled *nos coordonnées*), opening and closing times (*horaires/horaires et jours d'ouverture/calendrier d'ouverture/nos horaires*), accessibility information (*accessibilité*), and admission fees (*tarifs*). Finally, the portion of a museum guide that encourages readers to contact the museum for further information or a visit is usually titled *contacts*, but may also be designated *contact, contactez-nous,* or *en savoir plus*.

In addition to the five mandatory moves described above, the following three optional moves were identified in the corpus:

1. Museum goal (*L'objectif*) (found in 17 guides)
2. Frequently asked questions (*Informations*) (found in 7 guides)
3. Code of conduct (*Mode d'emploi du musée*) (found in 3 guides)

These moves may be optional for several reasons. A museum's goal (*objectif*), while often embedded in the introduction section, could be excluded due to space constraints or if the purpose of the museum is implicit based on the contents of the guide. Authors may decide that including museum guidelines and a code of conduct (*mode d'emploi du musée*), also labeled *bonne pratique*, is not necessary. Finally, some guides lack sufficient space for frequently asked questions (*informations* or *vos questions*), and visitors may be encouraged to contact the museum directly.

To describe the **register** of museum guides, we will look at three aspects: field, mode, and tenor. It is clear based on the high-frequency lexical items that a museum guide's **field** of discourse, or what the guide is about, covers the museum in question, that is, its contents and layout, as well as the policies in place for accessing and navigating its premises.

High-frequency lexical item	Frequency	No. of texts
musée(s)	345	20
tarif(s)	74	10
siècle	68	15
salle(s)	67	10
collections	66	17
ville	58	15
personnes	51	12
jours	49	17
expositions	42	13
visite	38	13
place	34	14
ouvert	22	13

Several words point to the macrostructure of the text, for example, *place* is frequently found in an address (e.g., *20 place des Terreaux*), located under *contacts*. *Siècle* is found in the museum introduction or in collection descriptions. *Informations pratiques* contains the widest variety of frequently recurring single-word lexical items (i.e., *musée, ville, personnes, jours, salle(s), expositions,* and *visite*) due to the breadth of this rhetorical move. An examination of **mode** – how a text will be used – reveals that museum guides are meant to be read before or during a visit to a museum, as indicated by the orderly description of a museum's contents and policies and the lack of dialogue between the author and reader.

Finally, the **tenor** of discourse, characterizing the relationship between a guide's author and audience, points to an expert-to-nonexpert relationship,

Text types

marked by the transparent yet detailed fashion in which the most important points of a collection's historical and cultural context are summarized for the reader, who may have no prior knowledge of the subject matter.

The greater part of a guide describes the museum's contents; therefore, the genre's **communicative function** is primarily **informative**. However, this inviting description is crafted to encourage readers to visit the museum (and perhaps to purchase a membership in the museum), revealing an underlying conative function. Finally, continued communication between the museum and its audience is sometimes solicited in the contact section, where visitors are directed to engage with the museum's social media via phatic posts outside the text.

Micro-textual features

At the micro-textual level, the predominant **mood** of French museum guides is indicative. The present indicative tense (*présent*) is used in statements describing museum contents and features, though past indicative tenses are found in narration, including *passé simple* in historical descriptions. Guides are dotted with commands (*impératif*), prompting visitors to visit.

An analysis of **cohesive devices** shows that demonstrative referencing occurs frequently in this genre. For example, the adjectives *ce, cet, cette*, and *ces* are used when describing works of art. Substitution in the form of pronouns standing in for nouns is almost non-existent in the corpus. However, another intersemiotic form of substitution occurs in some brochures, where icons and images represent museum policies that might otherwise be written out (e.g., a handicap symbol replaces the word *accessibilité* or a clock replaces *horaires*). The liberal manipulation of graphic elements in brochures results in ellipsis, as headings indicating a transition from one rhetorical move to another may be completely omitted. Therefore, readers must rely on the brochure's visual arrangement to locate the information typical of each move. This form of ellipsis is rare in museum guides designed as websites, which follow a more standard design.

With respect to the use of conjunctions as cohesive devices, *et* and *ou* are often found coordinating like items in museum content descriptions (e.g., *Les collections zoologiques et botaniques débutent dès 1843: mammifères, oiseaux, insectes et planches d'herbiers de la région*). As far as lexical cohesion is concerned, a quick look at the high frequency of nouns (see table) shows that the repetition of single-word lexical items is an important lexical cohesive device employed in museum guides.

The extremely high frequency of *musée* in the corpus alludes to this word's importance in the genre. To determine how *musée* might relate to other words in guides, we looked at the strength with which it collocates with other content words in our corpus.[8] This allowed us to group words that pair strongly with *musée* into three frequent domains: museum names, museum types, and museum visiting information. The table of collocations and domains shows several examples of pairs resulting from this analysis, lending further credence to the claim that museum guides are essentially about the museums they describe.

Most frequent lexical item	Strong collocates	Domains
musée	*Baron* *Marcel-Maulini* *Delacroix*	Museum names
	d'art *des beaux-arts* *contemporain*	Museum types
	informations *pratiques* *horaires*	Museum visiting information

---

Sample text: French museum guide

Musée de la Résistance et de la Déportation

Le Musée
Musée d'histoire, il traite à l'aide de photographies, de textes, de documents originaux les thèmes liés à la Seconde Guerre mondiale : le nazisme depuis son origine, la guerre et le régime de Vichy, la résistance franc-comtoise, nationale, européenne, la Libération.

La place réservée à la déportation et à la "Solution finale" contribue à sa singularité. À cette présentation didactique s'ajoutent des collections de peintures, dessins et sculptures réalisés en camp de concentration et en prison. Durant l'Occupation, de 1941 à 1944, cent résistants appartenant à des groupes franc-comtois furent fusillés à la Citadelle.

"Ne pas témoigner serait trahir"

Labellisé : « Musée de France »
   OUVERTURE : 1971
   CONCEPTION : Denise Lorach, ancienne déportée, créatrice du musée, François Marcot, historien, Guy Langlois, décorateur.
   Avec le soutien de l'ensemble des associations de déportés et résistants de Franche-Comté, de la Ville de Besançon, des Conseils généraux du Doubs, du Jura et du Territoire de Belfort, du Conseil régional de Franche-Comté, du Ministère de la Culture.
   Le bâtiment des Cadets dans lequel se trouve le musée fut construit en 1682 sur ordre de Louvois.
   Casernement qui abrita jusqu'à 600 Cadets du Roi, il constitue l'ossature transversale du quadrilatère fortifié par Vauban.
   Ø
Niveau 1
SALLE 1 > Début du nazisme (1919-1924)

• Naissance de la République allemande
• Début du parti nazi
• Putsch de Munich

122   **Text types**

> Documents nazis, tracts, brochures, affiches, insignes et objets de propagande de Vichy
> SALLE 6 > La France Libre
>
> - L'appel du 18 juin 1940
> - Premiers ralliements
> - Les Français Libres au combat
> - L'union autour du Général de Gaulle
>
> SALLE 7 > Les débuts de la résistance en France
>
> - Une résistance individuelle et spontanée
> - La naissance de la presse clandestine
> - La formation des mouvements
> - Le tournant de la guerre : fin 1942-début 1943
>
> Tracts et objets de différents pays, affiches de la libération.
>
> Key: noun phrases – highlighted in gray
> *Source*: Musée de la Résistance et de la Déportation de Besançon

Sample French museum guide analysis

For a better idea of how the described features appear in French museum guides, we will analyze a *guide de visite* provided by the Musée de la Résistance et de la Déportation de Besançon – Citadelle, which is located in the Bourgogne-Franche-Comté region of Eastern France. This history museum is similar to a number of others documenting French resistance against Nazi occupation during World War II.

At the macro-textual level, the guide is a double-sided trifold brochure employing visual cues, such as images and variations in color, text orientation, and the use of space, to guide readers along a determined path through the text. It includes all mandatory rhetorical and sub-rhetorical moves, plus one optional move. Aside from the museum introduction (*à propos du musée*), labeled *Le Musée* in this guide, the only other labeled moves are found in the *informations pratiques* area located on the back side of the brochure. The text contains information on several areas not observed in most of our corpus due to the organizational structure of this particular museum (i.e., *administration – conservation, centre de ressources*, and *restauration*). Perhaps due to space constraints, *informations pratiques* and *contacts* are merged.

Mandatory rhetorical move	Sub-rhetorical move	Mandatory or optional?
Nom du musée	*None*	Mandatory
À propos du musée	*L'objectif*	Optional
Expositions/Collections	*None*	Mandatory
	Visite	Mandatory
Informations pratiques, Contacts	*Horaires*	Mandatory
	Accessibilité	Mandatory

The text has a length of 911 words (excerpted in the sample), slightly under the average text length of texts (987 words) included in the corpus. The field of discourse covers the history of the French resistance movement against Nazi occupation during World War II. The guide's secondary, conative function is communicated via the gravity of the brochure's emotional imagery. The phrase *Ne pas témoigner serait trahir*, centered in a large font size beneath the introduction, transmits a pressing need to remember the historical events depicted in the collection.

At the micro-textual level, the mood of this guide is primarily declarative based on the predominance of two tenses: *présent* and *passé simple*. In terms of cohesive devices, the repetition of noun phrases (highlighted in gray) creates a parallel structure among the lists. Ellipsis, which is related to the visual arrangement of the brochure and indicated as Ø above, is observed in the omission of headings that normally signal the rhetorical moves *expositions/collections* and *contacts* in other museum guides. Hyponymy is employed to designate the specific types of objects (e.g., artifacts, documents, propaganda, and memorabilia) found in three exhibition spaces. Finally, the coordinating conjunction *et* is used to group words and phrases of equal rank, forming clusters of like items throughout the text.

124   **Text types**

GERMAN

Museum guides present the translator with a number of genre-specific challenges, from rendering culturally relevant content to preserving embedded author ideologies, all while targeting a highly heterogeneous, potentially international readership. Corpus-based analysis can be helpful in guiding the translator's decision-making, based on patterns rendered at both the macro-textual and micro-textual levels. To illustrate this, a corpus of content from 30 museum websites from German-speaking parts of the world was compiled. This content was taken from the "About Us" or start page of each website as it appeared in 2016. For this particular genre, neither word length nor sentence length emerge as prototypical. We see an average length of 350 words, with a broad range of 225 to 753. The average number of words per sentence is 17, with a range of 11 to 22. To a large extent, website usability guidelines likely inform the maximum text length on any given webpage.

Macro-textual features

An analysis of **rhetorical moves** within this subset of museum guide content highlights the following as prototypical, appearing in at least 20 of the 30 texts:

1. Museum name (*Name des Museums*)
2. Brief catchphrase or slogan directly below the name (*Slogan*)
3. Description of general offering (*Gesamtüberblick*)
4. Detailed description of highlights (*detaillierte Beschreibung*)
5. Important historical dates (*wichtige historische Daten*)

Historical dates are particularly widespread and appear in the context of all museum types – not just those involving history. These dates can be a primary selling point in German-language museum guides, signaling the credibility of a museum and potentially reflecting a cultural time orientation. This credibility is also established, albeit to a lesser extent, through the inclusion of quotes from famous people, as seen in six of the 30 texts. Some of the rhetorical moves one would expect in an English-language museum guide are not commonplace in German-language guides, such as a formal welcome (in only 3/30 texts), hours of operation (3/30), pricing information (2/30), special attractions (7/30), and number of visitors (4/30).

To mitigate the need to scroll, websites often make use of a "more information" hyperlink that directs the reader to a different page containing more detailed information. Interestingly, we only see this strategy used 4 times in the corpus, suggesting a preference for German-language sites to pack more content into "About Us" webpages. This, in turn, might result in a longer text length and greater tolerance for the need to scroll than is common in other languages.

The **mode** of discourse for this genre is both persuasive and expository. The primary objective is to encourage readers to visit the museum, and factual information is provided in support of this overarching aim. Again, dates and lexical items pertaining to history take on a persuasive function in German-language museum guides. For example, the word *Geschichte* (history), is the second most frequently occurring noun in the corpus, appearing 41 times and in 20 texts. Other temporally and historically oriented lexical items in the corpus are listed in the frequency table.

German lexical item	English equivalent	Frequency	No. of texts
Jahr-	year	38	11
Jahrhundert-	century	31	11
Vergangenheit	past	7	3
Zeiten	times	7	5
historisch-	historic	15	4
jährlich-	annual	5	5
Kulturgeschichte	cultural history	5	4

The list of frequently occurring nouns and verbs further reveals a persuasive/ expository mode while also outlining the field of discourse.

German lexical item	English equivalent	Frequency	No. of texts
Museum	museum	109	28
Sammlung	collection	39	13
Ausstellung	exhibit	42	13
Kunst	art	21	6
Besucher	visitor(s)	13	10
zeigen	to show	13	9
präsentieren	to present	10	9
Sonderausstellung	special exhibit	10	9
Themen	themes	10	8
finden	to find	9	6

In terms of **tenor**, the discourse of museum guides takes place between a given museum and an anonymous reader, who can be regarded as a prospective customer. Corpus wordlist data reveal that this readership is the general public; relatively little terminology suggests expert-to-expert communication. The customer relationship is enhanced through extensive use of direct address, using the formal you (*Sie*) in conjunction with action verbs, such as *besuchen* (visit), *tauchen* (dive), *entdecken* (discover), and *probieren* (try). As is typical for the German-language, the formal "you" is used in conjunction with other lexico-grammatical constructs to preserve a sense of distance between text sender and receiver:

> *Möchten Sie selber fahren?* (Would you like to take the wheel yourself?) → distance preserved through the constellation of the formal you, a modal verb, and a rhetorical question; navigieren *Sie bitte* (please navigate) → distance preserved through formal you and use of please

126 **Text types**

A further connection between sender and receiver is created through the 55 instances of *Wir/uns* (we/us), forms of sender self-reference.

Micro-textual features

At the micro-textual level, a quick analysis of the first two sentences in each text reveals a strong tendency for declarative sentences. Of these 60 sentences, 54 are declarative, 1 is interrogative, and 2 are subjunctive. On the surface, this would seem to point to a strong **informative** function. However, given the fact that the German-language prefers distance, it is not surprising that we see no imperatives. That said, many of the declarative sentences do not simply present factual information but take on a persuasive function by encouraging the reader to do something, as seen in the following example:

German passage
Sie sehen, spüren und erleben den Alltag in der DDR.
Declarative English translation
You see, sense, and experience everyday life in the GDR.
Imperative English translation
See, sense, and experience everyday life in the GDR.

This example points to an important consideration in the German–English translation of museum guides, namely syntactic shifting from declarative sentences to imperative sentences in addressing target language linguistic and cultural preferences.

We do not see a prototypical pattern for this genre in terms of sentences being simple, complex, or compound. An analysis of the first sentence in each text yields the following breakdown: 11, 6, and 13, respectively. As far as self-referencing is considered, there is a strong preference for proper noun forms rather than pronouns, such as *we*, even if this implies repeating the same proper noun across the span of two juxtaposed sentences. We see such juxtaposition when the name of the museum is mentioned in 17 of the 30 texts. In 15 instances, the proper noun form is repeated across sentences. In only two sentences does "we" take the place of the proper noun in the second sentence. This tendency can also be regarded as a lexicogrammatical distancing strategy. Such repetition results in the frequent use of lexical recurrence as a cohesive device at the micro-textual level in German-language museum guides.

In contexts involving the mention of main attractions and highlights (as opposed to the names of the museums), we see much less use of lexical recurrence and greater use of lexical parallelism, as seen in the following set of examples from the corpus:

German instances of lexical parallelism	*English translations*
200.000 Jahre Geschichte und kulturelle Entwicklung/4.500 Objekte	200,000 years of history and cultural development/4,500 artifacts

(Continued)

(Continued)

German instances of lexical parallelism	English translations
Berlin/die deutsche Hauptstadt	Berlin/the German capital
zeitgeschichtliche Dauerausstellung/lebendige Zeitreise	contemporary permanent exhibit/lively travel through time
Sammlung/faszinierende Stücke	collection/fascinating pieces

Such lexical variation can be regarded as a cohesive device strategically used in line with a persuasive function, namely presenting the museum in an appealing light from multiple interrelated angles.

As mentioned above, one of the fundamental components of museum guides is culturally relevant content that may or may not need to be explicated in translation for a target readership. Low-context languages, such as German and English, tend to be explicit. In other words, there may be less need to explicate in translation since the content is more likely to be explicitly described in the source text. This tends to be the case in the museum guides found in this corpus, as reflected in the following examples:

German passage with culturally relevant content	English translation
… das Bomann-Museum, eines der größten und bedeutendsten Museen in Niedersachsen.	… the Bomann Museum, one of the largest and most important museums in Lower Saxony.
eine Einrichtung des Landes Mecklenburg-Vorpommern	an institution of the state of Mecklenburg-Vorpommern
die römische Stadt Nida	Nida, the Roman city

High-context languages, on the other hand, such as Arabic, French, Russian, and Spanish, tend to be more implicit, suggesting a potential need for greater explication of culturally relevant content.

Sample text – German museum guide

DDR Museum Pforzheim

Lernort Demokratie
Angetrieben durch die Sorge um die demokratische Zukunft, will das DDR-Museum ein Haus für Demokratieerziehung sein. Die pädagogische Ausrichtung des Museums will für die elementaren Menschenrechte sensibilisieren und das Demokratiebewusstsein stärken. Demokratie soll nicht als selbstverständlich, sondern als dauerhaft zu schützendes und fortlaufend weiterzuentwickelndes Gut angesehen werden.

Das DDR-Museum in Pforzheim will die Erinnerung an die DDR-**Geschichte** im Kontext gesamtdeutscher Relevanz wach halten, besonders für die jungen Generationen, für die die deutsche Wiedervereinigung selbstverständlich ist.

„Eine Demokratie ist nicht einfach da, und – vor allem – sie bleibt nicht von allein. "Joachim Gauck

Das DDR-Museum Pforzheim wurde von Klaus Knabe **1998** im September gegründet ist mit über 4000 Besuchern **jährlich**, dass einzige Museum in den

128   Text types

> westlichen Bundesländern, welches die deutsche **Geschichte** des **20. Jahrhunderts** mit Schwerpunkt auf die **Geschichte** der DDR-Diktatur (**1945-1990**) darstellt.
>
> Das Museum will Demokratiebewusstsein fördern, Menschenrechte thematisieren und die Auseinandersetzung mit der DDR- Diktatur fördern.
>
> DDR-**Geschichte** soll erklärt aber nicht verklärt werden. Besonders junge Menschen sollen für die **geschichtlichen** und politischen Themen deutscher **Geschichte** begeistert werden. Die Themen Flucht, Freikauf von DDR–Häftlingen durch die Bundesrepublik Deutschland und Ankommen der DDR-Bürger im Westen bilden einen Schwerpunkt des Museums. **Zeitgeschichtliche** Bezüge und Dokumente aus dem Großraum Pforzheim stellen einen authentischen Bezug her.
>
> Das DDR-Museum Pforzheim verfügt über eine bedeutende Sammlung mit Exponaten aus allen gesellschaftlichen Bereichen der DDR- **Geschichte**. Das Museum hat seit **15 Jahren** Erfahrung mit der Vermittlung von DDR-**Geschichte** und wurde im **Jahr 2014** konzeptionell neu ausgerichtet.
>
> **Zeitzeugen**, so genannte lebendige **Geschichtsbücher** führen durch die Ausstellung.
>
> Key – historical or time marker – bold; lexical parallelism – highlighted in gray
> *Source: www.pforzheim-ddr-museum.de/*

Sample German museum guide analysis

The sample museum guide excerpt is taken from the website of the DDR-Museum Pforzheim. At the macro-textual level, it exhibits all five of the prototypical rhetorical moves identified in the corpus for this genre: (1) name, (2) brief catchphrase, (3) description of the general offering, (4) detailed description of highlights, and (5) interspersed important historical dates. Lexical items referring to history or other time markers (in bold) occur 17 times in this text. They function in conjunction with a famous quote from a former president of Germany, Joachim Gauck, to encourage readers to visit the museum.

At the micro-textual level, as far as cohesive devices are concerned, both lexical recurrence and lexical parallelism are strategically used. For example, we see the name of the museum, DDR-Museum, used 5 times. Not once do we see a self-referent placeholder (we or us) being used in place of the proper noun name, nor do we see direct address of the receiver (you), suggesting a lexicogrammatical preference for social distance. The text contains three instances of intra-sentential lexical parallelism (highlighted in gray) for the purposes of presenting the museum's main attractions from slightly different angles. Although visuals are not part of the corpus-based analysis presented here, it is worth noting that the picture on the website consists of a photograph of the museum from the outside. In this sense, social distance is also visually preserved in that we see no visitors or people of any kind. A quick glance at the visuals found on other museum websites in this corpus suggests a similar pattern.

The low-context, relatively explicit nature of German-language museum guides is seen in descriptions that co-occur with culturally relevant lexical items. For example, *DDR-Dikator* (GDR dictatorship) is explicated through a juxtaposed parenthetical containing concrete dates (1945–1990). Most source-text readers would be aware of this timeframe and, in this sense, the dates do not fill a conceptual gap. This is a situation where the source text, and, if translated into English, the corresponding target text, would be equally explicit. That said, there are other instances of culturally relevant content in this sample text that would benefit from explication in the context of English translation:

German cultural content	Possible explicitation through translation
Pforzheim	Pforzheim, *35 km north of Stuttgart* ...
Joachim Gauck	Joachim Gauck, *former German president* ...
Deutsche Wiedervereinigung	reunification of Germany *in 1990*

This sample text consists of 261 words, slightly lower than the mean of 350 found in the representative corpus for this genre. In this content's original online environment, the reader needs to scroll to access all of the information on the page. Despite the web medium, we see no occurrences of a hyperlinked "more" or "more information" directing visitors to additional information on separate webpages. As seen in the corpus, such hyperlinking and redirecting is only seldom used in German-language museum guides.

130 **Text types**

RUSSIAN

In today's world, where one can travel far and wide, in person or virtually, museums attract a highly multilingual audience. For this reason, museums invest in localizing their online and printed materials into multiple languages. In this section, we analyze a corpus of ten traditional (non-interactive) Russian museum guides, which range from the world-renowned Pushkin Museum of Art in Moscow to Novosibirk's Museum of Nature in Siberia to the Road of Life Museum in a small town in the Leningrad Region, near Lake Ladoga, which provided a winter transport route to and from the besieged city of Leningrad from 1941–1944. For this project, we included guides with word counts between 1,000 and 1,200 words. While every museum is unique, we found that their guides share certain structural and textual features.

In the corpus, we identified several Russian variants to refer to "museum guide": *Путеводитель по музею, Гид по музею, Брошюра музея*, and *Буклет*.

Macro-textual features

At the macro-textual level, museum guides are characterized by the following mandatory **rhetorical moves**:

1. Name of the museum, e.g., Государственный музей изобразительных искусств им. А.С. Пушкина (The Pushkin State Museum of Fine Arts)
2. Museum background information, which discusses the museum's mission and history
3. Information on the museum's exhibits

Optional rhetorical moves include:

1. Brief introductory statement, typically attention-getting (e.g., Дом-музей Велимира Хлебникова – единственный в мире Дом-музей поэта [Velimir Khlebnikov's Museum is the only museum of the poet in the world])
2. Visiting information, which may include the museum's address, maps, working hours, tours, admission fees, accessibility information, and so on. Some collocations pertaining to this section are listed below:

    a. Адрес музея (Museum's address)
    b. Проезд/Схема проезда (Directions)
    c. Время работы (Open hours)
    d. Выходной (день) (Day off, i.e., Closed on)
    e. Телефоны для справок и записи на экскурсии (Phone number for inquiries and tour reservations)

3. Museum guidelines, such as Правила поведения (Code of conduct), which may include prohibitions, e.g., На территории музея не курят (Smoking is prohibited on museum property) or friendlier notes, such as В музее можно фотографировать (Photography is permitted)

4. Soliciting action to convince the reader to visit the museum, return to the museum, or become a member, e.g., Мы всегда рады видеть вас! (We are always happy to see you!)
5. Individuals involved with the museum, e.g., the name of the director (Директор музея)
6. Author information, e.g., Автор текста (Author of the text)

To attract visitors, museum guides frequently employ photographs, pictures, and drawings. In addition, some contain floorplans and maps.

The data analysis shows that, in addition to museum-related terminology, such as экспозиция (exposition/display) (53), коллекция (collection) (46), посетитель (visitor) (28), выставка (exhibition) (22), and собрание (collection) (21), many lexical items pertain to the discursive **fields** of art and history (see table).

High-frequency lexical items	Frequency
год (year)	77
история (history)	39
литературный (literature, *adj*)	37
россия, российский (Russia(n))	36
искусство (art)	34
время (time)	33
работа (in this context: work of art)	28
век (century)	24
предмет (item)	20
произведение (искусства) (work of art)	18

As for the **mode** of discourse, museum guides are written to be read; they mediate communication between museum staff and visitors. In terms of **tenor**, museum guides are written primarily by experts for those visiting a museum, the latter being either nonexperts or experts.

The primary **communicative function** of museum guides is **informative** and uses **conative** language, since their goal is both to provide facts and to call upon the reader to visit a museum. We also see elements of the expressive function when the author shows passion for the topic and resorts to literary devices.

Micro-textual features

At the micro-textual level, museum guides display features of the higher register, such as present and past active participles (e.g., включающий, хранящий, повествующий, устоявшийся), past passive participles and their short predicative forms (e.g., посвящен(ный) [11 instances], расположен(ный) [9], подарен(ный) [3]), some verbal adverbs (включая [2] the verb являться as a copula [7 instances in four

132   **Text types**

texts], and reflexive verbal forms (e.g., находится [14], планируется [3], открылся [3]).

Using Derek Offord's classification of Russian styles, museum guides combine official/business style (e.g., in greetings, introductions, regulations, or general information) with academic style (e.g., in formal historical accounts). Some guides contain elements of literary style, such as questions to the reader (А знаете ли вы, что ... [And do you know that...?]), syntactic structures with adjectival phrases preceding nouns (нетронутый по сей день паркет [untouched until this day wooden floor]), archaic lexical items (ныне instead of сегодня to refer to today), or marked word order (И звонким эхом ... звучат на ней молодые веселые голоса ... [And with a resonant echo ... young happy voices resound here ...]).

Punctuation-wise, it is worth noting that three of the ten museum guides in the corpus use three or four exclamation points per text, which contributes to their expressive function.

Interestingly, on the sentence level, museum guides have a shorter average sentence length (11.5 words per sentence) than business letters or user manuals, both of which average 15 words per sentence. This may indicate that museum guides use fewer complex and compound sentences. The most frequent conjunctive devices in the corpus are и and а (over a hundred of occurrences of each), the conjunctive relative pronouns который (62 occurrences) and что (42), and the conjunction где (9). We also noted a number of complex sentences that do not use explicit conjunctive devices to connect clauses, such as У музея высокий научный рейтинг, материалы опубликованы в изданиях ... (The museum has a high scientific rating, its materials are published in ...). In English, we would probably need to explicitate such an implicit cohesive link.

Other **cohesive devices** include referential devices, such as pronouns его (58), ее (22), их (18), он (22), она (10), они (8), Вы (7), Ваш (3), and свой (32); этот and its forms (53 occurrences); and the adverb of place здесь (33). Participles also contribute to textual cohesion when they reference preceding nouns. Throughout this corpus, lexical cohesion appears to be created primarily through repetition.

Sample text – Russian museum guide

НА ДОРОГЕ ЖИЗНИ

Трасса, теперь именуемая «дорогой жизни», была проложена по льду Ладожского озера. Вдоль нее располагались ремонтные мастерские, на каждом километре стояли регулировщики, через каждые 5 километров были расположены пункты забора воды. Зенитная артиллерия и истребители защищали неба над магистралью, дорожники перекрывали трещины во льду и воронки от вражеских бомб деревянными мостами. Дорога жила своей жизнью и давала жизнь стоящему за ее спиной огромному городу.

В навигационный период перевозки на «Дороге жизни» осуществлялись судами Северо-Западного речного пароходства в охранении боевых кораблей Ладожской военной флотилии. Воздушный мост над Ладогой осуществляли в основном транспортные самолеты Ли-2.

ФИЛИАЛ ЦЕНТРАЛЬНОГО ВОЕННО-МОРСКОГО МУЗЕЯ «ДОРОГА ЖИЗНИ»»

Филиал Центрального военно-морского музея «Дорога жизни», расположенный в поселке Осиновец Всеволожского района Ленинградской области, был создан на основании приказа Главнокомандующего Военно-Морским Флотом № 443 от 14 ноября 1968 г. Он открыл свои двери для посетителей 12 сентября 1972 г. Здание музея находится у берега Ладоги, недалеко от мыса Осиновец, откуда начиналась легендарная дорога жизни. Музей посвящен беспримерному подвигу защитников блокадного Ленинграда, воинов Ленинградского и Волховского фронтов, моряков Ладожской военной флотилии, тружеников «Дороги жизни». В пяти залах собраны многочисленные реликвии Великой Отечественной воины: флаги и знамена, различные виды оружия, модели кораблей, самолетов и автомашин, документы, фотографии, личные вещи участников событий военной поры. На открытой площадке музеи экспонируются крупногабаритные предметы вооружения и морской техники, мемориальные корабли и суда, транспортный самолет Ли-2. За каждым экспонатом – судьба человека, воинский подвиг.

…

Экспонаты второго зала рассказывают о ледовой трассе 1941–1942 г. С началом ледостава на Ладожском озере людские перевозки прекратились. Для обеспечения города продовольствием и боеприпасами оставался один путь – по льду озера. Санно-гужевые обозы двинулись в путь 20 ноября 1941 г., на следующий день прошла первая автомашина. Так появилась Военно-автомобильная дорога № 101 (ВАД-101) протяженностью 29 километров, проходящая по трассе мыс Осиновец – острова Зеленцы – село Кобона. Зимняя дорога располагалась всего в 20–25 километрах от берега, занятого противником. Вражеские самолеты почти ежедневна проводили множественные ожесточенные налеты на трассу. В экспозиции зала хранятся блокадные продуктовые карточки ленинградцев, карта-схема обороны города, боевое знамя 225-го артиллерийского зенитного дивизиона, личные вещи, боевые награды и документы защитников Ленинграда. На многочисленных фотографиях запечатлены шоферы и ремонтники, герои-летчики и девушки-санитары. санные обозы, колонны автомашин, «ледовые лазареты», различные моменты из жизни Военно-автомобильном дороги № 101.

Source: Excerpted from cdn.navalmuseum.ru/Files/pdf/1430994750broshyura_dzh.compressed.pdf

Sample Russian museum guide analysis

For the sample analysis, we chose a brochure of the Road of Life Museum that was published to mark the 70th anniversary of the Soviet victory in the Great Patriotic War, or World War II. The exposition is part of the Central War and Navy Museum (Центральный Военно-морской музей). At the macro-textual level, the brochure contains all three mandatory rhetorical moves – the name of the museum, background information, and information on the museum's exhibits. The brochure begins with the preface by the director of the museum, Ruslan Nekhai, in which he discusses the significance of the Road of Life during the war. The preface is followed by a section on Lake Ladoga, with a detailed description of the lake and its history. The next section is devoted to the history of the Ladoga Navy during the Great Patriotic War. The main section of the brochure contains information about the Road of Life Museum display and its five exposition halls. The brochure concludes with a section about the future of the museum. On the back of the brochure, we find the contact information

134 Text types

(phone, address, transportation, open hours), as well as the names of those who participated in the creation of the brochure, including the museum's director.

For the purposes of the sample analysis, we chose a 430-word excerpt which contains descriptions of the Road of Life, as well as information on the three (of five) exposition halls. The mode of discourse of the brochure is informative and conative, since it describes the exhibit with the goal of attracting visitors. The tenor of the discourse is expert-to-nonexpert. In terms of the field of discourse, the brochure's main topic is the history of the Road of Life and the museum itself – the excerpt contains six repetitions of the phrase дорога жизни (the Road of Life) and multiple synonymic references to it (магистраль, дорога, трасса), as well as repetitions of the word музей (museum) and филиал (museum branch). The museum describes the difficult years of World War II and the siege of Leningrad, hence the use of such military terms as артиллерия (artillery), вражеские бомбы (enemy's bombs), боевой корабль (military ship), военная флотилия (navy fleet), самолет (plane), главнокомандующий (commander-in-chief), военно-морской флот (Navy), блокадный Ленинград (besieged Leningrad), and more. The root воен- (related to the military) is repeated a total of 10 times.

At the micro-textual level, the brochure's word choices are indicative of official writing style; for example, the brochure contains many short passive adjectives (8 occurrences), such as проложен (laid out), расположен (located), создан (created), посвящен (devoted to), собран (collected), and представлен (exhibited), запечатлен (photographed), and reflexive verbs (12 occurrences), such as располагаться (to be located), осуществляться (to be carried out), находиться (to be located), начинаться (to start), and экспонироваться (to be exhibited). The excerpt under analysis is written mostly in the past tense, which is consistent with the historical aspect of the writing.

For grammatical cohesion, the brochure relies on conjunctions, primarily the conjunction и (and) (16 occurrences) and one complex conjunction то, что (that which). Lists are also frequent and punctuated by commas. As for lexical cohesion, the excerpt resorts to repetition (both actual and lexical), as noted above, as well as several pronouns (он [he/it], она [she/it], ее [her/its]) and omissions. Verbal adjectives represent cohesive links when they refer to previously mentioned nouns.

SPANISH

So, what is a museum guide specifically? The text type contains information that spans from the museum's *mission* to its organizational rules. These are different kinds of information: orienting oneself in a museum is a different order of experience than understanding its value as a private or public good or as a cultural-historical repository. The museum guide serves a promotional function as well, supporting cultural and heritage tourism. In Spanish-speaking countries, as elsewhere, museums frequently have physical classrooms within the museums proper and generate many textual materials related to outreach, including digital captioning for virtual classrooms, leaflets, and worksheets. These guides may contain information related to these activities in addition to the museum itself.

A list of the roughly ten basic rhetorical moves of the museum guide in Spanish reveals its fundamentally informative function. Quantitative and qualitative analysis will be conducted on a corpus of ten museum guides taken from Spanish museum websites and published or updated between December 2015 and December 2016. Spain has a museum system of legendary quality and variety. The shortest text in the corpus is 1,116 words in length, while the longest is 10,347. The average word in this corpus contains 4.9 characters, and the mean sentence length is 17 words. Depending on the inclusion of optional moves, a given text in this text type may range from the simplicity of a brochure to the comprehensiveness of a catalogue.

Macro-textual features

The composite features, or **rhetorical moves**, of a Spanish-language museum guide are as follows:

1. Name of the museum, address and general information (*Nombre y dirección del museo* and *información general*) (found in 10 texts)
2. Introduction and institutional history (*Introducción y historia de la institución*) (found in 10 texts)
3. Goals/mission (*Misión y visión*) (found in 8 texts)
4. Hours and pricing structure (*Horas y tarifas*) (found in 9 texts)
5. Detailed information on the exhibitions (*Información específica de las exposiciones*) (found in 10 texts)
6. Museum floor plan (*Planos del museo*) (found in 5 texts)
7. Masterpieces or highlights (*Obras maestras y obras destacadas*) (found in 3 texts)
8. Programming (*Actividades*) (found in 5 texts)
9. Museum rules (*Normas del museo*) (found in 2 texts)
10. Resources (*Recursos*) (found in 3 texts)
11. Soliciting action, including fillable forms (*Formularios o más información*) (found in 3 texts)
12. Bibliography (*Fuentes o referencias*) (found in 1 text)
13. Credits, Curators, Investments, and Patrons (*Colaboradores, Patronos o Patrocinadores*) (found in 3 texts)

Only name and general information, exhibit information, and introduction and institutional history proved to be obligatory moves for this sample; other moves,

Text types

such as goals/mission and hours and pricing, are quasi-obligatory. Institutional history is always or nearly always the first major rhetorical move in the samples surveyed, followed by, or interwoven with, the museum's goals or mission. Roughly a third included masterpieces, further resources, and requests for action on the visitors' part. A bibliography appeared in only one text; in another, Museo de Huesca, citations are made but no bibliography is given. At least one publication is merely a *dossier informativo* (information package), and limits discussion to the exhibits; another low-frequency textual feature is the at-a-glance summary of events, which is optional. In at least one case, the hours are given but not the pricing (Museo de Cádiz). Masterpieces, when they are identified, may be allocated a few sentences all the way up to several pages. Maps of the city where the museum is located are sometimes given rather than a floorplan of the museum itself. The goals of one museum in the corpus, the Museo de Huesca Arte y Género, describes its own role as not only *reflecting* but also *influencing* society and norms of inclusivity:

> *El Museo expone cultura pero también fabrica cultura, por lo que es agente activo en esta discriminación expositiva. Por eso, los Museos debemos reivindicar de manera activa la presencia de la mujer en el terreno artístico y social.*
>
> (The Museum not only reflects culture, but also creates culture and is an active agent in this expository action. We, therefore, as Museums should actively defend the presence of women in artistic and social settings.)

The corpus reveals many words describing goals in terms of reintroducing, reinterpreting, reclaiming (*reintroducir, reinterpretar, reconquistar*) something, showing that museums actively attempt not only to preserve the past but also to challenge received ideas. Newness (e.g., *nueva*, 27 instances; *nuevos*, 15) and renovation (restoring, remodeling, reorganizing) figure highly in the corpus (e.g., the lemma *renovar*: 1; > *renovación*: 11; > *renovado*: 5; and > *renovada*: 2). One corpus text starts with a provocative interrogative about whether one must be a naked woman to be admitted to that particular art museum, a cheeky reference to the painterly tradition of the nude (although perhaps not appropriate wit for all museumgoers in all cultures).

Let us consider some of the most common nouns in the data:

Lexical items	Frequency
museo	420
sala	158
taller	102
visita	98
planta	89
siglo	87
colección	80
greco	74
salas	67

(Continued)

(Continued)	
Lexical items	*Frequency*
bachillerato	65
obras	65
alumnos	64

The highest-frequency nouns in the wordlist for all texts reflect the physical building and what museumgoers do there, such as *museo, sala, taller, visita, planta, colección*, and one instance of a historical referent in the top 40 terms, *siglo*, and one proper noun, *(El) Greco*, a noted painter. In summary, many of these are **meronyms** (x, a constituent part of y), or **holonyms** (x, which contains y), either parts or wholes of the educational structure, the classification structure, or the architectural structure of the museum. The *orienting* function of the text is reflected in the high frequency of such words as *desde*, a temporal/spatial preposition indicating movement from an origin, with a massive 93 instances in ten texts, and "locating" or "movement" propositions *entre* (61 entries), *a través* (40), *hacia* (24), and *a lo largo de* (16). Genitive *de la* constructions reach 556 in the clusters, followed by prepositional phrase *en la* (194). Coordinating conjunctions and articles (*y la, y el, y los*, and *y las*) occur 159 times.

The **communicative function** of texts may be informative, expressive, operative, or a combination thereof. The primary function here, as noted, is primarily informative. The text is written in formal language in an institutional voice, free of identifying style or individual appeals or welcomes. The audience may vary widely, from children to non-native speakers of the language to scholars specializing in the subject matter; that is, from nonexpert or novice to expert readers. Nevertheless, the texts in many cases project a hospitable invitation to explore.

Micro-textual features

At the micro-textual level, we find corpus evidence of the indicative mood, in particular, and almost exclusively; in uses of tense, the instances of past tense are invariably related to art history, institutional history, and museum acquisitions and modifications. Predictably, most verbs occur in present perfect conjugations (32), a peculiarity of peninsular Spanish writing used to describe past-tense events.

Cohesive devices are in evidence, such as *este* (97) and *esta* (74), but there are very few substitutions (*ambos/as* [6]). There are no instances of *ni/ni* (neither/nor) and scarce use of forms of "same" (*mism-* [19]). Where conjunctions and prepositions are concerned, the highest frequencies are *con* (354), *por* (259), *o* (99), *sobre* (61), *hasta* (51), and *sin* (40).

Sample text – Spanish museum guide

NORMAS GENERALES El presente folleto es un avance de información con respecto a cada uno de los apartados que lo componen, por lo que pueden estar sujetos a modificaciones, aplazamientos o cancelaciones. Para conocer las normas generales relativas a cada apartado deberá visitar la página web correspondiente a cada organizador o actividad. En relación a los espectáculos y conciertos organizados en cualquiera de los emplazamientos reflejados en este folleto: las puertas se cierran a la hora anunciada para el inicio de los mismos. Solo se permite la entrada si hay descanso. Está totalmente prohibida la toma de fotografías, filmaciones y grabaciones a personas ajenas a la organización. No está permitido fumar en el interior de los recintos.

Todo arte me he otorgado su belleza, y me ha concedido su esplendor y perfección. Quien me ve cree que, con mis congéneres, me dirijo al jarrón deseando obtenerlo. Mas quien mira y contempla mi hermosura, la percepción ocular a su imaginación engaña, pues ve, por mi diáfana luminosidad, a la luna llena situar dichosa en mí su halo. No estoy sola, pues mi jardín manifiesta maravilla nunca antes vista. Versos del poema de Ibn Zamrak (Granada, 1333–1394) que adornan las jambas del arco del mirador de Daraxa o Lindaraja*

VEA, Verano cultural en la Alhambra, es la plasmación del conjunto de actividades que tiene lugar tanto en el Conjunto Monumental de la Alhambra y generalife como en otros edificios, jardines o patios sitos en la colinas de la Sabika y del Mauror y en la ciudad de Granada. Como fruto de una rica agenda cultural, el presente folleto aglutina la diversidad de actividades (propias, participadas u organizadas por otros agentes culturales) poniendo de relieve especialmente aquellas que tienen lugar solo durante el verano y que además gozan de una amplísima relevancia internacional. Descubrir, conocer y disfrutar se aúnan en una experiencia única e inolvidable si junto con la visita a los monumentos, se pasea por la Alhambra verde, se aprecian los museos y exposiciones, se participa en las actividades educativas o se complace con los espectáculos y conciertos que tiene lugar durante más de tres meses. Cada una de las artes ha ido enriqueciendo este patrimonio vivo y realzando su encantadora belleza para componer día a día, entre todos los visitantes, creadores, artistas, investigadores o gestores, un mosaico de experiencias que después se expandirán por todo el mundo y harán de la cultura un hecho más universal y cercano, más responsable con su preservación, un legado incalculable para las siguientes generaciones. *Editado en Leer la Alhambra. Guía visual del Monumento a través de sus inscripciones. José Miguel Puerta Vílchez y Patronato de la Alhambra y Generalife, Edilux, 2010

...

Generalife, Alcazaba y jardines del Partal ** Visita general a la Alhambra (Palacios Nazaríes, Generalife, Partal y Alcazaba) y a los siguientes monumentos: Bañuelo, casa morisca Horno de Oro, palacio de Dar al-Horra, casa del Chapiz y casa de Zafra ***Visita a los jardines de la Alhambra (Generalife, Partal y Alcazaba) y a los monumentos indicados anteriormente **** Visita Nocturna a los Palacios Nazaríes de la Alhambra y a los monumentos indicados anteriormente ***** Bañuelo, casa morisca Horno de Oro y palacio de Dar alHorra. El Corral del Carbón tiene entrada libre y gratuita

HORARIOS Conjunto Monumental de la Alhambra y el Generalife • Visitas Alhambra general o jardines, de lunes a domingo de 8.30 a 20 h • Visita Nocturna, de martes a sábado de 22 a 23.30 h • Visitas para granadinos, todos los domingos de 14 a 20 h (previa reserva en la web del Patronato o presencialmente en el Corral del Carbón) Monumentos en las visitas combinadas

MUSEO DE LA ALHAMBRA Patronato de la Alhambra y Generalife El Museo de la Alhambra ocupa la parte baja del palacio de Carlos V, distribuyéndose en siete salas ordenadas cronológicamente con piezas artísticas de la etapa hispanomusulmán, desde el emirato al periodo nazarí. En sus salas se puede ver la evolución decorativa y técnica de piezas de cerámica, madera con uso arquitectónico y mobiliario, tejidos, metales, vidrio etc., Destacan, entre otras piezas, el jarrón de las Gacelas, las puertas de la Qubba Mayor, las puertas de alhacena del palacio de los Infantes o la pila califal de ciervos y leones. Desde los primeros momentos en que los palacios de la Alhambra son habitados por los Reyes Católicos, el ajuar que queda es protegido, reutilizado y disfrutado en la nueva corte. A lo largo de los siglos los objetos y restos arquitectónicos conservados se disponían decorando las estancias, de la misma forma se almacenaban en diferentes espacios del recinto hasta ir creando un museo de forma natural, origen del actual.

La Alhambra es un Conjunto Monumental creado a lo largo de más de seiscientos años por culturas tan diversas como la musulmana, la renacentista o la romántica. La visión de los jardines de la Alhambra, el rumor de la brisa entre los árboles unido a los sonidos del agua, nos aíslan del ruido cotidiano; y nuestro paseo se transforma en una experiencia única. El Conjunto dispone de un rico y variado programa de visita y actividades que a continuación le detallamos.

Key: various features discussed in sample analysis – highlighted in gray
Source: Excerpts drawn from www.alhambra-patronato.es

Sample Spanish museum guide analysis

Our sample text begins with a title page: *VEA: Verano cultural en la Alhambra Y EN SUS ESPACIOS MONUMENTALES DE GRANADA* and the publication's sponsoring agency, the *Consejería de Cultura*. The acronym VEA (*Verano en la Alhambra*) also means "look" (the imperative). The first main textual introduction, on page 2, is the museum rules, opposite the table of contents on the right. The format of the brochure is bitext columns with bicolor *en face* English translation, which itself internationalizes the reader profile. Page three begins with an epigraph:

Todo arte me he ortogado su belleza,	All of the arts have bestowed their beauty upon me
y me ha concedido su splendor y perfección.	and have granted to me their splendor and
	perfection.
Quien me ve cree que, con mis congéneres,	Those who see me believe that, as is the nature of
me dirijo al jarrón deseando obtenerlo.	my kind, I am speaking to the vase in the hope of
	obtaining it for myself.
Mas quien mira y contempla mi hermosura,	And whoever sees and contemplates my beauty,
la percepción ocular a su imaginación engaña,	his eyes betray his imagination,
pues ve, por mi diáfana luminosidad,	for he sees, by my diaphanous radiance,
a la luna llena situar dichosa en mi su halo.	the full moon happily setting her halo upon me.
No estoy sola, pues mi jardín manifiesta	I am not alone, for my garden reveals
maravilla nunca antes vista.	a marvel never witnessed before.
Versos del poema del Ibn Zamrak (Granada, 1333-1394)	Verses from the poem by Ibn Zamrak (Granada, 1333-1394)
que adornan las jambas del arco	etched on the jambs of the arch of the
del mirador de Daraxa o Lindaraja *	mirador de Daraxa or Linaraja *

As rhetorical moves, epigraphs are prefatory, contrapuntal, contextualizing, or summative, and this one clearly has a poetic function, that of setting the mood for the visit. Thus, the first contrast is evident: from norms of expected behavior to an appeal to the senses and emotions. In no way should the epigraph be considered an empty signifier or merely decorative. This poem is physically inscribed on the grounds, points to Mozarabic aesthetics, referencing the garden itself in the poem's thematics, and introduces local art through the verbal medium. The line breaks of the second English stanza are enjambed rather than end-stopped, creating a break in

140 **Text types**

the continuity of the poetic form. Our text sample circles back at the end to the leitmotif of the gardens as a natural, idyllic refuge: *La visión de los jardines de la Alhambra, el rumor de la brisa entre los árboles unido a los sonidos del agua, nos aíslan del ruido cotidiano.*

Evaluative adjectivization in the text, such as *experiencia única e inolvidable* or *un legado incalculable,* signals an informative but also conative function to the brochure, stressing the emotional impact of the visit. All of these examples are highlighted in the sample text in gray.

Metaphors used in the text, though perhaps they are dead metaphors, are drawn from art and architecture: *poner de relieve, componer un mosaico de experiencias.* Word cluster data reveal common multi-word strings such as *exposiciones temporales* (13 instances, in 50% of the texts). The declarative mood largely characterizes the text in question, with an occasional subjunctive. Passive constructions (*se pasea*), which avoid direct address or commands, are also present. Types of sentences in the sample text are compound and complex (44 sentences with a mean of 42.159 words per sentence, the highest in the corpus, and well above the corpus mean of 17); the type/token ratio is approximately 35.

In regard to tense, the historical present is used in the text as a way of making the past more salient. For example, *Desde los primeros momentos en que los palacios de la Alhambra* son *habitados por los Reyes Católicos, el ajuar que queda es protegido, reutilizado y disfrutado en la nueva corte* (emphasis added). We see the present coexist on the same page with the future, which is used to express the organizational goals of expanding, universalizing, and preserving the legacy of the site.

Notes

1 The only corpus in which "of" ranks higher is that of news articles, where it ranks second and is also spread across all the corpus texts.
2 The only other corpora in which "in" ranks higher is that of news articles and recipes, where it ranks sixth in both cases and is spread across each text as well. The only other corpus in which "at" ranks equally and can also be found in all the texts is that of news articles.
3 "Of the" ranks highest in the museum guides corpus, and although "in the" and "at the" rank just one spot higher in the news articles corpus, they are spread across 10% fewer texts.
4 The only other corpus in which "including" ranks higher and is more widespread is that of news articles (41st place and 90% of the texts).
5 This is not only the case when it comes to the names of common or world knowledge (e.g., famous paintings, historical events, species, etc.) but also when it comes to the names of certain venues and/or their collections. For example, the information that the Smithsonian Institute provides in several different languages includes consistent use of proper noun equivalents related to its museums, galleries, and zoo, and many of these equivalents are employed by the users of these languages in non-translation contexts as well.
6 The only other corpus where "and" ranks as highly and is as widespread is that of recipes.
7 The example sentence that illustrates the third move in the Phillips guide also uses "and" to link related clauses.
8 Collocation strength was calculated based on Mutual Information score and Log Dice using LancsBox (Version 3.0.2). The results were compared to ensure collocates ranked similarly using both statistical measures.

5 Patient education materials

Patient education brochures, pamphlets, and other materials are a way that experts can provide clear, reliable, and accessible information on a wide variety of health issues, including disease prevention and management, lifestyle choices and wellness, smoking cessation, and the risks of current public health threats, such as dengue fever. They may also teach the public to be critical consumers, for example, by providing information on how to read nutrition labels. These materials streamline the communication of care options regarding common short-term interventions such as surgeries. Such texts are geared toward helping patients and their caregivers advocate for themselves, and their use has increased as patient-centered care has come to include patients, parents, and their families in health-related decision-making.

Patient education materials are produced primarily by specialized health foundations, government agencies, chemical and drug companies, insurance companies, and doctors (Mayor and Blanca 2005: 133). They are distributed or made available during or at the conclusion of health interviews, but also at health fairs and screenings, and in other places where health promotion is the goal. Often broadly called "handouts," these writings may be discussed with a provider and then kept for reference at home. The most typical print formats are bookmarks, communication toolkits, wheels, door hangers, fact sheets, rack cards (front and back printed, high gloss heavy card stock), bifold and trifold brochures, comic books and booklets. In many cases, the material can be downloaded as PDFs or streamed online in tutorials. Today, digital interactivity and message tailoring are widespread.

Ornia (2016: 141) locates patient education material as the general communication variant of the expository and instructive medical text type hybrid, along with medical advertisements in general media, commercial articles about medical devices, and posters. Information dissemination is their primary function, but in another sense, if we remember that behavioral change is a kind of learning, these texts aim to improve patient compliance and self-management, which are key factors in improving health outcomes.

Authors and translators of patient education materials strive to write in plain language. The reading comprehension level of patients in public clinics was shown to be at approximately grade 6.5 (Davis et al. 1991), and nearly half of patients did not understand written material (Vivian and Robertson 1980), in part due to the vastly elevated reading level at which it was written (Jimison 1997: 143). Patient education materials can be produced in, or translated into, videos or other formats for low-literacy patients, in both low-literacy and very-low-literacy versions. It is telling that in English, an instrument, the Patient Education Materials Assessment Tool (PEMAT), written by the Agency for Healthcare Research and Quality (AHRQ), exists to measure the understandability and action-ability of print and audiovisual education materials. It considers the variable domains of layout, organization, visual aids, content, word choice, and phraseology in measuring understandability. Direct address, tangible tools (planners and check-lists), manageable steps, visuals, and instructions on performing calculations help assess actionability. These criteria are applicable in non-language-specific contexts to virtually any such materials used around the world.

ENGLISH

Patient education brochures are a common resource for providing patients and their caregivers information about health issues affecting them, so that they may manage or improve their health status. Therefore, this genre of patient education resource can be characterized as both informative and conative. The corpus in this chapter includes 12 patient brochures from seven different entities: the Centers for Disease Control and Prevention, the University of Pittsburgh Medical Center, the American Heart Association, the American Stroke Association, Johns Hopkins University, Johns Hopkins Health System, and the National Institutes of Health. The brochures include between 432 and 4,340 words and have an average of 1,086 words. Of the 12 corpus texts, four range from 432–685 words, seven range from 750–1,192 words, and one text contains 4,340 words.

Macro-textual features

Patient education brochures often include the following seven **rhetorical moves**, typically in the following order:

1. Informative title (found in all 12 brochures)
2. Explanation of the condition, disease, or behavior (found in 9 of the brochures)
3. Explanation of the causes or risk factors (found in 6 of the brochures)
4. Explanation of the symptoms or consequences (found in 11 of the brochures)
5. Explanation of treatment or remedies (found in 11 of the brochures)
6. Prevention or management tips (found in 9 of the brochures)
7. Links to other sources of information or resources (found in 11 of the brochures)

An informative title, the first move, is included in all of the brochures. In nine cases, it is purely descriptive (e.g., "Smoking Facts"), while in three cases it is both descriptive and conative (e.g., "For People with Diabetes or High Blood Pressure: Get Checked for Kidney Disease," "Stop Smoking!"). Nine of the twelve brochures include the second move, a section explaining the condition, disease, or behavior in question. Examples of explanation headings include "What is blood pressure?" and "Facts on Men and Heart Disease." The third move, a section explaining the causes or risk factors, occurs in half of the 12 brochures, with headings such as "How is Hepatitis B spread?" or "What are the causes?" The fourth and fifth moves, explanations of symptoms/conse-quences and treatment/remedies, can be found in 11 of the 12 texts, and head-ing examples of each move include "What can happen?" and "How to quit (smoking)." Prevention or management tips, the sixth move, are found in nine of the texts (e.g., "CDC recommends that the first dose of vaccine be given to your baby before leaving the hospital," "Remind your doctor and diabetes edu-cator to examine your feet!"). Finally, 11 of the 12 brochures provide links to other resources, the seventh move, in instances such as, "For more on the 'Be

144 **Text types**

Smart About Your Heart' programs, and lots of other useful diabetes information, visit ..." or "If you want help to stop smoking."

As a means to communicate directly with patients and encourage them to follow a treatment or management plan, patient education brochures make ample use of the second-person pronouns "your" and "you," which are the fourth (339 instances) and ninth (223 instances) most frequent words in the corpus, respectively, and occur, in both cases, in 92% of the brochures.[1] Examples of phrases including "your" and "you" are "after your last cigarette," "will ask you to give a blood sample," and "in the morning before you eat." Note that "you" includes both subject and object uses. The possessive pronoun "your," for its part, can be found in particularly frequent and widespread clusters such as "your blood" (47 instances, 67% of the texts), "your doctor" (29 instances, 58% of the texts), "your heart" (27 instances, 50% of the texts), and "your health" (13 instances, 58% of the texts), which rank 4th, 12th, 14th, and 28th, respectively. Translators of patient brochures will likely have to think carefully about how they go about translating second-person pronouns. Depending on the target language, there may be options when it comes to conveying the second person (e.g., formal/informal, singular/plural), and translators may be better off selecting one way or another in order to adequately meet genre writing expectations in the target language. Moreover, the second person may not be deemed appropriate in any of its forms, and translators may have to resort to other discursive strategies.

Micro-textual features

The conative function of patient education brochures is also carried out via modal verbs. They are used in this corpus to communicate that a patient "can," "may," "should," or "must" do something, especially when they are conjugated in the second person. "Can" ranks 13th in the corpus with 171 appearances spread across all the brochures. In no other corpus does this modal verb rank as high.[2] "You can" is the most frequent cluster with "can," ranking 15th with 26 appearances occurring in 67% of the brochures. An example where this cluster appears is "there are things you can do to" or "You can get vaccinated at ..." "May" ranks relatively high at 33, with 56 appearances occurring in 92% of the brochures.[3] The cluster "you may" is tied with another "may" cluster (i.e., "may be") as the most frequent "may" cluster, with a rank of 30 and 10 appearances in 50% of the texts. Usage examples of "you may" include "You may also want to look into ..." and "you may want to use an insulin pump." "Should" ranks relatively high as well at 60 (23 appearances in 92% of the brochures).[4] Though "you should" is not the most frequent "should" cluster, it appears in 5 instances and in 42% of the brochures in phrases such as "If you have diabetes and heart disease, you should keep LDL lower" or "You should eat a diet that's good for the heart." Though by no means frequent in this corpus, "must" nevertheless occurs in 4 instances, which occur in two of the brochures. In one of these brochures, it occurs only with "you," in "You must eat on a regular schedule ..." and "You must treat it right away." Care must be taken when translating modals in cases where nuanced options exist in the target language.

Options might be both lexical, in ways similar to "can" or "may" or "should" or "ought" in English, or morphological, where a difference in tense entails a difference in force (e.g., "should" vs. "must").

Patient education brochures frequently include language indicating possibility, as diseases, medical conditions, behaviors, and the outcomes of treatment and management plans may be uncertain or may be judged only as potential, depending on the circumstances. Two of the modals discussed above, "can" and "may," are frequently used to indicate that something might happen, exist, or be true in specific clusters in the corpus under study. For instance, "can" may be observed in "can be," which ranks highest as a cluster in the patient brochures corpus at 18, with 23 appearances in 67% of the brochures.[5] Usage examples of "can be" include "it can be spread easily" and "Over time, there can be nerve problems and poor blood circulation." "Can cause" is the next most frequent cluster featuring "can." It ranks 23rd, which is the highest-ranking for this cluster in any of the other English corpora. It appears 18 times and in 42% of the brochures, in examples such as "Nerve damage can cause numbness" and "high blood pressure can cause kidney disease."[6] Two other frequent "can" clusters, following "can cause," are "it can" (17 instances, 67% of the brochures) and "can help" (14 instances, 58% of the brochures). They rank 24th and 27th, respectively, and higher in the corpus of patient brochures than in any of the other English corpora.[7] Usage examples include "it can spread easily" and "This can help keep your blood vessels healthy." "May be" is the other most frequent "may" cluster, which is tied with "you may." It, of course, also ranks 30th and has 10 appearances, but it appears in 58% instead of 50% of the texts.[8] An example of "may be" in context is "your heart problems may be worse and strike when you are younger."

Patient education brochures do not rely only on modals to convey possibility. Take as an example the adjective "likely" (16 instances, 42% of the brochures). Ranking 67th, it is by far more frequent in the patient brochures corpus than in the news articles and instruction manuals corpora, where it also appears. In 13 of these 16 instances, "likely" appears in the cluster "likely to" and, in 11 of them, in "more likely to." Usage examples of both clusters include, "People with diabetes were just as likely to smoke as those without diabetes" and "Jaundice Symptoms are more likely to occur in adults than in children." In the remaining 3 instances, "likely" does not directly precede an infinitive with "to," for example, in instances such as "Four times more likely!" Adjective phrases with "likely" may be challenging to translate, as there may not be an equivalent adjective phrase to seamlessly render it into other languages. Translators might have to resort to other phraseological structures or alter the target syntax considerably to adequately convey the same probabilistic meaning.

One last example conveying possibility is "risk" (55 instances, 100% of the brochures), which ranks 34th. In none of the other English corpora does "risk" rank nearly as high. In fact, certain collocations or clusters of the word "risk" occur only in this particular text type, and none of the other English corpora analyzed in this book have these clusters. The following are frequent such examples:

Collocation	Frequency	Appearance in texts	Rank
risk for	18	83%	23
risk factors	15	58%	26
at risk	13	75%	28
your risk	13	42%	28
at risk for	11	67%	30

An example of one of these contexts is the collocation "risk for," which appears in one text as "raises your risk for heart attack and stroke." A "risk factors" example is "people with certain risk factors." "At risk" can be found in "People with diabetes who smoke are putting their lives at risk." "Your risk" is used in "make healthier choices to reduce your risk." And the question "Are babies at risk for Hepatitis B" features "at risk for." It may be challenging to translate "risk" clusters when they include the prepositions "at" and "for," as the translator may need to employ non-parallel target structures or make significant syntactic adjustments to effectively transfer the meaning of these clusters.

Patient education materials are often written to be accessible to a broad audience, taking into account different potential readers and their literacy skills. The Centers for Disease Control and Prevention (2009: 6), for example, recommends keeping sentences short, "if possible, between eight to ten words." Though for the most part the sentences in the patient brochures corpus tend to be straightforward and relatively brief, there is some evidence of sentential complexity. This complexity manifests itself in the considerable frequency of "if you," which ranks sixth and appears in 40 instances and in 75% of the texts.[9] Take, for example, the phrase "if you" in the example "Even if you have no symptoms, you may still be at risk for heart disease." This phrase shows how a conditional or if-clause can add length to sentences and exceed, for example, the CDC's recommendation to limit sentence length to eight to ten words. Translators, depending on their languages and a particular set of target genre writing expectations, may find it difficult or inappropriate to maintain a short sentence length or conditional phraseology and may have to translate in an alternative way.

Sample text – English patient education materials

Understanding and managing high blood pressure

Check. Control. Change.

What is blood pressure?

When your heart pumps blood through the blood vessels, the blood pushes against the walls of your blood vessels. This creates blood pressure. Your body needs blood pressure to move the blood throughout your body, so every part of your body can get the oxygen it needs.

Healthy arteries (the blood vessels that carry oxygen-rich blood from the heart to the rest of the body) are elastic. They can stretch to allow more blood to push through them. How much they stretch depends on how hard the blood pushes against the artery walls.

...

Causes of high blood pressure

High blood pressure cannot be cured. It can, however, be managed very effectively through lifestyle changes and, when needed, medication. In most cases, the cause of high blood pressure is not known. In fact, high blood pressure usually doesn't have symptoms. This is why it is sometimes called "the silent killer."

However, there are known risk factors for high blood pressure. These are conditions that are known to increase the risk for getting high blood pressure. Risk factors fall into two categories: those you can control, and those that are out of your control.

Risk factors that are outside of your control

Family history: Just as hair and eye color can run in families, so can high blood pressure. If your parents or other close blood relatives have high blood pressure, there's an increased chance that you'll get it, too. This is why it's important to get your blood pressure checked on a regular basis. The American Heart Association recommends checking at your regular healthcare visit or every 2 years for people whose blood pressure is in a normal range.

...

Risk factors that you can control

Lack of physical activity: Not getting enough physical activity as part of your lifestyle increases your risk of getting high blood pressure. Physical activity is great for your heart and circulatory system in general, and blood pressure is no exception.

An unhealthy diet, especially one high in sodium. Good nutrition from a variety of sources is critical for your health. A diet that is too high in salt consumption, as well as calories, saturated fat, and sugar, carries an additional risk of high blood pressure. On the other hand, making healthy food choices can actually help lower blood pressure.

...

Drinking too much alcohol. Regular, heavy use of alcohol can cause many health problems, including heart failure, stroke, and irregular heartbeats. Drinking too much alcohol can increase your risk of cancer, obesity, alcoholism, suicide, and accidents. It can also cause your blood pressure to increase dramatically.

In addition to these risk factors, there are others that may contribute to high blood pressure, although how is still uncertain. These include: Smoking and tobacco use: Using tobacco can cause your blood pressure to temporarily increase and can contribute to damaged arteries, which can make high blood pressure worse.

...

Monitoring, treating, and managing high blood pressure

If you've been diagnosed with high blood pressure, it's very important to follow the treatment plan your healthcare provider gives you. This will almost certainly include changes to your diet and level of physical activity, and may include medication, too.

Keep track of your heart health at Heart360!

You can take control of your blood pressure and other vital cardiovascular information by signing on at the American Heart Association's website, www.heart360.org/cholesterol.

Source: "Understanding and Managing High Blood Pressure," reprinted with permission from the American Heart Association. Brochure content has been discontinued; for more current content, go to www.heart.org

Sample English patient education text analysis

A brochure titled "Understanding and Managing High Blood Pressure" has been selected to contextualize and further analyze the textual features discussed above. The brochure comes from both the American Heart Association and the American Stroke Association. Its highly descriptive title leaves nothing to the imagination and fulfills the first rhetorical move. The second page, in keeping with the second move, features a four-paragraph explanation of blood pressure, preceded by the heading "What is Blood Pressure." The third move explains the causes of high blood pressure and begins on the fourth page under the descriptive heading "Causes of High Blood Pressure." This move is comprehensive to the extent that it includes two subheadings – "Risk factors that are outside of your control" and "Risk factors that you can control" – and covers all of pages 4 and 5. The brochure includes the fourth move by explaining the physical consequences of high blood pressure. This move features the heading "How High Blood Pressure Affects the Body" and spans four paragraphs. The fifth move in this brochure features a very self-explanatory heading, titled "Monitoring, Treating, and Managing High Blood Pressure." Spanning some five pages, this section is comprehensive and includes seven subheadings: "Eating healthy," "Physical activity," "Maintaining a healthy weight," "Reducing stress," "Limit (or avoid) alcohol," "Avoid or quit tobacco," and "Home blood pressure monitoring." Located under the previously mentioned third move subheading, "Risk factors that you can control," the sixth move takes the form of prevention tips. This move includes a number of controllable risk factor categories, such as "Lack of physical activity" and "An unhealthy diet, especially one high in sodium." Each category is accompanied by an explanation and tips to prevent high blood pressure. For example, the former category is accompanied by the following text: "Not getting enough physical activity as part of your lifestyle increases your risk of getting high blood pressure. Physical activity is great for your heart and circulatory system in general, and blood pressure is no exception." Finally, the brochure includes the seventh move by referring readers to other sources. Under the heading "Keep Track of Your Heart Health at Heart360!," the brochure reads "You can take control of your blood pressure and other vital cardiovascular information by signing on at the American Heart Association's website, www.heart360.org/cholesterol."

This brochure makes ample use of second-person pronouns "your" (122 instances) and "you" (55 instances), so much so that they constitute 36% and 25% of all the instances of these two pronouns in the entire corpus. Here it should be noted that the selected brochure is the most voluminous in the corpus at 4,340 words, which is a little over 4 times longer than average. An example of a phrase where "your" is used in several instances is "Your body needs blood pressure to move the blood throughout your body, so every part of your body can get the oxygen it needs." In addition to "your," the brochure includes the reflexive "yourself" in five out of its six total corpus appearances in phrases such as "reminding yourself of your goal." Subject and object uses of "you" include "The older you are, the more likely you are to ..." and "a support network helps you get through tough times." "You" also appears in the contractions "you've" (3 instances) and "you're" (11 instances). The brochure includes examples of all the frequently occurring "your" clusters discussed in the above section. "Your blood" appears in 21 instances (45% of all the corpus cases), of which 20 are "your blood pressure" (2/3 of all the corpus cases) and one is "your blood vessels." "Your doctor" appears in only 3 instances, but it may be because the brochure includes 13 instances of "your healthcare provider" (50% of the total corpus cases), which encompasses doctors as well as other healthcare professionals such as nurses or physician assistants.[10] "Your heart" appears in 8 instances (30% of all the corpus cases), of which three are "your heart and circulatory system." Finally, the remaining "your" cluster discussed in the previous section, "your health," appears in 2 instances (just 7% of all the corpus cases).

As explained in the previous section, the modals "can," "may," and "should" are considerably frequent in the corpus. Their frequency in the selected brochure is also considerable, with "can" appearing in 71 instances (42% of the total corpus cases), "may" in 11 (20% of the total corpus cases), and "should" in 6 instances (26% of the total corpus cases). Though, as described in the previous section, "must" is by no means a frequent modal in the corpus, it does appear once in the brochure as such. In the other instance, it is a noun ("a healthy diet is a must"). When modals are conjugated in the second person, they may directly encourage the reader to act. "You can," which happens to be the most frequent "can" cluster in the corpus, occurs in 11 instances in the brochure (42% of the total corpus cases). "You may," the "may" cluster that happens to be tied with "may be" as the most frequent, occurs once in the brochure (10% of the total corpus cases). "You should," though not the most frequent "should" cluster in the corpus, occurs once (20% of the total corpus cases). "You must" does not appear in the selected brochure, as it is not the brochure in which the two total corpus instances of "you must" appear.

As discussed in the previous section, the modals "can" and "may" indicate possibility. In the brochure, the cluster "can be" occurs in 7 instances (30% of the total corpus cases), "can cause" in 10 (56%), "it can" in 4 (24%), and "can help" in 5 instances (36%). "May be," the remaining cluster discussed in the previous section and whose corpus frequency ranks highest with that of "you may," occurs in 2 instances (20%). The adjective "likely" also indicates possibility and, as mentioned in the previous section, ranks highest by far in the brochures corpus. It is also very much present in the selected brochure, in which it appears seven times (44%). In 5 of these 7 instances, it appears in the cluster "likely to" (38%) and in four of them, in "more likely to" (36%). The brochure also includes two of the three total corpus appearances where "likely" does not precede a to-infinitive. These 2 instances are "The older you are, the more likely you are to get high blood pressure" and "Once your blood pressure is under control, you will likely be tested less often."

The final frequent corpus example indicating possibility is "risk," which ranks higher by far in the brochure corpus than in any of the other English corpora. In the selected brochure, "risk" appears 17 times, representing 31% of all its corpus appearances. The frequent "risk" clusters discussed in the previous section all appear to different extents in the selected brochure: "risk for" (4 instances, 22% of the total corpus cases), "risk factor(s)" (5 plural instances [1/3 of the total corpus cases], 3 singular instances [100% of the total corpus cases]), "at risk" (2 instances, 15%), "your risk(s)" (5 singular instances [38% of the total corpus cases], 1 plural [100% of the total corpus cases]), and "at risk for" (1 instance, 9%). Though not discussed in the previous section, "risk of" appears 5 times, which constitute more than half of the 9 total instances of this cluster in the corpus, for example, "Being overweight increases your risk of cardiovascular disease and diabetes."

Finally, the selected brochure employs the conjunction cluster "if you" in 5 instances, representing just 13% of all of its appearances in the corpus. Nevertheless, the brochure does employ three other variations of this phrase where "you" is modified: "if your" (2 instances), "if you've" (1), and "if you're" (1). An example of the first possessive case is "If your parents or other close blood relatives have high blood pressure, there's an increased chance that you'll get it, too." The second case, the contraction conjugated in the present perfect, appears in "If you've been diagnosed with high blood pressure, it's very important to follow the treatment plan your healthcare provider gives you." And the third and last case, which is also a contraction but in the present continuous, appears in "If you're having side effects from the medications you're prescribed, talk with your doctor." To conclude this analysis, notice how these various "if you" sentences easily exceed the CDC's recommendation to limit sentence length to eight to ten words. Conjunctions such as "if" in patient education materials may very well lengthen sentences and potentially complicate readability, depending on the audience.

CHINESE

Patient education materials provide concise health information in many formats, including pamphlets, fact sheets, booklets, and posters, which can be in print or electronic form. In this corpus of Chinese patient education materials, there are nine texts. The total word count in terms of Chinese characters is 15,288 and the average word count is about 1,700. Patient education materials are typically a long piece of writing, which is supported by the mean length (in terms of Chinese characters) of the materials included in the Chinese corpus, which is about 1,700 characters. The lengths of the nine corpus texts shows range from 910 characters to 2,282, depending on the complexity of the materials. The themes of the texts cover eye hygiene, oral hygiene, ischemic cardiomyopathy, chronic obstructive pulmonary disease, gingival bleeding, tips for drinking honey water, tips for liver protection, festival diet, and common diseases and disorders.

Macro-textual features

At the macro-textual level, we begin by isolating the conventional features, or **rhetorical moves**, of patient educational materials. They are:

1. Informative title
2. Body consisting of headings or sub-moves:

   1. Description of disease or ailment (基本知识)
   2. Causes (致病因素)
   3. Symptoms or consequences (表现/症状)
   4. Treatment (治疗方法)
   5. Prevention tips (预防措施)
   6. Precautions and warnings (注意事项)

Based on the Chinese corpus, every text has a title and a body, which often include a few sub-moves. "Prevention tips" is the most frequent sub-move and occurs in seven of the nine texts. Five texts have the sub-move that describes the disease or ailment, while the sub-moves that outline causes, symptoms or consequences, and precautions and warnings occur in four texts each. The treatment sub-move occurs in three texts. The exact wording of the sub-moves is inconsistent, although the Chinese phrases above would make perfect sense. Some headings in the texts are in the form of questions rather than phrases.

As far as register is concerned, one way to reveal the **field**, or the topic or domain of a text, is to examine its terminology and lexical items. A quick look at the word frequency list makes clear that the terminology and lexical items in this text type relate to patient education (see table).

High-frequency lexical items	Frequency	High-frequency lexical items	Frequency
食物 (food)	39	传播 (spread)	19
预防 (prevention)	39	艾滋病 (AIDS)	18

(Continued)

Text types

(Continued)

High-frequency lexical items	Frequency	High-frequency lexical items	Frequency
吃 (eat)	30	人体 (human body)	17
喝 (drink)	29	近视 (myopia)	16
出血 (hemorrhage)	25	病毒 (virus)	16
牙龈 (gum)	23	功能 (function)	16
脂肪 (fat)	23	口腔 (oral cavity)	15
治疗 (treatment)	23	孩子 (children)	15
症状 (symptom)	22	健康 (health)	14
注意 (precaution)	22	咀嚼 (chew)	13
患者 (patient)	21	疾病 (disease)	12
饮食 (diet)	19		

All of the lexical items in the table describe either diseases/disorders, patients, or treatment. As for the mode of discourse, patient education materials are usually texts written to be read by the audience to learn about a disease or disorder. They can also contain dialogues, as shown in one of the texts in this corpus, which is an interview with a doctor.

When it comes to the **tenor** of discourse in patient education materials, the relationship between the author and the audience is usually expert-to-nonexpert. This is evidenced by the non-technicality of the terms used in the materials, as shown in the table.

The **communicative function** is informative. The purpose of patient education materials is to inform the reader about a disease or disorder and to encourage certain actions through the use of imperative sentences.

Micro-textual features

At the micro-textual level, the corpus data point to a preference for the declarative or indicative **mood** in patient education materials. Almost all the sentences in the corpus were statements. The mood can also be interrogative, and many sentences in one text in the Chinese corpus were questions.

As regards **cohesive devices**, the use of **reference** is rare in the Chinese patient education materials. Personal pronouns, including 我 (I), 我们 (we), 你 (you), 他 (he), 他们 (they), and 自己 (oneself), occur 17 times total in the corpus. Among demonstrative reference devices, 这, the Chinese equivalent for *this*, appears 13 times in the corpus; 这 also appears in many words or phrases in the corpus, such as 这样 (this way, occurring 5 times), 这种 (this type, occurring 4 times), 这些 (these, occurring twice) and 这个 (this one, occurring twice). 那, the Chinese equivalent for *that*, appears twice in the corpus. The cohesive device of **substitution** is scarcely used in the Chinese materials; in this regard, only 8 occurrences of 其他 (other) were found. By contrast, **ellipsis** is a widely used cohesive device in Chinese, in which subjects and objects are optional if they can be implied by the context.

The Chinese patient educational materials also make extensive use of additive, causal, and temporal **conjunctions** (see table).

Conjunctions	Frequency
如果 (if)	21
并 (and, also)	19
因为 (because)	14
而且 (moreover)	6
所以 (therefore)	5
为了 (in order to)	4
然后 (then)	1
不仅 (not only)	1
以便 (so as to)	1
只要 (as long as)	1

The use of conjunctions is generally less frequent in Chinese than in English. Also, directions (i.e., prevention tips and precautions) in the Chinese materials are in the form of lists, which reduces the need for conjunctions. **Lexical cohesion** is arguably the most common form of cohesion in Chinese. In the case of patient education materials, each step is described by one simple sentence or one compound sentence; in compound sentences, lexical repetition occurs dozens of times in this Chinese corpus.

In the corpus of Chinese patient education materials, when offering prevention tips, simple sentences starting with a verb are the norm. For statements, simple sentences, compound sentences, and complex sentences seem to appear equally frequently.

In the Chinese corpus, there is a high occurrence of **nouns**, as shown in the table.

High-frequency nouns	Frequency	High-frequency nouns	Frequency
食物 (food)	39	口腔 (oral cavity)	15
牙龈 (gum)	23	孩子 (children)	15
脂肪 (fat)	23	疾病 (disease)	12
症状 (symptom)	22	护肝 (liver protection)	12
患者 (patient)	21	原因 (reason)	12
因素 (factor)	21	口腔溃疡 (mouth ulcer)	11
饮食 (diet)	19	肝脏 (liver)	11
艾滋病 (AIDS)	18	建议 (proposal)	11
人体 (human body)	17	水果 (fruit)	11
病毒 (virus)	16	眼睛 (eye)	10
功能 (function)	16	情况 (situation)	10

The nouns in the corpus can be classified into three domains: (1) nouns describing human organs, such as 牙龈 (gum), 口腔 (oral cavity), 肝脏 (liver), and 眼睛 (eye); (2) nouns describing diseases or disorders like 艾滋病 (AIDS) and 牙周病 (periodontitis); and (3) nouns related to diagnosis, such as 症状 (symptom), 原因 (reason), 建议 (proposal), and 饮食(diet).

In addition to nouns, another word category that is highly recurring in this genre is **verbs**, as evidenced in the table of high-frequency verbs.

154 Text types

Verbs	Frequency
预防 (prevent)	39
引起 (cause)	35
吃 (eat)	30
治疗 (treat)	23
咀嚼 (chew)	13
发生 (happen)	12
接触 (contact)	11
休息 (rest)	11
咳嗽 (cough)	11

Sample text – Chinese patient education materials

小学生用眼卫生

注意用眼卫生要做到"二要二不要"

（1）二要：

①读书写字姿势要端正，保持"一尺一拳一寸"，即眼睛离书本一尺，身体离桌沿一拳，手指离笔尖一寸；

②连续看书写字一小时左右要休息片刻，或向远处眺望一会。

（2）二不要：①不要在光线太暗或直射阳光下看书、写字； ②不要躺着、走路或乘车时看书。

看电视怎样注意卫生？

①每次看电视不要超过2小时，连续看电视1小时后，应起来活动5-10分钟；

②观看者应离电视屏幕2米以上；

③电视机安放高度应与观看者坐时的眼睛高度相一致；

④室内最好开一盏3-8瓦的小灯，以减轻屏幕与周围黑暗的强烈对比，这对避免眼睛疲劳有好处。

怎样预防近视？

①注意用眼卫生； ②坚持做眼保健操；

③劳逸结合，睡眠充足；

④注意营养，加强锻炼，增强体质；

⑤定期检查视力，发现减退及时矫正，防止近视加深。

学生预防近视的方法

学生预防近视的方法有哪些？ 近视现在越来越普遍，现在最好的方法就是做好近视的预防，注意用眼卫生，或者是做眼睛保健操、改掉一些不良的用眼习惯.下面就针对于"学生预防近视的方法有哪些"做一下介绍。

1、在学习中注意适当以听代读，以减轻眼睛看近负荷。避免连续看近时间过长。阅读、写字、操作电脑等连续看近40分钟后应休息、看远处10～15分钟。尽量控制每天累计看近时间，最好不要超过6小时。

2、纠正不良看近姿势。阅读时，注意眼睛与书的距离要保持在约33厘米，操作电脑时眼睛距离35厘米大的电脑屏幕不应少于60厘米，距离38厘米的电脑屏幕不应少于70厘米。姿势要端正，不能躺着看书或边走边看。

3、注意改善需要较长时间看近的环境。教室光线要明亮，桌面、黑板不要反光过强，左右两侧都应有窗户，不要太高、太小，以坐在教室任何位置都能看到窗外为宜，并定期调换坐位;孩子在家的书桌应放在外面无遮挡物的窗前，台灯应放在左前方，光线要柔和，如白炽灯，**最好**为25~40W之间，位置以不直接照射**眼睛**为宜。

4、**如果**在持续**看近**时出现**眼睛**干涩、发红，有灼热感或异物感，眼皮沉重，看东西模糊，甚至出现眼球胀痛或头痛，说明已经出现视觉疲劳症状，要立即停止**看近**，可以做眼保健操，还可以用湿热毛巾热敷双眼来缓解视觉疲劳。<u>如果</u>通过上述处理，仍无明显好转，<u>那</u>就需要到医院看眼科医生了。

Key: conjunctions – underline; lexical repetition – highlighted in gray

Sample Chinese patient education text analysis

At the macro-textual level, the sample text offers tips to primary school students for good eye health and for preventing myopia. This text appears on over 1,000 Chinese websites. It has a title and a body, which contains one sub-move, i.e., offering prevention tips. The text has 912 characters and is shorter than the average (1,700 characters) in this text type. The mode of discourse is imperative and the tenor of discourse points to an expert-to-nonexpert relationship. The communicative function is informative and operative for the reasons given above.

As far as the micro-textual features are concerned, the imperative mood is evidenced in the common use of 应 (should)，要 (should)，不要 (don't)，and 最好 (had better), and the present tense is used to give suggestions concerning eye health. In terms of cohesive devices, reference and substitution are almost absent in the sample text; only 这 (this) occurred once. As most sentences in this sample text are imperative, the subjects are implied; otherwise, ellipsis does not occur. Conjunctions are used (see underlined words) such as 如果 (if) and 或者 (or). Lexical repetition that occurs in the same step of the education materials (see words highlighted in gray) appears about 20 times, while there are no hypernyms or synonyms. See table for instances of repetition in the sample text.

Repetition	Frequency	Repetition	Frequency
眼睛 (eye)	8	电脑 (computer)	3
不要 (don't)	7	方法 (method)	3
看近 (look near)	7	看书 (reading)	3
注意 (need to)	7	屏幕 (screen)	3
近视 (myopia)	6	小时 (hour)	3
电视 (television)	4	写字 (write)	3
厘米 (centimeter)	4	学生 (student)	3
卫生 (hygiene)	4	最好 (best)	3
预防 (prevention)	4		

The sample text is characterized by simple sentences. In the sample, there are 12 simple sentences, 9 compound sentences, and 6 complex sentences.

156 Text types

FRENCH

French patient education materials (*matériels destinés aux patients*) address the common questions and concerns of individuals suffering from ailments or considering medical procedures. Materials generally take the form of handouts distributed by health care establishments, medical associations, and other entities operating in the health care sector. To gain insight into the current textual features of this genre, we assembled a collection of 15 patient education handouts published by 14 different sources within the last 5 years. Texts in the corpus range in length from 1,263 words to 5,993 words, with an average of 2,533 words. The range of 1,270 words is primarily due to the depth at which a given ailment or procedure is covered. This genre is decidedly consistent regarding the nature of information found in each mandatory rhetorical move.

Macro-textual features

We begin our analysis at the macro-textual level by outlining the following mandatory **rhetorical moves**:

1. Informative title (*Titre informatif*)
2. Body of the handout (*Contenu du guide*)

   a. About the illness (*À propos de la maladie*)
   b. Causes (*L'origine/Les causes*)
   c. Symptoms (*Symptômes*)
   d. Treatments (*Traitements*)
   e. Prevention tips (*Prévention*)

3. Additional information (*Contacts utiles/Pour en savoir plus*)

Informative titles (*titres informatifs*) typically engage readers with a catchy appeal to view the contents of the handout (e.g., *C comme cirrhose : apprendre à vivre avec une cirrhose*). They are followed by the body of the handout (*contenu du guide*), which is divided into five sub-rhetorical moves. The first defines an ailment (*à propos de la maladie*). The second and third contain a statement of the ailment's causes (*l'origine/les causes*) and symptoms (*symptômes*), respectively. The final two sub-rhetorical moves outline available treatments (*traitements*) and prevention tips (*prévention*). Both *prévention* and *l'origine/les causes* may address risk factors (*facteurs de risque*). Finally, contact information or links to authoritative sources where patients can find further information are found under *contacts utiles/pour en savoir plus*. Two optional rhetorical moves include the highly recurrent diagnosis (*diagnostic*) and the less frequent table of contents (*sommaire*).

We will look at three aspects to describe the **register** of patient education materials: field, mode, and **tenor**. Based on the frequent lexical items listed in the table, this genre's **field** of discourse, or what the handouts are about, concerns the description, treatment, and personal impact of ailments.

High-frequency lexical item	Frequency	No. of texts
maladie	259	13
personne(s)	158	13
traitement	149	13
vie	113	13
risque	101	13
médecin	88	13
santé	87	13
symptômes	87	13
prise en charge	68	11
patients	75	11

An examination of **mode** – how a text will be used – reveals that patient education materials are designed to be read. Though questions are found in several handouts, these questions are rhetorical and serve as prompts for readers to uncover facts about an ailment. Questions are followed by responses and, therefore, do not invite readers to a dialogue with authors (e.g., *Qu'est-ce qu'une cirrhose ? Il s'agit d'une maladie grave du foie, qui s'accompagne de lésions irréversibles*). The **tenor** of discourse, characterizing the relationship between the genre's authors and audience, points to an expert-to-nonexpert relationship, as reflected in the straightforward descriptions of specialized medical concepts.

The **communicative function** of the genre is primarily informative. Handouts provide a structured overview of their subject matter so that patients can make educated decisions when discussing an ailment or procedure with a physician. However, because readers are encouraged to use handouts as guides to effective communication with medical professionals, patient education materials additionally have a conative dimension.

Micro-textual features

At the **micro-textual level**, the predominant **mood** of French patient education materials is indicative. The third-person singular *présent* is commonly used to state facts in the active voice (e.g., *Le maladie de Parkinson **est** une maladie neurologique dégénérative*). As mentioned above, questions are merely rhetorical. Finally, authors in a few of the handouts instruct readers to engage in or to avoid a behavior using the imperative (e.g., *Un conseil : **participez** activement à votre propre thérapie*).

An analysis of **cohesive devices** shows a preponderance of definite and indefinite articles frequently accompanying ailments, treatments, and patients. For example, *personnes* are ordinarily affected by an ailment (e.g., *les personnes diabétiques/porteuses d'un syndrome de Lynch/séropositives au VIH*). Demonstrative references, of which inflections of the adjective *cet* form the majority, regularly collocate with *maladie*, *guide*, *risque*, and *brochure*.

Article	Collocate	Frequency
une	maladie	258
un	traitement	149
la	maladie	131
les	personnes	105
le	traitement	54

Three personal referents are noteworthy. The pronoun *je* is found in handouts written from the reader's perspective (e.g., *Est-ce que je peux me faire vacciner ?*). *Me* is used in a similar fashion (e.g., *Quels sont les signes qui doivent m'alerter ?*). *Vous*, by far the most common personal pronoun, spurs readers into action (e.g., **Vous discutez** *de votre maladie et* **posez** *les questions qui vous préoccupent*).

References employing third-person singular personal pronouns stand out as **substitution** devices. For example, the pronoun *elle* replaces a feminine word in the following two-sentence definition: *La dialyse est la solution alternative.* ***Elle permet de débarrasser le sang des toxines.*** Lexical cohesion is established via hyponymy, where answers contain specific words corresponding to general words in questions (see table).

Question	Answer
Quels sont les **profession-nels** *impliqués ?*	*Votre* **médecin traitant généraliste** *et/ou votre* **cardiologue** *réalise le* **bilan.**
Quels sont les **dangers de la cirrhose ?**	*La cirrhose peut entraîner des* **complications sérieuses :** œdème généralisé, hémorragies internes, troubles de la conscience *pouvant aller jusqu'au* **coma.**

Finally, with respect to the use of conjunctions as cohesive devices, the vast majority are coordinating conjunctions but are not necessarily found in compound sentences. These sentences may nevertheless be quite long. For example: *Elle améliore votre qualité de vie en vous aidant à prendre conscience des bénéfices de votre traitement* ***et*** *en vous apprenant à décrire à votre médecin l'évolution de votre maladie* ***et*** *à reconnaître d'éventuels effets indésirables des traitements.*

Sample text – French patient education materials

Ne laissez pas le DIABETE vous priver de vos yeux.

Comprendre **la maculopathie diabétique**

Qu'est-ce que **la maculopathie diabétique** *?*

La maculopathie diabétique est la principale cause de malvoyance chez les personnes diabétiques. Cette maladie atteint la **macula, zone centrale de la rétine** qui joue un rôle essentiel dans la vision des détails. La vision périphérique est conservée, mais la vision centrale est atteinte et peut entraîner un handicap visuel qui rend difficile l'exécution de certaines tâches au quotidien (lire, reconnaître les visages, percevoir les détails…).

Deux formes de maculopathie diabétique

La maculopatique œdémateuse (aussi appelée « œdème maculaire diabétique ») est la forme la plus fréquente. Elle concerne 10% des patients diabétiques et peut être traitée. Plus rare, **la maculopathie ischémique** est incurable et entraîne souvent une déficience visuelle majeure.

*Qu'est ce que **la rétinopathie diabétique** ?*

Cette pathologie oculaire est liée à la présence trop importante de sucre dans le sang qui finit par altérer les petits vaisseaux de **la rétine**. Elle concernerait un million de personnes en France. On estime par ailleurs que la quasitotalité des diabétiques de type 1 (insulinodépendants) et plus de 60% des diabétiques de type 2 développeront **une rétinopathie diabétique** durant les 20 premières années de leur diabète. En l'absence de traitement, **la rétinopathie diabétique** évolue vers **une déficience visuelle** (ou malvoyance), voire **une cécité**.

Elle est ainsi la première cause de cécité avant 65 ans. A tous les stades de **la rétinopathie diabétique**, **un œdème maculaire** peut se former.

…

La rétine est une fine membrane tapissant la surface interne du globe. Elle comprend deux parties :

- la rétine centrale ;
- la rétine périphérique.

En cas de maculopathie diabétique, seule la rétine centrale est atteinte. D'un diamètre de 5 à 6 mm, elle est située au pôle postérieur de l'œil. Elle comprend :

- la macula (« tache » en latin), zone de couleur jaune-marron située au centre de la rétine, dont elle occupe 2 à 3% de la surface seulement.

…

Caractéristiques

La maculopathie œdémateuse est caractérisée par un épaississement de la région maculaire, lié à l'accumulation de sang et de liquide dans la macula. Cet épaississement se produit lorsque les vaisseaux sanguins de la rétine se mettent à gonfler et à fuir. **L'œdème** qui en résulte brouille la vue et provoque une perte progressive de vision au centre de la rétine, qui peut à la longue évoluer vers **une cécité**.

…

Ensuite, quelle que soit la nature de votre diabète, vous devrez faire des examens oculaires de contrôle tous les ans, même si votre vision vous paraît normale. En cas d'anomalies visuelles ou de rétinopathie diabétique évolutive, ces examens peuvent être plus fréquents. Votre ophtalmologiste vous indiquera alors le rythme à suivre pour faire contrôler votre vision.

Key: meronyms – highlighted in gray; article-ailment pairs – bold

Source: Institut d'Education Médicale et de Prévention

160 Text types

Sample French patient education text analysis

To gain a better understanding of French patient education materials, we will analyze a handout on diabetic maculopathy. The text was published by L'Institut d'Education Médicale et de Prévention, which prepares materials in collaboration with medical professionals and key players in the French health care sector and engages in media awareness campaigns on public health issues.

From the macro-textual perspective, the table contains a list of all the rhetorical moves in the order they appear. *Symptômes* is repeated in this handout.

Heading from table of contents	Move(s) under each heading	Level	Mandatory?
Ne laissez pas le DIABETE vous priver de vos yeux.	*Titre informatif*	Rhetorical	Yes
Sommaire	*Sommaire*	Rhetorical	No
Contenu du guide	*Contenu du guide*	Rhetorical	Yes
Comprendre la maculopathie diabétique *La maculopathie ischémique* *La maculopathie œdémateuse ou œdème maculaire diabétique*	*À propos de la maladie* *L'origine/Les causes* *Symptômes*	Sub-rhetorical (under *Contenu du guide*)	Yes
Du dépistage au diagnostic	*Diagnostic*	Sub-rhetorical (under *Contenu du guide*)	No
	Symptômes	Sub-rhetorical (under *Contenu du guide*)	Yes
Les piliers de la prévention	*Prévention*	Sub-rhetorical (under *Contenu du guide*)	Yes
Les traitements existants *Vivre avec une maculopathie diabétique*	*Traitements*	Sub-rhetorical (under *Contenu du guide*)	Yes
Contacts utiles	*Contacts utiles/Pour en savoir plus*	Rhetorical	Yes

The field of discourse covers the condition of diabetic maculopathy, or damage to a specific part of the eye caused by diabetes mellitus. The back-and-forth between questions and answers serves as a rhetorical device used to engage readers in what is a primarily informative text. Because these questions, statistics (found under *prévention*), and other information summarize the fundamental aspects of a complex medical condition, the tenor of discourse points to an expert-to-nonexpert relationship.

At the micro-textual level, the mood of this handout is largely indicative. It contains many statements of fact made using the present tense (*présent*), most often the third-person singular of *être* in definitions (e.g., *La rétine **est** une fine membrane tapissant la surface interne du globe*). However, *imperatif* is sometimes used to instruct patients to take specific steps (e.g., *Comment se préparer* *à un examen du fond d'œil avec dilatation de la pupille ? **Prévoyez** de venir sans maquillage sur les yeux ni lentilles de contact).*

In terms of cohesive devices, because the authors have chosen to directly address their readers, the second-person plural pronouns *vos, vous,* and *votre* are the most frequent personal referents. For example, the text reads: *Votre ophtalmologiste vous indiquera alors le rythme à suivre pour faire contrôler votre vision* (emphasis added). Articles, too, play a role in tying the subject matter of this text together. The collocation frequency table contains the five most frequent collocations using definite and indefinite articles. The article-ailment pairs (bold in the sample text) reflect the larger pattern observed in the full corpus.

Collocation	Collocation frequency with definite/indefinite article	Total frequency in sample text
maculopathie	19	23
rétine	17	17
macula	15	17
rétinopathie	6	8
maladie	6	10

Substitution and hypernymy/hyponymy are present in the text, as exemplified by these sentences: *Qu'est-ce que la **rétinopathie diabétique** ? Cette **pathologie oculaire** est liée à la présence trop importante de sucre dans le sang qui finit par altérer les petits vaisseaux de la rétine. **Elle** concernerait un million de personnes en France.* Here, *pathologie oculaire,* a hypernym of *rétinoapathie diabétique,* is used in the answer to define the technical term. The definition extends into the next sentence, where the concept is substituted by the pronoun *elle.* This cohesive device occurs throughout the sample text and in the corpus.

Finally, parts of the eye and of vision are signaled by meronyms found throughout the text, which indicate that they are part of a larger concept – i.e., in the case of the sample text, these terms form part of the eye. Synonyms are sometimes used for the purpose of clarity or when an ailment or a related concept has more than one generally accepted designation. In most cases, these synonyms can be found offset from the text in parentheses or quotation marks. In other cases, synonyms are given in a doublet, indicated by *ou* to show another option for the term.

162   Text types

GERMAN

Hospitals and medical care facilities worldwide, particularly in large metropolitan areas, tend to be inherently multilingual and multicultural communicative environments. A high demand for medical interpreting, both onsite and remote, attests to this. From informational, emotional, and at times, legal standpoints, it is crucial that patients have access to medical content, such as information guides, in a language they can readily understand, if not in their native language. A corpus of 12 patient information guides was compiled for the purposes of discerning how such expectations and preferences are patterned in German-language texts. These guides were retrieved online from various medical care facility websites in 2016.

Macro-textual features

A macro-level analysis of **rhetorical moves** highlights the following as prototypical (in no set order), appearing in at least 8 of the 12 texts:

1. Title/heading (*Titel/Überschrift*)
2. Genre framing (as a patient information leaflet) (*Benennung als Infoblatt*)
3. Naming of medical facility/company (*Benennung der medizinischen Einrichtung/Firma*)
4. Disease/condition description (*Krankheits-/Zustandsbeschreibung*)
5. Treatment description (*Beschreibung der Behandlung*)
6. Associated risks (of contraction, of treatment, and of not receiving treatment) (*Risiken und Begleiterscheinungen*)
7. Contact information (*Kontaktinformationen*)

A formal patient greeting, like one might find more frequently in English-language patient guides, appears in only 4 of the 12 texts, perhaps signaling a distancing strategy between text author (medical care provider) and reader and placing a stronger emphasis on strictly informative text type conventions. Moves that mention symptoms and diagnostics occur in seven of the texts, pointing toward disease descriptions, treatment options, and risks as more prototypical components. The headings and subheadings found in the disease, treatment, and risks moves frequently appear as rhetorical questions (in 7 out of 12 texts), suggesting a structural means to engage the reader.

As was the case in some of the other German-language genres analyzed in this volume, the exclamation mark is frequently used (15 times across six texts) in patient information guides for the purpose of added emphasis and for framing text as mandatory reading. These examples are taken from the corpus:

German passage	English translation
Lassen Sie sich impfen!	Get vaccinated!
Bei privaten Auslandskrankenversicherungen gilt ausschließlich der jeweilige Vertrag!	For private travel health insurance, solely the respective contract applies.

(Continued)

Patient education materials   163

(Continued)

German passage	English translation
Immer Lotionen verwenden, nie Pasten, weil diese aufgrund ihrer Konsistenz die Hautatmung beeinträchtigen!	Always use lotions instead of pastes, as these reduce skin perspiration due to their consistency.

While the overall length of German-language patient guides does not emerge as prototypical, the average sentence length is 14 words. With the exception of one text in our corpus, which has a mean sentence length of 20 words, all of the texts fall within a range of ± 2 words in relation to this overall average. Not unlike the instruction manuals analyzed in this volume, sentence length is relatively fixed for the purpose of enhancing readability and predictability. Highly field-specific content, as rendered through the nouns taken from the corpus (see table), is packaged into relatively short sentences. These nouns also establish the **field** of discourse as involving medical care.

German field-specific term	English equivalent	Frequency
Noroviren	noroviruses	12
Tuberkolose	tuberculosis	12
Bleaching	whitening	11
Krätze	scabies	10
Ergotherapie	occupational therapy	8
Sanierung	decontamination	8
Erreger	pathogen	6
Hygienemassnahmen	hygienic measures	6
Händedisinfektion	hand disinfection	6
Impfung	vaccination	6
Fahrtüchtigkeit	fitness to drive	5

The mode of discourse for this genre is both informative and didactic. The informative stance is supported by frequent definitions and descriptions of symptoms, treatment options, and risks. The didactic stance, which is secondary, comes in the form of concrete patient instructions, such as how to prepare for appointments and procedures. Regarding **tenor**, communication takes place between medical care providers or facilities and a layperson audience consisting of patients and their caregivers. The formal "you" (*Sie*) is used a total of 95 times across all 12 texts to directly address the reader. The layperson audience orientation as well as the highly informative communicative function of this genre are highlighted through the juxtaposition of field-specific medical terminology and more general language descriptions or explanations, as seen in the following examples from the corpus:

164 **Text types**

German field-specific term and general language explication	English equivalent
Influenza, eine "echte" Grippe	Influenza, a "real" cold
Wörtlich übersetzt bedeutet Fibromyalgie "Faser-Muskel-Schmerz"	Literally translated, fibromyalgia means muscle fiber pain
Die Zeit zwischen Ansteckung und Ausbruch der Erkrankung (Inkubationszeit)	The time between infection and signs of illness (incubation period)
Die Ultraschalldiagnostik (Sonographie)	ultrasound diagnostics (sonography)
Die Untersuchung des Enddarmes (Endosonographie)	rectal examination (endosonography)
die festen (parenchymatösen) Organe des Oberbauches	upper abdominal solid (parenchymatous) organs

It is interesting to note that either the field-specific or general language variant often appears in parentheses in German-language patient guides. German-language texts often use such parentheticals for framing content as highly important. The same does not hold true in English-language texts, implying a potential need for re-structuring when translating German texts into English by avoiding parentheses. Occasionally, the layperson equivalent of a field-specific medical term appears in quotes in German-language patient guides. It might be advisable to omit these quotation marks when translating into English so as not to risk having the English-speaking reader interpret the content as questionable or even sarcastic.

Micro-textual features

Micro-textual analyses reveal that the vast majority of sentences in the corpus, as one might expect, are declarative and present factual information. These sentences do not follow any specific syntactic template, as we might expect in operative text genres. As previously mentioned, we see interrogative sentences relatively frequently in the form of rhetorical questions in headings and subheadings. The subjunctive mood is often embedded in declarative sentences as a form of subtle hedging. This can be regarded as a distancing strategy as well so that medical care providers are not held liable for treatment that proves to be ineffective or statements/claims that might not apply in all cases. The table illustrates constructs used to establish a subjunctive mood along these lines.

German subjunctive mood construct	Frequency	Example	English translation
kann (EN: could)	9	*Gelegentlich kann es nach einer Impfung zu Rötungen kommen*	Occasionally, vaccinations might lead to redness.
können (EN: could)	19	*Die Schmerzen können quälend und belastend sein*	The pain may be excruciating and burdensome.
meist- (EN: usually)	5	*Die Behandlung erfolgt meist stationär*	Treatment is usually in patient

(Continued)

(Continued)

German subjunctive mood construct	Frequency	Example	English translation
möglicherweise (EN: possibly)	2	*… welche möglicherweise Noroviren verursacht haben*	… which were possibly caused by noroviruses
oft (EN: oftentimes)	4	*Auch sind die Resultate oft nicht optimal*	Oftentimes, the results are also not optimal

Such hedging is likely used just as often (if not more often) in English-language patient information guides as a way of mitigating liability. In the context of German to English translation, the empty referent *es* (it), as used, for example, in the hedging construct *kann es* (it could) may need to be reformulated in a more active fashion, as rendered in the following two examples:

German passage containing empty referent
Durch die Behandlung kann es vorübergehend zu einer erhöhten Empfindlichkeit der Zahnhälse kommen
Literal English translation
Through treatment, it may temporarily result in the tooth necks being more sensitive
Modulated English translation
Treatment may temporarily result in …

German passage containing empty referent
bei geschwächtem Immunsystem kann es aber auch zu schweren Infektionen kommen
Literal English translation
due to a weakened immune system, however, it can lead to severe infection
Modulated English translation
A weakened immune system, however, may lead to severe infection

Simple sentences emerge as the preferred sentence type, contributing to readability and the purpose of conveying factual information. The first two sentences in each of the 12 patient information guides reveal the following breakdown: 15 simple sentences, 1 compound sentence, and 6 complex sentences.

As far as **cohesive devices** are concerned, patient guides frequently make use of lexical recurrence when referring to illnesses and in headings and subheadings, as the table of frequently occurring nouns in our corpus illustrates.

German term	English equivalent	Frequency
Patient/-en	patients	59
Behandlung	treatment	33
Arzt	physician	30
Erkrankung	illness	22
Klinik/-en	hospital/-s	25
Untersuchung	examination	14

(Continued)

166 Text types

(Continued)

German term	English equivalent	Frequency
Infektion	infection	13
Beschwerden	symptoms	11
Informationen	information	11
Medikamente	medications	11
Krankheit	illness	10
Lunge	lung	10
Schmerzen	pain	10

In this genre, we also see frequent utilization of hypernymy/hyponymy, substitution, and synonymy as cohesive devices. An analysis of the first two full sentences in each of the texts found in the corpus reveals that one of these three cohesive devices is used in 9 out of the 12 patient guides. This often comes in the form of general language definitions and descriptions after the mention of field-specific nouns, as seen in the following example:

German passage
ERKRANKUNG
Das Fibromyalgiesyndrom (FMS) ist bei den meisten Betroffenen eine dauerhaft bestehende Erkrankung. Wörtlich übersetzt bedeutet Fibromyalgie "Faser-Muskel-Schmerz"
English translation
Illness
For most patients, fibromyalgia syndrome (FMS) is a long-term illness. Literally translated, fibromyalgia means muscle fiber pain.

Sample text – German patient education materials

DRK Kliniken Berlin
Information für Patienten und Angehörige.
Information Krätze (Skabies)
www.drk-kliniken-berlin.de
…

Was ist Krätze?

Krätze ist eine ansteckende und stark juckende Hauterkrankung. Verursacher sind Krätzemilben. Die begatteten Milbenweibchen graben kleine Gänge in die Haut und legen dort ihre Eier ab. Nach etwa drei Wochen entwickeln sich daraus geschlechtsreife Krätzemilben. Diese neue Generation von Milben ist dann in der Lage, sich zu vermehren.

Vorkommen und Verbreitung

Krätze breitet sich in Gemeinschaftseinrichtungen wie Schulen und Altenheimen sehr schnell aus. Besonders dort, wo viele Personen auf engem Raum zusammen sind, ist das Ansteckungsrisiko besonders hoch und erfordert bei Verdachts- und Erkrankungsfällen eine rasche Reaktion durch eine sinnvolle Kombination von Hygienemaßnahmen und Behandlung der Erkrankten. Die Krätze ist auch in den Industrienationen eine sich zunehmend ausbreitende Erkrankung. Bisher galt sie hauptsächlich als eine Erkrankung von Obdachlosen und in ähnlichen Verhältnissen lebenden Menschen.

Wie wird Krätze übertragen?

Die Krätze wird bei engem körperlichen Hautkontakt mit infizierten Personen, d. h. von Mensch zu Mensch, übertragen. Dazu zählen meist auch pflegerische Tätigkeiten. Die Infektion wird oft erst nach Wochen bemerkt, denn erst zu diesem Zeitpunkt kommt es zu einem juckenden Ausschlag, der besonders nachts bei Bettwärme oft unerträglich wird.

Welche Körperteile werden befallen?

- Häufig findet man Milben in den Bereichen:
- Fingerzwischenräume, Handgelenke
- Armbeugen
- Gesäß
- Haut um den Bauchnabel
- im Brustwarzenbereich
- oft im Genitalbereich
- bei Babys und Kleinkindern auf Handflächen und Fußsohlen, auch Gesicht und Kopf

Welche Symptome treten bei Krätze auf?

Milbengänge; feine rötliche Linien, deren Ende als Aufenthaltsort der Milbe dient.
Bläschen auf der Haut; in der Mitte ist die Milbe als kleiner schwarzer Punkt sichtbar.
Starker Juckreiz; durch Kratzen kommt es an diesen Stellen zu kleinen oberflächlichen Hautverletzungen, in deren Folge u. U. ein Hautausschlag mit Eiterbildung erkennbar wird.

Wie sieht die Behandlung der Krätze aus?

Ganzkörperbehandlung mit einem Anti-Skabiesmittel, das genau nach Anweisung des Arztes angewandt werden muss.
Bettwäsche, Kleidung und Handtücher täglich wechseln und bei 60° C waschen.
Nicht waschbare Textilien:
Eine wirksame Methode ist z. B. das Lagern in fest verschlossenen Behältnissen.

Es gilt das Infektionsschutzgesetz!

Danach dürfen Personen, die an Krätze erkrankt sind, Schulen, Kindergärten oder ähnliche Einrichtungen nicht besuchen bzw. dort tätig sein, bis nach ärztlichem Urteil eine Ansteckungsgefahr ausgeschlossen ist. Eltern sind verpflichtet, über die Erkrankung ihres Kindes die Einrichtung zu informieren.

168 Text types

> ### Wie kann man einer Weiterverbreitung vorbeugen?
>
> Neben einer konsequenten Behandlung der offensichtlich betroffenen Patienten und der bereits geschilderten Behandlung von Kleidung ist eine konsequente Behandlung der Kontaktpersonen besonders wichtig. Als <u>Kontaktpersonen</u> gelten <u>alle Menschen, die in den letzten drei Wochen vor Ausbruch der Erkrankung engen körperlichen Kontakt zum Patienten hatten</u> *(z. B. Umarmung, Hautkontakt)*. Diese Menschen sollten sich ebenfalls behandeln lassen, unabhängig davon, ob sie bereits <u>Beschwerden</u> wie <u>Juckreiz oder Hautveränderungen</u> bei sich feststellen.
>
>   Kontaktpersonen sollten auch im häuslichen Bereich auf die intensive Reinigung von Möbeln wie Polstersessel und Betten achten. Der Fußboden und Bodenbeläge können dazu mit einem starken Staubsauger sicher von Milben befreit werden. Der Einsatz <u>chemischer Mittel</u> zur Entwesung milbentragender Gegenstände ist in den meisten Fällen nicht erforderlich, der Einsatz von <u>Desinfektionsmitteln</u> ist sinnlos!
>
> Key: rhetorical questions – highlighted in gray; explicitation – italics; hypernymy/hyponymy, substitution, synonymy – underline
>
> *Source: Excerpts taken from "Information für Patienten und Angehörige. Information Krätze (Skabies)," Dr. Marlies Höck*

Sample German patient education text analysis

The sample patient information guide was retrieved from the DRK Kliniken Berlin website in 2016. It provides information on scabies, including a description, symptoms, contraction, treatment options, and prevention. This text exhibits all seven of the moves identified above as prototypical for the genre. It consists of 692 words with an average sentence length of 14.7 words, which reflects the mean for this genre, as documented in our corpus.

Rhetorical questions (highlighted in gray) are frequently used in the context of headings and subheadings for framing purposes and for establishing interaction between text sender and receiver. We see 2 instances of explicitation in parentheses (italics) to further enhance the informational communicative purpose of the text.

Explicated parenthetical content in German	English equivalent
Krätze (Skabies)	scabies
Enger körperlicher Kontakt (z.B. Umarmung, Hautkontakt)	close bodily contact, such as hugging or skin-to-skin contact

The second of these examples represents a situation where it might be advisable to avoid parentheses in favor of commas in English translation so that the information, which is important, is not mistakenly regarded by the reader as non-essential.

Two exclamation marks highlight critical information in this sample text.

German passage with exclamation mark	English translation
Es gilt das Infektionsschutzgesetz!	The Protection against Infection Act applies!
der Einsatz von _Desinfektionsmitteln_ ist sinnlos!	The use of disinfectants is pointless.

Here, the second example represents a situation where it might be advisable to use a period as end punctuation when translating into English in that the use of exclamation marks in English-language patient guides tends to be reserved for content that represents danger.

At the micro-textual level, we see extensive utilization of hypernymy/hyponymy, substitution, and synonymy (underlined content) as cohesive device strategies to enhance informativity and readability. The examples marked up in the sample text all involve intra-sentential cohesive devices. Lexical recurrence is also quite common, with the following vocabulary appearing at least 3 times in the corpus:

German term	English equivalent	Frequency
Krätze	scabies	11
Kliniken	hospitals	9
Behandlung	treatment	6
Milben	mites	6
Erkrankung	illness	4
Diagnose	diagnosis	3
Haut	skin	3
Juckreiz	itching	3
Krätzemilben	scabies mites	3
Patienten	patients	3

RUSSIAN

The genre of comprehensive patient education brochures is relatively new in Russia. In the former U.S.S.R., patients frequently relied on their physicians for medical information, as well as friends, family, TV, periodicals, and a few specialized encyclopedias. Today, patient education materials are generally available in print and on the internet. This genre is of particular importance to translators in the United States, since U.S. health providers often deal with non-English-speaking clients, including those who would prefer to read patient education materials in Russian.

While Russian instruction manuals and business letters have attracted the interest of translation researchers, patient education materials in Russian remain understudied. To analyze the textual features of this genre, we gathered a corpus of ten Russian patient education texts from seven different online sources. All texts were published in 2015–2016 and range from 740 to 1,230 words in length.

Macro-textual features

At the macro-textual level, we isolated the following mandatory **rhetorical moves**:

1. Title
    - Информация для пациента/ов
    - Материалы по санитарному просвещению пациентов
    - Памятка пациента
    - Брошюра пациента
    - Буклет (Минздрава России)
    - Памятка для населения

2. Introduction, which typically explains what a condition or issue is and why it is important to address
3. Body, which typically includes information about prevention, transmission, and treatment

The body may have subheadings, such as профилактика/защита/как предупредить (prevention), пути передачи (transmission routes), Что делать, если (what to do if), лечение (treatment), etc. However, there is not much consistency in the subheadings among the texts. Some texts have very few subheadings.

These are the most frequent optional rhetorical moves:

- Name of the organization that created the brochure
- Motto (Дать шанс здоровью можешь только ты! [Only you can give a chance to [your] health!])
- Learn more (phone number, website, etc.)
- Name of author

The texts are frequently accompanied by statistics, graphs/tables, and pictures.

The **field** of discourse in the patient education corpus encompasses medical issues, as the frequency table shows.

Lexical item	Frequency
Дети/ребенок (children/child)	105 (75/30)
Заболевание (disease)	82
Инфекция (infection)	44
Орган (organ)	40
Холестерин (cholesterol)	38
Риск (risk, n.)	34
Профилактика (prevention)	34
Прививка (vaccine)	32
Вакцина (vaccine)	31
Воспалительный (inflammatory)	30
Является (to be copular verb in present tense)	27
Кровь (blood)	25
Возраст (age)	24
Организм (body)	22
Уровень (level)	21
Население (population)	20

As for **mode,** the Russian patient information materials are written to be read by those seeking medical information and advice. These materials may be given to patients by their health providers or sought and found by patients on the internet. In terms of the relationship between the author and the reader, or **tenor,** patient information materials are written by experts in the field for an audience of primarily nonexperts. The **communicative function** of patient education materials is informative and includes conative language. They aim to provide readers with basic medical knowledge on a topic and to persuade them to follow a certain course of action in order to stay or get healthy.

Micro-textual features

At the micro-textual level, we found a tendency to use structures indicating necessity; the most common of which are listed here:

- Verbs in the imperative mood, mostly in the respectful Вы-form, such as помните (remember), старайтесь (try), избегайте (void), следуйте (follow), соблюдайте (adhere to), ограничьте (limit), не забывайте (do not forget), etc.
- Нужно/необходимо + infinitive (one should/must), such as нужно использовать (one should use), необходимо избегать (one should avoid)
- Нельзя + infinitive (one should/must not), such as нельзя хранить (one must not keep)
- Constructions with стоит + infinitive, стоит помнить, не стоит забывать (one must not forget)

As is typical for informative and instructional texts, the tense used is primarily present, with occasional past-tense forms (e.g., for citing research statistics).

The texts in the corpus vary widely in terms of the author's involvement with or detachment from the reader. Below are examples illustrating the two ends of this continuum. Close involvement is shown by using personal pronouns, which also make the text less formal; e.g., in the brochure for children and their parents on healthy eating, informal personal pronouns are used to address children, while the formal is used for their parents:

- Овощи и фрукты содержат витамин С, который укрепляет твой иммунитет (Vegetables and fruit contain vitamin C, which strengthens your immune system)
- Это позволит Вам корректировать его ежедневный рацион (This will allow you to adjust his daily diet)

Detachment is shown through features indicating formality, such as nominalizations, reflexive verbs, verbal adjectives, and the absence of first- and second-person personal pronouns and their forms; e.g., in the brochure about cancer (about 1,030 words), the following was found:

- Numerous nominalizations, especially with the suffix -ени- (возникновение, ограничение, предупреждение, исчезновение, потребление, etc.), which alone accounted for over 50 occurrences of nominalization in the text
- About 20 occurrences of reflexive imperfective verbs (e.g., риск наблюдается [risk is observed])
- Over 20 verbal adjectives, both active (e.g., накапливающийся [accumulating]) and passive (e.g., вызванный [caused by])
- No instances of second-person personal pronouns; the only instance of the pronoun мы (we) is found in a picture captioned Против рака мы сильнее только вместе (Against cancer, we are stronger only when we are together).

While such variations in formality across the corpus of Russian patient education materials can be attributed to the specific audience targeted by each text (in the cases above, children and parents vs. adults), they may also point to the fluidity of this text type in Russian, which is consistent with its relatively recent emergence.

The cohesive patterns we observed are generally consistent with formal instructional writing. In terms of **reference**, over 55 instances of the indicative pronoun это were found, whereas few personal pronouns were used (see discussion above).

Regarding **conjunctions**, they are typical of Russian formal writing. The most frequent conjunctions are *и* (found in all ten texts), что (ten texts), а (ten texts), но (nine texts), если (eight texts), или (eight texts), and чтобы (six texts). The conjunctive relative pronoun который is frequent, with over 40 occurrences. Moreover, lists are employed across all the texts in the corpus, contributing to cohesion and clarity of delivery.

In terms of **lexical cohesion**, Russian patient education materials appear to resort to reiteration via repetition (as seen from the above table of the most frequent lexical items) and collocations, such as воспалительное заболевание (inflammatory illness), уровень холестерина (cholesterol level), вирусный гепатит (viral hepatitis), and медицинская помощь (medical assistance).

It is interesting to note that some Russian patient education materials contain references that are hard to imagine in the U.S. For instance, an otherwise dry brochure on lice prevention and treatment takes on a slightly antique flavor in the following paragraph:

В отличие от целого ряда заболеваний, которые человечество практически победило, педикулез прошел сквозь века. Еще до нашей эры Геродот писал о том, что египетские жрецы так тщательно выбривали головы для того, чтобы обезопасить себя от неприятных насекомых – вшей.

(Unlike a whole range of diseases that humankind has essentially conquered, lice have persisted for centuries. In ancient times, Herodotus wrote that Egyptian priests shaved their heads completely because they wanted to save themselves from nasty insects, such as lice.)

Sample text – Russian patient education materials

Не бояться, а знать!

(профилактика онкологических заболеваний)

В современном мире онкологические заболевания являются одними из главных причин смерти, при этом многие виды рака за последние годы «помолодели» и встречаются у людей возраста 25–35 лет. К сожалению, невозможно полностью защитить себя и своих близких от этой болезни, но существует эффективная профилактика рака, которая позволяет свести риск заболевания к минимуму.

Факторы, приводящие к развитию онкологических заболеваний

…

Ионизирующее излучение. Ионизирующее излучение является канцерогенным для человека и приводит к возникновению большинства злокачественных опухолей. Выявлено, что канцерогенность альфа-лучей выше, чем гамма-лучей.

Заболеваемость злокачественными новообразованиями зависит не только от вида ионизирующего излучения, но и от дозы, времени воздействия ионизирующего излучения, а также от возраста, в котором человек подвергся облучению. После бомбардировки Хиросимы и Нагасаки рост заболеваемости лейкозом достиг пика через восемь лет. Повышение заболеваемости другими опухолевыми заболеваниями произошло значительно позже, и риск его был выше для тех, кто получил облучение в раннем возрасте.

…

Канцерогенные химические вещества. Опухоли, вызываемые канцерогенными веществами, могут быть как местными, так и отдаленными. Возникновение отдельных опухолей связано с циркуляцией химического канцерогена по организму. Многие канцерогенные вещества обладают специфическим действием на определенные органы независимо от путей поступления. Между первым воздействием канцерогенного агента и возникновением опухоли проходит определенный промежуток времени – латентный (скрытый) период. Длительность латентного периода обратно пропорционально дозе канцерогенного агента. С канцерогенными химическими веществами человек контактирует на производстве (профессиональные канцерогены), в быту (загрязнение воздуха, курение).

…

Курение. На основании экспертной оценки установлено, что курение связано с возникновением рака губы, языка, других отделов полости рта, ротоглотки, гортаноглотки, пищевода, поджелудочной железы, гортани, бронхов, легких, мочевого пузыря и почек.

Заболеваемость раком легких, трахеи и бронхов у мужчин в 2–5 раз превышает соответствующий показатель у женщин. Однако в последние годы она стремительно растет и у женщин, что, безусловно, вязано с увеличением потребления табачных изделий женщинами. Риск развития злокачественного новообразования увеличивается пропорционально количеству выкуренных сигарет. Наиболее губительное действие курение оказывает на молодой организм. У лиц, начавших курить в раннем возрасте, отмечается высокий риск возникновения рака легкого, мочевого пузыря, желудка. Не исключено мутагенное влияние табачного дыма на половые клетки плода у курящих беременных женщин. Отказ от курения приведет к снижению заболеваемости злокачественными новообразованиями на 25–30%.

...

Профилактика онкологических заболеваний

Современная медицина различает три вида активной профилактики рака: первичную, вторичную и третичную.

Цель **первичной профилактики** заключается в предотвращении канцерогенеза – процесса появления опухоли. В ходе профилактики необходимо остановить контакт с канцерогенами. Также в первичную профилактику входит повышение иммунитета организма, нормализация образа жизни и питания. Очень важным является отказ от курения и злоупотребления спиртными напитками, физическая активность, здоровое питание.

Вторичная профилактика включает обнаружение и борьбу с предраковыми заболеваниями, выявление, профилактику и лечение рака ранних стадий. К мероприятиям вторичной профилактики относятся: мазки на онкоцитологию (рак шейки матки), профилактические осмотры, выявление групп риска, маммография (рак молочной железы), профилактическое КТ легких у курильщиков, тест на ПСА (рак простаты).

Третичная профилактика рака отвечает за предотвращение повторного возникновения опухоли (рецидив) и появления метастазов у излеченных больных.

Как предупредить рак самостоятельно?

Основными простыми действиями по профилактике рака являются:

- регулярная физическая активность и предупреждение ожирения;
- отказ от курения;
- уменьшение потребления алкогольных напитков;
- ограничение в потреблении копченой и острой пищи;
- питание в профилактике рака также играет существенную роль. Употребляйте больше овощей и фруктов с большим содержанием витамина С (киви, цитрусовые), каротина (помидоры, редька, морковь), а также капусту, чеснок, цельные зерна злаковых культур;
- регулярные осмотры у врача, прохождение дополнительной диспансеризации по месту жительства.

Будьте здоровы!

Против рака мы сильнее только вместе!

Source: Excerpts taken from mari-el.gov.ru/minzdrav/drb/DocLib2/Forms/AllItems. aspx, written by Filonova

Patient education materials   175

Sample Russian patient education text analysis

For the analysis, we selected a text that was mentioned above – a patient education brochure on preventing oncological diseases. The brochure was published in 2015 on the website of the Ministry of Health of the Mari El Republic (the city of Yoshkar-Ola). The author of the text is a medical doctor, N. Filonova. The length of the brochure is approximately 1,030 words and has been excerpted here.

The brochure contains the mandatory rhetorical moves – title, introduction, and main sections. The title of the brochure is Не бояться, а знать (Don't be afraid, but know), with an explanatory subtitle профилактика онкологических заболеваний (prevention of oncological diseases). The text begins with a brief introduction (italicized) discussing how widespread oncological diseases are in today's world. The main part begins with the list of factors that lead to oncological problems, such as incorrect diet, radiation, cancer-causing chemicals, smoking, genetic factors, and age. Following the list is information on prevention, including a list of ways to prevent the disease. The brochure concludes with Будьте здоровы! (Stay healthy!).

In terms of the mode of discourse, the brochure is both informative and conative, since in addition to educating the reader, it calls on readers to pursue a healthy lifestyle to help prevent cancer. The tenor of the discourse is expert-to-nonexpert. As for the field of discourse, the brochure contains medical information on cancer. Below is the list of the most frequently used words and expressions:

Lexical item	Frequency	Lexical item	Frequency
рак	28	злокачественный	10
заболевание/заболеваемость	19	возникновение	10
опухоль	14	канцерогенный	8
профилактика	14	канцероген	8
риск	13	злокачественные опухоли/новообразования	7

At the micro-textual level, as mentioned earlier, the text is rich in nominalizations, reflexive suffixes, and verbal adjectives, which is typical for official writing. The text is written primarily in the present tense, except for the paragraphs referring to the history of nuclear explosions and their consequences. Third-person verb forms prevail. For cohesion, the text resorts to conjunctions (such as и [and] (38), а [but] (8), как [such as] (6), также [as well as] (5), что [that] (4), and который [which] (4), etc.). For lexical cohesion, the author of the text refers to frequent repetitions of the word рак (cancer) along with the hypernyms болезнь (disease), заболевание (illness), and онкологическое заболевание (oncological disease), and the metonyms опухоль (tumor), злокачественная опухоль (malignant tumor), and злокачественное новообразование (malignant formation). In terms of syntax, both simple and complex sentences are used. The average sentence length is 14.3 words.

SPANISH

Different geographies will reflect health concerns particular to their respective populations, which is evident in patient education materials. For example, materials targeted for Latino/a populations reflect higher health risks for certain conditions such as spinal irregularities in childbirth, and so folic acid campaigns are more extensive in Spanish. In general, the language found in patient education materials and elsewhere represents a significant component of medical care. As one of our samples claims, *Nuestro objetivo es informar al paciente y cuidar de él* (Our goal is to keep patients informed and care for them). For this particular corpus, the focus is on the Dominican Republic, a country in the Caribbean. Not surprisingly, tropical diseases figure prominently in the sample.

Ten representative texts from the Dominican Republic, published online between December 2015, and December 2016, were collected in order to analyze their composite features, or rhetorical moves. The corpus contains 12,933 words, for an average of 1,293 words per text. The minimum text length was 550 words, while 3,172 words was the maximum. One particular feature that merits mention is the standardized type/token ratio, which gives us a rough sense of the lexical density. This figure is somewhat low in this text type, suggesting that the language used in patient education materials is in line with the expert-to-nonexpert discourse. The average sentence contains approximately 25 words.

Macro-textual features

At the macro-textual level, the following **rhetorical moves** were found:

1. Title (*Título*; indicates the subject matter, often phrased as a question: e.g., *¿Tiene diabetes?*; *¿Cuál método de planificación le conviene más?*) (found in ten texts)
2. Author or sponsoring agency (*Autor o patrocinador*; usually a physician or medical board) (found in nine texts)
3. Body (*Cuerpo del texto*; explaining the disease or health issue, its causes, symptoms or consequences, treatment, and prevention and management tips) (found in ten texts)
4. Fill-in sections (*Formularios*; health diary, checklists, log sheets for recording readings, names, and phone numbers, and other actionable data) (found in zero texts)
5. Additional information or Soliciting action (*Información adicional*; contact information or links to specialized organizations where the reader can find further information; may include related links or posts) (found in seven texts)
6. Product information leaflets (PILs) (*Folleto informativo*; attached to the back or in an inside pocket) (found in zero texts)

In the corpus, we find the majority of titles phrased as rhetorical questions. In one text, we find the patient information appearing on an official blog, including follow-up links to related articles of interest, a hypertextual extension of the text. In another text, tabs for individual questions can be accessed according to the user's preference. In at least one case, the author's photograph appears before the main text, and virtually all texts include illustrations. In the sample studied, no fill-ins or product information leaflets were included, as the texts were collected from the digital environment.

Let us begin our macro-textual analysis of the text type under consideration with an examination of **register**, which consists of **field** (the realm of experience the text invokes), **tenor** (the relationship between author and audience and their respective roles), and **mode** (whether the text is spoken or written, and its traces of discourse markers of each). Regarding **field**, of the top 40 words in the data, the top nouns in descending order of frequency are as follows: *cirugía* (59), *salud* (46), *virus* (46), *enfermedad* (40), *zika* (40), *casos* (37), *paciente* (noun; 35), *viajeros* (35), *Brasil* (34), *riesgo* (33), *hernia* (32), *ombligo* (31), and *cáncer* (30). These words describe procedures, disease and types of disease, factors related to disease incidence (e.g., risk), goals of treatment (health), places where diseases are endemic, and patients and travelers (those most concerned with the information or most affected by disease exposure). This allows us to define the **field**, or semantic domain, of our corpus as disease screening, prevention, and treatment. The nouns alone make it hard to judge whether the information is for specific purposes, such as medical tourism, but it is clearly concerned with health risks and therapies for a lay population. In terms of **tenor**, the authors of such text types are not always known, but they are presumed to be seeking a therapeutic alliance with the readers. They are generally health promoters or health allies who write factually but with attention to the sensitive nature of health and illness, often in culturally responsive ways.

Impersonalization characterizes the text, in that we are not aware of the writer's standing, persona, or editorial presence. The social distance, while present – the very fact of a medical organization producing information is a claim to authority – is not marked or textualized. Curiously, no forms of address (*tú* or *usted*) appear in the corpus. Identity-marking pronouns, used for the implied author, are invariably plural (the possessive *nuestro/a/os/as* appear, 10 total instances). One text offers advice on elective plastic surgery and is structured as a Q&A that seeks to address both the informational and emotional concerns of the patient. Materials in Spanish are frequently designed to project a sense of "we" rather than accentuating the distance between providers and patients. For example, the Center for Disease Control in the U.S. has a brochure titled *Las latinas somos unas madres extraordinarias* ... (We Latinas are extraordinary mothers) showing Latinas with a young infant on the cover. In other words, the implied author may be characterized as an implicit member of the target readership, reducing the social distance to zero.

Micro-textual features

In some cases, information in patient education materials is intended to 'fine-tune' existing knowledge, for example, by drawing distinctions between similar terms *cirugía reconstructiva* and *cirugía estética*, or even by helping readers unlearn misinformation, which is a **metalinguistic** function that empowers readers to use language to participate responsibly in their own treatment solutions. The use of heading questions has the effect of disarming readers, who are, as we noted, mostly nonexperts, by echoing questions they want answered. The questions are therefore often written from the patient's perspective (*¿Cómo debo prepararme para el MRI?*) The ratio of graphics to text is quite high for the same reason. Motivational language, often using exhortatives, is typical in headings: *¡Ahora es el momento de mantenerse usted y su bebé saludables!* This is a measure of what is called deontic modality, the degree to which the text gives permission, offers advice, or demands action, and in response, the degree to which a reader feels obligated to act. This text type runs the gamut in this metric, although it should be noted that a word such as *debe* (must or should) features 18 times in seven texts (70%) in our data, an indication that at least some prescriptive action is called for. Inasmuch as the tone in the above example is motivational for new mothers, we can also call this an instantiation of the **conative**, or appellative, function of language, in that it seeks to persuade the reader to act.

In regard to **mode**, medical brochures and pamphlets are short texts that provide overviews and are often meant to be read in one sitting. Checklists and numbered tips are common writing strategies for information processability and learning facility. The text type is written but shows oral, interactive elements, such as anticipating questions, as noted above, lower lexical density than texts written for experts, and direct address to patients (note the use of *nosotras* above). The patient education text is not spontaneous or time-bound in the sense that it responds to a single event but rather, in many cases, it is responding to recent, critical, and ongoing health crises, often known as "emerging diseases." These are highly edited texts that use authoritative medical information and dispense entirely with personal opinion or conjecture. They are written with comprehension as a priority.

Patient education materials 179

PRUEBAS DE DETECCIÓN.

❏ ZIKA PCR en Tiempo Real.
❏ Virus ZIKA Ac IgM (ELISA).
❏ Virus ZIKA Ac IgG (ELISA).

❏ Diferenciación Dengue/Chikungunya por PCR. (Prueba opcional para diagnóstico diferencial).

REFERENCIA Laboratorio Clínico como parte de su compromiso con el sector salud, se mantiene incorporando a su menú, pruebas de gran importancia diagnóstica para la clase médica y la comunidad.

Por tal razón pone a disposición las pruebas para la detección de la infección por el virus Zika:

❏ ZIKA PCR en Tiempo Real
❏ Virus ZIKA Ac IgM (ELISA)
❏ Virus ZIKA Ac IgG (ELISA)

❏ Diferenciación Dengue/Chikungunya por PCR
(Prueba opcional para diagnóstico diferencial).

ZIKA, actualización:
La Fiebre de Zika es una infección aguda causada por el virus Zika (VZIK), que pertenece a la familia viral Flaviviridae, género Flavivirus, que agrupa a virus transmitidos por mosquitos del género Aedes como los virus del Dengue, de la Fiebre Amarilla y del Nilo Occidental, entre otros.
En Mayo del 2015 la Organización Panamericana de la Salud (OPS) reportó la transmisión de casos autóctonos confirmados en Brasil y desde esa fecha, son más de 20 los países de Las Américas que han confirmado la transmisión de VZIK.
http://www.cdc.gov/zika/geo/index.html

La OPS advierte que el VZIK se ha "propagado en forma explosiva" en Las Américas, con un pronóstico de tres a cuatro millones de posibles infecciones en la región durante el presente año, y se ha relacionado con numerosos casos de malformaciones congénitas, particularmente la microcefalia.

Sin embargo, se sabe que solo una, de cada cuatro personas infectadas, desarrolla síntomas, no obstante aun asintomáticos tienen el virus en sangre y por tanto pueden trasmitir la infección. (PAHO Alerts Caribbean About Zika Virus Infection).Home Updates & Emerging Issues.
Treinta y cuatro países y territorios hacen reportes de transmisión local vectorial del virus del Zika en la Región de las Américas desde 2015.

El período de incubación: es de 2 a 7 días después de la picadura del mosquito vector. No se ha documentado más de una infección por VZIK en la misma persona, por lo que se asume que la respuesta inmune protege de por vida. Comúnmente la enfermedad dura entre 4 y 7 días. Los reportes de varios países, relacionan la transmisión de Zika con un incremento de pacientes con fiebre leve, conjuntivitis no purulenta y exantema, que puede ser el cuadro que alerte de la transmisión de este virus.

Las características clínicas pueden coincidir con las de Dengue y Chikungunya, que también se transmiten por mosquitos Aedes, por tanto, con esas coincidencias clínicas y epidemiológicas, es imprescindible mantener una estrategia en el diagnóstico. En este sentido la OPS ha propuesto un algoritmo que permita en los países endémicos de Dengue y con circulación

Avalados por el Colegio Americano de Patólogos (CAP)

Sample Spanish patient education text analysis

The text we selected for analysis, *Zika: Pruebas de detección* (Zika: Screening Tests), contains many of the above-mentioned textual features and will be used to demonstrate micro-textual features of patient education materials. The text was taken from *Referencia Laboratorio Clínico* (www.labreferencia.com), an ISO-certified clinical lab. Its length is 1,395 words, with 484 distinct words. The mode is expository, offering a comparative guide to symptomology of commonly confused diseases. The text seeks to inform the public about screening

180 **Text types**

and the risks associated with this vector-borne zoonotic infection. It also aims, through differential diagnosis, to distinguish zika, dengue, and chikungunya, which are frequently confused or misdiagnosed. The tenor of discourse is an expert medical provider or institution to other providers and researchers but also to the lay public. The organization works directly with patients and medical professionals in the country and internationally. The text's lexis includes Anglicisms and a mix of registers, which are given sequentially, suggesting a broad array of health literacy expectations with respect to the targeted readership.

The text, in effect, is written *para la clase médica y la comunidad*, indicating a dual audience profile of both medical professionals and lay readers. The key clue that the text is at least partly for public consumption is the sourcing of some material from English-language research from the Center for Disease Control, which protects the population from "health, safety and security threats" (www.cdc.gov/about/organization/mission.htm). The CDC aims its resources at travelers, policymakers, parents, lab workers, health departments, other specialists, and everyday people alike. The reference to such canonical authorities reflects the high standing of the source text, while also conveying a desire to make the text accessible. The internationalization of health care research has led to multilingual sourcing of this kind (e.g., citing from "PAHO Alerts Caribbean About Zika Virus Infection: Home Updates & Emerging Issues"). Sources from other countries influence terminology both in the authoring and in the translation of such texts. Diagnostic information about this health threat in the Americas would be of interest in other languages due to the high volume of travel to and from the region, to the north of the continent especially, and due to the rapid spread of diseases.

In terms of mood, the text is written primarily in the declarative mood, with the exception of a number of impersonal phrases expressing obligation and followed by subjunctives. As for cohesive devices, the passive is used in place of personal pronouns, while demonstrative references (*esto, eso, esos, estos*) are very few. Cohesion is accomplished through hypernymy (e.g., *caso*, a substantive for more specific references) and synonymy, such as *trastornos, infecciones*, and the like.

Regarding noun phrases and verb phrases (nouns, compound nouns, verbs, verb phrases), there is a notable doubling of terms in some instances, where the lay term and the Greek-derived technical term (*artralgia, mialgia*) are both supplied:

> Dolores en las articulaciones (artralgia) y dolores musculares (mialgias) pueden estar presentes con variada importancia.
> (Joint pain (arthralgia) and muscular pain (myalgia) can occur to varying degrees.)

Elsewhere, we see Latinate terms (maculo, lit. "spot"; prurito, lit. "itching"):

> Rash o erupción en piel (maculo-papular), con prurito (picazón) que puede acompañarse de edemas (hinchzón o inflamación) más frecuentemente en la parte distal de las extremidades superiores e inferiores, muy llamativas en el tronco, sobre todo en la espalda, incluso detrás del cuello y los oídos.

Patient education materials · 181

(Skin rashes or breakouts (maculopapular) with pruritis (itching) can accompany edema (swelling or inflammation) most frequently at the end of the upper and lower extremities, particularly in the torso and primarily on the back, including behind the neck and ears.)

This doubling reflects the proliferation of synonyms or borrowings in the field and addresses the potential register differences among its intended readership. Elsewhere, *exantema* is used as a synonym, without harmonizing it with the other terms used in the text for "rash." This synonymy indicates a conceptually and lexically dense text, requiring a rather high level of medical knowledge for the reader to process it fully – at least relative to texts written exclusively for patients. Many multisyllabic terms, such as *etiopatogenia*, require knowledge of medical roots if not pathology as well. The reader is supplied the Spanish-language abbreviation VZIK for the zika virus.

The types of sentences are compound and complex. Tenses are primarily present tense, past tense, and present perfect tense, both to trace the history of the disease or findings related to it and to lay out treatment procedures, for which the infinitive is also employed as an imperative. The passive voice is used extensively to stand for the medical community as a whole: the "passive voice of authority" (e.g., in the last line, *Se considera que la respuesta inmune protege de por vida*). The use of the passive is notable in the following passage, in which the research conducted, and the alert issued both lack agents (or an agentless third-person plural is used), as in *Las investigaciones consideran*:

> *En el transcurso de le enfermedad se han descrito síndromes neurológicos (meningitis, meningoencefalitis y mielitis), que se describieron en el brote de Polinesia francesa (2013–2104) y en la actual epidemia en la región de Las Américas. Por ello, se reitera la alerta a los servicios de salud ante la posible aparición, con el fin de que puedan tener la adecuada preparación para la identificación y atención apropiada de los casos.*

Notes

1 The patient education brochures corpus is where "your" ranks highest. "You" ranks higher in only two other corpora: that of instruction manuals and that of business letters, where it ranks sixth in both cases.
2 The only other corpus where "can" ranks somewhat closely is that of instruction manuals, where it ranks 18th and also appears in all of the texts in the corpus.
3 Though "may" ranks higher in the business letters corpus at 26, it appears in considerably fewer texts at 64%.
4 The only corpus where "should" ranks higher is that of business letters, where it ranks 48th but appears in only 24% of the texts.
5 The only other corpus where "can be" occurs is that of instruction manuals, where it ranks 66th and occurs in 80% of the texts.
6 The only other corpus where "can cause" is found is that of instruction manuals, where it ranks much lower at 117 and occurs in 40% of the texts.
7 The only other corpus where "it can" appears is that of instruction manuals, where it ranks considerably lower at 112 and is spread across 60% of the texts. "Can help" only occurs in the patient education brochures corpus.

182 Text types

8 The only other corpus where "may be" ranks higher is that of business letters, where it ranks 20th but occurs in a considerably smaller percentage of texts, 15%.
9 Though "if you" ranks higher in the business letters corpus, it is only by two points and it occurs in 20% fewer texts. On the other hand, "if you" ranks the same in both the patient brochures corpus and the instruction manuals corpus, though in the latter corpus it appears in 100% of the manuals (i.e., in 25% more texts).
10 Note that "your healthcare provider" appears only in the selected brochure and one other brochure in the corpus.

6 News reports

The news report or article is a genre of text that presents information about recent happenings or events that may be of interest to a wide variety of people. News articles appear in newspapers or news magazines, which are typically published daily or weekly in print or online and are often routinely read as a means to keep up on current events. Journalistic texts may be divided according to their ostensible level of objectivity:

> *informative genres* (the typical news report, containing factual descriptions of events), *interpretative genres* (such as reportage, in which information is selected, interpreted and narrated by the journalist) and *argumentative genres* (in which the [style of the author], who is often not a journalist, prevails, such as the opinion article or the column).
>
> (Bassnett and Bielsa 2009: 68, emphasis added)

"Hard" news, features, and editorials are three kinds of texts that vary in their use of style, personal opinion, level of detail, and subject matter. News reports or articles, the archetypal variety of informative "straight" news, Fairclough argues (2003: 30–2), derive from a "network" of prior texts – speeches, interviews, or written documents – creating a "genre chain" that allows different kinds of discourse to transform and enter into others. Therefore, lines are often blurred between texts as well as processes, that is, the stages of news gathering, writing, and dissemination, which can include translation, "transediting," and other kinds of rewriting, for example, reworkings of feeds from wire services:

> News agencies produce raw information, but also more elaborate pieces of ready-to-print news reports, analysis and comment, which subscribing news organizations can freely reproduce, fully or in part, introducing any alterations or rewriting they consider necessary, without even acknowledging the source.
>
> (Bassnett and Bielsa 2009: 34)

While the news report may lay claim to impartiality, the ideological stance or attitude of writers can in fact be demonstrated through analysis. News reports, classified as expository text types, may be contrasted usefully with editorials, which belong to the argumentative text type. The two are distinguished by what

Hatim and Mason (2005: 151) call *evaluativeness*, or the managing of a textual orientation to steer a reader to a particular conclusion. Editorials, among other kinds of media discourse, are often studied using critical discourse analysis, which can shed light on unequal power relations embedded in texts and relations between social actors. News reports may have a focus that is local, regional, national, or international. Even print news and online news have important distinctions: online news, for example, has been characterized by its hypertextuality and its "process-rather-than-product nature" (Chovanec 2014: 4).

ENGLISH

The corpus in this chapter includes ten news articles taken from five different newspapers: the *Chicago Tribune*, the *Los Angeles Times*, the *New York Times*, *USA Today*, and the *Washington Post*. The articles include between 604 and 1,500 words and have an average of 1,052 words. They cover mostly national and world news stories in areas such as politics, business, or terrorism. News articles are typically written by journalists, whose duties involve the gathering and editing of news for publication or broadcast in the media.

Macro-textual features

News articles are often drafted with the following six **rhetorical moves**:

1. Headline (usually a concise and catchy statement about the story)
2. Byline (providing date and name of the writer)
3. Relevant picture or video (often accompanied by text)
4. Lead paragraph (containing the who, what, when, where, why, and how of the story)
5. Explanation paragraph (providing further important details or facts that should answer any questions the readers might have about the story as they read it)
6. Additional (least essential) information
7. Final paragraph (kicker or conclusion)

Each of the articles in the corpus includes a headline, the first move. In nine of these ten cases, the headline is written, in order to save space, without auxiliary verbs, articles, conjunctions, or relative pronouns where possible (e.g., "Berlin attack latest in disturbing terror trend," "Outcry at Loyola after students learn athlete accused of rape was enrolled for 3 years," "American voters wanted change in 2016, but will they get the change they wanted?"). A byline, the second move, is also included in each of the articles; however, in one case, the author or authors are not referred to by name, but rather by affiliation with the wire service. As for the third move, there is a picture in eight cases and a video in the remaining two. The pictures and videos are accompanied by text in all but one case: a picture of a tweet, whose inherent text helps summarize the article and thus speaks for itself. In five of these nine cases, the picture or video is accompanied by a sentence or two that summarizes the story or event, while in the remaining four cases, all of which are pictures, the text only describes the picture (i.e., it is a true caption).

In the case of the fourth move, it is interesting to note that the lead paragraph of each of the articles includes the information that is most important or essential to the story, with supporting information of diminishing importance placed in subsequent paragraphs.[1] To capture the essentials of the story, the lead paragraph in all but one case is composed of a single sentence of considerable length and complexity. An explanatory paragraph, the fifth move, is present in all cases but one and varies from one to two sentences in length. The one article that does not contain such a paragraph includes in its place a relevant quote containing further important details about the story. The sixth move, additional information, is

186   Text types

featured in each of the articles in the form of paragraphs of different lengths. Interested readers may appreciate having these paragraphs at their disposal, but editors could, in theory, edit them out for space or other reasons. Finally, the seventh move, or final paragraph, takes the form of a two-sentence summary in one case, whereas in the other nine cases it is a one-to-two-sentence "kicker." "Though *kicker* has long referred to the line above a headline, some have started using the term to describe a surprising or poignant revelation at the end of an article" (Merriam-Webster.com, n.d.). In more than half of these nine cases, the kicker is a direct quote (four cases) or reported speech (one case).

Micro-textual features

Overall, journalistic writing is expository. News articles generally seek to inform or provide information about facts and explain and discuss important circumstances surrounding them. Though the intention in most cases is to do so objectively, a certain ideological positioning may be sustained to varying degrees, since news is also a "social and ideological product" (Kaniklidou 2018: 80). To provide a detailed and correct account of the facts and surrounding circumstances, journalistic writing often exhibits precision and explicitness. Evidence of this may be found in the particularly high frequency of words such as "of," "in," "on," or "at," which rank 2nd (296 instances), 6th (245 instances), 11th (91 instances), and 15th (68 instances), respectively, as the most frequently occurring words in the corpus and which appear in each of the news reports.[2] These prepositions are frequently used to indicate belonging to, relating to, or connection with someone or something (e.g., "Section 12-A of the 1953 act"); location (e.g., "memorial service at the Kaiser Wilhelm Memorial Church," "fist-sized burn on the chest"); positioning (e.g., "his alleged role in the coup attempt," "just in front of a Christmas bazaar"); and time (e.g., "failed military coup in July," "Putin on Wednesday indicated"). Moreover, they appear in several of the most frequent word clusters. Across 90% of the texts, "in the" appeared 60 times, "of the" appeared 53 times, "at the" appeared 23 times, and "on the" appeared 18 times. Across 70% of the texts, "in a" appeared 16 times and "at a" appeared 14 times. Though not as frequent as the previous preposition examples, "including," a preposition used to introduce examples that are part of a particular group or amount, ranks the highest in frequency (as 41st with 16 appearances) and is the most widespread (at 90%) in the news articles corpora than in any of the English corpora in this volume. An example with "including" is "...policy changes to stop the practices, including improving transparency of prices, preventing..." Translators of journalism who are under tight deadlines risk inappropriately calquing these prepositional uses or others if they do not pay close attention to the reoccurring descriptive structures in news reports.

Further evidence of the level of detail or description that goes into news reporting may be found in "that," "who," and "which," whose frequency ratio in the news reports corpus ranks significantly higher (as the 8th, 26th, and 34th most frequently occurring words, respectively) than their frequency ratio in any of the other English-language corpora used in the present volume. "That" and "who" also occur in all of the corpus texts, which is not always the case in the other corpora, and "which" appears in 90% of the texts, which is the highest percentage in any of the corpora. "That" occurs significantly more frequently than "who" and "which" in the corpus because it is used as a pronoun in different circumstances (e.g., "That's what was missing," "to concoct a framework that could replicate"), conjunction (e.g., "Weaver said that she was"), or adjective (e.g., "throughout that lengthy span"), whereas "who" and "which" are wh-words, whose use in the corpus ranges from interrogative pronouns (e.g., "it's not clear which path Trump will take," "the insults flung every which way," "in a national debate over who and what was to blame") to relative pronouns (e.g., "working class Americans who are often recipients of such aid," "an attack which killed"). In addition, "that" may be employed in lieu of "who" in restrictive clauses (e.g., "a nationwide hunt for an unidentified attacker that the Islamic State announced had answered the terror group's call to"). Nevertheless, "that" is especially frequent in news reports due to its many appearances as a conjunction and as a pronoun, namely a relative pronoun. Take, for example, the only cluster in the corpus in which "that" appears: "that the." It is the sixth most frequent cluster, appearing in 22 instances and in 70% of the texts. It features "that" as a conjunction (e.g., "given that the managers were," "Bild reported that the suspect was") in 16 instances and as a relative pronoun (e.g., "an indication that the," "suggestions that the") in the remaining 6 instances. However, in the vast majority of instances in the corpus, the wh-words ("which" and "who") are used to introduce relative clauses. Especially when "that," "who," and "which" are used as relative pronouns, translators should take care to analyze whether they are being used to introduce restrictive or nonrestrictive clauses, as different languages may have different pronoun usage and punctuation rules depending on the type of clause. Moreover, translators must be prepared to handle the complex syntax that the use of these words as both relative pronouns and conjunctions entails, as both communicate descriptive information in sentential form as subordinate clauses. Finally, the translator must notice when "that" is omitted as either a conjunction (e.g., "Daveed Gartenstein-Ross … said many Islamic State followers are incorrectly labeled lone wolves") or a relative pronoun (e.g., "the words the gunman uttered"), which may occur frequently depending on the context, venue, or particular writer and which may not be possible to replicate in the target language. For example, the cluster "said the" – which appears in 10 instances and in half of the texts in the corpus – occurs in phrases where the conjunction "that" is omitted, except in one instance ("39% of voters said the ability to create change").

A final area of interest is how often verbs are used in the past tense, which is necessary when reporting on events or happenings. The two most frequent past-tense verbs in the news reports corpus are "said" and "was," which, respectively, rank as the 10th and 12th most frequent words, occur in 98 and 87 instances, and are spread across all the news reports. In the other English corpora reported on in this volume, neither these two verbs nor any others in the past tense are anywhere near as frequent or widespread, if they occur at all. An example in which both of these past tenses are put to use is "Since it was in financial distress, Mr. Schuette said, Flint was not permitted to." Translators working on different past-tense verbs will have to pay close attention to how they translate them into languages with more than a single temporal distinction for the past, depending on the context. Moreover, they will need to be ready to handle different syntactic placements of phrases with "said," which may not always be at the beginning of the sentence (e.g., "The paper said he had been"), but rather toward the middle (see the example above) or the end (e.g., "'This is no sweeping judgment of refugees,' he said.").

Text types

Sample text – English news report

Moscow doubts killer of ambassador in Turkey was a lone wolf

December 21, 2016, 6:47 AM | MOSCOW

The spokesman for President Vladimir Putin on Wednesday indicated Moscow doesn't believe the gunman who killed Russia's ambassador to Turkey acted on his own, but refused to explain the reasons for the suspicion.

"We shouldn't rush with any theories before the investigators establish who was behind the assassination of our ambassador," said spokesman Dmitry Peskov, who offered no suggestions about who those people might be.

The ambassador, Andrei Karlov, was killed Monday evening in front of stunned onlookers at a photo exhibition in Ankara. The assassin, Mevlut Mert Altintas of Ankara's riot police squad, was killed in a police operation.

[Picture Caption: Karlov started his diplomatic career in 1976, after graduating from the Moscow State Institute of International Relations. (December 19, 2016)]

On Tuesday, Russia flew a team of 18 investigators and foreign ministry officials to Turkey to take part in the probe. Their plane returned with Karlov's body and his family. Russian officials and Turkish Foreign Minister Mevlut Cavusoglu who was visiting Moscow met the family at the Vnukovo airport late Tuesday.

Ankara has not made public any theories. But a senior Turkish government official, who spoke Tuesday on condition of anonymity because he was not authorized to release details to the press, said it was unlikely Altintas acted alone.

The official said the killing had all the marks of being "fully professional, not a one-man action."

Independent Turkish security analyst Abdullah Agar said Altintas' behavior and the manner in which he carried out the attack "gives the impression that he received training that was much more than riot police training."

…

Turkey has been rife with speculation about Altintas' motive and possible links.

On Tuesday evening, a Turkish Foreign Ministry official said Cavusoglu spoke with U.S. Secretary of State John Kerry by phone and provided information on the assailant.

The official, speaking on condition of anonymity in line with government rules, said Cavusoglu also told Kerry that both Turkey and Russia "know" that a movement led by U.S.-based Muslim cleric Fethullah Gulen was behind the attack.

Turkey has accused Gulen of orchestrating a failed military coup in July aimed at toppling President Recep Tayyip Erdogan and accuses the cleric of wanting to destabilize Turkey. It is pressing the United States to extradite Gulen to Turkey to stand trial for his alleged role in the coup attempt. Gulen has denied the accusations.

During the phone call, Kerry raised concerns about "some of the rhetoric coming out of Turkey with respect to American involvement or support, tacit or otherwise, for this unspeakable assassination yesterday because of the presence of Mr. Gulen here in the United States," Kerry's spokesman John Kirby said. "It's a ludicrous claim, absolutely false," Kirby said.

"We need to let the investigators do their job and we need to let the facts and the evidence take them where it is before we jump to conclusions," Kirby added.

> Much of Turkey's media, both broadcast and print, has reported claims that the gunman had links to the Gulen movement, including reports of Gulen literature being found in his home, and of him having studied at a Gulen-run school.
> Associated Press
> Copyright 2016, Chicago Tribune
>
> Source: www.chicagotribune.com/nation-world/ct-russia-ambassador-assassinated-turkey-20161221-story.html

Sample English news article analysis

A news report from the *Chicago Tribune* has been selected to further analyze and contextualize the features discussed above. As indicated in the byline, or second move, the article was published on December 21, 2016, and written by the anonymous "Tribune news services • Contact Reporter" (i.e., this is the exception mentioned in the section above that does not refer to the journalist or journalists by name). The article's headline, the first move, reads "Moscow doubts killer of ambassador in Turkey was a lone wolf." The headline attempts to both summarize the story in a single concise sentence and draw attention to it with the metaphor "lone wolf," which could have been replaced with a descriptive-but-less-catchy phrase like "acted alone." To save space, the headline is also stripped of a conjunction and a couple of definite articles. That is, it could be rewritten in another context as "Moscow doubts whether the killer of the ambassador in Turkey was a lone wolf." The headline also uses the single-word metonym "Moscow" to refer to Russia's government, which serves the dual function of saving words and provoking the reader's attention in order to interpret its implied meaning.

The third move in this article is a photograph of soldiers carrying the victim's casket in the company of his widow. The text accompanying the picture – "A gunman shot and killed Russia's ambassador to Turkey, Andrei Karlov, as he gave a speech at a photo exhibition in Ankara on December 19, 2016" – clearly summarizes key details and does not attempt to describe what is occurring in the photograph or who is in it. The combination of this photo and the accompanying text offer enough support for the reader to quickly determine what exactly took place after having read the headline and before proceeding to the lead paragraph (the fourth move): "The spokesman for President Vladimir Putin on Wednesday indicated Moscow doesn't believe the gunman who killed Russia's ambassador to Turkey acted on his own, but refused to explain the reasons for the suspicion." The lead directly relates back to the headline and adds supporting details, pointing out that no reasons for believing that the killer was a lone wolf were provided by Russian officials. Like the headline, the lead omits the conjunction "that" after "indicated" and "believe." Finally, to capture the essence of the story in a single sentence, the lead resorts to certain sentential complexity, making use of the relative pronoun "who," which, as pointed out in the previous section, is of high frequency in the corpus, and employing the adversative conjunction "but," which in this case connects another clause at the end of the sentence.

The explanatory paragraph, the fifth move, comprises the following two sentences: "The ambassador, Andrei Karlov, was killed Monday evening in front of

Text types

stunned onlookers at a photo exhibition in Ankara. The assassin, Mevlut Mert Altintas of Ankara's riot police squad, was killed in a police operation." This provides yet more information about the actual assassination (i.e., the news-worthy event) and in this way especially complements the text accompanying the photo in the third move. This time, the gunman is identified by name and with some background history, and we find out that he himself was also killed, in addition to the fact that the assassination of the Russian ambassador occurred before "stunned onlookers." This explanatory paragraph also echoes in 4 different instances the high corpus frequency of prepositions of place, time, or belonging and the level of detail that they afford the writer: "in front of stunned onlookers," "at a photo exhibition," "started his diplomatic career in 1976" "killed in a police operation," "the assassin, ... of Ankara's riot police squad," or "claims that the gunman had links to the Gulen movement, including reports of Gulen literature being found in his home, and of him having studied at a Gulen-run school."

The sixth move, additional paragraphs, can be found in this article more or less to the same extent as in the others. Here is the paragraph immediately fol-lowing the explanatory paragraph:

> On Tuesday, Russia flew a team of 18 investigators and foreign ministry officials to Turkey to take part in the probe. Their plane returned with Kar-lov's body and his family. Russian officials and Turkish Foreign Minister Mevlut Cavusoglu who was visiting Moscow met the family at the Vnukovo airport late Tuesday.

In this additional paragraph, more details are revealed, but they are not essential to get the gist of the story. This stretch of text begins with a preposition of time, *on*, whereas, for example, the sentence in the third move above ended with this preposition in the phrase "on December 19, 2016." It also nearly ends with the frequent preposition of place "at," which indicates where the parties met. Finally, this paragraph uses the relative pronoun "who" to introduce how the Turkish Foreign Minister could meet with the victim's family when they landed in Russia.

The final paragraph (i.e., the seventh and final move) can be described more as a kicker than as a summary. This single-sentence final paragraph ends the article by revealing how the Turkish press has already arrived at the "surpris-ing" conclusion that the shooter was involved with the Gulen movement – a movement led by U.S.-based Muslim cleric Fethullah Gulen – whereas from reading the lead paragraph, we learn that Russia refused to release why they believed the gunman was not a lone wolf. Moreover, the last few paragraphs preceding the kicker indicate that the U.S. feels that conclusions should not be made before investigators have finished gathering evidence. The single-sentence kicker is of considerable length and complexity in large part due to its ending with the long participial phrase beginning with "including," which adds consid-erable end-weight with its additional information.

To conclude this analysis of a sample news report from the corpus, it should be pointed out that in all the examples of moves discussed, the past tense is used (e.g., "was," "indicated," "killed," "returned," "met," "had"). It goes without saying that this verb tense is the norm when narrating past events. In particular, the use of reported speech is characteristic of the news. For instance, "said," one of the two most frequent past-tense verbs in the corpus, appears in the selected article 7 times, in addition to other reported speech verbs such as "shouted" or "added." These speech verbs can be found in the beginning, middle, or end of the sentence. For example, "said" comes after the quote it refers to in the following sentence: "'We shouldn't rush with any theories...,' said spokesman Dmitry Peskov, who offered no suggestions..." In this case as well, "said" precedes the subject, which is also characteristic of news reports and makes it possible to seamlessly attach a "who" clause at the end of the sentence. Finally, in the case of "said," in all cases where the conjunction "that" could have been used, it was not. Take for example the following: "Agar said the words the gunman uttered in Arabic were from a passage frequently cited by Jihadists." This sample article, therefore, can be said to exemplify many of the rhetorical moves characteristic of this genre in English.

192 **Text types**

CHINESE

News reports provide information about current events and are closely associated with newspapers. In China, most newspapers are state-owned. In order to understand the current state of Chinese-language news reports, a corpus of 13 texts was collected from 13 different sources, all published in the last 5 years so as to document current textual conventions. The sources were all state-owned national newspapers from the Chinese mainland, such as *People's Daily*, *Jiefang Daily*, and *Economic Information Daily*. The average length of a Chinese news report in this corpus is 1,158 characters. A quick look at the 13 corpus news reports shows that the minimum length is around 914 characters and the maximum is around 1,495, depending on the complexity of the news report.

Macro-textual features

At the macro-textual level, we begin by isolating the conventional features or **rhetorical moves** of Chinese-language news reports:

1. Headline (标题)
2. Byline (署名)
3. Lead paragraph (引入段)
4. Explanatory paragraph (解释说明段)
5. Additional Information (附加信息)

Of these, moves one, three, and four are found in all 13 texts, while moves two and five appear in almost all of the texts. Other optional moves that may be found in a news report are 副标题 (subheadline, or *deck* in journalistic speak, found in seven texts) and 结论 (conclusion, found in ten texts).

Register consists of three aspects: the **field** of discourse, that is to say, what the text is about; the **mode** of discourse, or how the language is used; and the **tenor** of discourse, which refers to the relationship between the author and the audience.

As far as the **field** is concerned, one way to find out about the topic a text describes and the discipline a given text type refers to is by looking at its terminology and, more generally, its lexical items. A look at the word frequency makes clear that the terminology and lexical items used in this text type relate to news. Some high-frequency words that illustrate this relationship are shown in the following table.

High-frequency lexical items	Frequency	High-frequency lexical items	Frequency
月 (month)	45	效率 (efficiency)	19
年 (year)	43	发展 (development)	18
日 (day)	37	问题 (problem)	18
旅游 (tourism)	28	农业 (agriculture)	18
经济 (economy)	23	股票 (stock)	18

(Continued)

(Continued)

High-frequency lexical items	Frequency	High-frequency lexical items	Frequency
中国 (China)	23	表示 (said)	17
美联储 (Federal Reserve)	21	记者 (reporter)	17
农民 (farmer)	19	调整 (adjustment)	17
加息 (increase interest rates)	21	全国 (whole country, nationwide)	17
农村 (rural area)	19		

The lexical items in this table cover a wide range of fields, including tourism, economy, agriculture, and so on, as the theme of news reports varies considerably.

As for the **mode** of discourse, news reports are usually texts written for readers who want to learn quickly about major events that have happened in the last day or recent developments in public affairs. To fulfill that need, news reports typically describe events logically and concisely. News reports are usually formal written texts; their style differs from spoken language, which is less formal and contains pauses or fillers.

Finally, the **tenor** of discourse tells us about the kind of relationship between the author and the audience, which can be equal or unequal (i.e., expert-to-expert or expert-to-nonexpert). When it comes to news reports, the author is usually among a small number of people with first-hand information, and the audience must rely on the information they provide. Indeed, since the author is the owner of the information, the audience may only see the tip of the iceberg or the so-called "truth" as presented by the author. That is to say, the audience's access to information is more limited than that of the author.

The purpose of a news report is to convey facts about major events to the audience, so its **communicative function** is informative. However, news reports may also contain conative features in that they rely on emotion and selected facts to "manipulate" the audience and engage their feelings accordingly.

Micro-textual features

In terms of **mood**, the corpus data point to a preference for the indicative in news reports. The pretense of objectivity in news reports is reflected in the fact that pronouns like 我 (I) and 你 (you) are rarely used.

As regards **cohesive devices**, the use of **reference** is rare in the Chinese news reports. Personal pronouns, including 我 (I), 你 (you), and 自己 (oneself), occur 6 times, in 5 of the 13 news reports. Among demonstrative reference devices, 这, the Chinese equivalent of "this," appears in many words or phrases in the corpus, such as 这种 (this kind), 这个 (this one), 这些 (these, the plural form of *this*), and这些年 (over these years). The news reports corpus also makes use of additive, causal, and temporal **conjunctions**, as evidenced in the conjunction frequency table.

Conjunctions	Frequency
和 (and)	47
并 (and, also)	24
而 (and, but)	15
但 (but)	12
同时 (meanwhile)	12
以及 (and)	11
或 (or)	8
由于 (because)	4
如果 (if)	4
只有 (only)	3
此外 (moreover)	3
虽然 (although)	2

Generally speaking, the use of conjunctions is less frequent in Chinese than in English. **Lexical cohesion** is arguably the most common form of cohesion in Chinese.

In the news reports corpus, there is a high occurrence of **nouns,** as shown in the noun frequency table.

High-frequency nouns	Frequency	High-frequency nouns	Frequency
景区 (scenic spot)	37	股票 (stock)	18
旅游 (tourism)	28	记者 (journalist)	17
爱心 (love)	25	全国 (whole country)	17
经济 (economy)	23	调整 (adjustment)	17
中国 (China)	23	证券 (securities)	15
农民 (farmer)	19	书屋 (bookstore)	15
农村 (rural area)	19	儿童 (children)	15
效率 (efficiency)	19	工作 (work)	15
发展 (development)	18	市场 (market)	15
问题 (problem)	18	融资 (financing)	15

The nouns used in the news reports can be generally classified into four domains: (1) nouns describing identities, such as 记者 (journalist), 农民 (farmer), 儿童 (children), etc.; (2) nouns describing places, such as 中国 (China), 农村 (rural area), 全国 (whole country), etc.; (3) nouns describing abstract concepts, such as 旅游 (tourism), 爱心 (love), 经济 (economy), etc.; and (4) nouns describing concrete concepts, such as 景区 (scenic spot), 书屋 (bookstore), etc.

In addition to nouns, another word category that is highly recurring in this genre is **verbs,** as evidenced in the verb frequency table.

Verbs	Frequency
加息 (increase interest rates)	21
表示 (claim, say)	17
进行 (proceed)	15
可能 (may)	14
创新 (innovate)	13
相关 (relate)	12
完善 (improve)	12

Sample text – Chinese news report

"河长制" 让江苏水质明显改善

　　作者：本报记者 郑晋鸣 本报通讯员 徐航 《光明日报》（ 2016年12月04日 02版 ）
　　"签订责任状当上'河长'后，河流的大事小情都与我密不可分。"指着杨屯河，江苏徐州安国镇镇长陈全更向记者细数河长的工作。2013年，徐州市施行"河长制"管护制度，由党政主要负责人任"河长"，直接对河流生态负责。就拿陈全更来说，他是安国镇19条河道的"河长"，除了一月2次定期巡河，在入村调研与检查中，陈全更也一定会去分管的河道看一看，只要发现河道里有漂浮物、违章建筑等，就会立刻着手解决。

"河长制" 是江苏在全国首创的一种河流生态保护新举措，它起源于一次史无前例的生态危机。2007年，太湖蓝藻暴发震惊全国，事件发生后，无锡从上到下痛定思痛，决心重整水生态，可这绝非易事：河道淤塞、生活污水、企业偷排污水……难题繁多，无从下手。面对这种情况，无锡首创"河长制"，让党政负责人担任起市内79条河流的"头"。1年后，这些河流的考核断面达标率就从53.2%提高到71.1%。尝到甜头的无锡人于2008年9月在全市推行"河长制"管理模式，标志着"河长制"的真正建立。4年后，江苏在全省推广这种模式。如今，"河长制"已走向全国，全国8个省市全面推行"河长制"，16个省区市在部分区域推行"河长制"。

说起"河长制"的好处，徐州张集镇镇长兼"河长"许东向记者讲了一个故事：2015年5月8日凌晨，一辆运送化学制剂的罐装车在徐宿高速古黄河服务区发生泄漏，3吨化学制剂随雨水流入镇上运料河的支渠。一位河道管护员发现异常后，立刻上报许东。许东随即赶赴现场，并调度大型机械，将支河两端打上土堰，防止污染水体外流。同时联系化工专家，确定专业处置方案，立即抽调人员及机械进行处理，制止了污染物的扩散。"放在以前，遇上这种情况，河道管护员须层层上报，事件处置会很慢，后果严重。"许东说，现在"一把手"任"河长　"，第一时间了解情况，可直接调配人员、机械与资金。"节省时间，就是在挽救生态。"

水污染的问题出在水里，根却在岸上。各种非法排放与乱丢乱倒，是水生态的最大敌人。针对这种情况，"河长"担起了监督检查的重任。江苏的每个社区与村委都会公布"河长"的联系方式，遇上乱排乱放的情况，百姓知道该拨谁的电话。"以前看到有人破坏水环境不知道向谁举报，现在有了'河长'，就知道该向谁反映，出了问题该是谁的责任了。"在南京市建邺区，市民张德贵对记者说。

近年来，江苏 "河长制"出台"升级版"，目标由原来的"水质达标"升级为"生态安全、供水安全、防洪安全"为一体的河道全面长效管护。目前全江苏727条骨干河道全都设有"河长"，河流水质得到明显改善。变"多头治水"为"一龙治水"，江苏以此造就了碧波清流。

Key: repetition – highlighted in gray

196 **Text types**

Sample Chinese news article analysis

All of the above-mentioned macro-textual characteristics are exemplified in the sample news report that will be discussed. The news report was from *Guangming Daily*, a national Chinese-language daily newspaper. The sample news report is about a river chief system (a river chief is responsible for the management and protection of waterways). The news report in question includes every conventional move: headline, deck, or subheadline, byline, lead paragraph, explanation paragraph, additional information, and conclusion. The text has 1,098 characters, a bit shorter than the average of 1,158 characters. The mode of discourse is informative, and the tenor of discourse points to an expert-to-nonexpert relationship, as well as an expert-to-expert one. The communicative function is informative, for the reasons outlined above.

As far as the micro-textual features are concerned, the indicative mood and the present or past tense are used to tell the reader what happened or to present recent developments. In terms of cohesive devices, reference and substitution are nearly absent in the sample text; only 我 (I) occurs, and only once. Conjunctions are also rarely used, with 并 (and) and 同时 (meanwhile) each occurring once. When it comes to repetition (see the words highlighted in the sample text), a large proportion falls into the categories of nouns describing identities, places, and abstract concepts. The table at the end of the analysis indicates how often these repeated phrases appeared. The sample news report is characterized mainly by repeated nouns, which is characteristic of a news report. Nouns generally emphasize the theme of the report.

Phrase	Frequency
河长制 (river chief system)	11
河长 (river chief)	9
江苏 (Jiangsu province)	8
河道 (river course)	8
生态 (ecology)	7
河流 (river)	6
许东 (Xu Dong, personal name)	4
全国 (whole country)	4
记者 (journalist)	4

FRENCH

The French news report (*article de presse*) can trace its origin to the advent of the printing press, though the latter nineteenth century heralded the concurrent publication of several new genres, including the modern *reportage*. While the communicative goals of genres such as the *analyse*, *éditorial*, *enquête*, and *interview* vary, the structure and language of news reports share several features. To better understand these features, we will focus on what is perhaps the most representative genre, the *reportage*, of which a corpus of 12 texts published by 12 separate sources within the last 5 years was compiled. The mean text type length is 1,032 words, with the shortest text having 219 words while the longest has 1,613 words. Differences in size are primarily due to depth of coverage. News articles written to keep readers up-to-date on current events are shorter, while reports on the causes of complex political or economic issues tend to be longer.

Macro-textual features

We begin our analysis at the macro-textual level by outlining the following mandatory **rhetorical moves**:

1. Headline (*Titre*)
2. Deck, or subheadline (*Chapeau*)
3. Byline (*Signature*)
4. Lead paragraph (*Accroche*)
5. Body (*Corps de l'article*)
6. Conclusion (*Chute*)

The *titre*, or headline, of a news report is a concise, catchy statement (*attaque*), generally following the title of the column (*rubrique*) of the newspaper of publication. It precedes the deck (*chapeau*, also known as the *chapô* or *sous-titre*), a supplemental headline that summarizes the report while enticing the audience to continue reading. A byline (*signature*) containing the name of an author or publisher and a date or time generally follows. The lead paragraph (*accroche*) develops the who, what, when, where, why, and how alluded to in the *chapeau*. Some texts also contain an image or photo with a descriptive caption (*légende*) near the beginning. The body of a report (*corps de l'article*) is the longest, most detailed section of the text. It may contain several optional headings (*intertitres*) as well as extracts (*exergues*) of important information presented in a larger font size. Some news reports contain boxed text (*encadrés*) with information helpful for understanding the topic of a report. The genre ends with a conclusion (*chute*), typically composed of a single paragraph.

To describe the **register** of French news reports, we will look at three aspects: **field**, **mode**, and **tenor**. It is clear based on the table that a news report's **field** of discourse, or what the report is about, covers the news being reported on, which varies from text to text and corresponds to topics of current events. The predominance of lexical items pertaining to current events is illustrated in the table, where only two of the most frequent words are found in three or more texts, and four out of seven items are exclusively found in reports on climate change.

High-frequency lexical item	Frequency	No. of texts	Domain
pays	187	9	General
émissions	72	2	
carbon	68	1	
climatique	50	2	Climate change
réduction	42	2	
accord	48	2	
réfugiés	44	3	Immigration, climate change

An examination of **mode** – how a text will be used – reveals that news reports are meant to be read and read quickly. The most salient aspects of the text are located at the top, followed by a progressively more detailed account as the report continues.

The **tenor** of discourse, which characterizes the relationship between a news report's author and audience, points to a hybrid nonexpert-to-nonexpert/expert-to-nonexpert relationship. Reported speech (often indicated by words like *selon*), taking the form of paraphrase and direct quotes, signals the journalist's role as an informed writer who synthesizes, explains, and contextualizes the claims and opinions of experts for an educated audience.

A French news report's **communicative function** is informative, as indicated by its clear, factual, and objective language, as well as the structured, general-to-specific manner in which the genre's rhetorical moves are laid out. However, the *titre* and *chapeau* fulfill a conative function of language, since they are written to catch the eye of potential readers.

Micro-textual features

At the micro-textual level, the mood of news reports is largely indicative. Specific indicative tenses express mood when recounting events in the past (*passé composé* and *imparfait*), present (*présent*), and future (*futur*). The present indicative tense is the most common structure used to express mood in our corpus.

An analysis of **cohesive devices** shows that both personal and demonstrative referencing occur at a similar frequency in this genre. The adjectives *ce*, *cet*, *cette*, and *ces* regularly qualify a range of nouns. Both personal and possessive pronouns are used as personal referents, the most frequent of which are the third-person *il/ils* and *sa/son/ses*.

Repetition is most apparent in the genre's macrostructure, where events are reported in increasing detail in the headline, deck (i.e., subheadline), and the body of an article. However, authors do not generally use the same words each time an event is repeated and may establish cohesion using synonyms to avoid undesirable repetition as a matter of style (e.g., by alternating between *Etats membres* and *pays membres* in reference to members of the European Union), as French stylistics exhibits a comparatively low level of tolerance for repetition. Authors make texts concise by replacing long, otherwise repetitive strings with acronyms (e.g., by using *OCDE* after the first instance of *Organisation de coopération et de développement économiques*). Finally, a typical form of ellipsis involves abbreviating formal designations following an initial reference (e.g., *Accord de Paris* becomes *Accord*).

The extremely high frequency and wide distribution of *pays* in our corpus alludes to this word's importance in French news reports. As mentioned above, one notable feature of the genre is its variable subject matter. While this may render the lexical aspect of news reports somewhat unpredictable, we are able to discern the way in which function words collocate with some content words. To determine how a frequent word like *pays* relates to its surrounding text, we looked at the strength[3] with which it collocates with function words and discovered that the prepositions *des* and *de* as well as the article *les* are strong collocates that accompany a variety of noun phrases.

Most frequent noun	Strong function-word collocates	Collocations in context
	des (pays)	des pays africains, des pays en développement, des pays européens
pays	les (pays)	les pays d'accueil, les pays développés, les pays situés en première ligne
	pays (de)	pays de l'Union européenne, pays de l'Est, pays de transit

Sample text – French news report

Crise des migrants : ce qu'a fait l'Europe, un an après la mort d'Aylan Kurdi

Plusieurs mesures européennes ont été prises depuis la publication de la photographie de la dépouille de ce jeune Syrien retrouvé mort noyé sur une plage turque le 2 septembre 2015, symbole de la crise migratoire.
LE MONDE | 02.09.2016 à 19h59 • Mis à jour le 02.09.2016 à 22h46

…

Ce drame migratoire particulièrement médiatisé a poussé ***les pays de*** l'Union européenne (UE) à prendre un certain nombre de décisions sur l'accueil des réfugiés tout au long de l'année.

…

L'Allemagne ouvre ses portes aux réfugiés
Face à des flux migratoires jamais vus depuis la seconde guerre mondiale, Berlin décide, dans la semaine suivant la mort d'Aylan Kurdi, d'assouplir ses règles d'accueil pour les ressortissants syriens, renonçant à les renvoyer vers leur point d'entrée en Europe.

…

Après s'être longtemps opposé à l'instauration de quotas de réfugiés à se répartir entre les Etats de l'Union européenne – un procédé soutenu par la chancelière allemande Angela Merkel –, le gouvernement français accepte, finalement, face à l'urgence de la situation, la proposition de la Commission européenne. Le 7 septembre 2015, François Hollande confirme que la France accueillera 24 000 nouveaux réfugiés sur deux ans, conformément au plan de répartition élaboré par la Commission européenne.

…

200 Text types

En juillet 2016, le premier ministre hongrois, Viktor Orban, a annoncé la tenue d'un référendum le 2 octobre sur le plan européen de répartition des réfugiés dans *les pays* membres de l'Union européenne.

...

Budapest estime que ces quotas obligatoires de répartition des migrants, adoptés en septembre dernier par les Vingt-Huit, violent sa souveraineté.

...

Le 13 septembre 2015, face à un flux de migrants trop important, l'Allemagne se voit débordée et prend la décision de rétablir provisoirement les contrôles à la frontière. Un geste fort dans l'espace Schengen où la libre circulation à l'intérieur des frontières *des vingt-six pays* est un des piliers du projet européen.

...

La décision de Berlin fait des émules, surtout dans *les pays de l'Est* qui rejetaient l'idée allemande de quotas de répartition des réfugiés. L'Autriche, la République tchèque et la Slovaquie, *pays de transit*, rétablissent les contrôles frontaliers, alors que la Hongrie et la Slovénie, principaux *pays d'entrée* dans la zone Schengen, décident d'ériger des clôtures de barbelés.

...

Et aujourd'hui ?
La majeure partie du flux passe désormais par l'Italie, en plus de la Grèce. Sur les 272 000 migrants et réfugiés ayant traversé la Méditerranée depuis janvier, plus de 112 000 Ø ont rejoint la péninsule italienne et 106 461 Ø la Grèce, tandis que 3 165 Ø ont péri en mer, selon un bilan de l'Organisation internationale pour les migrations (OIM) publié à la fin d'août.

...

Par ailleurs, le plan temporaire de « relocalisation » de réfugiés depuis la Grèce et l'Italie vers *d'autres pays de* l'UE, censé incarner la solidarité européenne, s'est embourbé. Selon la Commission européenne, en un an, il a concerné moins de 4 500 personnes, sur 160 000 Ø prévues d'ici septembre 2017.

Key: synonymy – highlighted in gray; personal referents – underline; noun phrases cited in analysis – bold and italics

Source: www.lemonde.fr/international/article/2016/09/02/crise-de-migrants-ce-qu -a-fait-l-europe-un-an-apres-la-mort-d-aylan-kurdi_4991868_3210.html

Sample French news article analysis

For an improved understanding of how the foregoing features appear in French news reports, we will analyze a *reportage* titled *Crise des migrants : ce qu'a fait l'Europe, un an après la mort d'Aylan Kurdi*, which was published in 2016 on the website of the French daily newspaper *Le Monde*. This publication is one of the most widely read French newspapers in the world and contains reports on an assortment of current events.

At the macro-textual level, the news report includes all mandatory rhetorical moves in the following order: *titre, chapeau, signature, accroche, corps de l'article,* and *chute*. It also contains two non-mandatory moves: a descriptive caption (*légende*) following a photograph and several bold-faced headings (*intertitres*). The length of this news report falls just above the average for this genre, at 1,224 words.

The field of discourse corresponds to the effects of an immigration crisis on the European Union, a common news topic at the time of publication. The tenor of discourse points to a hybrid nonexpert-to-nonexpert/expert-to-nonexpert relationship, marked by the author's reporting of immigration data, summary of the views of policy-making bodies, and explanation of related humanitarian and political implications. Several typical lexical items identified in the larger corpus appear in the report, including *réfugiés* (14), *pays* (10), and *accord* (2). The informative nature of the report is clear based on the highly structured general-to-specific manner in which the story develops, though the conative headline – *Crise des migrants : ce qu'a fait l'Europe, un an après la mort d'Aylan Kurdi* – grabs the reader's attention with its reference to a shocking event that received global coverage.

In terms of micro-textual features, the mood of this news report is primarily indicative, with the *présent* being the tense used most frequently to describe reported events, followed by the *passé composé* and *imparfait*.

In terms of cohesive devices, personal referents outnumber demonstrative referents in this news report. Among these, *ses* is the most frequent and is found in sentences such as the following, where it appears alongside the demonstrative adjective *cet*: *Mais **cet** accord est aujourd'hui compromis, la Turquie menaçant de revenir dessus si elle n'obtient pas de Bruxelles l'exemption de visas pour **ses** citoyens dans l'espace Schengen.*

Synonymy results in cohesion where members of the European Union are referred to interchangeably as *Etats de l'Union européenne*, *Etats membres*, *pays de l'Union européenne*, *pays membres de l'Union européenne*, and *les Vingt-Huit*. Countries, political unions, and organizations also receive multiple designations. For example, France is referred to as *l'Hexagone*, the European Union as *l'UE*, and *Organisation internationale pour les migrations* as OIM. Words depicting refugees, immigration policies, and geographical areas are likewise varied. Ellipsis (indicated as Ø) is employed to avoid the repetition of nouns modified by numeric values (*En 2015, 354 618 **migrants** avaient traversé la Méditerranée, dont 234 357 Ø avaient rejoint la Grèce et 116 147 Ø l'Italie*).

As is the case with the larger corpus, the noun *pays* is a lexical item of interest in this news report. Below, it can be seen in noun phrases alongside all three of its strong function-word collocates (*de*, *des*, and *les*).

---

*L'Autriche, la République tchèque et la Slovaquie, **pays de** transit, rétablissent les contrôles frontaliers, alors que la Hongrie et la Slovénie, principaux **pays d'**entrée dans la zone Schengen, décident d'ériger des clôtures de barbelés.*

*Un geste fort dans l'espace Schengen où la libre circulation à l'intérieur des frontières **des** vingt-six **pays** est un des piliers du projet européen.*

*En juillet 2016, le premier ministre hongrois, Viktor Orban, a annoncé la tenue d'un référendum le 2 octobre sur le plan européen de répartition des réfugiés dans **les pays** membres de l'Union européenne.*

Finally, hyperlinks to related reports published by *Le Monde* function as an intertextual cohesive device tying various parts of the newspaper together and further informing readers.

202   Text types

GERMAN

As Christiane Nord (1988) points out, newspaper articles commonly serve as a genre of choice as material for use in translation practice courses, particularly when teaching aspects of text analysis. While there may not currently be a high demand for newspaper article translation, this may soon change as news content enters an era of synchronous and asynchronous multilanguage text production. This trend is already evident when examining online content for several German-language newspapers, such as *Die Zeit*.[4] To better understand how German-language news articles are structured, a corpus of 30 full-length articles, which appeared in regional newspapers throughout Germany in November, 2016, was compiled.

Macro-textual features

The following **rhetorical moves** are commonplace, appearing in at least 20 of the 30 texts:

1. Headline (*Überschrift*)
2. Deck, or subheadline (*Unterüberschrift*)
3. Author (*Autor*)
4. Date of publication (*Erscheinungsdatum*)
5. Location (*Ortangabe*)
6. Lead (addressing 5 W's; *Einleitung*)
7. Body containing specific details (*Hauptteil*)

A subheadline appears in 21 of the 30 texts, suggesting that the headline itself often carries the most weight in attracting the reader's attention. We see a strong preference for directness in German-language headlines: 28 out of the 30 contain nothing in the way of wordplay or other literary devices. The same holds true for 17 of the 21 subheadlines. In this particular corpus, the author's full first and last names appear in 22 out of 30 and in abbreviated form (first and last initial) in the remaining eight texts. A city is mentioned at the outset of the article in 21 of the 30 texts. Interestingly, 17 of the texts also provide a concrete time (hours:minutes), which may be explained by the fact that these articles appeared online and may have been updated as events unfolded. Generally speaking, the rhetorical moves typical in German-language news articles are similar in type and scope to English-language news articles, except, perhaps, for the absence of wordplay.

The articles selected for inclusion in the corpus all fell within a range of 300–600 words. This does not suggest a prototypical text length of German-language news articles as many potential articles for inclusion were deliberately filtered out due to not falling within this range. What does seem to be at least somewhat typical is average sentence length (in words). The mean sentence length in this corpus is 15 words, and 27 out of the 30 texts are between 12–18 words in length.

All of the texts in this corpus contain regional news, and we see quite a bit of lexical variation when attempting to establish a given field of discourse. In depicting potential cross-regional topics of interest, the table of nouns represents lexical items that occur at least 5 times and appear in at least 5 of the 30 articles.

German lexical item	English equivalent	Frequency	No. of texts
Euro	Euro(s)	16	7
Polizei	police	9	5
CDU	CDU (Christian Democratic Union of Germany)	8	7
Unternehmen	company	8	5
Zukunft	future	6	5
Möglichkeit	possibility	5	5

This list points to central themes of finance, politics, and potentially crime, as one would expect in English-language news articles as well. The **mode** of discourse is largely expository, with a strong focus on delivering objective, factual information. Corpus wordlist data show that evaluative language is kept to a minimum. Two subtle exceptions are the evaluative words *nur* (only) and *offenbar* (apparently), which appear 23 and 8 times respectively. The use of the subjunctive for reported speech keeps the register non-evaluative. This is a deliberate lexicogrammatical strategy in German-language news articles because, in this fashion, anything that might come across as subjective or evaluative is readily attached to a speaker and directed away from the article writer.

In terms of **tenor**, the sender of German news articles is listed by name and the audience consists of anonymous readers. We see no instances of author self-reference or direct address to the readership. Since the corpus analyzed here consists of regional newspapers, the audience is potentially narrower in scope than the readership of national newspapers. Interestingly, as we have seen in other genres in this volume, potential region-specific content that might not be readily understood by readers external to the given region tends to be explicated in the vast majority of cases. Proper nouns, such as politicians, geographical locations, and buildings, tend to be explicated in the source language. This tendency further highlights the low-context nature of German-language texts. From a globalization perspective, it is interesting to note that Anglicism usage is sporadic, with only three lexical items (*job*, *fair*, and *shot*) appearing with a collective frequency of seven in the entire 12,431-word corpus. Perhaps this trend is specific to regional German-language newspapers and we would see more widespread usage of Anglicisms in national newspapers.

Micro-textual features

At the micro-textual level, as we might expect, the vast majority of sentences are declarative, further highlighting an expository function. A quick examination of the first sentence in each of the 30 articles reveals the following breakdown: 25 simple, 0 compound, 5 compound-complex. The prevalence of simple sentences indicates the importance of getting information across clearly and succinctly at the beginning of the article. At the syntactic level, we see

Text types

patterned usage of intra-sentential punctuation in the first sentences of 10 of the 30 texts (four dashes, five colons, and one semicolon), which likely contributes to the relatively long average sentence length of 15 words. In contrast, English-language news articles might feature end punctuation in passages where these intra-sentential punctuation marks appear, resulting in shorter sentences.

A marked feature of German-language news articles is the use of temporal and spatial deictic expressions, as seen in the table of examples taken from the corpus.

German deictic expression	English translation	Frequency
hier	here	21
dann	then	16
jetzt	now	14
dort	there	13
nun	now	13
derzeit	at the moment	5
künftig	in the future	4
gestern	yesterday	3
inzwischen	in the meantime	3
demnächst	soon	2
derweil	meanwhile	2
heute	today	2
morgen	tomorrow	1
später	later	1

These deictic expressions can be regarded as presuppositions, and their comprehensibility is based on knowledge shared by both the text sender and receiver. Indirect quotes, making use of the subjunctive for reported speech, seem to be preferred over direct quotes. We see a total of 15 direct quotes in seven different texts in our corpus. When direct quotes are used, the speaker tag precedes the quote, which itself immediately follows a colon for 11 of the 15 quotes, as seen in the following example:

German direct quote
Und auch die Stadt Elterlein gefällt der Amerikanerin: "Es ist klein und hübsch und deutsch."

English translation
The American also likes the city of Elterlein. "It's small, beautiful, and German," she says.

Micro-textual analysis of article headlines and subheadlines reveals some interesting trends. Eighteen of the thirty headlines consist of noun phrases, highlighting a linguistic preference for nominalized constructs in the German language. In the context of German to English translation, such headings might call for denominalization in the form of a transposed shift to verb constructs. When verb phrases do appear in headings, we see the active voice used 8 times and the passive voice 4 times. When examining lexical relations between headings and subheadings, we see 10 instances of synonymy, as seen in the examples from the corpus given here, and only one instance of lexical recurrence. Lexical variation emerges as a preferred cohesive device in shaping the reader's situational model.

German headline/subheadline containing synonymy
DDR-Vergnügungspark
Für die Berliner Spreepark *gibt es immer noch kein Konzept*
English translation
DDR amusement park
Still no plans for Berlin's Spreepark

German headline/subheadline containing synonymy
Saar-Uni forscht mit Stanford
Institut für IT-Sicherheit Cispa der Saar-Uni kooperiert mit kalifornischer Elite-Uni
English translation
Saarland University to conduct research with Stanford
Center for IT-Security CISPA at Saarland University to cooperate with Californian elite university

---

On the whole, both headlines and subheadlines are relatively explicit. We see only sporadic use of ellipsis (5 instances in all), involving the omission of articles (3 times) and forms of the verbs *haben* (to have) and *sein* (to be).

Sample text – German news report

Bienendieb in Menden

Mann stiehlt Honig aus Bienenkasten
Sankt Augustin. Eine Streuobstwiese in Menden war erneut Ziel von Kriminellen. Eine Überwachungsanlage filmte jedoch den Mann, der die Bienenkästen öffnete und den Honig entwendete.

Von Thomas Heinemann, 03.11.2016

Erneut hat ein mutmaßlicher Bienen- und Honigdieb auf der Streuobstwiese nahe der Marienstraße in Menden zugeschlagen. In der Nacht zu Dienstag kam ein Mann auf das Privatgrundstück und entwendete den Honig. Die beiden von vorherigen Raubzügen geschwächten Bienenvölker von Imkerin Nicole Saturna werden diesen erneuten Eingriff vermutlich nicht überleben, sagt Diplom-Biologe Andreas Fey, Eigentümer und Projektleiter der Streuobstwiese.

Nach der Halloweennacht, in der auch die Streuobstwiese nicht von Vandalismus verschont geblieben war, hatte Fey nach dem Rechten sehen wollen. Nicht die kleinen Sachbeschädigungen weckten seine Neugierde: „An einem Bienenkasten stand ganz leicht der Deckel hoch. Erst dadurch ist mir aufgefallen, dass etwas nicht stimmte." Fey, der nach den letzten Raubzügen technisch aufgerüstet hatte, inspizierte eine versteckt installierte Spezialkamera. Diesmal hatte die Falle zugeschnappt: Um 3.17 Uhr am Dienstagmorgen filmte die mit unsichtbaren Infrarotscheinwerfern ausgerüstete Kamera einen Mann.

206 Text types

> **Taschenlampe im Mund**
>
> Mit Taschenlampen im Mund und in der rechten Hand – das zeigen die mittlerweile der Polizei übergebenen Videoaufnahmen ganz deutlich – öffnete der Mann die Bienenkästen, suchte die letzten vollen Waben, bürstete verbliebene Bienen mit einem Kamm zur Seite und entwendete den Honig. Danach räumte er die Waben zurück, als ob nichts geschehen sei.
>
> „Es ist wirklich eine Dreistigkeit", sagte Fey, der bereits eine stattliche Belohnung für Hinweise aus der Bevölkerung ausgelobt hatte, am Mittwochnachmittag: „Mir ist sehr daran gelegen, den mutmaßlichen Dieb schnellstmöglich dingfest zu machen. "Der nun gefilmte Mann sei nicht zum ersten Mal in die Fotofalle getappt.
>
> Bereits am 26. Oktober sei er auf dem Privatgrundstück gewesen, offenbar um die Kästen auszukundschaften. Fey vermutet einen Profi: „Die Handgriffe waren sehr routiniert und schnell. Er wusste genau, was er da tat." Erneut war die Polizei vor Ort, um eine Strafanzeige aufzunehmen. Polizeisprecher Burkhard Rick bestätigte auf Nachfrage, dass Ermittlungen gegen unbekannt eingeleitet wurden.
>
> Key: intra-sentential punctuation – highlighted in gray; temporal deictic expressions – underline
>
> *Source: www.general-anzeiger-bonn.de/region/sieg-und-rhein/sankt-augustin /Mann-stiehlt-Honig-aus-Bienenkasten-article3396044.html*

Sample German news article analysis

The sample news article appeared online in the November 3 edition of the *General-Anzeiger*, a daily regional newspaper in Bonn. The topic is the theft of honey from a private beehive. This article exhibits all seven of the prototypical moves found in German-language news articles. The headline consists of a noun phrase *Bienendieb in Menden* (bee thief in Menden), and we see synonymy used as a cohesive device to link the headline, *Bienendieb*, with the subheadline, *Mann* (man). The subheadline also contains ellipsis in that the article before *Mann* is dropped. The headline and subheadline highlight the informative nature of this expository genre: who, what, and where are already revealed.

With 15.22 words on average per sentence, this article is right at the mean sentence length of 15 that is prototypical for this genre. All of the sentences are declarative. This article is interspersed with intra-sentential punctuation in the form of dashes and colons (highlighted in gray). Several of these instances represent situations where end punctuation might be preferred when translating into English, as illustrated in the following example:

German passage with intra-sentential punctuation
"Es ist wirklich eine Dreistigkeit," sagte Fey, der bereits eine stattliche Belohnung für Hinweise aus der Bevölkerung ausgelobt hatte, am Mittwochnachmittag: "Mir ist sehr daran gelegen, den mutmaßlichen Dieb schnellstmöglich dingfest zu machen."
English translation
"It's really takes a lot of nerve," says Fey, who, on Wednesday afternoon, already offered a handsome reward to anyone who is forthcoming with information. "For me, it's very important that the suspected thief is arrested as soon as possible."

We see 4 instances of direct quotes and 2 instances of reported speech that make use of the subjunctive. In this particular text, two of the direct quotes are immediately preceded by a colon, which seems common when it comes to quote structuring. As is prototypical for the genre, we see deliberate utilization of temporal deictic expressions, as seen in the table of temporal deictic expressions. Comprehending these references relies on extratextual knowledge.

German temporal deictic expression	English translation
In der Nacht zu Dienstag	In the night to Tuesday
Dienstagmorgen	Tuesday morning
Dannach	afterwards
Mittwochnachmittag	Wednesday afternoon

208 **Text types**

RUSSIAN

Translators of journalism know that news reports are written differently in different locales, with textual features dependent not only on linguistic and cultural traditions but also on current trends related to the Russian political climate. To describe the textual features of contemporary Russian news reports, we gathered a corpus of ten articles, all published in 2016 and ranging from 800 to 1,400 words in length. The articles were collected from five online news sources popular among Russian readers (www.kp.ru, www.vz.ru, tass.com, www.gazeta.ru, and www.russian.rt.com).

Macro-textual features

At the macro-textual level, we identified the following mandatory **rhetorical moves**:

1. Headline (заголовок) (subheadline: двойной заголовок)
2. Byline with the author(s), date, and in several instances, time (подпись автора)
3. Lead paragraph (лид, or ведущий/главный абзац)
4. Explanatory paragraph (пояснительный абзац)
5. Additional information (дополнительная информация)
6. Conclusion (концовка)

We found no major optional rhetorical moves in the corpus. Interestingly, none of the articles in the corpus had a deck, or subheadline. Most articles contained numerous hyperlinks and photos related to their topics, both of which may prove worthwhile to study. Headlines are another fruitful research topic, since they are meant to persuade the audience to read the article.

In terms of register, the **field** of discourse in news reports varies depending on the topic of the article. Based on the list of the most frequent nouns, it appears that socio-economic and political issues current to the year 2016 are the primary field of the corpus (see table). To illustrate how widespread the issues are across the corpus, we also provide the statistics on the number of texts where each lexical item occurs. As one can see, most of the nouns are names of geographical locations (with Russia being the most frequent), while some are politicians' names (Putin, Poroshenko) and several others are words common to formal political discourse (время, вопрос, сторона, рубль, деятельность, договор). Consistent with the text type, the abbreviation ТАСС occurs in five texts. ТАСС is the central Russian news agency, and the abbreviation stands for Телеграфное агентство Советского Союза (Telegraph Agency of the Soviet Union). The mention of острова (islands), along with Japan and its capital Tokyo, indicates the long-lasting Kuril Islands dispute between Russia and Japan. One article discusses problems encountered by disabled people in Russia, hence the frequency of the word инвалид. It is worth noting that if we had selected corpus texts from, let's say, entertainment news, our results would have been different.

High-frequency nouns	Frequency	No. of texts
Россия, РФ (Russia, Russian Federation)	46	6
Остров (island)	29	2
Время (time)	27	6
Латвия (Latvia)	26	1
Москва (Moscow)	26	7
Сторона (side, in a conflict, negotiation, etc.)	24	6
Япония (Japan)	22	2
Инвалид (a disabled person)	22	1
Рубль (ruble)	17	2
Вопрос (issue, question)	17	3
Путин (Putin)	16	3
Крым (the Crimea)	16	2
Территория (territory)	16	4
Токио (Tokyo)	14	2
Порошенко (Poroshenko)	11	2
США (U.S.A.)	11	4
Украина (Ukraine)	11	3
ТАСС (the central state news agency in Russia)	8	5

In terms of the **mode** of discourse, news reports are written to be read by their audience. As for **tenor**, news reports target a large general audience but are also read by experts, so the relationship between the author and the reader in news reports is both expert-to-nonexpert and expert-to-expert.

The **communicative** function of news reports is primarily informative; however, since mass media today hold significant influence over its readership, news reports also use conative language, and at times are emotive or expressive texts.

Micro-textual features

At the micro-textual level, news reports display features of a higher **register**. Offord refers to the style of journalism as *публицистический*, noting that its function is not only to inform but also to persuade (Offord 2005:16). When the balance between informative and conative/persuasive functions is shifted to the former, the register is close to academic writing and official or business styles, which are often impersonal and factual (Offord 2005: 59).

The prevalence of a higher register is supported by the following grammatical and syntactical characteristics found in the corpus:

1. Active participles, e.g., соответствующий (4), желающий (4), ведущий (3), командующий (3), сидящий (3), входящий (2), выступающий (1), живущий (1), идущий (1), борющийся (1), принадлежащий (1)
2. Passive participles and their short forms, e.g., насыщенный (3), пропущенный (1), обусловленный (1), просроченный (1), обозначенный (1)

210 **Text types**

3. Verbal adverbs, e.g., не теряя, защищая, возглавляя, меняя, осуществляя, позволяя, выступая (each occurring once)
4. Reflexive verbs with -ся, which add to the impersonal nature of news reports, e.g., оказаться (5), считаться (2), полагаться (1), подразумеваться (1)
5. The verb являться used as copula (4 occurrences)
6. Reporting verbs, which indicate complex sentence structures, in the present tense, e.g., считает (5), полагает (1), заявляет (1), сетует (1), or past tense, e.g., сказал (10), заявил (9), пояснил (7), отметил (5), рассказал (4), подытожил (1). Most of the past-tense reporting verbs listed here occur in masculine form (25), while seven occur in the feminine and four in the plural.

In terms of sentence structure, news reports contain both simple and complex or compound sentences. This makes sense given the communicative function of targeting a broad audience and the importance of readability.

As noted above, news reports contain vocabulary pertaining to the fields of politics and economics. A closer look at the frequency list reveals the use of abbreviations, compound words, official or formal clichés, and some catchphrases. The catchphrases contribute to the news reports' conative and emotive functions.

- Abbreviations: США (11), РФ (10), ПЗЗ (10), ТАСС (8), СССР (7), НКО (4), КПРФ (1)
- Compound words: Госдума (12), законопроект (5), Росимущество (4), межконтинентальный (2), замглавы (1)
- Official or formal clichés: по словам, по информации, как известно, с одной стороны – с другой стороны, по предотвращению, стало известно, нормализация отношений
- Catchphrases: ставят наглое условие

The use of the simple comparative form *маневреннее* (more maneuverable) points to the formal nature of this text type.

As for cohesive devices, we found the following tendencies. The **reference** devices, such as его (36 across nine texts), ее (9 across seven texts), их (15 across seven texts), appeared with great frequency, as did the reflexive possessive pronoun свой in all its forms (35 times). **Conjunctive** devices, such as и, (то) что, но, если (то), хотя, поскольку, чтобы, когда, etc., were also common. The conjunctive relative pronoun который was used over 60 times.

Regarding **lexical cohesion, reiteration,** and **collocations** appear to be frequent, as shown in the word frequency discussion above. Reiteration is achieved via repetition (see frequency table), synonymy or near-synonymy (Россия – РФ), hyponymy (страна – Россия), and meronymy (Япония – Токио). Collocations are consistent with the text type semantic field, e.g., мирный договор (peace treaty, 6 occurrences in two texts), категорически против (decidedly against, 3 occurrences in two texts), and совместная экономическая деятельность (joint economic activity, 3 occurrences in one text).

News reports   211

> **Sample text – Russian news report**
>
> В споре за курилы токио склоняется к важной уступке москве
>
> Текст: Андрей Резчиков
>
> **Появились признаки того, что Япония согласна начать «совместную эконо-мическую деятельность» на Курильской гряде. Это может означать, что Токио делает большой шаг навстречу Москве – японскому бизнесу придется заключать сделки в российской юрисдикции, тем самым признавая россий-ский контроль над островами. Россия наверняка сможет продемонстрировать Японии ряд встречных жестов.**
>
> Во вторник появились признаки того, что Япония склоняется к новой важной уступке в споре за Курильские острова. Москва дала понять, что Токио согласен начать наконец «совместную экономическую деятельность» на островах. Правда, сами японцы пока этого не подтверждают.
>
> «Прорабатывается вариант совместного заявления президента и премьер-минис-тра. Речь идет об активной совместной хозяйственной деятельности на четырех островах», – заявил помощник президента Юрий Ушаков, уточнив, что подразуме-вается доступ компаний к работе, инвестиции. По его словам, к подписанию по итогам переговоров готовятся 10 межгосударственных документов, до 15 коммерческих. Также около 50 контрактов могут подписать представители деловых кругов, пишет с его слов РИА «Новости».
>
> Сам Путин заявил во вторник, что Россия хочет полной нормализации отношений и считает отсутствие мирного договора между странами анахронизмом. Однако «совместная экономическая деятельность» на островах возможна только после решения политических вопросов. «Что касается островов Южной Курильской гряды, то здесь разные варианты возможны; мы готовы рассмотреть совместную работу и на одном острове, и на двух, и на трех, и на четырех», – сказал президент. «Важны условия, но условия должны быть максимально либеральными», – считает глава государства.
>
> Президент отметил, что журналист сразу же поставил вопрос о том, будто бы хозяйственная деятельность может развиваться на островах, суверенитет над котор-ыми будет осуществлять Япония. «Но если будет это так с первого шага, то тогда второго шага не нужно, потому что вопрос можно считать закрытым. Мы так не договаривались», – сказал Путин.
>
> Key: grammatical cohesive links – highlighted in gray
>
> *Source: www.vz.ru/politics/2016/12/13/847251.html*

Sample Russian news article analysis

For our analysis, we chose a news report on the situation with the Kuril Islands. The report was published in December of 2016 on the popular Russian news website https://vz.ru. Moscow and Tokyo have a long-standing dispute over ownership of the Kuril Islands, and this article discusses the possibilities of col-laborative economic activity on the islands. The article is about 830 words in length. For the analysis, we chose an excerpt of about 280 words. The article contains all six obligatory rhetorical moves (headline (В споре за Курилы Токио склоняется к важной уступке Москве [On the Issue of Kurils, Tokyo is Inclined to Yield to Moscow]), byline with the name of the author (Andrei Rezchikov), date and time of publication (December 13, 2016, 22:15), lead paragraph (in bold), explanation paragraph, additional information and conclusion. No optional rhetorical moves were noted (which is true for the entire corpus).

As for the communicative function, the article is primarily informative. According to Offord's classification of Russian genres (2005), this article belongs to the style of political journalism (reporting). The tenor of discourse appears to be expert-to-nonexpert, although the article may also be read by experts. The mode is written – this article is written to be read. The field of discourse is concerned with politics, namely, with the dispute over the Kuril Islands between the governments of Russia and Japan. To refer to the governments, the article frequently uses the names of the two capitals – Moscow and Tokyo. In the excerpt, the following frequently used words represent the field of discourse: Курилы/Курильские острова (the Kuril Islands) – 4 times; Япония (Japan) – 4 times, Токио (Tokyo) – 3 times, Москва (Moscow) – 3 times, Путин (Putin) – 3 times, Россия (Russia) – 2 times, российский (Russian) – 2 times, спор (argument) – 2 times. The political nature of the discourse is represented in such vocabulary units as большой шаг (a big step), японский бизнес (Japanese business), российская юрисдикция (Russian jurisdiction), российский контроль (Russian control), встречный жест (action in return), важная уступка (important concession), совместное заявление (collaborative statement), межгосударственный документ (document concluded between governments), etc. This choice of vocabulary indicates official style of writing.

At the micro-textual level, the excerpt contains characteristics of the official Russian style – in this case, political journalism. Grammar-wise, we find multiple instances of reflexive verbs (10 instances) and short adjectives, such as согласен (agrees, 2), возможен (is possible, 2), and готов (ready, 1), which is typical of this register. Two verbal adverbs are found (уточнив [having clarified] and признавая [admitting]). As noted above, vocabulary is formal and related to politics, and official phrases are frequent: дать понять (to let someone know), прорабатывается вариант (a possibility is being considered), and пишет с его слов (writes based on his words). The passage also displays hedging; e.g., появились признаки того, что (there are signs that; it appears that), это может означать (this may mean), пока (so far), and могут подписать (may sign), etc. From the standpoint of syntax, the text contains many complex sentences, such as quotations, sentences with verbal adverbs, and sentences connected with conjunctions, primarily что (that, 9 instances). The multiple quotations of officials also contain complex sentences. The quotations are introduced with verbs such as заявлять (to declare), сказать (to say), and считать (to believe). Some quotations carry a more informal tone, such as мы так не договаривались (this was not our deal).

From the standpoint of cohesion, we find many conjunctions, primarily что (that, 9) and и (and, 6). The verbal adverbs also represent non-conjunctive links between parts of sentences. The lead paragraph contains a dash, which in this case is used to express a cohesive link between clauses. The grammatical cohesive links are highlighted in gray. In terms of lexical cohesion, actual and synonymous repetition is used. For example, the Japanese government is referred to as Токио (Tokyo), Япония (Japan), and японцы (Japanese people). No instances of lexical omission are noted.

SPANISH

Spanish-language news has journalistic traditions that combine features of informative texts with those of persuasive ones, such as the *publirreportaje* (advertorial). Readers of news in Spanish, especially in Spain, have seen the rise of "reportaged news," including the use of interpretive and creative exposition, the pursuit of a human-interest angle, and even the introduction of literary techniques (Parratt 2011: 144).

Datasets available in Spanish news corpora, such as CREA, for example, illustrate such features as contrastive adverb use and collocational profiles (see Butler 2008, for example). Our interest here will be to survey ten Peruvian news reports of various orientations, which were collected and surveyed with a view of identifying their general textual features. The texts were published during a 12-month period (December 2015 to December 2016), and their subject matter largely treats matters of regional and national economics, such as agrarian reform, illegal crops, bureaucracy, overregulation, and the modernization of trains to Machu Picchu. Environment, education, science, law, and health are the principle intersecting themes of the Peruvian news collected. In terms of text type size the dataset for Peruvian news reports runs to 13,184 running words for the ten texts, for an average of approximately 1,300 words. The range of lengths, from 755 words to 2,797, reflects the type of reporting, the depth of coverage, the quality of the newspaper, and even the location of the article in the publication.

Macro-textual features

The following are the rhetorical moves associated with this genre:

1. Headline (*Título*; catches the reader's attention; found in ten texts)
2. Deck, or subheadline (*Subtítulo*; may offer detail, a subtheme, or angle on the story; found in three texts)
3. Byline (*Citas bibliográficas*; the crediting of who wrote the text, the date, and the writer's affiliation and/or biography; found in ten texts)
4. Lead (or Lede) (*Párrafo introductorio*; contains who, what, when, where, why, and how; found in eight texts)
5. Body (*Cuerpo del texto*; development of the article; present in ten texts)
6. Conclusion (*Conclusión*; implications of the news item; present in six texts)
7. Attribution (*Documentación*; documentation of sources, for example in footnotes; found in two texts)
8. Photographs, captions, and quotations (*Fotos, leyendas y citas*; evidential support for the veracity of the claims; found in six texts)

The most attention-grabbing of these moves are the headline (importantly, often written by an editor), the subhead, and the lead. Only the headline, byline, and body appear in all ten texts. However, "body" is a flexible category – development is a subjective dimension of writing – so there may be as few as seven moves. The lead paragraph in this text type is written as a broad-based pyramid containing the most salient features of a story and its "angle," or perspective.

214   **Text types**

Then, following the inverted pyramid image, the multiple paragraphs of the body delve deeper into specifics. In cases where the writer wishes to bring attention to an idea by starting with a single case, thus personalizing the story, the lead comes later, after an inductive exploration of a person involved. For example, text #3, analyzed below, introduces linguists in training before arriving at the need for the profession and an available training program. If these anecdotal leads are included in our count, our total moves from eight to ten. In an editorial from the data, a quotation from the body – a "callout" – is isolated to function as a kind of subheading or epigraph. This is an optional stylistic choice in some publications; the lead in such cases would more properly be a *thesis* and may or may not appear in the first paragraph(s). Bylines may avoid the author's name altogether, as in summations of a presidential address.

Photographs, captions, and quotations are largely optional text-typological features. Editorial articles, for example, are more likely to include a photograph of the author. Even though quotations are used in a preponderance of the textual evidence, they are not necessarily obligatory or even quasi-obligatory; they are used as one kind of authoritative evidence, expert opinion, or in some cases as layperson or nonexpert opinion, a weaker kind of evidence. Where photographs are present, captions are invariably used as well. Some photographs are stock images that do little but illustrate the article's theme. One text out of the ten uses graphs to present information visually and schematically; the same text also uses photographs.

A conclusion in the traditional sense of a summation of an argument or its logical ramifications – for example, a succinct conclusion in one of the texts – constitutes a call for action and thus exerts an exhortative function. Another concludes with an unmistakable reiteration of the argument and a restatement of the unsolved problem posed at the outset of the article. Conclusions are present only diffusely or indirectly in this corpus. In one case, for example, a text ends with an anecdote of sorts and a quotation; such an ending does not constitute a conclusion in the sense we are using here, as a rhetorical shift. Section headings within the news report appear in at least one case, another optional feature. In text #4, the lead and the subheading are arguably the same, or indistinguishable.

Register, or the context, consists, in Hallidayan terms, of three elements: **field**, **mode**, and **tenor**. The first of these categories, **field**, proved elusive in this corpus. High-frequency nouns from the top 100 lexemes reveal a bewildering array of subjects (in descending order of frequency): *animales, país, universidad, gobierno, ley, años, China, comercio, región, fauna, tráfico, empresas, estado, servicios, sistema, Trump, carne, fines, Iquitos, Machu Picchu, economía*. In this sense, the field of news reports from a corpus analysis perspective can be said to depend upon the particular texts chosen, and a sample so small cannot yield statistically meaningful trends in subject matter (though in terms of structural and rhetorical data, it can be quite significant). From the lexis and other cues, we can determine that the articles address the common or nonexpert reader more than the specialized or expert one. The **mode** of discourse is highly determinant of textual meanings, such as its cohesive relations (Halliday 1989: 26), which we will consider below. Finally, **tenor**, where news reporting is concerned, reflects the distance or closeness of interactants in a communicative situation. Tenor also, significantly, refers to how much the writer seeks to influence the reader, for example, by using language that displays attitude or affect, thus exercising unequal power (González-Rodríguez 2006: 157). We find such tenor variables in the following examples: *trumpear*, a neologism in one of the texts, *Trumpear a Trump*, which means roughly "to beat Trump at his own game." Another tenor variable is the coverage of certain politicized issues, such as *abuso* (abuse, 3 instances in one text) and *corrupción* (corruption, 9 instances in three texts). Corruption and abuse are value judgments until a conviction occurs, and they are usually discussed publicly by those who wish them remedied. Our sample text below links interpreter-translators to human rights protection, a clearly ideological subject position. Similarly, we also noticed the appearance of terms in the wordlist such as *justicia* (8 occurrences in three texts) and even more telling, *justicia social* (5 in two texts), a politically polarizing term with roots in Catholicism and nineteenth-century progressivism, which refers to rectifying unequal distribution of wealth and power in society. Its mere presence in a text is enough to strongly suggest activist sympathies.

To determine the texts' **communicative functions**, we consider the obvious informative function but also the degree to which the texts, individually and collectively, show interpretive commentary, influence, and opinion. The news report maps onto a range of functions and is not reducible to a mere transfer of information.

Micro-textual features

Cohesive devices, such as reference, substitution, ellipsis, and lexical cohesion, are found in statistically significant numbers. The frequency of *pero* (41 in eight texts or 80%) and [*sin*] *embargo* (15 in five texts or 50%) suggests a systematic balance between various sides of an issue, characteristic of this text type.

In terms of tense, the headlines are written in the present tense, which can create ambiguity around whether the action is present continuous (something happening now), present habitual (a standing truth) or present historical (a true past tense). We will see a particular case in our sample text analysis below.

One particular use of a noun phrase form is noteworthy. The corpus evinces the use of the article with the country name, *El Perú* (23 instances in six of ten texts), a practice by no means universal among Spanish speakers.

Sample text – Spanish news report

Traductores e intérpretes: una reserva para los derechos humanos

Por: Luis Andrade Ciudad

Yoly Soto Palomino trabaja en el Ministerio del Ambiente como asistente de la Dirección General de Educación, Cultura y Ciudadanía Ambiental. Ella aprendió el quechua cuando era niña por compartir la vida con sus abuelos en Ayacucho, en un tiempo en que saber quechua era un conocimiento silencioso, en un entorno marcado por violencias de toda índole, pero, en especial, contra todo lo que sonara a indígena. En esa época, Yoly Soto no podía adivinar que, tiempo después, un punto a su favor en su postulación a un puesto de trabajo en el Estado sería hablar esta lengua originaria, en su variedad *chanka* o ayacuchana.

Desde su ingreso al sector público hace más de una década, a pesar de que sus jefes valoraban este punto en su currículum, Yoly Soto tuvo pocas ocasiones para poner en práctica el conocimiento del idioma. Hace unos meses, ella se enteró de la convocatoria al Octavo Curso para Traductores e Intérpretes en Lenguas Originarias lanzada por el Ministerio de Cultura, y tomó una decisión arriesgada. Pidió una licencia de un mes, sin goce de haber, para hacer el curso, al que tuvo que postular, obviamente sin la seguridad de que saldría elegida. Una vez conocidos los resultados – que se publicaron días después de que saliera su resolución de licencia –, Yoly viajó a Quillabamba, Cusco, donde se capacitó durante tres intensas semanas en aspectos básicos de traducción e interpretación, compartiendo experiencias y expectativas con más de treinta hablantes de diferentes variedades de quechua, aimara, harakbut y matsigenka.

Hoy la funcionaria está entre los 260 **traductores e intérpretes** oficiales formados y certificados por el Estado peruano, y se encuentra laborando intensamente por fortalecer los mecanismos para garantizar la interculturalidad en su sector. Por ejemplo, ha trabajado, como parte de sus prácticas en el oficio, con el personal de Trámite Documentario, para crear una ventanilla de atención destinada a hablantes de lenguas originarias, y también es parte del equipo que organiza activamente el Taller de Educación Intercultural Ambiental, que se llevará a cabo en julio próximo, con el fin de poner en agenda la introducción de un enfoque intercultural en el candente problema del cambio climático. "Soy ayacuchana, huamanguina de nacimiento, yo sé hablar el quechua gracias a mis abuelos campesinos, que aun sin saber leer ni escribir, me transmitieron esta riqueza única, la mejor herencia, que es el quechua", afirma.

Dina Ananco Ahuananchi, de padre awajún y madre wampis, es también traductora e intérprete formada y certificada por el Estado, egresada del tercer curso organizado por el Ministerio de Cultura. Ella hizo estudios de Literatura en la Universidad Nacional Mayor de San Marcos y es una de las capacitadas con mayor conciencia sobre la necesidad de profundizar esta especialización, que ciertamente no se puede lograr de manera apropiada en un periodo de tres semanas. Como traductoraintérprete wampis, fue convocada por el Poder Judicial en mayo del 2014 para participar en el juicio por la tragedia de Bagua, junto con Isaac Paz, traductor intérprete awajún.

Pese a lo desafiante del juicio, a las limitaciones de la formación y a tener un hijo muy pequeño que atender, Dina Ananco se las ha ingeniado para cumplir este encargo estatal de la mejor manera, trasladándose periódicamente desde Lima hasta Bagua para asegurar que cada uno de los acusados del pueblo wampis pueda declarar en su lengua originaria, como les corresponde por derecho. Inicialmente criticada por algunos medios por haber preguntado con insistencia sobre el significado de algunos términos jurídicos durante las primeras audiencias en que participó,[*] ella afirma ahora con humildad, refiriéndose a todos los actores participantes en el juicio:

> Yo sé que hay momentos en que saben que nosotros nos equivocamos o nos olvidamos de algunas palabras, pero también saben que tenemos todo el compromiso de poder hacer un buen trabajo en la sala. Creo que va generándose confianza y vamos aprendiendo, en realidad, todos juntos.[†]

En un taller de **traductoresintérpretes** organizado por el proyecto "Traduciendo culturas para los derechos lingüísticos en el Perú" en julio del 2015, Dina Ananco se refirió en estos términos al significado del trabajo de interpretación y traducción que está realizando: "Es una forma de reencontrarme con mi pueblo y con mi lengua, porque estoy aprendiendo, en constante aprendizaje". Yoly Soto y Dina Ananco tienen perfiles profesionales, socioculturales y lingüísticos muy distintos, pero ambas comparten un sentimiento muy claro de orgullo por pertenecer a uno de los 47 pueblos que en el Perú hablan una lengua originaria, orgullo que sin duda se ha reforzado a través de la formación que han recibido en el curso sobre traducción e interpretación.

Justamente uno de los hallazgos más saltantes que hemos identificado en el proyecto "Traduciendo culturas para los derechos lingüísticos en el Perú" es que los **traductores e intérpretes** capacitados por el Ministerio de Cultura tienen como principal motivación para hacer el curso un fuerte compromiso por visibilizar y revitalizar sus lenguas originarias, las que entienden como un elemento central de la identidad de los pueblos indígenas de los que forman parte.

...

Con todos los problemas que tiene por atender, la iniciativa de formación y certificación de intérpretes en lenguas originarias es una de las acciones más creativas, consistentes y arriesgadas que ha desarrollado la Dirección de Lenguas Indígenas del Ministerio de Cultura para fortalecer los derechos de los pueblos indígenas. El éxito de esta iniciativa no es solo, ni principalmente, resultado de buenas decisiones de gestión estatal. Tal vez el factor más importante ha sido el compromiso por la interculturalidad y por la construcción de ciudadanía que han mostrado los capacitados, compromiso que queda bien ilustrado por las historias de Yoly Soto y Dina Ananco. Esta actitud, reforzada y afinada a través de las capacitaciones, constituye una reserva que tiene nuestro país para el trabajo a favor de los derechos humanos en el futuro cercano, en un contexto desafiante en que ninguno de los planes de gobierno de los candidatos presidenciales dedica suficiente espacio a estas preocupaciones como parte de sus prioridades para los años que vienen.

*Ver, por ejemplo, <http://acento.com.do/2014/bbcmundo/8146846elbaguazolacomplejidad deunjuicioenelqueloscargosnotienentraduccion/>

†Entrevista realizada por Rosaleen Howard en el marco del proyecto "Traduciendo culturas para los derechos lingüísticos en el Perú". El proyecto ha sido financiado por el Arts and Humanities Research Council (Consejo Científico para las Artes y las Humanidades) del Reino Unido. Los investigadores son la especialista en estudios de traducción Raquel de Pedro Ricoy (Universidad HeriotWatt, Escocia, Reino Unido) y los lingüistas Rosaleen Howard (Universidad de Newcastle, Inglaterra, Reino Unido) y Luis Andrade Ciudad (Pontificia Universidad Católica del Perú).

Key: various features discussed in sample analysis – highlighted in gray

Sample Spanish news article analysis

The text chosen for a brief analysis is "Traductores e intérpretes: Una reserva para los derechos humanos." Regarding macro-textual features, the opening paragraph introduces us, via an anecdotal lead, to a Quechua speaker who learned the language of her ancestors from a young age, despite implied societal resistance to indigenous languages. The first and second paragraphs contextualize the learning of this minority language with words such as *violencias*, *decisión arriesgada*, *sin la seguridad*, characterizing the rigors of preparation but also noting support from the State certification program. The low status of her native tongue is couched in terms such as a *conocimiento silencioso*, a metaphor for being unheard and thus unvalued. The technical term *lenguas originarias* establishes the primacy of indigenous languages in Peru, and the author includes the concept of defending interculturality in the discussion of the importance of translators and interpreters, as well as their potential for

Text types

helping address pressing problems such as global warming. The author details actions to ensure that court testimony can be given in an appearing party's native language, and the reader is reminded that it is the litigant's right to do so. Very unusually, the legal interpreter profiled, the second one discussed in the article, admits to gaps in knowledge but defends them in light of the intention to improve and serve. Both interpreter-translators are proud of their heritage, a motivating factor in pursuing this work: *un fuerte compromiso por visibilizar y revitalizar sus lenguas originarias, las que entienden como un elemento central de la identidad de los pueblos indígenas de los que forman parte*. That is, language revitalization – preventing language death – ties this work to linguistic human rights and to the identities of marginalized segments of society, despite, the author reiterates, the political risks. The training course is called creative in its fostering of civic commitment (*ciudadanía*) by training members of a linguistic minority to be interpreters. This is a human-interest story that also reinforces certain national values (inclusion and cultural memory) and highlights a program that offers individuals the opportunity to foster a pluralistic society. The article ends with a somewhat veiled plea for such efforts to appear in government platforms in the future.

In terms of micro-textual features, the narrative hangs on two cohesive devices, or "pegs": the two candidates' persistence and the government's will to create a linguistics program despite the challenges or problems (*tuvo pocas ocasiones para poner en práctica; con todos los problemas; pese a lo desafiante*).

The sample text consists of 1,509 words, 576 types or distinct words, and a type/token ratio of 39. Mean word length is 5.2 characters, the second-longest in the dataset. Its sentences were easily the longest in mean number of words, over 42, nearly double the overall mean of 24.5. Sentence type is typically both compound and complex.

Tense is elided altogether in our sample news report, wherein no textual clues are available for the reader to determine whether the emphasis is that translators and interpreters are working now for human rights, or if they are a perennial resource. The effect of nominalization is to shift focus from the temporal to the notional. Chovanec (2014: 1) has identified this as a problem of temporal deictics, or the "way past-time temporal events are encoded" to emphasize recency. Shifts between the headline and subheadline and other types of "process chaining" may also occur in texts. The shift from immediacy to news that is not time-bound characterizes the shift from "hard news" to "soft news" (Bell 1991: 14).

Notes

1 In journalism, sequencing information from the most important to the least important is referred to as the inverted pyramid.
2 The news articles corpus is where "of" is most frequent. Moreover, "of" appears in all the corpus texts. In the case of "in" and "at," the only corpus where their frequency ranks as high and where their occurrence is as widespread is that of recipes and museum guides, respectively. "On," for its part, ranks just one spot higher in the instruction manuals corpus, where its occurrence is also as widespread.
3 Collocation strength was calculated based on Mutual Information score and Log Dice using LancsBox (Version 3.0.2). The results were compared to ensure collocates ranked similarly using both statistical measures.
4 Die Zeit, www.zeit.de/english/index

7 Business letters

Business correspondence is core to commercial communication and transactions in general. Business letters are the means by which companies and institutions establish and manage interactions with customers, clients, or other businesses or entities. Such letters are known for their formulaic writing style, brevity, and standardized format/presentation. Even though business letters may address different needs and purposes, many of their features remain constant.

Pragmatic considerations such as politeness in business discourse are especially vital to note, as they go well beyond the conveyance of information. Pilegaard (1997), for example, has shown that politeness in business discourse maps to the sender's status, reminding us that the social matrix envelops and conditions formal exchanges of information. Indeed, López Ferrero and González Arias count politeness among the characteristics of quality written business texts: clarity and readability; economy; objectivity; unbiasedness; politeness; contemporaneity; simplicity; formality; and precision and correctness (2015: 513–4). And we might perhaps add a culturally specific refinement long prized in public and private Hispanophone discourse: elegance. Naturally, meeting multiple discourse goals at once can be a daunting or contradictory project – economy and formality may be at odds, for example. Other typifying features of business discourse in Spanish include the formal form of address (Ud.); avoidance of pronouns directly referencing parties to the transaction, impersonal expressions replacing them; and employment of the first-person plural to signal "corporate responsibility" and "gravitas" (Gorman and Henson 1996: 2).

Commercial texts have been analyzed in accordance with their macrofunctions: correspondence (our focus here), promotion, internal communication, public administration communication, and texts required by politeness (Sanz Pinyol and Fraser 2003). Commercial texts may also be classified by speech acts: persuading, requesting, proposing, explaining, recommending, analyzing, motivating, answering, and announcing (Portocarrero and Gironella 2003).

220   **Text types**

ENGLISH

For the analysis of the lexicogrammatical features of business letters, a corpus of 33 texts was compiled. The texts range from 108 to 544 words with an average length of 233 words. When looking at the word length of most of the texts, all but three of the 33 business letters contain fewer than 400 words. In fact, 11 are below 199 words long, 12 are below 299 words, and 7 are below 399, with only 2 in the 400-word range and 1 in the 500-word range.

Macro-textual features

Business letters display eight mandatory **rhetorical moves**:

1. Sender's address
2. Receiver's address
3. Opening greetings
4. Statement of the purpose of the letter
5. Elaboration of the subject of the letter
6. Soliciting action
7. Closing salutation
8. Signature

These mandatory moves, which usually occur in the order outlined above, can be identified in all 33 business letters, except for in a few cases in which the soliciting action move was absent. The absence of this move occurs in 3 cases when the intention of the business letter is to thank the recipient rather than request an action from them.

In addition to these mandatory moves, there appear to be four more optional moves:

1. Subject line (occurs 12 times in the entire corpus)
2. Supporting details (occurs 14 times)
3. Conclusion (occurs 4 times in the corpus)
4. Enclosure (occurs 5 times in the corpus)

In terms of **register**, the **field** of discourse of the business letters making up the corpus revolves around customers' bank account or credit card information and/or balances, health insurance plans and the selling or renewal of products or services. Indeed, a brief look at the frequency list of words in the corpus shows that some of the high-frequency words are account, credit, bank, card, service(s), health, customers, plan(s), balance, renewal, and products. Here is a breakdown of the number of instances in which these terms occur in the corpus and the number of texts in which they can be found.

The **mode** of discourse refers to a text written to be read insofar as business letters are missives that companies generate and then send to customers. Last but not least, the **tenor** of discourse is such that the addressee need not

Lexical item	Frequency	No. of texts
account	50	15
credit	46	9
bank	30	11
card	30	7
service(s)	39	19
health	25	6
customers	31	17
plans	36	9
renewal	12	5
products	11	6
balance	12	9

belong to the discourse community of the companies sending the letters; therefore, the language used is typically not technical in order to be accessible to as large an audience as possible.

As far as the **communicative function** is concerned, business letters in the corpus can be classified as **informative,** with a greater degree of **conative** language, since business letters are generally aimed at informing the customer or potential customer of certain products or services. In this corpus, the informative function is usually conveyed by such phrases as "This letter is to confirm that," "This letter is to notify you of" or "Please let this letter serve to confirm that," to name just a few. Some expressions that use conative language to convey the informative nature of these texts are: "If you have any questions, please talk to your agent or call our customer service team" or "If you have any questions about the matter, please do not hesitate to call." In addition to this main function, another common type of language used is **phatic,** which is conveyed by opening and closing salutations in many instances, where the aim is to establish some sort of contact between the addresser and the addressee with greetings such as "Dear Sir/Madam," "Dear + name of the person," with the latter trying to establish a direct connection with the reader by calling them by their first name.

Micro-textual features

As far as **cohesive devices** are concerned, there is frequent use of noun pronouns (you and we), possessive adjectives (*your* and *our*) and demonstrative items (*this* and *that*). The table below shows some of the most common lexical items used for referencing.

The three main types of conjunctions used in the whole corpus are "and," which occurs 168 times, "or," which occurs 52 times, and "if," which occurs 34 times. When taken together, the high frequency of these words could be indicative that business letters may make frequent use of compound sentences, although conditional clauses are at times used as well but with much less frequency.

Referencing item	Frequency
you	166
your	160
this	76
we	65
our	63

Substitution does not seem to be a very common lexical device in business letters. Indeed, in the whole corpus, the following were the only 5 instances of it:

If you wish to set restrictions on any card you **may do so** by contacting Cardmember Service.

Your expertise in coordination with the Architects, Engineers, and the General Contractor helped achieve the very best outcome in performance from **all** involved.

The two entities are entirely different and **neither** have filed a Power of Attorney from EquiCredit of DE …

As a result, some individuals will see lower rates for this new coverage in 2014, while others will see higher rates.

Google is free to offer its Google Wallet application in a manner that doesn't require integration with the secure element, and many payment applications **do just that**.

Likewise, there are no major instances of **ellipsis** in the text that stand out other than the types of ellipses used in everyday English. For example, pronouns are omitted after the preposition "and" to avoid redundancy, which is usually considered common usage of the language rather than a peculiarity of business letters.

The fact that both ellipsis and substitution are not widely used in business letters is in line with the need for these letters to be clear, straightforward and unambiguous so as to allow the reader to understand the message being conveyed.

As far as lexical cohesion is concerned, **repetition** seems to be the preferred method of linking lexical items to create cohesion and coherence in a business letter. Using repetition as a lexical cohesive device allows for unambiguity and clarity as previously pointed out.

In terms of tenses, two tenses prevail in business letters, namely the present tense (161 instances when considering the many occurrences of "is," "are" and "have") and the future "will" (79 instances). In addition to these two tenses, there is some minor usage of the modal verb "may" (36 instances) and the present perfect (25 instances).

Lastly, the body of each of the letters contains many of the rhetorical moves (e.g., stating the purpose, elaborating it and soliciting action) and contains a nice balance of noun and verb phrases. In other sections, however, noun phrases are common. In particular, the opening greeting move features a noun phrase typically pre-modified by the adjective "Dear," and the closing salutation is typically conveyed by the adverb "Sincerely."

Sample text – English business letter

UnitedHealthcare
September 30, 2013
Re: Discontinuance of Plans

Dear Valued Employer,

We at UnitedHealthcare Insurance Company would like to thank you for allowing us to provide your employees with their health insurance benefits. It has been our pleasure to serve you.

We are writing to inform you that your current policy will be discontinued or not Ø renewed at your next renewal at least ninety (90) days from now, on (March 1, 2013) because UnitedHealthcare Insurance Company will no longer offer your current health plan in the State of Colorado. This notice is being provided to you in accordance with the provisions of your group contract and Colorado's insurance law.

This discontinuance triggers a special enrollment period which allows you to select a new health plan. You will have sixty (60) days from the date your plan ends to enroll in a new plan.

Your options include:

- Purchasing another small group health plan from us;
- Purchasing a small group health plan from another carrier; or
- Purchasing a new plan through Connect for Health Colorado, where you may qualify for federal financial assistance (www.connectforhealthco.com).

You should schedule the start date of your new plan to match the end date of your current plan to avoid a gap in Ø coverage.

We will send a Ø notice explaining this change to each of your employees currently Ø covered by the plan(s)

We thank you for your continued commitment to UnitedHealthcare. If you have any questions, please contact your UnitedHealthcare Renewal Account Executive, Broker or call 1•866-432•5992.

Sincerely,

Elizabeth C. Sobug
President and Chief Executive Officer
UnitedHealthcare Colorado

Source: UnitedHealthcare

224 **Text types**

Sample English business letter text analysis

The sample business letter under analysis is a 2013 Health Insurance Company letter. From a macro-textual point of view, the letter is characterized by all of the mandatory moves as outlined in the section above, namely:

1. Sender's address (redacted)
2. Receiver's address (redacted)
3. Opening greetings (the name of the customer has also been redacted)
4. Statement of the purpose of the letter
5. Elaboration of the subject of the letter
6. Soliciting action
7. Closing salutation
8. Signature (redacted)

In addition to these mandatory moves, there is also a non-mandatory move, the subject line, which informs the reader of the content of the letter, in this case, "Discontinuance of Plans."

The text is 263 words long, which is pretty close to the average size of a business letter as outlined above. The shortness and concision of a business letter may also be attributed to the fact that its purpose is to be direct and straightforward in informing the reader.

As far as the register is concerned, a brief look at the list of high-frequency words in the letter shows that the field of discourse centers on the termination of a healthcare plan. Indeed, some of the most frequently occurring keywords are plan (11), health (6), insurance (4), and the lemma discontinu- (3 times). Both the mode and tenor of discourse of this particular letter match the mode and tenor of discourse of business letters in general.

The communicative goal of this letter is primarily informative. It is mainly aimed at informing the reader of the termination of their health insurance, but later on in the letter, toward the end, it encourages the reader to contact the company in order to obtain further information about the notice (exhibiting a greater degree of conative language). It also exhibits phatic language to some extent, which is aimed at establishing contact with the reader and terminating the communication through an opening and closing salutation, respectively. In this case, the opening salutation is very generic "Dear Valued Employer," and the closing one is "Sincerely," which seems to be the preferred way of closing the channel of communication at the end of a business letter, as pointed out above.

From a micro-textual point of view, the preferred method of referencing in this letter seems to be the possessive adjective *your*, which occurs 12 times and the personal pronoun *you* occurring 10 times and to a lesser extent the pronoun *we* (4 times) and the possessive *us* (3 times) and *our* (1 time). There is fairly scant use of conjunctions in this text, e.g., *or* (3 times), *and* (2 times), *because* (1 time) and *if* (1 time). Based on these findings, one might conclude that the the compound sentence is the predominant type of sentence used in this text, but a closer look at the use of the conjunctions in the sample text reveals that both *or* and *and* are used to link phrases rather than two or more independent clauses. As a matter of fact, there are no compound sentences; instead, there are five simple sentences and eight complex ones, the latter featuring relative clauses, non-finite subordinate clauses (using an infinitive or gerund), and conditional clauses (if).

In line with what was stated above, neither substitution nor ellipsis appear to be widely used in such letters due to the need to be unambiguous and clear to the reader. In this respect, the letter in question has zero instances of substitution and only 4 instances of ellipsis (one verbal, two clausal and one deictic – through the omission of the possessive adjective *your* before the word *coverage*).

As far as lexical cohesion is concerned, the text is highly repetitive, reusing key terms such as plan (10 times), health (6), insurance (4) and United-Healthcare (4; this is the name of the company) throughout the short text. Some of the synonyms used in relation to these keywords are *policy* (instead of *plan*, which occurs only once in the whole text) and the verbal phrase *no longer offer* to convey the meaning of *discontinue* (only used 1 time).

In terms of tenses, as seen in the general corpus, the text displays a high frequency of present tense (5) and future tense (4) and a few cases of modal verbs (*would* and *should*, each of which occurs once) and the present continuous (2 instances). The imperative mode is used instead in the soliciting action move to persuade the reader to take some sort of action.

Lastly, noun phrases are used in the sender's and receiver's address moves, in the subject line, as well as in the opening salutation where the noun phrase is usually modified by the adjective "dear." When it comes to the body of the text, which in this case includes a statement of purpose, the elaboration of the subject of the letter, and the solicitation of an action, the language used is characterized by a mix of noun (roughly 50) and verb phrases (approximately 30). The closing salutation move, however, is usually conveyed by the adverb "Sincerely" followed by the sender's name.

226 **Text types**

CHINESE

A business letter is a formal written letter intended for exchanging information between business firms, customers, suppliers, employees, government agencies, and others. It may take many forms, for instance, a business letter could be a letter between companies, a cover letter, recommendation letter, or any other formal correspondence in business settings. In order to understand the current state of Chinese-language business letters, a corpus of 33 business letters was collected from various sources, all published in the last 5 years so as to make sure to capture current textual conventions. A business letter is typically not a long piece of writing; the average length of a Chinese business letter in the Chinese corpus in terms of characters is about 320 characters. A quick look at the range of lengths of the 33 business letters shows that the minimum length is around 71 characters and the maximum around 977. Most of the letters were between business firms; one was between government agencies and one between Chinese universities.

Macro-textual features

We begin by isolating the conventional features of Chinese-language business letters, or **rhetorical moves**. They are:

1. Opening salutation (称呼语)
2. Body (正文)
3. Complimentary close (结束语)
4. Name (署名)
5. Date (日期)

It is worth noting that as a business letter could be sent in the name of a member of a company or the company itself, the name here in move 4 could be either a personal name or a company name. In some cases, the position of the sender is also provided in this move. There are basically three forms of move 4, namely, signature, company seal, and the combination of the two.

In addition to these five conventional moves, which were found in all of the 33 business letters in the corpus, there are a few optional moves: (1) 信头 (heading, found in one business letter), which includes sender's name, zip code, telephone number, fax number and some other information; (2) 事由 (subject heading, found in six business letters), which indicates the subject of the letter and usually appears right after the opening salutation; and (3) 附件 (enclosures, found in three business letters), which is often placed at the end of the letter.

While the content of the rhetorical moves of Chinese business letters is generally the same as that of their English counterparts, the order of the moves is often different. Beyond that, a rhetorical move called "typist initials," which is used in some English business letters to indicate the person who typed the letter, is rarely seen in Chinese business letters.

In terms of **register**, it is worth looking at the three characteristic aspects of register: the **field** of discourse, or what the text is about; the **mode** of discourse, or how the language is used; and the **tenor** of discourse, or the relationship between the author and the audience. As far as the **field** is concerned, one way to find out about the topic of a text is to look at its terminology and, more generally speaking, its lexical items. A quick look at the frequency word list produced by Wordsmith Tools makes it clear that the terminology and lexical items used in this text type relate to business. Some of the high-frequency words which point to this are:

High-frequency lexical items	Frequency
公司 (company)	154
合作 (cooperate)	30
项目 (program)	26
双方 (both parties)	23
贵司 (your company)	22
进行 (conduct)	22
我司 (our company)	21
有限公司 (limited company)	19
工作 (work)	17
人才 (talent)	17
我方 (our company)	17
希望 (wish)	16
市场 (market)	14
服务 (serve)	13
合同 (contractual)	13
贵方 (your company)	13
提供 (provide)	13

All of the lexical items in the table above describe either aspects of commercial activity or related behaviors.

As for the **mode of discourse**, business letters are texts written to be read by the recipients to serve a specific purpose in business communication. The language used in business letters tends to be formal, concise, and usually includes a large amount of terminology. Emotional expressions and a colloquial style are generally avoided. Finally, the **tenor of discourse** indicates the status and role relationships of participants, which could be either equal (expert-to-expert) or unequal (expert-to-nonexpert or layperson). When it comes to business letters, either relationship could obtain as both the sender and the recipient are actors in commercial activities and might both be considered as experts in the field, although unequal relationships are also possible between Party A and Party B. Different business letters may therefore display different tenors of discourse as the participants and purposes may vary.

The **communicative functions** of the business letter tend to be **informative**, with occasional uses of **conative, phatic,** or **vocative** language. As an indispensable part of business communication, business letters are used to sell products or services, request material or information, answer customer inquiries, and serve a variety of other business functions. In a nutshell, business letters basically aim at providing information/materials to the recipients or triggering

228　**Text types**

a certain action/reaction from them. However, it is also possible to state that business letters have a certain degree of expressive function when the purpose is to maintain good public relations.

Micro-textual features

The corpus data point to a preference for the indicative mood in business letters. Most of the sentences in the body of the letter are indicative, and pronouns such as 我司 (our company, 21 times)/我方 (our company, 17 times) and 贵司 (your company, 22 times)/贵方 (your company, 13 times) are frequently used. Another common mood used in Chinese business letters is the imperative, which is indicated by terms such as 请 (please, 25 times), and 希望 (wish, 16 times). The subjunctive mood is used less often (如果*if* is found only 5 times in the corpus).

As regards **cohesive devices**, **reference** is commonly used in Chinese business letters. Pronouns including 我 (I), 我们 (we), 您 (you), 我司 (our company)/我方 (our company) and 贵司 (your company)/贵方 (your company) occur 58, 46, 15, 21/17, 22/13 times, respectively, in the 33 business letters. Among demonstrative reference devices, 本/此 and 该 as the Chinese equivalents for *this* and *that* appear in many words and phrases in the corpus such as 本项目 (this project), 本次 (this time), 此事 (this event), 此价格 (this price), 该项目 (that project), and 该公司 (that company). Analysis shows that there are also a reference device of comparison in the corpus which is displayed in four occurrences of 其他 and one occurrence of 其它 (both mean "other"). The cohesive device of **substitution** is rarely used in the Chinese business letters; in this regard, only one clausal substitution device, 这样 (as such), was found. By contrast, **ellipsis** is a widely used cohesive device in Chinese, in which subjects and objects are optional if they can be implied by the context. Leaving aside simple sentences, which are relatively rare in business letters, the omission of subjects and objects occurs many times in compound sentences in the corpus of Chinese business letters. The corpus also makes use of connectors as well as additive, causal, and temporal **conjunctions**, as evidenced in the table below:

Conjunctions	Frequency
并 (and, also)	32
由于 (as, because of)	11
但 (but)	9
如果 (if)	5
因此 (therefore)	4
而且 (moreover)	4
不仅 (not only)	4
同时 (meanwhile)	3
否则 (otherwise)	3
以便 (so as to)	2
虽然 (although)	2
可是 (however)	1

Generally speaking, the use of conjunctions is less frequent in Chinese than in English. However, the preference for compound sentences in Chinese business letters fuels the need for conjunctions. **Lexical cohesion** is arguably the most commonly used form of cohesion in Chinese. In the case of business letters, pronouns that represent the two participants or parties as well as subject-related terms, which must be clarified to avoid any misunderstanding, occur many times in the corpus.

In the corpus of Chinese business letters, there is a high occurrence of nouns as shown in the following table:

High-frequency nouns	Frequency	High-frequency nouns	Frequency
公司 (company)	154	商品 (goods)	9
项目 (project)	32	品牌 (brand)	9
双方 (both parties)	23	定金 (deposit)	9
贵司 (your company)	22	问题 (problem)	9
我司 (our company)	21	事宜 (matter)	9
有限公司 (limited company)	19	报价 (quote)	9
人才 (talent)	17	时间 (time)	8
我方 (our company)	17	业务 (business)	8
市场 (market)	14	情况 (situation)	7
贵方 (your company)	13	企业 (enterprise)	7

The nouns used in the Chinese business letters can be roughly broken down into three categories: (1) pronouns describing the participants, such as 双方 (both parties), 贵司 (your company), 我司 (our company), etc.; (2) nouns specific to commerce, such as 市场 (market), 商品 (goods); and (3) nouns that are relatively general, such as 问题 (problem) and 时间 (time).

In addition to nouns, another word category that is highly recurring in this genre is verbs, as evidenced in the table below:

Verbs	Frequency
合作 (cooperate)	30
进行 (conduct)	22
工作 (work)	17
希望 (wish)	16
服务 (serve)	13
提供 (provide)	13
设计 (design)	10
发展 (develop)	9
支付 (pay)	9
收到 (receive)	8
支持 (support)	7
需要 (demand)	7

230 Text types

Sample text – Chinese business letter

广东省××进出口公司
电挂：43333　　　　　地址：×市江南大道108号
电传：44327 TNB CN 电话：
编号：×工出字〔2009〕21号

××总经理台鉴：
事由：建立业务关系
　　从我驻意大利使馆商务处来信中获悉，贵公司希望与我国经营工艺品的外贸公司建立业务联系，我们高兴地通知贵公司，我们愿意在开展这类商品的贸易方面与贵公司合作。
　　我公司经营的工艺品有绣品、草竹编、灯具、涤纶花、珠宝首饰以及仿古器物和书画等，这些品种均制作精美，质量上乘。特别是涤纶花，式样新颖，色彩鲜艳，形态逼真，可与鲜花媲美，目前在欧、美、亚等洲许多国家，极为畅销，深受消费者的喜爱。现寄上涤纶花样照一套，供∅参考。欢迎∅来信联系∅。
　　顺颂∅
商祺
　　附件：涤纶花样照一套。

广东省××进出口公司
×年×月×日

Key: lexical repetition – highlighted in gray; connectors – underline

---

Sample Chinese business letter text analysis

At the macro-textual level, the business letter selected as an example was sent by a company to establish a business relationship with another company, which is very typical in Chinese business correspondence. The business letter includes every conventional move: 称呼语 (opening salutation), 正文 (body), 结束 (complimentary close), 署名 (name), and 日期 (date); it also includes all the optional moves listed in 1.1: 信头 (heading), 事由 (subject heading), and 附件 (enclosures).

The text has 304 characters and is a bit shorter than the average (320 characters) of this genre. The mode of discourse is informative and the tenor of discourse points to a relatively equal relationship seeing that both participants are inclined to carry out cooperation. The communicative function is informative based on the reasons discussed above.

As far as the micro-textual features are concerned, the indicative mood and the simple present tense are used in the sample letter. In terms of cohesive devices, the use of compound sentences fuels the need for cohesive devices in the body part of the sample. While demonstrative references are generously used, substitution is absent in the sample text; ellipsis (represented by the symbol ∅ in the sample text) is used 4 times; conjunctions are not used whereas connectors (see underlined words in the sample text) such as 特别是 (especially) and 现 (now) are. Lexical repetition (see words highlighted in gray in the sample text) appears 5 times in the body part while there is one hypernym (工艺品, crafts) and no synonyms; in the entire letter, there are instances of repetitions, as shown in the table below:

Repetition	Frequency
贵公司 (your company)	3
涤纶花 (polyester flower)	3
我们 (we)	2
经营 (manage)	2
工艺品 (crafts)	2

The sample business letter is characterized mainly by compound sentences; in the sample, there are four compound sentences and only one simple sentence in the body part. As for the lexical-grammatical features of the conventional moves, 信头 (heading), 署名 (name), 日期 (date) as well as 附件 (enclosures), they are characterized by noun phrases. As for 称呼语 (opening salutation), 事由 (subject heading), 正文 (body) and 结束 (complimentary close), two main word categories prevail, namely, nouns (33 instances) and verbs (20 instances).

232 **Text types**

FRENCH

French business correspondence is characterized by a high level of formality and tends to be impersonal in nature. In order to understand the characteristics of French business letters, a corpus of 19 texts was collected from several sources. Business letters are typically concise and short, which is supported by the average length of the texts included in the French corpus, approximately 156 words. A quick look at the range of length of the 19 letters in our corpus shows that the minimum length is around 82 words and the maximum around 203, depending on the topic of the letter. However, most of the letters range between 110 and 160 words.

Macro-textual features

We begin our analysis by distinguishing between the following **rhetorical moves**:

1. Correspondents' information (*Coordonnées des correspondants*)

    *   Sender's address (*Expéditeur*)
    *   Recipient's address (*Destinataire*)

        *   Recipient's formal name, title, and company

    *   Location (*Lieu*)
    *   Date (*Date*)

2. Subject line (*Objet*)
3. Opening salutation (*Vedette/ appel/ appellation*)
4. Body of the letter (*Corps de la lettre*)
5. Polite pre-closing (*Formule de salutation clichée*)
6. Closing salutation (*Formule finale de salutation*)
7. Signature (*Signature*)

    *   Sender's title (*Qualité du signataire*)
    *   Signature (*Signature*)
    *   Sender's name (*Nom du signataire*)

The correspondents' information (*coordonnées des correspondants*) includes the sender's address (*expéditeur*). However, when preprinted company stationery is used, the header customarily includes the corporate logo, name, address, phone/ fax number along with the company type information (e.g., SA or SARL), trade registration number and ownership interest (e.g., number of shares of stock). This letterhead content may be automatically inserted as a header or included manually by the writer. In addition to the sender's contact information, the address of the person or company to whom the letter is addressed (*destinataire*) is listed over a space of six lines, beginning with the sender's name and title and ending with this person's company name and address. This information is followed by a location (*lieu*), more specifically, a city, and date of correspondence (*date*), which is found on the line directly underneath the name of the city. Both the *lieu* and *date* are found in the upper right-hand quadrant of the first page (see sample text). The date is always spelled out and preceded by the definite article *le*, then the days, month and year (*le 25 octobre 2017*). Cardinal numbers are used for days except when a day falls on the first of the month (e.g., *le 1er novembre 2017*).

A subject line (*objet*) introduces the main topic of a piece of correspondence. This is followed by an opening salutation (*la vedette / l'appel / l'appellation*) consisting of a designation corresponding to the recipient, where an equivalent of sir(s) or madam(s) is used (e.g., *Monsieur/ Messieurs* or *Madame*). This designation is always followed by a comma. In business correspondence, the salutation does not include an adjective such as "Dear ..." (e.g., *Cher* ... or *Chère* ...), as this type of adjective is typically used in private correspondence between individuals acquainted with one another on a more personal level.

The body of a letter (*corps de la lettre*) consists of an introduction, a development, and a conclusion communicating the purpose of the letter in detail. The introduction could reference a previous call, meeting or correspondence with the recipient, or it may simply serve the purpose of presenting the recipient with a new business opportunity or a promotional offer. The development (middle) addresses the main purpose of the letter, which could be to request something, express satisfaction or regret, or issue an apology. The body of a business letter ends with a polite pre-closing formula expressing a desire, gratitude, or regret, and reflecting the content of the letter (e.g., *Dans l'espoir d'avoir satisfait à votre demande*; *En vous remerciant à l'avance*; *Avec le regret de ne pas pouvoir satisfaire votre demande*). Closing salutations (*formules finales de salutation*) are very formulaic and always include three parts separated by a comma in which the middle part corresponds to the designation used in the opening salutation (e.g., *Nous vous prions d'agréer, Monsieur, nos salutations distinguées*; *Veuillez recevoir, Madame, nos respectueuses salutations*). The signature (*signature*) is another move that consists of three parts: the first element indicates the status or title of the sender, the second consists of an actual signature, and the third is occupied by the sender's full name.

In addition to these mandatory moves, which appear throughout the corpus, the use of references (*références*) to previous correspondence initiated between the parties constituted another recurrent move. In fact, almost half of the texts in our corpus contained a reference line above the subject line. These references were usually indicated by the phrases *Vos références* and *Nos références*, or by their abbreviations, *V/R*, *N/R*, *Vos réf*, or *Nos réf*. They consist of an order number and the initials of the author of the letter in lower case. Some letters include supplementary information about the sender's company, usually referencing banking information (e.g., an account number or SWIFT code). Three letters mention enclosures (*pièces jointes*) and specify documents enclosed at the end of the letters. Such information is not always required because this depends on the subject and the goal of correspondence. Usually, the number and type of enclosures or attachments are mentioned underneath the subject line and preceded by the abbreviation *PJ:*.

In terms of register, the prevailing terminology and lexical items point to a field of discourse occupied by typical business letters. Several high-frequency words are telling in this regard:

High-frequency lexical items	Frequency
vous	82
nous	67
votre	50
monsieur	43
rue	22
lettre	19
nos	20
objet	17
contrat	14
demande	14
code	13
date	12
madame	11
notre	11
ville	11

The lexical items in the table relate to forms of address and the sections of a business letter; they primarily reference the generic elements contained in all business letters. None of the highly frequent lexical items indicate the topic or purpose of the letters except for "contract," which occurs in three of the texts, suggesting that these letters are referencing a contract. As for the **mode** of discourse, business letters are texts written to be read by their recipients (e.g., businesses, clients, suppliers, or employers) in order to request or provide information with the expectation of a response. Business correspondence follows a standard format and strict style. There are none of the indications of spontaneity used in spoken language, such as fillers and pauses.

The **tenor** of discourse is situational in the sense that the relationship between the author and audience can be either expert-to-expert, as is the case for business-to-business correspondence, or expert-to-nonexpert, such as when individual customers are being addressed. Though formality is maintained among the various letters in our corpus, levels of technicality differ according to the subject and purpose of a given letter. The **communicative function** of French business letters is primarily **operative**, as reflected in the use of **phatic** language, which is employed to establish or maintain communication, and **conative** language, which is used to engage or persuade the audience into taking certain actions or reacting in a specific way. A tertiary, informative function aimed at communicating information or updates on business operations and transactions is also discernible. Stylistically speaking, French business letters do not reflect the personalities of their authors and they express no originality or creativity. Instead, they maintain a standard, neutral tone.

Micro-textual features

The corpus data indicate a preference for the indicative mood and tenses. There are approximately 94 instances of the present tense (*présent*), 96 instances of the infinitive (*infinitif*), and 23 instances of the future tense (*futur*). The imperative, subjunctive, and past indicative are not used in business letters, while the conditional is used minimally. The indicative mood and tenses are notably the most common since they are used to relate facts and objective statements and help writers express respect and a high level of formality.

Regarding **cohesive devices**, the personal referents *nous, vous, votre, nos*, and *vos* along with the definite articles *le, la*, and *les* are the preferred method of referencing, with the formal, plural form of address *vous* occurring 82 times, in all texts; *nous* occurring 67 times in 13 separate texts; *je* occurring 18 times in 7 texts; the possessive determiner *votre* 50 times in 16 texts; *notre* 11 times in 6 texts; *nos* 20 times in 10 texts; and *vos* 8 times in only 4 texts. Since the professional tone of business letters relies on formality and politeness, it is expected that recipients will constantly be addressed using the formal *vous*, and, inversely, the sender of a letter will always use the second-person plural *nous* since he or she is speaking on behalf of a company. The predominance of these pronouns suggests some kind of direct interaction between senders and recipients. Demonstrative determiners (*ce, cette*, and *ces*) are present in situations where decisions, services, deadlines or expectations are being referenced.

Substitution is extremely infrequent in our business letters corpus. For instance, the third-person masculine subject pronouns *il* and *elle* are used a total of six times as substitutes for other words or as impersonal subjects beginning impersonal expressions. The pronoun *y*, which replaces prepositional phrases indicating location, appears 3 times in 3 texts. The pronoun *en*, which can be used to replace words introduced by a verb followed by *de, du, de la, de l'*, or *des*, occurs 32 times in a total of 13 texts, in only one of which it serves as a substitute. In the remaining 31 instances, *en* was used as either a preposition or an adverb. This lack of substitution may suggest that statements in business letters tend to be spelled out and that full references are consistently used to avoid any ambiguity or misunderstanding. As for **connecting words**, mainly additive and causal connecting words are found in our corpus, as indicated by the lexical items below:

Connecting words	Frequency	No. of texts
pour	35	15
et	32	16
avec	8	7
ou	8	3
si	7	4
ainsi	4	3
aussi	2	2
afin	1	1
mais	1	1
bientôt	1	1

236 Text types

The most frequent preposition is *pour*, which expresses causation, intent, and motivation, or the duration of future events. In this corpus, *pour* is used 34 times in phrases expressing causation and only once in reference to future events. The use of additive and causal conjunctions suggests that the sentences used in business letters are typically compound or complex.

High-frequency nouns	Frequency	No. of texts
monsieur	43	18
rue	22	13
lettre	19	15
objet	17	16
contrat	14	3
demande	14	10
code	13	10
date	12	6
madame	11	4
ville	11	4
disposition	10	10

As far as lexical cohesion is concerned, a quick look at the list of high-frequency nouns in the corpus shows that repetition is predominant when it comes to addressing the recipient of a letter, here using the designation *Monsieur*. Since the business letters selected for this corpus do not represent a single sub-type of business letter, the most frequently used nouns denote formal elements normally found in business letters. The nouns occurring in business letters can be classified into three higher-level categories: (1) nouns found in formulaic forms of address; (2) nouns found in contact information elements; and (3) nouns reflecting the topic or domain of correspondence.

Sample text – French business letter

Le bon tissu
Tissus de qualité
S.A. au capital de 1.691.525 euros
B.P. 4467 – 69 241 Lyon CEDEX 04 – Téléphone 04 72 10 10 80 – Télécopie 04 78 27 72 34
SIRET 954 504 33 000 11 – APE 171 K – RCS Lyon B 954 504 833

CCP 1361643 V Lyon	Monsieur Charles Rossi
BPLL Lyon Agence 001	Directeur Achats
N° compte : 00201905807	S.A.R.L. Ma Maison
Guichet : 00000	Bâtiment A

(Continued)

Business letters   237

(Continued)

Clé RIB : 46   94 avenue Gambetta
N° banque :   75984 PARIS CEDEX 20
Code IBAN :
SWIFT / BIC :

Vos références : 729/AT 20   Lyon
Nos références : MC /jl   le 8 novembre 2003
Objet : Votre appel d'offres du 31 octobre
P.J. : catalogue – tarif – conditions

Monsieur,

Nous vous remercions de votre lettre du 31 octobre dernier **et** de l'intérêt que vous portez à notre entreprise.

Notre catalogue illustré ci-joint **et** le tarif correspondant vous permettront d'apprécier la gamme entière de nos tissus ameublement. Sous ce pli, vous trouverez également nos conditions pour grossistes.

Au cas où vous seriez intéressé par certains de nos produits, nous aurons le plaisir de vous adresser des échantillons sur simple demande.

Restant à votre entière disposition **pour** tous renseignements complémentaires, nous vous prions d'agréer, Monsieur, l'expression de nos sentiments distingués.

Le directeur commercial
[signature]
Robert Bouchez

Key: personal pronouns – highlighted in gray; connecting words – bold

Source: Calliope and Isabelle De Ridder; www.calliope.be/french/res/FRmodules.html

Sample French business letter text analysis

In order to illustrate several of the features described above, we will analyze a sample business letter published on the Calliope website, which is an online writing center developed at the University of Antwerp. The center uses authentic texts to illustrate writing conventions across languages. At the macro-textual level, the business letter includes every mandatory move corresponding to the parties' information, a location and date (*Lyon le 8 novembre 2003*), a subject line (*Votre appel d'offres du 31 octobre*) and so on. The sample also includes several non-mandatory moves, such as company information (*S.A. au capital de 1.691.525 euros*), use of references (*Vos références : 729/AT 20*) and enclosures (*P.J. : catalogue – tarif – conditions*). The text is 187 words long, which falls within the average length range of this genre. The mode of discourse is phatic in the sense that the letter is being used to follow up on previous correspondence and aims at maintaining communication while inviting the recipient to take action by requesting samples if interested in the product. The tenor of discourse points to an expert-to-expert relationship since the sender is referencing the recipient's prior request for information concerning the purchase of fabric in bulk. The field of discourse corresponds to requests for proposals, as the subject line indicates that this letter was written in response to a request of this nature.

238 Text types

As far as the text's micro-textual features are concerned, the predominant mood and tense are indicative (3 instances of simple present tense and 4 instances of simple future). In terms of cohesive devices, the preferred method of referencing is personal referencing through the use of the personal pronouns (highlighted in gray in the sample text) *nous* (*3 instances*), *vous* (7 instances), *votre* (3 instances), *notre* (2 instances) and *nos* (2 instances). Definite articles are used only 5 times (2 *l'*; 2 *le*; 1 *la*) in the text as a reference device; whereas substitution and omission are completely absent in line with the general trend observed in the French business letters corpus. As for connecting words (in bold in the sample text), the sample business letter makes use of the additive conjunction *et*, the conditional conjunction *au cas où*, and the preposition *pour*. Finally, the sample business letter is characterized mainly by compound and complex sentences, which number at 1 and 4, respectively.

Business letters   239

GERMAN

In today's global economy, translation of business content accounts for one of the largest areas of demand within the language industry.[1] A steady stream of translated business correspondence from German into English is particularly evident in the automotive and pharmaceutical industries. As a text genre, the business letter can take on many forms and purposes. Corpus-based analysis can shed light on some of the features that emerge as prototypical. For this purpose, a corpus of 35 German-language business letters was compiled. The letters appeared online within the past 10 years and represent a mix of industries and a mix of purposes (to inform, to request, to complain, to thank, etc.).

Macro-textual features

At the macro-textual level, we see quite a bit of variety in terms of the scope of **rhetorical moves**. The following can be described as prototypical in that they appear in at least 20 of the 35 letters:

1. Company name/contact information (*Firmenname/Kontaktdaten*)
2. Date (*Datum*)
3. Subject line (often in bold font) (*Betreff*)
4. Opening salutation (*Anrede*)
5. Main body (consisting of 1–8 paragraphs) (*Brieftext*)
6. Closing (consisting of the person's title, name, and signature) (*Grußformel*)

The subject line (appearing in 24 out of 35 letters) is often preceded by the word *Betreff* (subject) to enhance directness. Transparency is also enhanced by two further common rhetorical moves, namely an internal reference number and external reference number (appearing in 13 and 14 of the letters respectively). German business letters make every effort to avoid ambiguity when it comes to defining the topic of correspondence as well as who is involved. It is not uncommon to see concrete dates mentioned (in 17 out of 35 letters) in framing previous correspondence.

Perhaps the most interesting strategy for enhancing directness found in German-language business letters is a convention in which the most important information is center-aligned, usually in bold font, offset from the text above and below and preceded by a colon. We see this strategy used in 14 of the 35 letters. The opening salutation in German-language business letters tends to be more formal. *Sehr geehrt-* (most honorable) occurs in 28 of the 35 letters. Follow-up contact might bring about a transition to a less formal form, *Lieb-* (Dear), but this is generally an exception as opposed to the norm. Even when there is a transition to a more informal opening, the closing tends to remain formal, with *Mit freundlichen Grüssen* (with friendly greetings) being more or less standard. This level of formality seen in the opening and closing reveals a cultural preference for distance.

We also see a relatively vast range in terms of text length in words for this genre, with the shortest business letter consisting of 82 words and the

Text types

longest, 592. The genre cannot be described as having a prototypical length. It is worth noting, however, that the majority (26 out of 35) of the letters consist of one to three paragraphs, with three being the most common (11 out of 35). An interesting syntactic pattern in German-language business letters is the prevalence of one-sentence paragraphs. Seventeen of the thirty-five letters found in the corpus contain at least one one-paragraph sentence. Paragraphs are rarely separated by line breaks. We only see this in 1 of the 35 letters.

In terms of register, the field of discourse central to business letters is rendered through the following double-digit frequency nouns:

German term	English equivalent	Frequency	No. of texts
GmbH	limited liability company	23	7
Telefon	telephone	21	16
Email	email	17	14
Zeichen	reference	16	12
BLZ	bank routing number	14	9
Datum	date	12	12
Konto	account	12	7
BIC	BIC (Bank Identification Code)	10	7
Sitz	registered office	10	8
Vorsitzender	chairman	10	7

This terminology reflects a strong semantic focus on commerce and business correspondence. Worth noting is the level of transparency in documenting bank information (routing number, account number, bank identification code) to an extent not commonly found in English-language business letters.

In terms of mode, German business letters are texts written to be read and are largely expository. Perhaps the strongest indicator of expository discourse is the widespread utilization of a subject line. We see the noun *Information/-en* (information) 6 times and a form of the verb *informieren* (to inform) 5 times, further highlighting an expository mode. With the exception of pockets of emotive language, such as *leider* (unfortunately) and *schade* (too bad), the letters primarily consist of non-emotive nouns and verbs.

In terms of tenor, sender and receiver identity tend to be explicit and transparent. A closer look reveals that a precise recipient is addressed in 21 out of 35 letters. A precise sender is stated in only 15 of the 35 letters. In situations where a precise recipient or sender is not provided, we see a more collective entity, such as *Sehr geehrte Damen und Herren* (Dear Ladies and Gentleman) or *Ihr Team* (Your team). As far as sender identity is concerned, it is common for the CEO or other high-ranking company entity who is distinct from the letter writer to be mentioned in the footer (14 out of 35 letters). The relationship between sender and receiver is framed as a formal one through the consistent use of the formal *you* (*Sie*) in direct address and series of titles preceding the last names of senders and receivers:

German title	English equivalent
Dr.	Doctor (Dr.)
Dr. med.	Doctor of Medicine
Frau	Mrs.
Herr	Mr.
Herr Kollege	Lit.: "Mr. Colleague"
Herr Rechtsanwalt	Lit.: "Mr. Lawyer"
Prof. Dr.	Lit.: "Professor Doctor"
Vorsitzender	Chairperson

Throughout the entire corpus, we see a person's first name being used in situations of address only 5 times. This showing of formality is a distancing strategy that is a central norm in German-language business letters. Addressing customers or colleagues on a first-name basis is generally avoided, even in situations where a relationship has been established for an extended period of time. A second common distancing strategy in German-language business letters is the strategic utilization of subjunctive modal verbs:

German subjunctive modal	English translation	Frequency
möchten	would like	9
wären	would be	8
würden	would (+infinitive)	4

Micro-textual features

At the micro-textual level, the mood of German-language business letters is predominately declarative based on the majority of sentences being statements. Of the 602 sentences constituting the corpus, only 21 exhibit end punctuation other than a period, namely an exclamation mark (19 times), and a question mark (2 times). Eighteen letters open with a complex sentence, fourteen with a simple sentence, and two with a compound sentence. The average sentence length of business letters in this corpus is 14.78 words. However, there is a relatively wide range of variety at the level of the individual texts, with the lowest being 7 words and the highest being 27. Sentence length is not standardized in a prototypical fashion as a genre convention in German business letters. As far as syntax is concerned, we do see a tendency for sentences to start with something other than the subject. This is the case for the first sentence in 25 out of 35 letters.

While we see lexical recurrence in German-language business letters, there tends to be a greater preference for lexical parallelism, as seen through the examples in the table that follows. These examples occur over the course of the first two main body sentences in the letters.

Text types

German synonyms	English equivalents
Gerät/gute Wahl	device/good choice
Impfmöglichkeit/Schutzimpfung	vaccination opportunity/preventative vaccination
Angebot/Artikel	offer/product
Anfrage/Wunsch	inquiry/wish
Hilfe/Unterstützung	help/support
2013/ein besonderes Jahr	2013/a special year

Parenthetical constructs are a common micro-level feature of German-language business letters. At least one appears in 16 of the 35 texts. In German, the content found in parentheses is often highly significant, whereas in English, parentheses often frame embedded content as secondary. This has implications for German into English translation in that it is often advisable to remove such parentheses, as seen in the following example:

German passage
   Kondensstreifen ... die bei bestimmten Witterungsverhältnissen (kalten und feuchten Luftschichten) länger anhalten, ...

English translation
Contrails that persist for a longer period of time in certain atmospheric conditions, namely cold and moist layers of air ...

It is also common to see a range of abbreviations in German-language business letters that may or may not take abbreviated forms when translated into English. We see at least one abbreviation in the main body of 13 of the 35 letters in the corpus, including the following list. None of these are proper nouns.

German abbreviation	Frequency	English equivalent
bzw.	5	or rather
ca.	4	approximately
d.h.	1	that is
evtl.	1	possible
inkl.	3	including
o.g.	2	aforementioned

Finally, ellipsis is rarely used as a cohesive device in German-language business letters. It appears only twice over the course of the first two main body sentences in the 35 texts.

Business letters 243

Sample text – German business letter

Arcor
Kundenbetreuung
Postfach 10 25 63
45025 Essen

Online-Kundenservice: www.kunden.arcor.de
Telefon: 018 10 70 010
24 Cent/Min. aus dem deutschen Festnetz
Telefax: 018 10 70 011
24 Cent/Min. aus dem deutschen Festnetz
Ihre Kundennnummer: — — — — — — — —

31.07.2007

Ihr Kündigungseingang

Guten Tag Herr XXXXXXXX,

hiermit bestätigen wir den Erhalt Ihrer Kündigung mit Eingang vom 30.07.2007.
Schade, dass Sie nicht länger mit Arcor-Sprache telefonieren möchten. Die Kündigung Ihres Vertrages haben wir unter Berücksichtigung der vertraglich vereinbarten Kündigungsfristen durchgeführt.

Wir bestätigen die Kündigung Ihres Vertrages für folgende Rufnummern:

XXXXXXXXXX — XXXXXXXXXXX — XXXXXXXXXX

Ihren Arcor-Sprache Anschluss werden wir zum 14.08.2007 abschalten.
Nach dem Kündigungstermin erhalten Sie mindestens noch eine Arcor-Rechnung. Selbstverständlich werden nur Leistungen bis zum Kündigungstermin abgerechnet. Ihre vertragliche Kündigungsfrist entnehmen Sie bitte Ihrem Auftragsformular.
Bitte beachten Sie, dass Sie nach der Abschaltung keine Telefongespräche mehr über Arcor-Sprache führen können und Ihre Rufnummern nicht weiter zur Verfügung stehen. Eine automatische Umstellung auf einen anderen Netzbetreiber erfolgt nicht.

Mit freundlichen Grüßen,
Ihr Arcor-Team

• erreichbar täglich von 6 bis 22 Uhr

Arcor AG & Co. KG	Pers. haftende Gesellschafterin:
Sitz: Eschborn	Arcor Verwaltungs AG
Eintrag im Handelsregister: AG Frankfurt am Main	Sitz: Eschborn
HRA Nr. 28013, Ust-IdNr: DE 178536670	Eintrag im Handelsregister: Frankfurt am Main
Vorstand: Harald Stöber (Vorsitzender)	

Key: one-sentence paragraph – highlighted in gray; lexical recurrence in conjunction with another word – underlined; prototypical framing – bold (centered)

244 **Text types**

Sample German business letter text analysis

The sample business letter was written in 2007 by Arcor, a German telecommunications company which was purchased by Vodafone in 2009, to a single end-user /customer (whose name was redacted). The purpose of the letter is to confirm the termination of telephone service. At the macro-textual level, it exhibits all of the prototypical moves found in this genre. We see a more informal opening, *Guten Tag Herr* XXXX (Good day Mr. XXXX), signaling an established business relationship between sender and receiver. It is worth noting that, despite this ongoing relationship, the recipient is still addressed as Mr. XXXX rather than on a first-name basis. While the sender signing off on the letter is collective (*Ihr Arcor-Team* /Your Arcor Team), we do see the common tendency in German-language business letters for the face of the company to be rendered by way of mentioning a high-ranking executive, in this case, the chairperson of the board.

The letter also contains the prototypical framing of the most important information by way of center-aligned, bold-faced content preceded by a colon, in this case, confirmation that the service of listed telephone numbers will be terminated. We also see two one-sentence paragraphs (highlighted in gray), both containing important dates.

Eight of the eleven sentences start with something other than the subject and many are complex in type. The content is quite explicit, with only one occurrence of ellipsis throughout. In this particular letter, we do not see prototypical usage of parentheticals or abbreviations. Perhaps the most prominent and deliberate cohesive device found in this letter is lexical recurrence in conjunction with another word for purposes of enhancing thematic focus and consistency (highlighted in gray). For example, we see multiple lexical items built around the base *Kündigung* (termination):

German term	English equivalent
Kündigung	termination
Kündigungseingang	termination receipt
Kündigungsfrist	termination period of notice
Kündigungstermin	termination appointment

RUSSIAN

Business letters belong to the field of official correspondence in commerce, administration, legal and diplomatic relations, and more. Unlike recipes, business letters are interpersonal and are rarely written for the public eye. Thus, to compile a relatively representative corpus of Russian business letters, we made sure that each letter originated from a different source. The topics also vary, ranging from a basic response and an inquiry to an open letter to President Vladimir Putin. All texts were published between 2011 and 2016. This corpus consists only of written letters available online, and not of electronic communication, which has its own textual characteristics.

The Russian Federation inherited from the U.S.S.R. a rather stringent system of standards, and business letters (деловые письма) are no exception. They are regulated by GOST Р 6.30–2003 entitled Унифицированные системы документации. Унифицированная система организационно-распорядительной документации. Требования к оформлению. The standard prescribes paper size (A4 or A5), the contents of the sender's and recipient's information, the grammatical cases to be used for the addressees, formats of signatures, structures of blank forms (if such are used in an organization), styles, and more.

The current research, however, is corpus-based, and aims at studying each genre descriptively, not prescriptively. For this reason, we will not analyze the correspondence between the GOST and the textual features found in the corpus – although that could be an interesting assignment. Nevertheless, it appears clear from the results of the corpus analysis that the genre of business letters is regulated and conforms to general norms of Russian business etiquette.

Macro-textual features

All the letters in the corpus contained the following **rhetorical moves**:

1. Sender's and recipient's information (sender's information comes either at the beginning or at the end of a letter)
2. Date
3. Introductory salutation
4. Body (reasons for writing)
5. Closing (actions required, conclusions, etc.)
6. Closing salutation
7. Sender's name

The contents of the sender's and recipient's information varied in the level of detail. In addition to the obligatory name of a person or company, the sender's and recipient's information optionally included the sender's and recipient's positions, addresses, phone/fax numbers, email addresses, websites, tax ID numbers, bank information, and internal reference numbers for the letter. While enclosures are not a part of the current corpus, business letters that include them tend to have a list of the enclosures at the end of the letter.

Notably, the introductory salutations showed fluidity in terms of punctuation (with the traditional exclamation point being gradually replaced by a comma, the latter being typical in the English letter-writing tradition), and in terms of forms of address (the traditional Russian name-patronymic and the relatively modern Господин/Госпожа), e.g., Уважаемый Сергей Семенович,/Уважаемый господин Сапков!/Уважаемые Дамы и Господа! Interestingly, one letter addressed the recipient in English but used an exclamation point (Dear Mr. Yee!).

During the macro-textual analysis, several optional rhetorical moves were identified: title of the letter (three letters), e.g., открытое письмо (open letter), заявление (request/notice/etc.), благодарственное письмо (thank-you letter); numbering of paragraphs to emphasize reasons or facts (two letters); official seal or place for seal (Место печати, often abbreviated as М.П.) (six letters); page numbering (e.g., стр. 1 из 1) (one letter); and even a fingerprint (one letter).

Another macro-textual feature indicative of this text type is the length of texts. The average text length in the business letters corpus was 276.25 words, with the shortest being 128, and the longest, 880. The body of the letters in the corpus varied in length from 1 to 11 paragraphs. Such variation may be due to the different communicative purposes of the letters. The 128-word letter was an informative letter in which the sender declined to sign documents electronically, while the 880-word letter was a letter requesting that the Mayor of Moscow reopen a criminal case.

Using Halliday and Hasan's (1985) description of register, business letters are described as follows: In terms of the **field** of discourse, the lexical analysis shows that business letters cover a wide variety of topics in the fields of business, law, politics, etc. As per Derek Offord's (2005) classifications of styles, business letters belong to official/business style (официально-деловой стиль) of a higher register (along with academic/scientific style (научный стиль) and the styles of journalism and political debate (публицистический стиль)). The table below lists high-frequency words found in the corpus.

High-frequency lexical items	Frequency
компания (company)	26
подпись (signature)	19
Россия (Russia)	15
форум (forum)	15
проект (project)	15
выставка (exhibition)	12
Российский (Russian)	12
кооператив (cooperative)	12
средства (means or resources)	10
письмо (letter)	9
федерация (federation)	8
группа (group)	8
являться (used as copula)	7
розыск (search, investigation)	7
Уважаемый (Dear, as in Dear Mr. Smith)	7

As one can see, the most frequent lexical items in the table above are nouns, which is typical for Russian formal language, and for the Russian language in general. The only verb that appears in the most frequent words list is являться. It is characteristic of formal language and is used as copula for "to be," which is omitted in the present tense in the modern Russian language.

Russian business letters are highly formulaic. The table below lists frequent linguistic formulas used in the corpus.

High-frequency formulaic expressions	Frequency
В размере (in the amount of)	7
Денежные средства (monetary funds)	7
В результате (as a result)	5
В отношении (regarding)	4
С уважением (respectfully)	4
За (свой) счет (at one's own expense)	4
В связи с (due to)	3
Извинения за (apologies for)	3
К сожалению (unfortunately)	3
Приложить максимум усилий (do as much as one can)	3
На основании (on the basis of)	3
По факту (as per the fact)	3
В сложившейся ситуации (in the current situation)	2
Настоящим письмом (by this letter)	2

Other formulaic expressions and business terms that occurred twice in the corpus included в случае (in the case of), в течение (during), с просьбой (with a request/requesting), вместе с тем (along with), общество с ограниченной ответственностью (limited liability company), основа процветания (basis for flourishing), платеж в размере (payment in the amount of), о продлении сроков (regarding extending the terms of), особое внимание (special attention), and others.

As a mode of discourse, business letters are written texts intended to be read by one or more entities involved in a formal relationship with the sender(s) – business partners, current and potential clients, employees and employers, administrators, lawyers, politicians, general public, etc. The **communicative function** of business letters may be **informative** or factual (e.g., informing a client of a new product or of a new delivery date) with a high degree of **conative** language, since the intention is one of generating interest, persuading, or creating an emotive relationship with the recipient, which can range from gratefulness to fear of consequences for action/inaction. In the current corpus, we identified four general types of business letters based on their communicative function:

1. Initial letters (introductions, offers, marketing materials, invitations) – e.g., an invitation to participate in an exhibition.
2. Responses (acknowledgments, accepting/declining an offer, etc.) – e.g., a response to an inquiry.

248   **Text types**

3. Conflictual letters addressing a problem that requires mitigation (complaints, threats, etc.) – e.g., a letter re: an intention to take action against publishing compromising information.
4. Personal-matter business letters (congratulations, gratefulness, apologies, etc.) – e.g., a thank-you letter.

Micro-textual features

At the micro-textual level, the corpus data points to a preference for nouns. In the corpus frequency list, the first 45 most frequent words are mostly nouns and prepositions. The 46th place is taken by the past-tense singular masculine verb form был (was), which occurs only 6 times in five texts. Still, the verbs found are indicative of business writing style. Below are the ten most frequently used verbs in the corpus (different verb forms are included in the count).

High-frequency verbs	*Frequency*
Быть (to be; in the present corpus only occurs in the past tense)	12
Являться (to be, used as copula)	6
Просить (to request; I request)	5
Сообщать(ся) (to inform)	4
Считать (to consider)	4
Выражать (to express)	4
Обращаться (to ask)	4
Благодарить (to thank)	3
Находиться (to be located)	3
Вызывать (to cause)	2

Other common micro-textual features include reflexive verbs, which contribute to the formality of the document. For example, the following verbs appear in the corpus: являться (6), обращаться (4), находиться (3), иметься (1), and казаться (1). Other features that appear in the text include verbal adverbs, with the following occurring a few times in the corpus: опровергая, воспользовавшись, зная, учитывая. The same can be said for verbal adjectives, which, in most instances, occurred more than once or twice in the corpus (e.g., обязующийся, сложившийся, взявший (взятку), заплативший, заслуживший, нижеподписавшийся, пострадавший, построивший, заботящийся, завершающий, and зависящий, among others).

Two other features, namely verbal nouns and noun chains, also contribute to the high frequency of nouns:

1. Verbal nouns; the suffix -ние is especially productive, as in внесение, воспрепятствование, завершение, заявление, изменение, использование, местонахождение, несоблюдение, одобрение, окончание, понимание, постановление, решение, совещание, стремление, умение, уважение, etc.
2. Nouns chains, e.g., предложенный вариант написания названия выставки (the suggested variant of spelling of the name of the exhibition), за несоблюдение условий контракта (for not following the terms of the contract), дата

принятия решения о приеме (the date of the making of the decision about the membership), and more.

Regarding cohesive devices, Russian business letters' use of first-person pronouns is rare, primarily limited to the formal dative form of вы – вам (10 times). This pronoun refers to the addressee of the message, which is consistent with the business letter text type meant for an addressee to take some action. Moreover, these second-person pronouns are typically capitalized in business letters like in other formal modes of communication. Their use in these business letters corresponds with a tendency to avoid the use of first-person pronouns (я/мы) to reflect the formal style and a certain degree of impersonality in the business letters text type. Russian allows for omission of such pronouns when the subject is clear from its verb form (e.g., настоящим сообщаю). Demonstrative pronouns, such as это and its forms, occur 7 times in the corpus.

Conjunctions are frequently used in business letters as a means of connecting clauses in complex and compound sentences, which is typical of Russian formal writing. The most frequent conjunctions are и, что, а, а также, в результате чего, благодаря (тому, что), ведь, где, чтобы, после чего, and поскольку. Verbal adverbs, such as those listed above, also create links between clauses in a sentence, and thus may be considered conjunctive cohesive devices.

Lexical cohesion is created primarily through repetition (see the table of most frequently used words). These words refer to parties involved in a situation or contract, events and projects these parties participate in, issues (e.g., monetary or legal), explanations and reasoning, etc. Not surprisingly, diminutives and particles were not found in the corpus of Russian business letters, which speaks to the formal nature of this text type.

Sample text – Russian business letter

Федеральное государственное казенное учреждение
«Федеральное управление накопительно-ипотечной системы жилищного обеспечения военнослужащих»
(ФГКУ «РОСВОЕНИПОТЕКА»)

Хорошевское шоссе, д. 38 Д, стр. 2, г. Москва, 123007
Тел. +7 (495) 693-56-65, факс +7 (495) 693-56-64
сайт: www.RUSVOENIPOTEKA.RU, Email: XXX@mil.ru

БЛАГОДАРСТВЕННОЕ ПИСЬМО

Руководство ФГКУ «Росвоенипотека» (Далее - Учреждение) благодарит Президентскую бизнес-школу за проведение тренинга «Деловая переписка».

В деятельности ФГКУ «Росвоенипотека» деловая корреспонденция занимает важное место, поэтому особое внимание уделяется составлению писем. Программа данного тренинга полностью отвечает запросу Учреждения и гармонично сочетает теорию и практику.

Данный тренинг позволил сотрудникам Учреждения не только повысить уровень владения языком в официально-деловой коммуникации, но и получить новые знания и навыки, необходимые при работе с деловой корреспонденцией.

> Сотрудники освоили методы работы с информацией, способы составления писем, рассмотрели структуру письма и приемы, позволяющие исключить ошибки при написании текста.
>
> Раздаточные материалы Ø составлены на высоком профессиональном уровне, включают большое количество примеров, в том числе и тексты Учреждения, что вызывает, безусловно, живой интерес. Данные материалы позволят и в дальнейшем совершенствовать навыки составления деловых писем и повышать эффективность деловой коммуникации.
>
> Начальник отдела кадров
>
> [подпись] С. Мешкова
>
> [круглая печать]
>
> «31» октября 2014 г.
>
> Key: various features discussed in sample analysis – highlighted in gray
>
> *Source: http://president-business-school.ru/776_____.htm*

Sample Russian business letter text analysis

The sample business letter is dated October 2014 and published on the website https://president-business-school.ru. This is a thank-you letter commending the President Business School for conducting excellent business communication training for ROSVOENIPOTEKA, a company that manages home mortgages for military personnel. At the macro-textual level, the letter contains all six mandatory moves typical for business letters – sender's information (company's name, address, phone, fax, website, and email), introductory line (in this case, it is the type of the letter – БЛАГОДАРСТВЕННОЕ ПИСЬМО [thank-you letter]), body explaining the reason for writing (to thank the President Business School), closing/conclusion (concerning the future use of the materials received at the training), sender's name, and date. The receiver's contact information is missing in this letter; the addressee is obvious since it is named multiple times in the body of the letter and the letter itself is published on the addressee's website. The length of the sample letter is 175 words (with 276.25 words being the average length of a letter in the corpus).

In terms of the mode of discourse, the letter is informative and conative, since it both describes the positive outcomes of the training and indirectly advertises President's Business School to other clients. It is likely that the sender knew that their letter would be published on the President Business School's website as an advertising move. The tenor of discourse appears to be expert-to-expert. As for the field of discourse, the letter's main goal is to thank President Business School for the training in business letter writing and to list the positive outcomes achieved through the training (the word *тренинг* is repeated three times). The type of the letter is clear from its title (БЛАГОДАРСТВЕННОЕ ПИСЬМО), and the verbal phrases used throughout the letter show positivity and accomplishment: благодарить (to thank), отвечать запросу (to meet the needs), гармонично сочетать (to harmoniously combine), позволить повысить уровень (to allow improving), получить новые знания (to gain new knowledge), освоить методы (to acquire methods), рассмотреть структуру (to study the structure), исключить ошибки (to avoid mistakes), вызывать интерес (to inspire interest), совершенствовать навыки (to improve skills), повышать эффективность (to increase effectiveness).

At the micro-textual level, the letter contains some verbal nouns (проведение [conducting], составление (2 occurrences) [putting together], владение [possession], написание [writing]) and one reflexive verb (уделяться [to be given]), which is consistent with the official style of writing. The most frequently used tense is present (7 occurrences), followed by the past tense (3 occurrences) and one instance of the future tense in the closing part of the letter (позволят [will allow]).

For grammatical cohesion, the letter relies on the additive conjunction *и* (7 instances) and lists. Some other conjunctions are used as well (не только, но и [not only but also], поэтому [because], что [which]). Two verbal adjectives are used to indicate referential cohesion (необходимый [necessary], позволяющий [allowing]). In terms of lexical cohesion, we see the repetition of the word тренинг (training) and учреждение (company). In fact, the word учреждение is used in place of the long name of the company ФГКУ «Росвоенипотека», which is indicated by the phrase "hereinafter referred to as" (далее – ...). This may be considered an instance of omission. In addition, the reference word данный (this) is used as a cohesive reference to the previous mention of a word that accompanies it. One more instance of omission was noted (indicated by Ø in the sample text).

Last but not least, the letter contains the signature of the author and a round seal. It should be noted that seals of various kinds are quite typical for Russian official documents.

252   Text types

SPANISH

Business letters in the Spanish-speaking world contain many sui generis elements in addition to features common to any work-related communication. To the untutored eye, Spanish-language business discourse may at times seem rhetorically laden, even wordy, full of verbal flights that recall older, more stylized forms of expression. The internationalization of English, Anglo-American business practices, and instant communication via web technology have attenuated this impression somewhat, although one still finds many frozen expressions, intricate clausal subordination, *cultismos* (high-register diction and archaic phraseological units), and oratorical style in business letters throughout the Spanish-speaking world.

Macro-textual analysis

The most frequent **rhetorical moves** of a business letter in Spanish are as follows (Flowerdew and Wan 2006: 135):

1. Letterhead (*Membrete*)
2. Inside address (*Nombre y dirección o Destinario*)
3. Reference (*Referncia*)
4. Date (*Fecha*)
5. Salutation (*Encabezamiento o saludo*)
6. Subject line (*Asunto*)
7. Body of the letter (*Cuerpo del mensaje*)
8. Preclose (Despedida)
9. Close (*Cierre*)
10. Signature (*Firma*)
11. Postscript (*Posdata*)

The obligatory moves, and indeed those found in all letters in our corpus, are date, salutation, body, close, and signature. In the salutation, close, and signature in particular, one finds formulas of address in Spanish that may be centuries old, and so codified as to require only an abbreviation, such as S. y Atto. S. (your attentive and loyal servant).

Business letters may make their rhetorical case using numbers, legal arguments, logic, and appeals to emotion. Language may veer into the promotional, as in one of our corpus texts, the Preclose of which, in an attempt to reassure nervous investors, invokes the company's sound financial history and client advocacy with what is virtually sloganeering:

> El prestigio y la solidez que tiene esta Institución hoy día es gracias a la visión de los socios fundadores y a la confianza y patrocinio de los socios. Visítenos. Oriéntese con nuestros asesores financieros los cuales han validado por 62 años que trabajamos por el bienestar de nuestros socios y la comunidad. Validamos que en CamuyCoop, Tu Gente está Contigo.

Micro-textual features

At the micro-textual level, the language data from WordSmith Tools' wordlist and keyword features show average word length of roughly five characters per word, although of 920 words, there are 377 tokens, for a type/token ration of just over 30%, and 249 of the words are relatively long, having between 8 and 18 letters; the mean sentence length for the corpus is 27.2 words, while the sample text has 35, the highest of the ten texts. These are long sentences with complex subordination, unvaried by any short sentences interspersed among them.

Cohesive devices appearing most frequently in the data include *esta carta* (5 occurrences in two texts); moreover, many definite articles appear, each distributed over nearly half of the texts:

Cohesive item	Frequency	No. of texts
este	28	9
esta	27	4
misma	12	4
estos	10	5
aquellos	9	1
esto	7	2
mismo	7	6
alguna	4	3
previo	4	2

Six references are displayed in one corpus text to an intertext, HIPAA legislation (Health Insurance Portability and Accountability Act of 1996), which exists in Spanish. *Siglas en inglés* appears 6 times in two texts, suggesting extratextual references to U.S. law or institutions, or to existing translations of them, as one would expect with official texts in use in Puerto Rico, an unincorporated territory of the U.S. As for prepositions and adverbs of time and manner, statistically most common are prepositions describing means (*a través de*; 13 in five texts) and temporal limits (*a partir de*; 8 in two texts).

Types of conjunctions recorded in the corpus include additive (the conjunction *y* appeared 199 times, or 2.5% of all text), adversative (*pero*: 6 instances in three texts); *aunque* (2 instances in two texts); and temporal adverbs (*hasta*: 6 instances in four texts; *cuando*: 4 instances in three texts; and *finalmente*: 2 instances in two texts).

Among the most common nouns are:

Nouns	Frequency
información	32
pago	30
salud	26

(Continued)

Text types

(Continued)

Nouns	Frequency
servicio	26
proceso	24
departamento	22
impuesto	17
ley	17
Código	16
cuenta	16
actualización	15
planilla	12

These nouns, considered collectively, provide insight into the **field** and show that business letters are frequently used to remind service users about renewing credentials, to offer guidance on how to apply for services, or to notify customers on how to remain in compliance (hence the many references to legal frameworks). Many business letters are also legal correspondence and vary widely in their subject matter, from health informatics cover letters to promotional offers to business lobbying. Business letters in Spanish are sometimes categorized as *jurídico-administrativos* (legal-administrative). The **tenor** of business letters can vary widely, depending on whether the text issues from an organization or an individual, or whether the communicative purpose is, for instance, to inform or to solicit. However, the sociolectical variable, in other words, the difference in status between the sender and addressee, is often highly marked and vertically differentiated in power: citizen to institution, or institution to customer. In some cases, business letters are exchanged between potential partners or social equals. The **mode** of business letters is highly formal, even impersonal, given the distance involved and the lack of personal acquaintance between interlocutors. Field, mode, and tenor constitute **register**.

The most frequently occurring verb in the data is *deberá* (15 tokens in three texts), followed by *debe* (11 in four texts), in keeping with official expressions of obligation. *Podrá* (10 in four texts) is fifth. This output suggests strongly that business letters concern legally permissible, available, or necessary courses of action for the immediate future. The high incidence of future tenses is itself noteworthy.

Sample text – Spanish business letter

10 de junio de 2016
Hon. José Nadal Power
Presidente Comisión de Hacienda y Finanzas Públicas
Senado San Juan, Puerto Rico

Estimado señor Presidente:

En la Corporación de las Artes Musicales (CAM) y sus subsidiarias se desarrolla una misión cultural muy importante en la actualidad considerando que es precisamente a través de este tipo de instituciones que se cimienta la identidad de los pueblos, se preserva el orgullo y se genera la fortaleza de espíritu indispensable para afrontar la adversidad. Sabemos que Puerto Rico se halla sumergido en una crisis económica sin precedentes y que es tarea de todos buscar soluciones viables para salir a flote y lograr nuevamente encaminarnos en la dirección de progreso que todos anhelamos para nuestra patria. Internamente nos hemos visto obligado a generar estrategias agresivas para ajustarnos a las reducciones presupuestarias cada vez más agudas que en caso de no variar, podrían suponer un verdadero riesgo futuro al sostenimiento de producciones culturales de excelencia. Ello debido a que tenemos un presupuesto cada vez más comprometido proporcionalmente con el pago de nómina y costos relacionados del convenio colectivo pactado, y al mismo tiempo más reducido para el desarrollo de los eventos y actividades programáticas. En términos concretos, los proyectos de resoluciones conjuntas bajo consideración de la Asamblea Legislativa proponen asignarnos $7,255,000 para el año fiscal 2016–2017. Tal cifra representa una reducción de $317,000 ó 4.2% al compararse con los $7,572,000 que nos fueron aprobados por virtud de las resoluciones conjuntas correspondientes al año fiscal 2015–2016. Sin embargo, salvo que esta respetada Comisión nos colabore modificando el lenguaje de las asignaciones contempladas bajo el P.C de la C. 894, estaríamos en riesgo de experimentar una reducción real ascendente a la cifra de $741,000 ó 9.8%, que tendría la consecuencia innegable de afectar trascendentalmente nuestra capacidad de cumplir con los servicios que prestamos a la ciudadanía. En específico me refiero a la partida de $424,000 que nuevamente se nos asigna por error para el pago de obligaciones con la Autoridad de Energía Eléctrica (AEE). Nótese que ni la CAM ni sus subsidiarias mantienen relación contractual ni obligación económica alguna con la AEE ya que todos los gastos de nuestro consumo energético están incluidos en los cánones de arrendamiento pactados con la Autoridad de Edificios Públicos (AEP). Es decir, una asignación de esa naturaleza resultaría inutilizable y constituiría una reducción adicional tácita del presupuesto asignado a la CAM y sus subsidiarias con cargo al Fondo General. Así las cosas, entendemos imprescindible reasignar los $424,000 incluidos en la RC de la C 894, de manera que dichos fondos nos sean destinados al pago de las obligaciones de arrendamiento de las facilidades de la CAM y sus subsidiarias bajo el renglón de Gastos Operacionales contenido en la RC de la C 893. Por un lado, ello garantizaría nuestro cumplimiento para con el pago de los contratos de arrendamiento con la AEP, estimados en $410,000 para el año fiscal 2016–2017 y, por otro lado, mitigaría el impacto económico propiciado por la eliminación de la asignación de $250,000 que nos fuere aprobada para tales fines durante el año fiscal 2015–2016. Hon. José Nadal Power Comisión de Hacienda y Finanzas Públicas Carta sobre Memorial de Presupuesto 10 de junio de 2016 A continuación se incluye una tabla que compara las asignaciones recomendadas en los proyectos de resoluciones conjuntas con las reasignaciones que peticionamos: Origen Propósito Asignaciones recomendadas Propuesta de reasignación RC de la C 893 Nómina y Costos Relacionados $4,440,000 $4,440,000 Gastos de Funcionamiento $1,331,000 $1,755,000 RC de la C 894 Orquesta Sinfónica de P.R. $800,000 $800,000 Teatro de la Opera Inc. $70,000 $70,000 Artes Escénico Musicales $190,000 $190,000 Pago de obligaciones con AEE $424,000 $0 Total $7,255,000 $7,255,000 Según se evidencia en la tabla antes incluida, la reasignación de los $424,000 bajo un renglón distinto al pago de las obligaciones de la AEE, NO representaría un aumento de la asignación global de presupuesto para la CAM y sus subsidiarias contra el Fondo General para el año fiscal 2016–2017. Sin embargo, la misma garantizaría mantener la operación de los servicios que llevamos a cabo y el pago de una nómina que durante el próximo año se estima

256   **Text types**

> aumentará a $6,280,000 como consecuencia de las aportaciones adicionales asociadas a los sistemas de retiro de los empleados. De dicha cantidad, $3,932,000 ó 63% corresponde exclusivamente al pago de nómina de los músicos de la Orquesta Sinfónica de Puerto Rico, regulado por convenio colectivo. Es decir, si no se aprobara la reasignación de los $424,000 bajo el renglón solicitado, el 92% de las asignaciones aprobadas para la CAM y sus subsidiarias con cargo al Fondo General se destinaría al pago ineludible de nómina, poniendo en riesgo nuestra operación y obligándonos a activar nuevamente, tal como se hiciera durante el presente año fiscal, una petición formal para el pago de nuestra nómina contra el Fondo Especial 141 que maneja la Oficina de Gerencia y Presupuesto. Esta fue la única alternativa que tuvimos disponible durante el año fiscal 2015–2016 para subsanar el defecto de la imposibilidad de uso de la partida que nos fuere asignada para pagos a la AEE. Recurrir durante el próximo año a la misma petición de auxilio que realizamos durante el presente año ante OGP en caso de que no se concrete la reasignación solicitada, nos sumergiría en un estado de total incertidumbre económica. Sin más que comentar, y esperanzado de que se hagan las enmiendas necesarias de conformidad a los planteamiento respetuosamente contenidos en esta carta de trámite, incluyo el Memorial de Presupuesto de la Corporación de las Artes Musicales y sus subsidiarias que se ha preparado para el año fiscal 2016–2017. Quedo a su disposición para atender cualquier duda que pueda surgir como parte del proceso evaluativo que lleve a cabo esta respetada Comisión.
>
> Atentamente,
>
> [firma]
>
> Key: various features discussed in sample analysis – highlighted in gray

Sample Spanish business letter text analysis

The text under analysis below is addressed to the Chair of the Ministry of Treasury and Finance in the Puerto Rican Senate and concerns a reduction in funding for an arts organization and a request for the shortfall to be remedied. The move-structure of the text may be analyzed as (1) claims (value of the arts); (2) context (dire economy); (3) justification for request (need to adapt to budget reductions); (4) documentation of the error in allocation (evidence thereof and legal and financial constraints); and (5) reiteration of consequences if the error is unresolved (economic uncertainty). The "throughline" of the letter's five rhetorical moves unites the claims to the specific request for patronage; the initial move – defending the arts – is not the overriding purpose of the letter, but is subordinate to, and serves as the rationale for, the request for financial rectification.

At the micro-textual level, patterns can elucidate strategies in business communication, such as the use of nominals linked with positive expectations of future performance in a CEO's letter to shareholders in an annual report. Not all features of a genre, of course, will be present in every textual instantiation, only features that are more typical or less typical of the genre as experts understand or employ it.

The future subjunctive mood in the text suggests a carryover from ancient legalistic discursive practice and represents a stylistic norm. Counterfactual scenarios are constructed through the use of the subjunctive mood and the conditional tense; in Spanish, these are considered more polite than if-constructions using the future tense.

Cohesive devices worth remarking upon include the use of *Las enmiendas* (changes) and the *reasignación* (reallocation [of funds]), which are referenced after the disputed allocations are first mentioned. Both metonyms stand for the funds, much as *asignar* is replaced by the substitution *reasignar*. The phrase *esperanzado que se hagan* (hopeful that they be made) elides the addressee, attenuating the request and avoiding a *face-threatening act*, to use the term from politeness theory (see note above on avoidance of pronouns). The text uses the *nos colabore* (literally, to cooperate with us; by extenstion, to remit) in order to euphemize the request for payment. The earmarking is deemed by the writer *inutilizable* (unusable), rather than phraseology that includes a subject (such as *No podemos utilizarlo*), which might appear more threatening.

Noun phrase constructions such as *esta respetada Comisión* establish a deferential tenor appropriate to one seeking funding. Using certain analysis techniques, we would likely find ingratiating phrases to occur in higher concentrations in the opening and closing of business letters across virtually any sample, as we can see unaided by statistics in our sample text. Noun phrases intensifying the writer's dilemma – *pago* in*eludible*, im*posibilidad de uso*, and *la consecuencia* in*negable de afectar trascendentalmente* (emphasis added) – combine with a verb phrase to convey a tone of urgency, particularly in light of the negative prefixes that make the argument determinant. A negative verb construction should also be taken into account: a reallocation *NO representaría* (would *not* constitute) an overall increase in the budget. The Spanish capitalizes the "NO" for emphasis.

The body of the letter establishes the problem to be addressed with metaphors built around the structural metaphor of *threat*, which dramatizes the author's lofty ideals in defending the role of cultural institutions in times of economic austerity:

> *se cimienta* la identidad de los pueblos, *se preserva* el orgullo y se genera *la fortaleza* de espíritu indispensable para *afrontar* la adversidad.

> (national identity is *strengthened*, our pride *protected*, and the *fortitude* of spirit so necessary for *squaring off against* adversity forged.)

At the macro-textual level, the abstract nouns that help define the values of the nation – identity, pride, spirit, enduring amid hardship – will be juxtaposed later in the letter with concrete, quantified need. Building and strengthening overlap with the semantic field of preparing for war. The next line uses the image of sinking (*plunged* in debt) with an exhortation to all Puerto Ricans to find solutions and *salir a flote* (to keep our heads above water, to right the ship), and *encaminarnos* (literally, to head for, but in keeping with the tenor and vehicle – the metaphor's component parts – of *debt as foundering*, the idea is to set sail toward progress). The isotopic structure, that is, the semantic network unifying the textual coherence thus far in our reading is: BRAVE DEFENSE and FLOATING/SAILING ARE ECONOMIC SURVIVAL. Aliveness is likened to *solvency*; geographic movement to *flourishing*. The author uses the extended metaphor of SUBMERSION IS CRISIS later in the text as well, and many more words from the semantic cluster appear in the corpus – language evoking aggression, risk, sustenance – but the above examples should suffice. This structure overarches the series of rhetorical moves discussed above.

In the corpus, we find the rhetorical use of both *patria* and *país* to refer to Puerto Rico. The use of *patria* in our sample text (… to head out toward progress, the fervent wish we all have for the country) reflects the interpersonal dimension of the text, or tenor variable. In the context, support for the arts amid Puerto Rico's mounting debt problems is presented as patriotic, and *Nuestra patria* constitutes an instance of antonomasia (whereby an epithet substitutes for a name), evoking nationalistic fellow feeling, *Puertoricanness*, in the implied reader. Given that Puerto Rico is not a country or nation, the connotative sense is closer to "beloved home" or "native land," something not merely political but with powerful affective dimensions. The political subtext of the business letter under study thus can be discerned, as the writer seeks to tap into a sense of commonweal and to psychologically motivate the political body to act in accordance with the writer's wishes.

Note

1 For further discussion, see Li (2013).

Appendix A

Sample grading rubric

	Unsatisfactory	Fair	Good	Excellent
Vocabulary and phraseology	Does not use vocabulary and phraseology that is appropriate for the target text; vocabulary is not domain-specific	Uses vocabulary and phraseology that is appropriate in some instances; relies heavily on calques or direct borrowing from the source language	Uses vocabulary and phraseology that conforms to target text conventions in most instances; few instances of calques or direct borrowing from the source language	Uses vocabulary and phraseology that fully conforms to target text conventions appropriate for the subject domain
Grammatical forms	The target text is agrammatical and does not use grammatical structures appropriate for the target language	The target text uses appropriate grammatical constructions and mood in some instances, but does not always adapt these to target text conventions	The target text uses appropriate grammatical constructions and mood in most instances; target text conventions are usually present	The target text relies on appropriate target language grammatical constructions and mood that are appropriate to the target text genre and subject domain
Syntax	Sentence and syntactic structures are inappropriate for the target language; domain-specific writing style and features are not present in the translation	Sentence and syntactic structures are appropriate to the target genre in some instances; domain-specific style and features are sometimes present in the translation, but inappropriately relies on the source language	Sentences and syntactic structures are appropriate to the target genre in most instances; domain-specific style and features are usually present, with only a few inappropriate borrowings from the source language	Sentences and syntactic structures are fully appropriate for target conventions in the specific subject domain; the translation does not inappropriately borrow source text structures

(Continued)

(Continued)

	Unsatisfactory	Fair	Good	Excellent
Coherence and cohesion	Appropriate cohesive markers are not present in the target text; target text is incoherent and inappropriate for the target text genre	Appropriate cohesive markers are present in the target text in some instances; some breakdowns in textual coherence are present and do not conform to target text conventions	Appropriate cohesive markers are present in the target text in most instances; few breakdowns in textual coherence are present and do not significantly impact the target text	Appropriate cohesive markers are present and comply with target domain and genre norms; the target text is coherent and adequately organized
Discourse organization	Appropriate rhetorical moves are not present in the translation; macro-level features of the translation do not conform to target text conventions	Appropriate rhetorical moves are present in some instances in the translation, but macro-level features in some cases are disconnected from micro-level features	Most of the necessary rhetorical moves are present in the translation; macro-level features are appropriate with only minor deviations from target language conventions	The target text is structured with appropriate cohesive markers that account for all necessary rhetorical moves; target text conventions are fully met
Cultural dimensions	The translation does not exhibit any indication of target language and cultural conventions; the translation does not adapt to target cultural dimensions	The translation takes into account basic cultural knowledge of the target language genre; the translation appropriately accounts for cultural differences in some cases, but not always	The translation takes into account cultural knowledge and target language genre conventions; the translation appropriately accounts for cultural differences when needed	The translation is fully informed by appropriate background knowledge of the target language and culture; translation decisions reflect cultural awareness and appropriateness

Appendix B
How to build a corpus

This appendix provides information on how the corpora for this coursebook were created. In particular, the sections below provide information related to some of the more important aspects of building a corpus, including how to identify, select, and evaluate texts that might be included in a corpus and how to digitize materials that are not already in an electronic format. At the end of the appendix, information regarding several readily available tools, resources, and references are provided to help aid anyone interested in conducting the analyses described in the coursebook for additional text-types or in different languages.

Specialized corpus selection criteria

According to Bowker and Pearson (2002: 9), a corpus is "a large collection of authentic texts that have been gathered in electronic form according to a specific set of criteria," and that is also *representative* of the language or language variety that one is aiming to investigate. According to this definition, the representativeness of a corpus depends on its purpose; that is, the purpose of the study drives the selection of "a specific set of criteria."

However, this definition also indicates that selection criteria are only one of the four factors differentiating a corpus from other collections of texts—the other three criteria are authenticity, size, and storage. The term *authenticity* refers to the idea that language used in the texts must be "natural" insofar as the purpose of a corpus is to document naturally occurring language. This means you should steer away from ad hoc documents that have been designed with a pedagogical purpose in mind. These documents cannot be regarded as containing natural language because often the language in it is tweaked and simplified to teach a certain concept/skill and hence is "artificial."

As for its *size*, the above-mentioned definition only states that it is to be "large," but they do not give any specific indications in this respect because its size depends on what the corpus is trying to achieve. Indeed, the authors show that when it comes to specialized or Language for Special Purposes (LSP) corpora, a corpus of 10,000 words can yield more relevant results than a general-purpose one like the BNC (British National Corpus), which consists of 100 million words. The fact that a corpus need not be a certain size in order to be defined as such is also stressed by Zanettin (1998: 618), another corpus linguistics expert, who states that when it comes to specialized corpora, it is possible to obtain relevant data from "a few texts."

262   Appendix B

The fourth and last factor defining a corpus is *storage*, and in this respect Bowker and Pearson (2002) are very clear that a corpus is a collection of texts stored in "*electronic form*" (emphasis added), which makes their analysis easier by allowing them to be processed by such corpus analysis tools as WordSmith Tools or AntConc. Unlike a manual analysis of texts, these tools make linguistic patterns stand out by means of word frequency lists and concordances. For the purpose of this study, all texts needed to be in an electronic format, and printed sources had to be digitized (see the section on OCR tools) and saved as text files (TXT) in order for corpus analysis tools to process them. As for the size, each corpus was to be around 10,000 words and did not contain fewer than ten texts. According to Bowker and Pearson (2002), you only need two or three occurrences of a lexical pattern in a specialized corpus to validate your hypotheses.

In this coursebook, the guidelines outlined below were used. When developing your first few corpora, you may want to use the same guidelines to keep the scope of work manageable.

1   *Corpus size*: 10,000 words as it is a specialized corpus.
2   *Text type size*: use full texts over excerpts in that the latter may not include important features of the text type under analysis.
3   *Number of texts*: choose around ten texts, preferably written by a wide range of authors so that the corpus is more representative of the entire community of specialists, also known as discourse community, rather than being representative of the language used by only a few.
4   *Medium or mode of text*: for the purpose of this study, we will be dealing with written-to-be-read texts.
5   *Subject*: each corpus will focus on different subject matter. The ones selected for this study are the following: food, mechanics, electronics or IT, tourism, journalism, economics, and advertising.
6   *Text type*: The choice of text types is driven by the purpose of a study. The text types that are to be investigated in this book are the following: recipes, instruction manuals, museum guides, news reports, business letters, and patient information.
7   *Authorship*: make sure the corpus is written by acknowledged members of the subject field. In this respect, you should steer away from anonymous sources which cannot guarantee trustworthiness and credibility (see the CARS checklist below). It is imperative to include respectable sources in your corpus in order to ensure that the texts are representative of the language used by a particular discourse community.
8   *Language*: make sure the texts you include in your corpus are original texts, that is to say, texts originally written in the language by native speakers. The texts should not be translations because the purpose of the study is to investigate non-translated language. If the authors are non-native speakers of the language, they may use non-idiomatic expressions that may alter your findings or data. This is also why it is important to investigate the author while checking sources using the CARS checklist guidelines. This will help you determine whether or not the author is a native speaker of the language in which the text is written. Also, keep in mind the region or country from which the texts are taken. The French spoken in the Caribbean may exhibit differences from the French spoken in Canada or France. The same holds

true for many languages, so building corpora for specific countries or regions allow a wide range of linguistic features to be observed.

9   *Publication date*: as a general rule, you should select recent documents so as to investigate the current state of each subject field under study. To this end, select texts written over the past year and only when necessary (e.g., due to a lack of relevant or reliable sources) expand the search to include those published over the past three to five years.

Whether you are using printed or online resources, you should make sure that, in addition to the CARS checklist guidelines, you follow the above-mentioned selection criteria. As you might have noticed, some of the selection criteria, such as publication date and authorship, overlap with the CARS checklist guidelines. Also, when saving files in TXT format, depending on the corpus analysis tools used and the language you are investigating, you might have to use different encodings to ensure that all of the diacritical marks, alphabets, or characters appear correctly. Each analysis program is slightly different, so be sure to check the instructions for your particular program. For instance, if you are using AntConc, you will need to use Unicode for Western languages and Unicode (UTF-8) for non-Western languages. If you are using WordSmith Tools, however, you can use Unicode for both Western and non-Western languages.

Using the above-mentioned encodings will ensure the respective tools will be able to read and process the files that you will be feeding them. One final point to consider in order to make the analysis more manageable—if the text contains tables or pictures, you should remove them so that the text can be easily read by corpus analysis tools.

How to find reliable sources on the web

When it comes to the World Wide Web, there are plenty of resources that one can access, read, watch, and share. However, not all of these resources can be considered scholarly or reliable because anyone can create and publish content on the internet. For the purposes of building a corpus of a specific text type, it is especially important to critically evaluate the texts for inclusion because, depending on many of the criteria outlined above, they may not have or share the characteristics of the text type. In terms of written works, this may result in texts lacking the appropriate lexis and text type conventions that are specific to a given discourse community.

Therefore, we use guidelines to evaluate online resources. Harris Robert developed the **CARS checklist**, which we adopted in developing these materials, that can help us differentiate between high-quality and low-quality information. The acronym CARS stands for: Credibility, Accuracy, Reasonableness, and Support. A detailed discussion of each of these evaluation criteria follows.

Credibility means that the source must be trustworthy and authoritative and must contain sufficient evidence that allows you to trust it. You can assess the credibility of a source by looking at the author's biography, education, and experience. The information you gather from these indicators of credibility allows you to make an informed judgment as to the level of expertise and authority the author has in the field and whether their opinion or the material can be trusted.

264　Appendix B

Accuracy means that the information provided must be factual, up-to-date, exact, and comprehensive, and it should not contain any misleading information. It is important that the information provided is current because what might have been true ten years ago may not still hold true today. For instance, information in rapidly developing fields like information technology may become outdated in a short period of time. In addition, it is important that the information be comprehensive, that is to say, the source has to tell the whole story not just part of it. Information gaps in a corpus creation task can affect its representativeness. For instance, in a recipe, the lack of certain steps (like cooking time or the ingredients section) can influence data analysis and be misleading. To evaluate the accuracy of a source, you should look at the publication date (i.e., was it recently published?) and then evaluate whether there are vague generalizations and how thorough the information is. Simply comparing a given number of texts belonging to the same text type can help you understand whether a certain text is comprehensive or not or contains vague statements.

Reasonableness means that the source must contain information that is objective, consistent, and fair. You can easily assess the reasonableness of an article by looking at how well-reasoned and balanced the information is, if it generally avoids bias (finding a source that is free of any kind of bias is not an easy task, but as a general rule, you should try to steer away from work that contains a biased tone, unless this is characteristic of the text type under review) and does not contain information that contradicts itself. This criterion requires you to read the text to be included in a corpus fully and attentively because this is the only way you can make sure the information in it is consistent and unbiased.

Support means that the source provides convincing evidence for the claims or information provided. You can easily assess the support of a source by finding out whether, when making claims, other works, articles, websites etc. are cited to back them up. To find this information, you should look at footnotes, bibliographies, or works cited lists. You could also evaluate the source using other sources to corroborate the information provided or claims made.

In addition to these indicators, for the purpose of this study, it would also be advisable to assess the source's intended audience because the language used varies depending on whether the audience is the general public, academics, experts or scholars. Indeed, it is the intended audience that determines most of the choices concerning the lexicogrammatical features of a particular text type and in general its style. By simply looking at the formality of the language used in a text and its overall style, one can infer the audience the author of the text is targeting.

Searching the web for reliable sources

Once you know how to evaluate online sources, you need to actually search for them on the web. To do so, there are some Google searching techniques that can speed up the search process and fine-tune your results by retrieving the most relevant information. For example, when searching the web for texts in Spanish, it is important to make sure the texts being collected are representative of the language region. To make sure you only get results from a certain country or region, you might have to limit your Google search to a certain country/region (for example Argentina instead of Spain if you are interested in language usage from Argentina).

Google Advanced Search features come in handy when you need to fine-tune an online search. You can access the Google Advanced Search page either from the homepage of Google by clicking on Settings and then selecting Advanced Settings from the menu or by simply typing "Google Advanced Search" in the Google search box on the Google homepage or any search engine.

When doing a Google search for an online source, make sure to keep in mind the CARS checklist. Let's say you want to find a recipe on the web that is indicative of the English language used in the United Kingdom, and you also want to make sure the results you get are fairly recent. On the Google Advanced Search page, next to the field "this exact word or phrase," type the search term "recipe." This command will retrieve only pages that contain the word recipe. Then scroll down to the "Language" field where you can choose from a drop-down menu the language you want your results to be in. In this case, since we are looking for recipes in English, we will select English from this menu. However, this command does not differentiate between the different types of English, so to fine-tune this search and limit the results to a specific country, in the field "region" choose the country you want to limit your research to. In this case, we will select the United Kingdom.

Alternatively, for some countries, it is also possible to limit the search to a certain domain or site by typing in the exact country code domain (e.g., ".uk" for the UK, ".it" for Italy, ".es" for Spain). The last field to adjust is the one that says "last update," which allows you to limit the search to a certain time-frame. Since the purpose of this study is to document the current state of a specific language, we can limit the search to the past year so that only texts/sources published over the last 12 months will be shown on the results pages. However, limiting the search to such a short timeframe may not yield enough relevant or reliable or credible sources. In these cases, it would be advisable to expand the search to the last three to five years. You can easily do this by clicking on the "last year" tab on the results page and selecting a specific start and end date. The dearth of online sources in languages other than English is not new to linguists working in corpus linguistics (see Maia 2003). This is an even bigger problem when working with specialized corpora, considering that non-English countries have yet to digitize all of their resources and make them available online. As a result, if limiting the search to the last year does not yield enough relevant/reliable results, the search should be expanded to include the last three to five years. We would not recommend going past the five-year threshold, because the further back you go in time, the higher the chances that the language variety and text types being documented will have undergone changes.

After adjusting the settings, Google will return the results of your search. In this example search, one of the first recipes that appears on the first page of the search results is titled "Mary's Black Forest Gâteau," hosted on the BBC Food Recipes website. After reaching the page, you then will need to assess the source using the CARS checklist. The recipe appears to be a reliable source since its author, Mary Berry, is, according to the BBC site itself, "one of the best known and respected cookery writers and broadcasters in the UK." Though the BBC is a respectable source of information, it is always good to do a brief search on the author online to see if other websites agree with what the recipe-hosting website says to avoid any bias in the information provided. By simply searching the author's name, you

266   **Appendix B**

can find additional information. The author in this example, Mary Berry, attended Bath College of Domestic Science and has published over 70 cookbooks and is also one of the judges on *The Great British Bake Off* show. Her books are available on Amazon and her name shows up in other major British newspapers such as *The Mirror, The Guardian*, and *The Telegraph*. Based on this information, the author appears to be a respectable and established figure in her field.

Then, the publication date should be checked. The actual webpage does not contain a publication date. This is quite common when reviewing web pages – not all websites provide a publication date or an author. Therefore, we might use Google's "last update" feature to help us filter out sites that do not contain a publication date and which contain information published past the timeframe we set for our search. When you set a timeframe for your search, Google shows the publication date next to the link to each and every webpage. The recipe by Mary Berry, for example, does not specify a publication date in the article but the link to said webpage on the first results page of Google shows the date of publication on the left side. This recipe was published on the BBC Food website on October 12, 2015. Unlike articles or books, recipes do not usually contain a bibliography or a works cited list, let alone footnotes; however, to assess whether the information being provided is supported by other sources, you can just look at other similar online recipes to determine whether the overall baking procedure and ingredients are the same. Of course, you might find differences when comparing recipes for a particular dish, but the main ingredients and process should be the same. Last but not least, as far as reasonableness is concerned, the one way you can assess it is by reading the recipe and making sure it is complete and consistent in all the steps. Once you have established that the source generally complies with the CARS checklist, you can go ahead and include it in your corpus of texts and move on to the next text.

How to assess printed sources

Though the CARS checklist by Harris was specifically developed to evaluate online sources, as a general rule, it is possible to assert that its guidelines can also apply to printed sources such as books or magazines. When evaluating a printed source, you should make sure to investigate the author (education, work, expertise, affiliations), the content (comprehensiveness, overall lack of bias, publication date, and works cited/references), and intended audience (style and place of publication for printed sources). If, after considering all these factors, the source turns out to have been written by an expert in the field, it is complete, current, relatively unbiased, and the style is reflective of the audience the book is targeting, then you can include this source in the corpus of specialized texts. However, you will need to digitize these documents and convert them into an editable format so that they can be more efficiently analyzed by means of corpus analysis tools.

OCR software – Digitizing printed material

If the sources you are using to collect some or all of the texts of a corpus are in print, you will have to digitize these paper copies by turning them into an electronic format that can be easily read by corpus analysis tools. Optical Character

Recognition (OCR) is a technology that converts different types of documents (scanned copies, PDF files, or images) captured by a scanner or any other digital device into editable and searchable text. Some scanners or cameras have built-in OCR software that can facilitate this process. Many libraries also have resources that can help you with this process.

Depending on how you scan the file, you may be able to save the text as a TXT file, or you might need to copy and paste the text into a word processor or program that would allow you to save the text in this format. However, if the output is a non-searchable/non-editable PDF, text file, or image, then you will need to use some type of OCR program to make this possible. There are online OCR tools that are freely available, and there are several that are integrated into commonly used software tools. For example, one such tool is integrated into Microsoft OneNote. This tool can be used to convert a picture into readable text. If you are scanning printed sources and want to use this Microsoft OneNote feature, make sure to save the scanned file as an image (i.e., JPG, TIFF). Then, drag and drop a saved picture or upload it into Microsoft OneNote, right-click on it, and then select "Copy Text from Picture." You can now paste the content of the picture into Microsoft Word or NotePad.

Another useful OCR tool can be accessed at www.onlineocr.net. This OCR tool supports 46 languages and extracts text from non-readable PDF files. One way to make the conversion process easier is to first convert the file into a Word document and then save the file as a TXT file. Otherwise, the complexity of the file might mean you need to edit the file after the conversion process is complete.

Yet another OCR tool worth mentioning is FreeOCR which uses the Tesseract OCR Engine. It supports most file formats (both PDF and image files). A free-to-use version can be downloaded from several websites. Ultimately, the choice of which tool to use will depend on the quality of the scanning/digitalizing process and the format of the output. These programs regularly change, and new services and programs are available online, so you may need to review what is currently available when you build your corpus. As mentioned above, some libraries can provide support for this type of work as well. Regardless of the tool that you use, you may still need to perform minor edits before they are ready to be processed by a corpus analysis tool to correct accent marks, corrupted characters or broken lines.

Corpus analysis programs and resources

WordSmith Tools – www.lexically.net/wordsmith/
AntConc – www.laurenceanthony.net/software/antconc/
Corpus Analysis Tools – https://corpus-analysis.com/

References

Abdelhak, Mervat, Sara Grostick, and Mary Alice Hanken. 2016. *Health Information – E-Book: Management of a Strategic Resource*. 5th ed. St. Louis, MO: Elsevier.

Abend, Lisa. 2007. "1080 Recipes: Why This Iberian Joy of Cooking Is Likely to Disappoint." *Slate*, October 31. www.slate.com/articles/life/food/2007/10/1080_recipes.html. Last accessed 14 May 2019.

Backinger, Cathy L. and Patricia A. Kingsley. 1993. "*Write It Right: Recommendations for Developing User Instruction Manuals for Medical Devices Used in Home Health Care.*" U.S. Department of Health and Human Services.

Backmann-Medick, Doris. 2009. "Introduction. The Translational Turn." *Translation Studies* 2(1): 2–16.

Baer, Brian James. 2016. "Teaching Translation through Text Types." In *Teaching Translation*, ed. by Venuti, Lawrence, 63–71. New York: Routledge.

Baker, Mona. 2011/2018. *In Other Words: A Coursebook on Translation*. New York: Routledge.

Bakhtin, Mikhail. 1986. "The Problem of Speech Genres." In *Speech Genres and Other Late Essays*, ed. by Emerson, Caryl and Michael Holquist, 60–102. Austin: University of Texas Press.

Bassnett, Susan and Esperança Bielsa. 2009. *Translation in Global News*. London: Routledge.

Beekman, John and Kathleen Callow. 1974. *Discourse Considerations in Translating the Word of God*. Grand Rapids, MI: Zondervan.

Bell, Alan. 1991. *The Language of News Media*. Oxford: Blackwell.

Bhatia, Vijay K. 1993. *Analyzing Genre: Language Use in Professional Settings*. London: Longman.

Biel, Łucja. 2017. "Enhancing the Communicative Dimension of Legal Translation: Comparable Corpora in the Research-informed Classroom." *The Interpreter and Translator Trainer* 11(4): 316–336.

Blum-Kulka, Shoshana. 1986. "Shifts of Cohesion and Coherence in Translation." In *Interlingual and Intercultural Communication: Discourse and Cognition in Translation*, ed. by House, Juliane and Shoshana Blum-Kulka, 17–37. Tubingen: Gunter Narr.

Bnini, Chakib. 2016. *Didactics of Translation: Text in Context*. Cambridge: Cambridge Scholars.

Bowker, Lynne and Jennifer Pearson. 2002. *Working with Specialized Language: A Practical Guide to Using Corpora*. New York: Routledge.

Bureau of Labor Statistics (BLS), U.S. Department of Labor, Occupational Outlook Handbook, Interpreters and Translators www.bls.gov/ooh/media-and-communication/interpreters-and-translators.htm. Last accessed 10 May 2019.

Butler, Christopher S. 2008. "Basically Speaking: A Corpus-Based Analysis of Three English Adverbs and Their Formal Equivalents in Spanish." In *Current Trends in*

Contrastive Linguistics: Functional and Cognitive Perspectives, ed. by Gómez González, María de los Ángeles, J. Lachlan Mackenzie, and Elsa M. González Álvarez, 147–176. Amsterdam: John Benjamins.

Byrne, Jody. 2012. *Scientific and Technical Translation Explained*. New York: Routledge.

Carreres, Ángela. 2006. "Strange Bedfellows: Translation and Language Teaching: The Teaching of Translation into L2 in Modern Language Degrees: Uses and Limitations." Paper presented at the *6th Symposium on Translation, Terminology and Interpretation in Cuba and Canada*. Havana, Cuba.

Catford, John C. 1965. *A Linguistic Theory of Translation*. London: Oxford University Press.

Centers for Disease Control and Prevention. 2009. *Simply Put: A Guide for Easy-to-Understand Materials*. 3rd ed. Atlanta, GA: Division of Communication Services. www.cdc.gov/healthliteracy/pdf/Simply_Put.pdf

Chesire, Keyne et al. 2018. "Teaching the Theory and Practice of Literary Translation across Multiple Languages." In *Translation, Globalization and Translocation*, ed. by Godev, Concepción, 101–115. Palgrave Macmillan.

Chovanec, Jan. 2014. *Pragmatics of Tense and Time in News: From Canonical Headlines to Online News Texts*. Amsterdam: John Benjamins.

Colina, Sonia and Barbara Lafford. 2017. "Translation in Spanish Language Teaching: The Integration of a 'Fifth Skill' in the Second Language Curriculum." *Journal of Spanish Language Teaching* 4(2): 110–123.

Conacher, Jean E. 1996. "Native Speaker to Native Speaker: Crossing the Translation Gap." In *Teaching Translation in Universities: Present and Future Perspectives*, ed. by Sewell, P. and I. Higgins, 161–182. London: Association for French Language Studies.

Cronin, Michael. 2017. *Eco-Translation: Translation and Ecology in the Age of the Anthropocene*. New York: Routledge.

Crystal, David. 2008. *Dictionary of Linguistics and Phonetics*. Hoboken, NJ: Blackwell Publishing.

Davis, T. C., M. A. Crouch, S. W. Long, R. H. Jackson, P. Bates, R. B. George, et al. 1991. "Rapid Assessment of Literacy Levels of Adult Primary Care Patients." *Family Medicine* 23(6): 433–435.

Epstein, Brett Jocelyn. 2009. "What's Cooking? Translating Food." *Translation Journal* 13(3) July. http://translationjournal.net/journal/49cooking.htm. Last accessed 14 May 2019.

Fairclough, Norman. 2003. *Analysing Discourse: Textual Analysis for Social Research*. New York: Psychology Press.

Flowerdew, John and Alina Wan. 2006. "Genre Analysis of Tax Computation Letters: How and Why Tax Accountants Write the Way They Do." *English for Specific Purposes* 25(2a): 133–153.

Gamero Pérez, Silvia. 2001. *La traducción de textos técnicos: Descripción y análisis de textos (español-alemán)*. Barcelona: Editorial Ariel.

González-Rodríguez, María José. 2006. "Tracing Context in the Discourse of the Media: Features of Language-In-Use in the British Press." *Revista Alicantina De Estudios Ingleses* 19: 149–168.

Göpferich, Susanne. 2010. "The Translation of Instructive Texts from a Cognitive Perspective: Novices and Professionals Compared." In *New Approaches to Translation Process Research*, ed. by Mees, Inger M., Fabio Alves, and Susanne Göpferich, 5–55. Frederiksburg: Samfundslitteratur.

Gorman, Michael and Maria-Luisa Henson. 1996. *Spanish/English Business Correspondence: Correspondencia De Comercio Español*. London: Routledge.

Halliday, M. A. K. and Ruqaiya Hasan. 1976. *Cohesion in English*. London: Longman.

References

Halliday, M. A. K. and Ruqaiya Hasan. 1985. *Language, Context, and Text. Aspects of Language in a Social-semiotic Perspective*. Victoria: Deakin University.

Halliday, M. A. K. and Jonathan J. Webster. 2014. *Text Linguistics: The How and Why of Meaning*. Equinox Publishing.

Halliday, Michael A. K. 1989. "Functions of Language." In *Language, Context, and Text: Aspects of Language in a Social-Semiotic Perspective*, ed. by Halliday, Michael and Ruqaiya Hasan, 15–28. Oxford: Oxford University Press.

Harris, Robert. 1997. "Evaluating Internet Research Sources." January 16. www.virtualsalt. com/evalu8it.htm. Last accessed, 29 August 2019.

Hatim, Basil and Ian Mason. 2005. *The Translator as Communicator*. London: Routledge.

Hatim, Basil A. 2001/2013. *Teaching and Researching Translation*. New York: Routledge.

Hatim, Basil A. and Ian Mason. 1997. *The Translator as Communicator*. London: Routledge.

Hervey, Sándor, Ian Higgins, and Louise M. Haywood. 1995/2002. *Thinking Spanish Translation: A Course in Translation Method: Spanish to English*. New York: Routledge.

Hidalgo, Encarnación, Luis Quereda, and Juan Santana. 2007. *Corpora in the Foreign Language Classroom*. New York: Brill.

Holquist, Michael. 1986. "Introduction." In *Speech Genres and Other Late Essays*, ed. by Bakhtin, M. M., Carol Emerson, and Michael Holquist, trans. by Vern W. McGee, ix–xxiii. Austin: University of Texas Press.

Jakobson, Roman. 1960. "Linguistics and Poetics." In *Style in Language*, ed. by Sebeok, Thomas A., 350–377. MA: MIT Press.

Jimison, Holly B. 1997. "Patient-Specific Interfaces to Health and Decision-Making Information." In *Promotion and Interactive Technology: Theoretical Applications and Future Directions*, ed. by Street, Richard L., Jr., William R. Gold, and Timothy Manning, 141–156. Mahwah, NJ: Lawrence Erlbaum Associates.

Kaniklidou, Themis. 2018. "News Translation and Globalization: Narratives on the Move." In *Translation, Globalization and Translocation: The Classroom and Beyond*, ed. by Godev, Concepción, 79–98. Cham, Switzerland: Palgrave Macmillan.

Krings, Hans P. 1986. "Translation Problems and Translation Strategies of Advanced German Learners of French (L2)." In *Interlingual and Intercultural Communication*, ed. by House, Juliane and Shoshana Blum-Kulka, 263–276. Tübingen: Gunter Narr.

Kumpulainen, Minna. 2018. "Translation Competence from the Acquisition Point of View: A Situation-based Approach." *Translation, Cognition & Behavior* 1(1): 147–167.

Kussmaul, Paul. 1995. *Training the Translator*. Amsterdam: John Benjamins.

Laursen, Anne Lise and Ismael Arinas Pellón. 2014. "Text Corpora in Translator Training: A Case Study of the Use of Comparable Corpora in Classroom Teaching." *The Interpreter and Translator Trainer* 6(1): 45–70.

Lavault, Elisabeth. 1985. *Fonctions de la traduction en didactique des langues*. Paris: Didier Érudition.

Laviosa, Sara. 2014. *Translation and Language Education: Pedagogic Approaches Explored*. New York: Routledge.

Lazzeretti, Cecilia. 2016. *The Language of Museum Communication: A Diachronic Perspective*. London: Palgrave Macmillan.

Le, Elisabeth. 2004. "The Role of Paragraphs in the Construction of Coherence – Text Linguistics and Translation Studies." *International Review of Applied Linguistics in Language Teaching* 42(3): 259–275.

Levý, Jiří. 1966. "Translation as a Decision-making Process." In *To Honor Roman Jakobson: Essays on the Occasion of His Seventieth Birthday*, 1171–1182. Den Haag: Mouton.

Li, Defeng. 2013. "Teaching Business Translation: A Task-based Approach." *The Interpreter and Translator Trainer* 7(1): 1–26.

López Ferrero, Carmen and Cristian González Arias. 2015. "Commercial Discourse." In *The Routledge Handbook of Hispanic Applied Linguistics*, ed. by Lacorte, Manuel, 512–530. New York: Routledge.

Lörscher, Wolfgang. 1991. *Translation Performance, Translation Process, and Translation Strategies: A Psycholinguistic Investigation*. Gunter Narr: Tübingen.

Lörscher, Wolfgang. 1996. "A Psycholinguistic Analysis of Translation Processes." *Meta* 41(1): 26–32.

Lotman, Juri. 1978/2019. "The Phenomenon of Culture." In *Essays on Cultural History*, ed. by Tamm, Marek, trans. by Brian James Baer, 33–49. New York: Palgrave Macmillan.

Maia, Belinda. 2003. "Some Languages are More Equal than Others. Training Translators in Terminology and Information Retrieval Using Comparable and Parallel Corpora." In *Corpora in Translator Education*, ed. by Zanettin, Federico, Silvia Bernardini, and Dominic Stewart, 43–53. Manchester: St. Jerome.

Mayor, Serrano and María Blanca. 2005. "Análisis contrastivo (inglés-español) de la clase de texto 'folleto de salud' e implicaciones didácticas para la formación de traductores médicos." *Panace@* 6(20): 132–141.

Malkiel, Brenda. 2009. "From Ántonia to My Ántonia: Tracking Self-Corrections with Translog." In *Behind the Mind: Methods, Models and Results in Translation Process Research*, ed. by Göpferich, Susanne, Arnt Lykke Jakobsen, and Inger M. Mees, 149–166. Copenhagen: Samfundslitteratur Press.

Malmkjaer, Kirsten (ed). 1998. *Translation and Language Teaching*. Manchester: St. Jerome.

Merriam-Webster, n.d. "How Journalists are Redefining the Word 'kicker.' The Word Has Long Had a Specific Meaning in Journalism. Now It Has Two." www.merriam-webster.com/words-at-play/kicker-definition-meaning. Last accessed 6 March 2018.

MLA Ad Hoc Committee on Foreign Languages. 2007. *Foreign Languages and Higher Education: New Structures for a Changed World*. www.mla.org/flreport.

Neather, Robert. Forthcoming. *Translating for Museums*. New York: Routledge.

Nord, Christiane. 1988. *Text Analysis in Translation: Theory, Methodology, and Didactic Application of a Model for Translation-oriented Text Analysis*. Amsterdam: Rodopi.

Offord, Derek. 2005. *Using Russian: A Guide to Contemporary Usage*. Cambridge: Cambridge University Press.

Olohan, Maeve. 2004. *Introducing Corpora in Translation Studies*. New York: Routledge.

Ornia, Goretti Faya. 2016. *Medical Brochure as a Textual Genre*. Cambridge: Cambridge Scholars.

Ortega, Simone. 1972. *1080 Recetas De Cocina*. Madrid: Alianza Editorial.

Parratt, Sonia. 2011. "Literary Journalism in Spain: Past, Present (and Future?)" In *Literary Journalism across the Globe: Journalistic Traditions and Transnational Influences*, ed. by Bak, John S. and Bill Reynolds, 134–147. Amherst: University of Massachusetts Press.

Pietrzak, Paulina. 2019. "Scaffolding Student Self-reflection in Translator Training." *Translation and Interpreting Studies*. doi: 10.1075/tis.18029.pie

Pilegaard, Morten. 1997. "Politeness in Written Business Discourse: A Textlinguistic Perspective." *Journal of Pragmatics* 28(28): 223–244.

Portocarrero, Felipe and Natalia Gironella. 2003. *La escritura rentable: La eficacia de la palabra en la empresa*. Madrid: Ediciones SM.

Presas Corbella, Marisa and Celia Martín de León. 2014. "The Role of Implicit Theories in the Non-Expert Translation Process." *MonTI Special Issue – Minding Translation* 1: 273–302.

Pym, Anthony. 2018. "Where Translation Studies Lost the Plot: Relations with Language Teaching." *Translation and Translanguaging in Multilingual Contexts* 4(2): 203–222.

Ravelli, Louise. 2009. *Museum Texts: Communication Frameworks*. London: Routledge.

References

Reiss, Katherina. 1971/2000. *Translation Criticism: Potential and Limitations. Categories and Criteria for Translation Quality Assessment*. trans. by Erroll F. Rhodes. Manchester: St. Jerome.

Reiss, Katherina. 1981/2004. "Type, Kind and Individuality of Text: Decision Making in Translation." Trans. by Susan Kitron. In *The Translation Studies Reader*, 2nd edition, ed. by Venuti, Lawrence, 168–179. New York: Routledge.

Risku, Hanna and Richard Pircher. 2008. "Visual Aspects of Intercultural Technical Communication: A Cognitive Scientific and Semiotic Point of View." *Meta* 53(1): 154–166.

Rocha, Josiany Salles. 2010. *Translation and Perspective Taking in the Second Language Classroom*. MA Thesis, Kent, OH, Kent State University.

Rodríguez-Inés, Patricia. 2014. "Electronic Corpora and Other Information and Communication Technology Tools." *The Interpreter and Translator Trainer* 4(2): 251–282.

Rolf, Eckhard. 1993. *Die Funktionen der Gebrauchstextsorten*. New York: de Gruyter.

Rosenblatt, Louise. 1978. *The Reader, the Text, the Poem: The Transactional Theory of the Literary Work*. Carbondale, IL: Southern Illinois University Press.

Sanz Pinyol, Gloria and Alba Fraser. 2003. *Manual de comunicaciones escritas en la empresa*. Barcelona: Graó.

Schäffner, Christina. 2001. *Annotated Texts for Translation: English-German: Functionalist Approaches Illustrated*. Buffalo, NY: Multilingual Matters.

Shreve, Gregory M. 2018. "Text Linguistics, Translating, and Interpreting." In *Routledge Handbook of Translation Studies and Linguistics*, ed. by Malmkjaer, Kirsten, 165–178. New York: Routledge.

Sinclair, John. 2004. *How to Use Corpora in Language Teaching*. Amsterdam: John Benjamins.

Scott, Mike. 2016. *WordSmith Tools* version 7. Stroud: Lexical Analysis Software.

Sola, Katie. 2016. "Here are the 20 Fastest Growing Jobs in America." *Forbes*, April 12. www.forbes.com/sites/katiesola/2016/04/12/here-are-the-20-fastest-growing-jobs-in-america/. Last accessed 29 May 2019.

Spivak, Gayatri Chakravurty. 2005. "Translating into English." In *Nation, Language, and the Ethics of Translation*, ed. by Bermann, Sandra and Michael Wood, 93–110. Princeton: Princeton University Press.

Swales, John. 1990. *Genre Analysis. English in Academic and Research Settings*. Cambridge: Cambridge University Press.

Takeda, Kayoko and Masaru Yamada. 2019. "'TI Literacy' for General Undergraduate Education." In *The Evolving Curriculum in Interpreter and Translator Education: Stakeholder Perspectives and Voices*, ed. by Sawyer, David B., Frank Austermühl, and Vanessa Enríquez Raído, 54–73. Amsterdam: John Benjamins.

Tirkkonen-Condit, Sonja. 1992. "The Interaction of World Knowledge and Linguistic Knowledge in the Processes of Translation. A Think-Aloud Protocol Study." In *Translation and Meaning*, ed. by Lewandowska-Tomasczyk, Barbara and Mary Thelen, 433–440. Maastricht: Faculty of Translation and Interpreting.

Trofanenko, Brenda and Avner Segall. 2014. "Introduction: The Museum as a Space of Pedagogical Ambiguity." In *Beyond Pedagogy: Reconsidering the Public Purpose of Museums*, ed. by Trofanenko, Brenda, 1–7. Rotterdam: Sense.

Vermeer, Hans J. 1989. "Skopos and Commission in Translational Action." In *Readings in Translation Theory*, ed. and trans. by Andrew Chesterman, 173–187. Helsinki: Oy Finn Lectura Ob.

Vinay, Jean-Paul and Jean Darbelnet. 1995. "A Methodology for Translation." In *Comparative Stylistics of French and English: A Methodology for Translation*, ed. and trans. by Juan C. Sager and M.-J. Hamel, 31–42. Amsterdam: John Benjamins.

Vivian, A. S. and E. J. Robertson. 1980. "Readability of Patient Education Materials." *Clinical Therapy* 3: 129–136.

Vyatkina, Nina and Alex Boulton. 2017. "Corporal in Language Learning and Teaching." *Language Learning and Technology* 21(3): 1–8.

Washbourne, Kelly. 2014. "Beyond Error Marking: Written Corrective Feedback for a Dialogic Pedagogy in Translator Training." *The Interpreter and Translator Trainer* 8 (2): 240–256.

Wilson, W. A. André. 1972. "Ingredients of good, clear style: A comparison of two versions of the Gospels in a West African language." *Bible Translator* 23(1): 135–144.

Zanettin, Federico. 1998. "Bilingual Comparable Corpora and the Training of Translators." *Meta* 43(4): 616–630.

Zanettin, Federico. 2002. "Corpora in Translation Practice." *First International Workshop on Language Resources for Translation Work and Research Proceedings.* https://files.ifi.uzh.ch/cl/yuste/postworkshop/repository/fzanettin.pdf. Last accessed 1 June 2019.

Zanettin, Federico, Silvia Bernardini, and Dominic Stewart (eds). 2000. *Corpora in Translator Education.* New York: Routledge.

Index

acronyms 93, 198
ambiguity 42, 78, 93, 215, 235, 239
AntConc 262–3, 267
audience 18–20, 26–7, 34, 47, 69, 91,
  114–15, 118–20, 152, 171–2, 192–3,
  197–8, 203, 208–10, 234, 264

Baker, Mona 10
Bakhtin, Mikhail 5–7
Bloom's taxonomy 10

CARS checklist 262–4, 265–6
clauses 102, 109, 112, 140, 187, 189, 212,
  249; conditional 221, 225;
  nonrestrictive 187; relative 48, 187, 225;
  restrictive 187; subordinate 187;
  temporal 48
coherence 7, 11, 222; intratextual 59;
  textual 9, 257
cohesion 4, 7, 11, 28, 93, 172, 175, 180,
  194, 198, 201, 268–9; grammatical 52,
  96, 134, 251; lexical 21, 24, 35, 38, 49,
  52, 93, 96, 132, 134, 172, 210, 212,
  249, 251; referential 251; textual 4, 7, 9,
  49, 103, 132
cohesive devices 9, 20–1, 27–8, 30, 34–5,
  48, 69, 78–9, 114–15, 120, 126–8, 152,
  157–8, 160–1, 165–6, 169, 201, 221–2,
  228, 230
cohesive links 132, 134, 211–12
collocations 9–10, 120, 140, 145–6, 157,
  161, 199, 210, 218
competence 2; cultural 6; textual 6;
  transcultural 2; translation 6
conative language 7–8, 34, 37, 67, 69, 99,
  102, 114, 120, 122, 143–4, 155, 157,
  209–10, 221

conjunctions 9, 20–1, 24, 28, 35, 37–8, 52,
  70, 72, 78, 80–1, 115, 153, 155, 185–7,
  189, 194, 224–5, 228–30, 237–8;
  adversative 189; subordinating 54, 64,
  67, 78

decision-making 10–11, 270

ellipsis 9, 20, 28, 30, 41–2, 44, 93, 95, 120,
  199, 201, 205–6, 222, 225, 228
evaluativeness 12, 184
exhortatives 178

field 8–10, 19, 26–7, 33, 46, 54, 76, 97–8,
  170–1, 177, 192–3, 212, 214, 226–7,
  245–6, 254, 263–4, 264–5

Halliday, M. A. K. 5, 8–9, 19, 26, 33, 46,
  48, 54
hypernyms 9, 24–5, 30, 38, 42, 44, 155,
  161, 169, 175
hypertextuality 78, 184
hyponyms 9, 42
hyponymy 52, 123, 158, 210

Jakobson, Roman 7

language combinations 12–14
Levý, Jiří 11
literacy 3, 142, 146, 180; digital 3; global
  3; translation 3
Lotman, Juri 10

markedness 12
meronyms 9, 38, 137, 159, 161
metonyms 9, 175, 189, 257
mode 8–9, 19, 26–7, 33, 46–7, 54–5, 76–7,
  97–8, 119, 155–7, 177–9, 192–3,

196–8, 214, 224, 226–7, 254

nominalizations 172, 175, 218
nonexperts 13, 19, 27, 41, 47, 131, 137, 171, 178, 214
Nord, Christiane 11
noun phrases 25, 31, 38, 117, 122–3, 199–201, 204, 223, 225, 231
nouns 21, 25, 29, 36, 39, 44, 49, 70, 98–9, 116–17, 120, 132, 153, 194, 196, 201, 229, 236, 247–8, 253–4; abstract 257; compound 10, 43–4, 180; concrete 42; mass 39; non-emotive 240
novices 1, 4–7, 11, 18, 137

OCR software 262, 266–7
omission 9, 28, 69, 72, 93, 115, 123, 134, 205, 225, 228, 238, 249, 251

PDF files 74, 82, 87, 95, 141, 267
pedagogy: language 2–3, 5, 14; translation 1, 3–5, 12, 261, 272
phatic language 7–8, 114, 120, 221, 224, 227, 234, 237
phraseology 58, 146, 257, 259
politeness 49, 69, 219, 235, 257
prepositions 107–9, 112, 186, 190, 235–6, 238, 248, 253; cluster 112; phrases 84, 137, 235; temporal/ spatial 137
processing: bottom-up 4; top-down 1, 4, 7

readability 17, 41, 58, 163, 165, 169, 210, 219
register 8, 19, 26, 151, 177, 180, 208–9, 212, 214, 220, 224, 226
Reiss, Katherina 11

repetition 9, 21, 24–5, 30, 34–5, 37–8, 52, 72, 79, 115–17, 134, 155, 195–6, 198, 222, 230–1
rhetorical moves 8, 18, 32–3, 83, 108, 111, 119–20, 122, 136, 156
rubric 13

scaffolding 10, 12, 14
Shreve, Gregory M. 4–5
skopos theory 11
source language 13, 17, 109, 127, 129, 180, 203
Spivak, Gayatri 1, 6–7, 272
substitution 9, 20, 24, 28, 30, 34, 41–2, 44, 48, 78, 120, 168–9, 222, 225, 235
Swales, John 8, 18, 26, 97, 135
synonyms 9, 24, 30, 38, 44, 155, 161, 181, 225, 230
synonymy 85, 90, 93, 166, 168–9, 180–1, 200–1, 205–6, 210
syntax 52, 175, 212, 241, 259; complex 187

target language 6, 8–9, 12–14, 61, 64, 108–9, 126, 129, 144, 146
tenor 8–9, 26–7, 46–7, 54–5, 76, 97–8, 131, 134, 175, 177, 214, 254, 257
text awareness 1–2, 7, 13
translationese 4, 7

Vermeer, Hans 11
visual aids 13, 17, 75, 81–2, 128, 142
vocabulary 9, 14, 41, 62, 169, 210, 212; controlled 42, 82–3, 85
vocative language 8, 227

Wilson, W. A. André 7
WordSmith Tools 58, 227, 253, 262–3, 267